DECISIVE BATTLES
OF THE TWENTIETH CENTURY

LAND-SEA-AIR

DECISIVE BATTLES

OF THE TWENTIETH CENTURY

LAND-SEA-AIR

Edited by
Noble Frankland and Christopher Dowling

BOOK CLUB EDITION

This edition published by
Purnell Book Services, Limited,
P.O. Box 20
Abingdon, Berkshire
by arrangement with Sidgwick and Jackson Limited

Printed and bound in Great Britain by
Morrison & Gibb Ltd., London and Edinburgh

Contents

Editors' Introduction

TECHNOLOGICAL ADVANCES in the twentieth century have made warfare vastly more destructive than in any previous age. The rise of the common man, as also the development of transport and the means of communication, have enabled armies to be, not only in word, but also in fact, nations in arms. The spread of democracy has enabled war and its passions to extend from the horizons of princes, governments, bankers and industrialists to those of every citizen in practically every country. War in the twentieth century has moulded the course of history and determined the lot of mankind to a greater extent than in any previous recorded age. Accordingly, the interest and importance of identifying and comprehending the decisive battles of this, the age of violence, have increased.

The twenty-three battles which are described in this volume in essays by different hands span approximately the first half of the twentieth century; one belongs to the decade before 1914, five to the First World War, fourteen to the geographically much larger Second World War, and two to the 'post-war' period. In making our selection we have of course advanced on to controversial ground. It may be argued that we have chosen too many battles or too few or that we have chosen the wrong ones. This may be so, for drawing up lists of battles is a subjective exercise. We have also had to match each potential title to an author with proper expertise. No doubt other editors might have included Gallipoli or the Ardennes; we have not done so. No doubt, too, there is a case for battles from the Russian, Spanish, and Chinese civil wars of this century. We did invite General Dayan in September 1973 to contribute a chapter on the Arab–Israeli War but he told us at the time that he had other preoccupations and within a month a further conflict broke out which might have rendered his chapter obsolete. At least we can say that the choice of our twenty-three battles is defensible and that it has been confirmed by each author, all of whom knew the title of our volume before they accepted our invitation to contribute to it.

The ways in which the twenty-three battles we have selected exerted their decisive effects were as different as were, in many cases, their locations and scales. The link between them all, their decisiveness, is more easily illustrated by examples than by theoretical definitions. Battles such as Tsushima, Tannenberg and Imphal–Kohima were all directly decisive in a military and tactical sense as well as being historically decisive stages in the destruction of the Russian and Japanese empires. These are examples of directly and classically decisive encounters.

In addition to the battles of this kind, however, we have included a quite different category, within which we have chosen Verdun, Jutland and Schweinfurt. Here the outcome was much less obvious and, to a great extent, more indirect. Verdun appeared to be an indecisive battle; it appeared indeed to epitomize the indecisive character of trench warfare during most of the 1914–18 conflict in the west. Verdun, however, did produce decisive effects of the first magnitude. The search for an alternative to such a nightmare induced the French to build the Maginot Line and the Germans to develop the fast-moving, deep-ranging Panzer column.

Jutland, minute by comparison with Verdun, but nevertheless the only full-scale naval action of the First World War and, of its kind, the last in history, also seemed to be a stalemate. It convinced the German High Command all the same that the threat of British blockade could be countered only by U-boat warfare. This was a policy which brought the United States into the war and sealed the fate of the German empire.

Schweinfurt, on a yet much smaller scale than Jutland, appeared to be a clear-cut victory in the air for the Luftwaffe over the American Eighth Air Force, whose strategic bombers were decimated in their unsuccessful attempt to destroy the German ball-bearing industry. Yet the result was to place in the ascendant the view that day bombers could survive only if they were escorted by long-range fighters and to stimulate dramatically the production of effective long-range fighters, notably the P51 Mustangs, which then, in conjunction with the bombers, wrested from the Germans the command of the air over Europe and opened the way for the successful and decisive Normandy landings.

Differences between direct and indirect effects and differences between the scales of battles are not necessarily reflected in the decisiveness of their results. Indeed, it may at first sight seem absurd to treat Dien Bien Phu in the same context as Stalingrad, where the forces involved were more than ten times greater: 1,300,000 compared with fewer than 120,000. Dien Bien Phu, however, like Singapore in February 1942, was a turning point in the history of Western civilization or Western imperialism in the Far East. The Tet Offensive of 1968, another battle on a small scale and some would even claim not a battle at all, was linked to Dien Bien Phu by General Giap. Here the Americans, who won the tactical victory, reaped a strategic defeat which was the prelude to their withdrawal from the Vietnam War. The three battles considered in conjunction may indeed be seen as the key which has unlocked the new world of South-east Asia.

Unfortunately for mankind, most of the battles of the twentieth century have been on the grand scale; they have been slow to resolve and imprecise in their consequences. Many of them have not, strictly speaking, been 'battles' at all, but protracted struggles of attrition sometimes waged over whole fronts or oceans. Thus the Battle of France, the Battle of Britain and the Battle of the Atlantic could more accurately be described as campaigns. In contrast, at Hastings, Waterloo and Sedan, where the rival commanders could survey the entire battlefield, decisions were reached in a matter of hours and they left in each case one side wholly triumphant and the other utterly ruined. Verdun, the longest identifiable land battle in hitsory, lasted ten months, left both sides exhausted and retained the secrets of its consequences for a succeeding generation to discover.

Indeed there have been few battles in the twentieth century which, at a single stroke, have changed the course of history; the Battle of France, which resulted in one of the most crushing victories in the history of warfare, is a notable exception. Armed forces, in the age of democracy, are remarkably resilient. Even Stalingrad did not destroy the German army beyond the hope and the power of recovery. It is no longer only generalship, discipline and operational skills which determine battles. Armed forces in the twentieth century have come to embody all the scientific, industrial and ideological resources of the modern state. But even in this century when warfare, within fifty years, has grown in potential more than in all previous history, the commander in battle may still control the fate of millions of his fellow human beings. If Montgomery had allowed himself to be drawn into a premature offensive he could have lost Alamein, and if Dowding and Park had succumbed to the pressure that was put on them to engage the Luftwaffe in an all-out fighter action they could have lost the Battle of Britain. At Jutland, Jellicoe could, in Churchill's well-known phrase, have lost the war 'in an afternoon', and there must now be reason to doubt whether Percival need have lost Singapore.

We have been fortunate to be able to harness the talents of a distinguished collection of authors to the making of this volume. We are delighted to be able to include contributions from five eminent American historians and one Australian – Professor Alvin D. Coox, Harrison E. Salisbury, Dr Stanley L. Falk, Professor Martin Blumenson, Professor Bernard Brodie and Dr Robert O'Neill. Several of the authors, in addition to their historical and literary prowess, have themselves reached high rank in the armed forces. These include General Sir William Jackson, who at this time is Quartermaster-General of the British Army, Lieutenant-General Sir Geoffrey Evans, who, in addition to writing about Imphal-Kohima, actually fought in the battle, and Air Vice-Marshal Stewart Menaul, who served with great distinction in Bomber Command's Path Finder Force during the Second World War. Sir John Wheeler-Bennett brings to his subject not only a lifetime of study but a first-hand and thorough personal knowledge of Hindenburg and his caste.

It is a truism that the understanding of history and especially the history of warfare depends upon an international viewpoint. It is perhaps also true that its best perspectives may be perceived through the eyes of historians both young and mature. We have therefore deliberately sought authors not only with various national viewpoints but of different generations.

NOBLE FRANKLAND

12 September 1975 CHRISTOPHER DOWLING

The Mikasa, *Admiral Togo's flagship at Tsushima.*
Left: His famous Nelsonian signal calling on every man to do his utmost

Chapter One

TSUSHIMA

Christopher Lloyd

THE DECAY OF the Chinese empire during the last half of the nineteenth century rendered a conflict between its neighbours, Russia and Japan, inevitable. The beginning of Russian expansion in the Far East may be dated from the establishment of Vladivostok as a naval base in 1860. After the Meiji 'restoration' of imperial power in 1867 Japan emerged from centuries of isolation to become a modern nation by adopting not only Western technology but also Western political attitudes, such as imperialist ambitions.

Thus, while Russia was extending her influence in Manchuria, Japanese influence was penetrating Korea on the excuse of securing the safety of her western seaboard. A long series of Japanese-inspired incidents culminated in 1894 with the Sino-Japanese War.

The officer who precipitated the conflict by attacking Chinese transports without a formal declaration of war (as he was similarly to attack Russian shipping ten years later) was Togo Heihachire (1847–1934). His career is an epitome of the development of the Imperial Japanese Navy. Just as Japan depended on Germany to improve her army, so she relied on Britain, as the leading naval power, to improve her navy. Togo was one of the carefully selected officers to be sent to England for training. For two years he served as a cadet on board H.M.S. *Worcester*, followed by a course on board the *Victory*, a mathematical course at Cambridge and a stay at Greenwich to superintend the construction of one of the many warships built for his navy, the cruiser *Fuso*. He was recalled to Japan in 1874. In 1894 he was in command of the light forces in the Yellow Sea.

Admiral Ito (who was to be supreme commander in 1904, as Togo was to be commander-in-chief at sea) defeated the obsolete Chinese fleet without difficulty in the brief Sino-Japanese War. In April 1895 the Treaty of Shimoneseki recognized the independence of Korea (which became, in fact, a Japanese puppet) and ceded rights in Manchuria and Formosa, with the neighbouring Pescadores, to Japan. This was too much for Russia, who forced Japan to disgorge the Liaotung peninsula and the vital base of Port Arthur. Fearing Russian ambitions in the Yellow Sea, other European powers followed suit at the expense of China, the French obtaining Pechili, Germany Kiaochow (Tsingtao) and Britain Wei-hai-wei, together with the lease of Kowloon on the mainland opposite Hong-Kong.

Japan's desire for revenge on Russia for robbing her of the fruits of victory led to a rapid development of her armed forces. But before committing herself to hostilities she safeguarded her diplomatic position by signing the Anglo-Japanese Alliance of 1902. Thereby Britain recognized her rights in Korea and undertook to prevent the intervention of a third party in the event of a conflict with Russia. The alliance was welcomed in Britain as a means of checking the expansion of a power which had for long been the source of uneasiness, particularly in India. For Japan, it was a signal for war.

It now seems incredible that Russia should have so seriously underestimated the advances made in Japanese military strength during the ten years since the Sino-Japanese War. When the 'Korean' party began to dominate the Tsarist government in 1903, negotiations were broken off and the viceroy and commander at Vladivostok, Admiral Alexieff, deliberately embarked on a policy of provocation. The army authorities underestimated the number of men Japan could put in the field by no less that two thirds and the Chief of the Naval Staff fatuously announced that since 'our fleet cannot be beaten by the Japanese fleet', enemy troops could not be landed in Korea. Having openly augmented the Pacific fleet, the Russian High Command then divided it by stationing two thirds at Port Arthur and the remainder at Vladivostok 1,000 miles away.

Since the principal aim of the Japanese was to land their armies in Korea and Manchuria, naval strategy aimed at neutralizing Port Arthur in order to control the Yellow Sea and prevent any reinforcements coming from Vladivostok. The Japanese fleet was the best trained and equipped in the world at that date. It may not have been as large as the British, but it was probably more efficient. A large flotilla of destroyers and torpedo boats were armed with 18-inch Whitehead torpedoes with a range of 3,000 yards, though most attacks were made at much shorter range. In 12-inch guns on board the battleships the weight of metal was much the same as that of the Russians, but Japanese ships carried more 6-inch quick-firing guns which did great execution in battle, and her ships were well in advance in the efficiency of their radio communication systems.

The Russian fleet, though actually larger, was remarkably inefficient, not so much in respect of gunnery or armour plating as in the engine room, in seamanship and above all in morale and leadership. Its ships were widely scattered in the Yellow Sea, the Pacific, the Baltic and the Black Sea, and when attempts were made to concentrate them the strategic methods adopted were suicidal.

Togo began the war by a pre-emptive strike with torpedoes at Port Arthur on the night of 8 February 1904. Though the number of hits was not high, two battleships were put out of action and the Russian squadron was startled into something like panic. A siege of the port by land and sea followed. Togo's ships suffered severely from Russian mines, but in May Admiral Makaroff (the only Russian officer of distinction) was accidentally killed when his flagship was blown up by one of his own mines and on 10 August, at the Battle of the Yellow Sea, Togo convincingly defeated, though he did not annihilate, the Port Arthur squadron, Admiral Vitgeft being killed early in the action. The Russians never emerged again, their ships being destroyed by army howitzers.

During this first phase of the war the Russian naval force in the Yellow Sea was reduced by seven battleships, six cruisers and twenty-nine destroyers, at a loss to the Japanese of two battleships, two cruisers and two destroyers. By his first victory over the Russians Togo gained a breathing space of several months to repair his ships while he awaited the approach of Russian reinforcements in the shape of the Baltic fleet, now destined for the Far East.

The decision to despatch this fleet on what was to prove the most suicidal mission in naval history was arrived at in April 1904, though the ships did not actually sail until October. The force, now called the 2nd Pacific Squadron, consisted of seven battleships – *Suvorov*, *Alexander III*, *Borodino*, *Orel*, *Oslyabya*, *Veliky* and *Navarin* – two armoured cruisers, four light cruisers, seven destroyers and nine transports. The first four battleships were new and powerful vessels of 13,000 tons, armed with two pairs of 12-inch guns in fore and aft turrets, with a secondary armament of twelve 6-inch quick-firing guns. Indeed, there was not much wrong with the ships at the outset, but it proved impossible to man them satisfactorily, the best engineers and gunnery personnel being already in the Pacific. The only attribute which the Russians certainly did not lack was fatalistic courage.

The squadron was placed under the command of Admiral Zinovy Petrovitch Rozhdestvensky, aged fifty-three, an irritable aristocrat who seems to have been convinced of the futility of his mission before he started. His orders were to reinforce the Port Arthur squadron after a voyage of 5,000 miles, the coal consumption being reckoned at 500,000 tons. Since Russia possessed no bases on the route to the Pacific, elaborate and expensive arrangements had to be made with the Hamburg–Amerika line to provide colliers at various points of call. No one seems to have imagined what the state of the hulls of the warships would be like after so long a voyage through tropical seas.

Before the Russian squadron left port, rumours were rife in the Baltic that the Japanese had somehow infiltrated the North Sea. Any accident was put down to sabotage and even clouds were mistaken for observation balloons during the passage through the Belt. When on the night of 21 October some fishing trawlers from Hull were seen off the Dogger Bank, several Russian ships fired on them (and on each other). The trawler *Crane* was sunk at a range of 100 yards and two men were killed. Two days later, before the trawlers returned, part of the Russian fleet was happily coaling off Brighton. When the fishing fleet did return, public protest almost amounted to a demand for war with Russia. The crisis was surmounted by diplomacy, the only explanation offered by Rozhdestvensky being that 'the incident of the North Sea was provoked by two torpedo boats which, without showing lights, under cover of darkness advanced to attack the vessel steaming at the head of the squadron. When the squadron began to sweep the sea with its search lights, and opened fire, the presence was also discovered of several small fishing vessels.'

There is no need to follow the sad progress of the Russian fleet as it crept down the coast of West Africa at an average speed of eight knots. Suffice it to say that somehow the fuel problem was surmounted and the ships reached the French harbour of Nossi-Bé at Madagascar in safety. Here Rozhdestvensky heard the news of the fall of Port Arthur, news which demolished the whole object of his mission. At the same time stories of the revolutionary movement in Russia reached the crews, the morale of which was so low that in some ships attempts were made to rival the notorious mutiny of the *Potemkin* at home.

While Rozhdestvensky awaited orders from St Petersburg he was told that a 3rd Pacific Squadron under Rear-Admiral Nebogatoff was on its way to join him. This consisted of one obsolete battleship, three armoured coast defence vessels of slow speed and a cruiser. When asked for his appreciation of the situation, Rozhdestvensky replied: 'I have not the slightest prospect of recovering the command of the sea with the force under my orders. The despatch of reinforcements composed of untested or badly built vessels would only render the fleet more vulnerable. In my view the only possible course is to use all force to break through to Vladivostok and from this base to threaten the enemy's communications.'

He realized that the British had stopped all shipment of coal further east and that he would have to run the gauntlet of the Japanese fleet in the Straits of Tsushima west of Japan because shortage of fuel made any more circuitous route impossible. He could remain no longer in a neutral port, so without further orders and without waiting for the arrival of Nebogatoff's squadron he put to sea. Having crossed the Indian Ocean, he heard at Sumatra that the Russian army had been defeated at Mukden; this was the event which decided the issue of the war. No wonder the general opinion in the fleet was thus expressed by an officer in a letter home: 'What hope is there for us now? We are fated to die; there is no turning back.'

Nebogatoff caught up with the main body at Kamranh Bay on the coast of Vietnam (then French Cochin China), but Rozhdestvensky, now in the depths of despair, had only one meeting with the man who was to become his second-in-command because of the death of the officer who held that post before the battle. Isolated even from his own officers, he proceeded to take this miscellany of forty-two ships northwards to an inevitable doom. The fleet sailed on 14 May.

'Togo is now the picture of health,' reported Captain W. C. Pakenham, R.N., appointed official observer on board the battleship *Asahi*. 'He said that now the fleet had been refitted the ships were as good as new.' With his tall build, his monocle, his high starched collar, his sangfroid as he watched the battle from a deck chair, it is not surprising that this representative of the Edwardian navy made a strong impression on the Japanese.

The Japanese were now in an impregnable position. Keeping his main fleet at Masampo on the southern tip of Korea near Pusan, Togo stretched a double line of scouting cruisers across the Straits of Tsushima. The island of Tsushima (meaning the Island of the Donkey's Ears) is separated by about fifty miles from Korea and it is about twice that distance eastward to the naval base at Shimonoseki on the Japanese mainland. Lying somewhat south-east of Tsushima is the much smaller island of Ikishima, so that the actual strait is narrowed to a breadth of about forty miles. It was through this gateway to the north that Rozhdestvensky was forced to go in order to reach Vladivostok with his miscellaneous collection of vessels. As Captain Semenoff wrote in his reminiscences of the battle: 'Once again and for the last time we were forcibly reminded of the old truism that a "fleet" is created by long practice at sea in time of peace and that a collection of ships of various types hastily collected, which have only learned to sail together on the way to the theatre of operations, is no fleet, but a chance concourse of vessels.'

When the Russian fleet was sighted by the auxiliary cruiser *Shinano Maru* some 150 miles south of the straits at 4.45 on the morning of 27 May 1905, it was steaming in two columns with a cruiser screen. Such was the variety of craft under his command that Rozhdestvensky was compelled to maintain an average speed of only nine knots, whereas Togo was able to manoeuvre at twice that speed. Hence there was plenty of time for the latter to leave his anchorage at Masampo in order to reach his chosen field of battle to the east of the island of Tsushima where the straits are narrowest. His own division of the fleet consisted of three powerful battleships, the *Mikasa*, the *Fuji* and the *Asahi*, and two armoured cruisers, with six other armoured cruisers under Rear-Admiral Kamimura attached. The plan was to attack the van of the Russian fleet with the biggest ships, leaving the cruisers under Rear-Admiral Dewa to harry the rear and reserving the torpedo flotilla for a night action.

At 1 p.m. Dewa's squadron came into view on the Russians' port beam about five miles away. According to Semenoff, some Russian ships opened fire by mistake, but the admiral signalled 'Ammunition not to be wasted'. All Russian signalling was done by semaphore, Rozhdestvensky fearing that wireless signals would betray his position. Togo, on the other hand, used wireless freely and by this means kept in touch with his far-flung ships. Thus the battle was the first occasion on which radio was used in action.

Just before battle was joined Rozhdestvensky made a tactical mistake which reminds one of Villeneuve's before Trafalgar, when an equally inexpert fleet came into action. He ordered the first and second divisions of heavy ships to increase speed and turn ninety degrees to starboard in order to stand between the Japanese and the weaker ships. Shortly afterwards he cancelled this in order to restore a line ahead formation, but he omitted to inform the division of ships astern of the change of plan and speed. The consequence was, according to Admiral Nebogatoff, that 'one vessel had to turn to starboard and another to port, so that there was absolute confusion'.

Togo's signal to engage had a truly Nelsonian flavour: 'The rise and fall of the Empire depends upon today's battle. Let every man do his utmost.' His main body was at that time north-east of the Russians. He now turned back westward across the line of the Russian advance about 8,500 yards ahead of the leading ship, his own flagship *Mikasa* leading. Rozhdestvensky opened fire at 2.08 p.m. After waiting a few moments to allow the range to shorten, the Japanese ships fired as they 'crossed the T' of the Russian ships, that is to say they brought a converging broadside fire to concentrate upon the leading Russian ships. As they found the range it was obvious to Semenoff, who had been in the Battle of the Yellow Sea, that the enemy were using a more sensitive fuse than before, so that the huge 12-inch shells (often to be seen turning over and over as they passed overhead) exploded on the slightest impact.

In the first phase of the action Russian fire was heavy and accurate, but the storm of explosives which hit the fleet during the next half hour was unprecedented and soon diminished its effectiveness. As Semenoff wrote: 'It seemed impossible even to count the number of projectiles striking us. I had not only never witnessed such a fire before but I had never imagined anything like it. Shells seemed to be pouring upon us incessantly, one after another. . . . The steel plates and superstructure on the upper deck were torn to pieces and the splinters caused many casualties. Iron ladders were crumpled into rings, and guns were literally hurled from their mountings. Such havoc would never be caused by the simple impact of a shell, still less by that of its splinters. It could only be caused by the force of the explosion.'

The leading battleships *Suvorov*, *Alexander III* and *Borodino* were wrapped in smoke and flame, their decks littered with debris, their turrets jammed, their crews unable to distinguish their target. The *Oslyabya*, lying fifth in the line, was the first to be put out of action. At 2.50 she sank, the first armoured battleship ever sunk by gunfire.

At 2.45 the flagship *Suvorov* was so crippled that she fell out of line, Rozhdestvensky himself being so severely wounded that he was no longer in control of the fleet. His last signal to Nebogatoff, now in command, was to press northwards to Vladivostok.

The Russian line had been forced to starboard by the impact of the Japanese attack on the port bow. The second phase of the battle opened after a short interval during which the Russian ships circled round the crippled flagship before resuming a northerly course at 3 p.m. By that time Togo had once more crossed their line of advance, so now he recrossed the line in order to head them off. When he was once more on their port beam, he inverted his order of sailing to bring the *Mikasa* back to the head of the line. The seamanship displayed by his captains during these intricate manoeuvres of simultaneous turns of all the big ships was of a very high order. Once his regrouping had been completed, the two fleets resumed a north-easterly direction on parallel courses for the next hour.

The *Alexander III* now led the line of a sadly damaged fleet in low visibility, clouds of smoke and a thin mist obscuring the field of battle. Far to the south the Japanese cruiser squadrons, commanded by Dewa, Kataaoko and Uric, had been in action for over an hour, but their weight of metal and the instability of their ships in a comparatively rough sea rendered their fire less lethal than that of the heavier ships of the fleet. Nevertheless, it sufficed to drive the transports towards the rear of the main body, many of them – including the huge ex-German liner *Ural* – being sunk by hits below the waterline.

The destroyer *Buiny* managed to take the wounded admiral off the flagship before she sank, but, as before, Togo was following every turn of the enemy as the Russians emerged from the pall of smoke with the burning *Borodino* leading, *Alexander III* having fallen astern. At 7 p.m. the latter was seen to capsize and soon afterwards the *Borodino* exploded.

Darkness was now falling. Togo ordered all his big ships to break off action, appointing a rendezvous at dawn well to the north. His losses so far had been minimal, the only ships to be badly damaged being the *Asama* and the *Mikasa* herself. Now it was the turn of the five squadrons of twenty-one destroyers and eighty torpedo boats, which had been held in reserve all day. Togo simply told them to pursue and destroy the enemy, but left them a free hand as to how to do it.

After an hour's respite the Russians began to distinguish low small craft rushing at high speed between their ships. The sea was swarming with torpedo craft. Though the expenditure of torpedoes was high, not a great number of hits were scored, the effect of the attack being rather to disperse the enemy fleet over a wide area north of the straits. Some, like the old battleship *Oleg*, bearing the flag of Admiral Enquist, turned south with two cruisers to shake off the enemy. Seventeen torpedoes were counted as they missed these ships, which ultimately reached Manila for internment.

At daylight on 28 May, with the promise of brighter weather and better visibility, Togo resumed the attack with his big ships. He was now 150 miles from where the battle had started and some of his cruisers were as much as sixty miles to starboard. Orders were given for them to close in on the rear, where they proceeded to sink some armoured cruisers and coast defence ships. At 11.30 Nebogatoff in the *Nikolai I* found himself surrounded eighteen miles south of the small island of Takeshima. Under heavy fire and with his own ammunition running short, he called a council of war to hear the advice of his officers. At the conclusion he announced: 'Gentlemen, I propose to surrender as the only means of saving our crews from destruction. Please give orders to run up the white flag.'

The flag was a tablecloth. When they saw it the Japanese could not believe that it signified surrender, so alien was such an action to their professional code. They made a careful approach to the four big ships and some firing continued before the surrender was negotiated, all Russian officers being permitted to retain their swords. More widely scattered ships, such as the coast defence vessel *Ushakoff* and the old battleships *Sissoy Veliky* and *Navarin* were sunk after a token resistance, the last of the Russian battleships, the *Dmitry Donskoi* (laid down as far back as 1885), capsizing after a gallant fight lasting two hours.

The destroyer *Biedovy*, to which Rozhestvensky had been transferred, was captured during the afternoon and he was taken ashore to a Japanese naval hospital scarcely conscious of what was happening. He recovered from his wounds and was acquitted at a court martial held on his return to St Petersburg. Nebogatoff, on the other hand, together with his chief of staff, was sentenced to be shot, the sentences being commuted to imprisonment. Rozhdestvensky died in 1909.

The only ships which reached Vladivostok were two destroyers and one light cruiser, *Almaz*. Out of the twelve Russian capital ships, eight had been sunk and the others captured. Five cruisers had been sunk and others captured. Seven destroyers were sunk. All this at a loss to the Japanese of three torpedo boats sunk and some damage sustained early in the action. Casualty figures were:

	Killed	*Wounded or taken prisoner*	*Total*
Japanese	117	583	700
Russian	4,830	5,917	10,747

Tsushima was the most complete of naval victories. In Europe it was hailed as a surprising success on the part of a small, quaint people without a full appreciation of its consequences. At that moment, exactly 100 years after Trafalgar, the 'splendid isolation' of Britain was at its climax. With a navy of forty-four battleships, she had nothing to fear from a French navy of twelve and a German navy of sixteen, and now her principal enemy was totally destroyed. Yet before the year was out she was to commit herself to a Continental alliance with France in order to face the German threat, with the realization that her interests in the Far East would be protected by her new Japanese ally.

For the Japanese, the consequences were more far-reaching, for she now virtually controlled the north Pacific. On the initiative of the President of the United States as a third party, the peace treaty signed at Portsmouth (New Hampshire) on 5 September 1905 granted all the Japanese demands – Port Arthur, the Liaotung peninsula and the southern half of the island of Sakhalin – as well as recognizing her protectorate of Korea. A year later the two largest battleships in the world were laid down in Japanese shipyards to mark her emergence as one of the world's leading sea powers.

On the face of it, David had killed Goliath. In fact, a well trained, well equipped, well led fleet had defeated a giant with feet of clay which was deficient in all those qualities. The Tsarist regime was staggering to its doom. The revolution which the war provoked in 1905 was merely postponed, whereas Japan was now in the front rank of world powers, whether considered from a political, economic or military point of view. National pride and confidence bred by such a complete victory led, inevitably and unfortunately, further along the path of imperialist expansion, at first at the expense of China, later at that of European and American interests in the Pacific and in South-east Asia. It is surely significant that Togo's disciple, Yamamoto, who served as a midshipman in the Battle of Tsushima, was commander-in-chief of the Imperial Japanese Navy at Pearl Harbor.

★ ★ ★

List of Ships Engaged

RUSSIAN			JAPANESE		
Class	*Ships*	*Displacement (tons)*	*Class*	*Ships*	*Displacement (tons)*
Battleship	*Knias Suvorov*	13,516	Battleship	*Mikasa*	15,200
	Imperator Alexander III	13,516		*Shikishima*	14,850
	Borodino	13,516		*Asahi*	14,850
	Orel	13,516		*Fuji*	12,320
	Oslyabya	12,674	Armoured cruiser	*Nisshin*	7,294
	Sissoi Veliky	8,880		*Kasuga*	7,294
	Navarin	10,206		*Idzumo*	7,294
	Imperator Nikolai I	9,672		*Iwate*	9,750
Coast defence	*General Admiral Apraksin*	4,162		*Adzumo*	9,436
Armour clad	*Admiral Senyavin*	4,684		*Asama*	9,700
	Admiral Ushakoff	4,684		*Tokiwa*	9,700
Armoured cruiser	*Admiral Nakhimoff*	8,524		*Yakumo*	9,850
	Dimitry Donskoi	6,200			
	Vladimir Monomach	5,593			

Note on Sources

Committee of Imperial Defence, *Official History of the Russo–Japanese War* (1910).
Falk, Edwin A., *Togo and the Rise of Japanese Sea Power* (1936).
Hale, J. R., *Famous Sea Fights* (7th ed. 1931).
Hough, Richard, *The Fleet that had to Die* (1958).
Nevikoff-Priboy, *Tsushima* (1936).
Semenoff, V., *Rasplata: the Reckoning* (1909).
Wilson, H. W., *Ironclads in Action* (1926).

The extent of the Russian disaster. Russian prisoners queueing for bread rations in the winter of 1914

Chapter Two

TANNENBERG

Sir John Wheeler-Bennett

(i)

THE BI-NOMENCLATURE of battles presents just one more hazard to the unwary historian. We do not know whether both the Athenians and the Spartans referred to the Battle of Aeguspotami as such, but in modern times the difference of names is marked. The British speak with pride and confidence of Waterloo and Jutland, but to the French and the Germans they are Mont St Jean and Skagerrak respectively, whereas in the American Civil War the Union historians have chosen to name battles after physical features and their Confederate colleagues after townships; thus Bull Run becomes Manassas south of the Mason and Dixon Line and Antietam is transformed into Sharpsburg.

This perversity of terminology is certainly true of the great engagement fought in East Prussia in August 1914. Though history remembers it as Tannenberg (it was nearly called Frögenau), it appears in the Imperial Russian archives as Soldau, though I am not certain what name Soviet military historians attach to it.

Nor must it be thought that the Battle of Tannenberg, which has established its place in history as (to quote one of its ablest students, Lord Ironside) 'the greatest defeat suffered by any of the combatants during the war', was the fruit of carefully prepared and long thought-out planning. It was in fact the improvised climax of a series of engagements in which the Germans had been far from dominantly successful. To understand the story of the battle fully it is necessary to know something of the background.

At the outbreak of hostilities three great strategic concepts were called into play, and within a month all had failed. For the Germans the Schlieffen Plan, disastrously modified by the younger Moltke, called for a sweep through Belgium and northern France aimed at the capture of Paris. The German General Staff anticipated a war on two fronts, but counted on being able to hold up a Russian advance until after the French had been decisively defeated and the German forces in the east could be reinforced.

General Joffre's Plan XVII was based on the supposition that the Germans would march through Belgium but that their front would not extend west of the Meuse. It was calculated that the enemy would have too few troops for a more extended operation, but the plan omitted to take into consideration the possible immediate employment of reserve divisions.

The Russian army in Europe, under the command of Grand Duke Nicholas, the Tsar's uncle, was divided into two army groups, one directed towards the invasion of East Prussia and the other towards the occupation of Galicia. Once these two aims had been achieved both army groups were to advance into Germany.

In Franco–Russian staff talks during 1912 and 1913 it had been stated that by 1914 Russia would be able to move against Germany on M (mobilization) + 13 days with 800,000 men, despite the fact that the Russian strategic railway system was hopelessly inadequate to the task and that her munitions and armaments industries were capable of producing barely two thirds of the estimated essential shell output and only fifty per cent of the necessary rifle ammunition.

An added difficulty for the Russians was that, in advancing into East Prussia, the two invading armies would inevitably be divided by the Masurian Lakes: the Russians could only continue their advance by sending one army to the north and one to the south of this chain of water. To make a success of this manoeuvre the closest and most efficient liaison was necessary. The Germans, therefore, though considerably inferior in manpower, had the potential advantage of being able to attack and defeat one of the advancing Russian armies while they were disunited, being then ready to turn upon the other.

Such was the theoretical position in the first week of August 1914, but neither on the Eastern nor the Western Front did things go according to plan. Much of this was due to the imponderables of war, among which was the question of relative individual personalities. The German Chief of the General Staff, General von Moltke, a nephew of the great architect of the German army, was a man of straw, terrified at the burden of responsibility which lay upon him, lacking the power of rapid decision, and destitute of that calm control which had enabled his famous uncle, once the mobilization of the Prussian army against France had been put *en train* in 1870, to retire to bed with Mrs Braddon's novel, *Lady Audley's Secret.*

Nor was the situation improved by the fact that the German holding force in East Prussia, the Eighth Army, composed of some eleven infantry divisions and one of cavalry, was commanded by Colonel-General Count Max von Prittwitz und Gaffron, who was not an officer of outstanding distinction or nervous fortitude, and who had acquired the uninspiring nickname of *der dicke Soldat* (the fat soldier). His chief of staff was General Count von Waldersee, a nephew of that officer whose uneasy task it had been to command the international force which had relieved the legations in Peking at the time of the Boxer Rising in 1900 and who had subsequently become Schlieffen's predecessor as Chief of the General Staff.

The real strength of leadership at Eighth Army G.H.Q. was Colonel Max Hoffmann, the senior general staff officer, and the quartermaster-general, General von Grünert. Both these men were of the best possible calibre of the German General Staff, than which, militarily speaking, one can offer no higher praise, and Hoffmann was fated to play a highly important role throughout the war.

On the Russian side, the commanding officer of the First Army, operating on the north of the front with headquarters at Vilna, was General Rennenkampf, a competent and dashing soldier but somewhat arrogant by nature, a characteristic which many of his colleagues attributed to his German ancestry. There was a not too kind joke in circulation on his appointment, that in invading East Prussia he was 'going to visit his German cousins'. Rennenkampf's colleague commanding the Second Army, which was on the southern sector of the front with headquarters at Warsaw, was General Samsonov, a veteran cavalry officer who had only recently been recalled from retirement, who had never before commanded as large a force as an army, and who was a chronic asthmatic. He had not the *panache* of Rennenkampf but he had achieved a reputation for dogged determination in executing orders.

The delicate and vital task of coordinating the movements of these two great armies, amounting between them to thirty infantry and eight cavalry divisions (which gave them a numerical superiority over the German Eighth Army of almost three to one in infantry and eight to one in cavalry) was General Jilinsky, who, as Chief of the General Staff before the war, had given pledges to Joffre which were almost impossible to fulfil. He now commanded the North-western Army Group, with headquarters at Bialystock. His burden, difficult enough in itself, was greatly complicated by the fact that between his two immediate subordinates, the commanders of his two armies, there existed a bitter quarrel of some ten years' standing.

In the Russo-Japanese War of 1904–5, both Rennenkampf and Samsonov had been cavalry divisional commanders at the Battle of Lianyang, during the Mukden campaign. Samsonov, with his Siberian Cossacks, bore the brunt of the defence of the Yentai coal mines, and after a gallant action was forced to retreat from his position. He blamed his failure in great measure on the inactivity and lack of support of Rennenkampf, who had been detailed to support him and made no secret of his views. In the bitterness of the general defeat the two officers, who had been keen rivals from their days at the Military Academy, met on the railway platform at Mukden and reproached each other with acrid recrimination. The dispute became heated; Samsonov boxed his opponent's ears and the two came to fisticuffs. An already disheartened army was thus treated to the uninspiring display of two major-generals rolling on the ground before the eyes of their scandalized staff officers, who eventually tore them apart. The Tsar forbade a duel but the former rivalry had developed into a passion for revenge, a fact which had apparently escaped the knowledge or the notice of those of the General Staff who were responsible for the appointments to the commands of the First and Second Armies. This fact was destined to be of great help to the enemy.

On 17 August Rennenkampf began his advance into East Prussia, marching due west in the expectation that Samsonov would come up from the south-east and strike the right flank of the German Eighth Army in support of his attack. Samsonov started his movement on the 19th, but had an infinitely more difficult terrain to traverse, for the sandy soil, soft roads and thick forests of Poland made both the marching of troops and the horse-drawn transportation of supplies formidable problems. Despite these obstacles, however, he calculated that he could reach his objective on time.

From the first, however, the Russian timetable was at fault, not only between Rennenkampf and Samsonov, but also between the units of the First Army itself, where a wide gap was left between the III and IV Corps. Discovering this, General von François, commanding the German I Corps, slipped through it on the 18th and attacked Rennenkampf from the rear at Stallupönen; causing widespread confusion and panic, he captured some 3,000 prisoners and withdrew without great loss.

It was during this first engagement that the German G.H.Q. made an almost incredible but highly advantageous discovery. The headquarters staffs of Jilinsky, Rennenkampf and Samsonov communicated with each other by wireless messages sent out either *en clair* or in so simple a code that a professor of mathematics attached to German headquarters as a cryptographer had no difficulty in reading it.

Nevertheless the action at Stallupönen, though a success for François and the I Corps, was an error of judgement on his part, for while large numbers of Russian prisoners were taken German losses were also considerable, both in men and material and in attacking power, which should in particular have been husbanded against the decisive battle. Moreover, no real advantage was gained by delaying Rennenkampf; on the contrary it was in the German interest that he should advance as rapidly as possible so that he might be crushed before the arrival of Samsonov.

After the initial check at Stallupönen, Rennenkampf continued his advance and by 19 August had reached Gumbinnen, where he took up battle positions. The German commander-in-chief, Prittwitz, favoured a further withdrawal but, under the influence of François, who as commander of the East Prussian Army Corps was unwilling to see more of his beloved province than was necessary given over to the horrors of war, agreed to give battle. On the following morning at dawn François made a surprise attack on the Russian right wing and drove it back some ten miles in disorder. On the left, Below's I Reserve Corps also scored a success, but in the centre Mackensen's XVII Corps launched an impetuous frontal attack, failed to reach its objectives, and was defeated and rolled back.

Prittwitz, viewing the situation from his headquarters at Wartenburg nearly seventy-five miles from the field of battle, was more impressed by Mackensen's defeat than by the successes of François and Below. His nerves, and those of his chief of staff too, were beginning to fray. Having accepted the aggressive advice of François, strongly supported by Hoffmann and Grünert, he now swung to the other extreme and rejected their counsel to continue the action on the following day. And when news arrived that Samsonov had at last emerged south of the Masurian Lakes and was therefore in a position to threaten the German right flank, Prittwitz lost his nerve altogether, ordered that the Battle of Gumbinnen should be broken off and that the whole Eighth Army should retire behind the River Vistula. He telephoned hysterically to Imperial Headquarters at Coblentz that he could not even hold the line of the Vistula unless strong reinforcements were sent to him forthwith.

This action on the part of the commander-in-chief was taken entirely against the advice of his G.S.O.1 Hoffmann and his quartermaster-general Grünert, but with the approval of his chief of staff Waldersee. Hoffmann and Grünert were not informed of the panic call to Coblentz, but had they known of the exact position at the Russian First and Second Army headquarters, their conviction that to advance was a better strategy than to retreat would have been greatly strengthened. Rennenkampf's staff was urging him, almost to a man, to break off the action at Gumbinnen, accept it as a reverse, and retreat accordingly. Samsonov's men were so exhausted physically by their gruelling march and so lacking in transport and supplies that he was virtually unable to assume the immediate offensive.

On both sides panic and lack of fortitude had played an important part. Almost from the first day of hostilities pleas for a Russian attack on a massive scale had flooded into Petersburg. The French ambassador, M. Maurice Paléologue, had besought the Tsar, as early as 5 August, 'to take the offensive immediately', and had received an affirmative assurance. As the tide of war turned against the Allies in the West and Plan XVII became increasingly unsuccessful, with the result that Paris seemed threatened, the stream of entreaties from Paléologue to the Russian Foreign Minister Sazonov, and from Joffre to the Russian chief of staff Janushkevitch, became a veritable flood. Unless Russia came immediately to the support of France, Paris would fall, the Western Allies would be defeated and the full might of Germany would turn upon Russia. It was for this reason that Jilinsky, under pressure from Grand Duke Nicholas and from Janushkevitch, but with little confidence of his own, had ordered the wretched Samsonov to press forward with accelerated speed and before his supplies had been assembled and transported. As a result the Second Army arrived at its rendezvous not only exhausted but without rations and without reserves of ammunition. Rarely in military history can an army have been in less good condition to launch a major and vitally important offensive.

But there had been psychological factors at Coblentz, in addition to the frantic appeals of Prittwitz. The approach of the Russian armies towards East Prussia had resulted in violent protests from a strong lobby composed of great landowners, chauvinists and patriotic Germans who could not bear the thought of their historic province, 'the cradle of the race', being given over to foreign invasion, its cities despoiled by barbaric hordes, and its people savaged by bands of Cossacks. The most forceful representations were made to the Kaiser himself and to the Imperial Chancellor, Bethmann-Hollweg, urging that reinforcements be immediately despatched to the aid of the Eighth Army, whose duty, it should be clearly stated, must be first to repel the Russian invasion and then to carry the war onto Russian soil.

These frenzied arguments were, of course, at complete variance with the principles of the Schlieffen Plan, as were the distracted appeals of Prittwitz. The Eighth Army was expected to hold its own, on strategy of its own devising, until such time as a decisive victory in the West could release massive reinforcements. Though the Battle of the Frontiers had been lost and the French counter-offensive in the Argonne broken, and a general retreat was in progress, the French, British and Belgian armies had not sustained a conclusive defeat.

The German successes in the West had been spectacular, however, and Moltke, according to his chief of operations Colonel von Tappen, had reached the conclusion that the great decisive Battle of the West had been fought and won. He took two important decisions: on 20 August he dismissed Prittwitz and Waldersee and appointed General Paul von Benckendorff und Hindenburg to the command of the Eighth Army, with Major-General Erich Ludendorff as his chief of staff, and on the 25th, in spite of contrary advice from his staff, he assigned the XI and Guard Reserve Corps to be transferred from the Western to the Eastern Front, with the promise of four more corps to follow.

At this moment Erich Ludendorff was the gleaming hero of the German army. After an extremely successful prewar record as Director of Operations, he had returned to the command of a brigade at the outbreak of hostilities and at the head of it had captured almost single-handed the Belgian citadel of Liège – an exploit for which the Emperor had decorated him with the highly coveted *Pour le Mérite* cross. He was an obvious choice to save the situation in East Prussia but he lacked seniority, and it was for this reason that Hindenburg was recalled from retirement in Hanover and given the command of the Eighth Army. He too was a popular choice, for he had family connections with both East and West Prussia, and had served as a staff officer at Königsberg.

Between the dismissal of one high command on 20 August and the arrival of the other on 23 August, there occurred a hiatus at Eighth Army G.H.Q., which was filled by the genius of Max Hoffmann. He at once grasped the opportunity – the god-given opportunity dreamed of by all senior staff officers – of drawing up plans in anticipation of his superiors. Indeed, so complete and uncontrovertibly excellent were they that when Hindenburg and Ludendorff did arrive there were few if any changes that they could suggest.

The decisive choice that had to be made was whether to attack Rennenkampf or Samsonov first. Hoffmann was of the opinion that the former, having received a 'bloody nose' at Gumbinnen, would not willingly risk getting another. Samsonov's army was, for the moment, the greater menace (Hoffman was apparently uninformed of the poor state of the Russian Second Army and was basing his calculation on terrain) and had to be dealt with first. Thus the orders which he issued in preparation for the advent of the new high command aimed at the concentration of the whole of the

Eighth Army for this purpose, the essential objective being not merely the defeat but the annihilation of Samsonov. Time was the essence of the plan, and Hoffmann therefore proposed to leave a weak but well masked force consisting of a cavalry division and some reserves and militia to hold Rennenkampf in check, and at the same time to envelop and destroy Samsonov.

In drawing up his plans, which Ludendorff adopted, Hoffman counted on one psychological factor: the bitter feud between his two opponents. He himself had been a military observer during the Russo–Japanese War, though with the Japanese armies. He had not therefore actually seen the brawl on the Mukden platform but he had received a first-hand account of it from his 'opposite number' with the Russians. When he became head of the Eastern Section of the German General Staff Hoffmann had made it his business to keep abreast of the progress of the quarrel. 'I used to tell our military attachés in Petersburg,' he told me, 'that they could buy the Russian order of battle for a few kopecks, but what was far more important was whether the row between those two was still going strong. In the last reports I got before the war, I heard to my great satisfaction that it was blazing as merrily as ever. You can imagine my relief when I found that they were both commanding on the Eastern Front.'

Some historians have tended to play down the influence which this inner knowledge had on Hoffmann's planning, but he certainly emphasized it to me when I talked with him in Berlin shortly before his death, and as he told the story he would add with a chuckle, sipping from his inevitable tumbler of neat cognac, 'If the Battle of Waterloo was won on the playing fields of Eton, the Battle of Tannenberg was lost on the railway platform at Mukden.' And so it certainly proved.

Samsonov spent 24 and 25 August resting his men, re-establishing his contact with supplies and preparing for an ultimate attack. In some preliminary skirmishing the Germans had retreated, and he seems to have had no idea of any immediate threat, nor to have thought that his communications with Jilinsky and Rennenkampf were being monitored 'loud and clear' by the Germans. What the German headquarters learned from these interceptions was checked and confirmed by the discovery in the pocketbook of a dead Russian staff officer of notes of the general movements of both the First and the Second Armies, evidently made at Jilinsky's army group headquarters. From these the Germans learned how far their opponents had departed from their general timetable. It was also indicated that Rennenkampf was in no hurry to march south. The attack on Samsonov could therefore proceed with comparative assurance.

The plan of operations was simple in conception but difficult of execution. The right and left wings were strengthened at the expense of the centre, which, lightly held, constituted the bait held out to Samsonov to tempt him to attack. By the evening of 25 August all was in order.

The drama upon which the curtain now rose did not take place in one self-contained act but in a number of detached scenes. The stage, which stretched over more than sixty miles of East Prussian territory, covered ground which prevented the formation of a continuous battle line. The battle called, therefore, for individual initiative on the part of the various German corps commanders and is particularly remarkable for the success of these independent actions.

Samsonov fell headlong into the temptingly baited trap and launched a terrible assault against the deliberately weakened German centre. But the position was held by the XX Corps, which was composed of troops drawn from the very district in which they fought, Allenstein men fighting for the defence of their own homesteads, and, though the line writhed and shook beneath the weight of successive Russian onslaughts by crack regimental formations, it did not break.

Meanwhile François on the right and Mackensen and Below on the left were driving forward against the Russian flanks. Towards evening the German centre abandoned its defensive tactics and took the offensive, making contact with François and enveloping Samsonov's main body in such a manner that it had no alternative but to retire eastwards.

But at German headquarters there was not complete composure of mind. Neither Hindenburg nor Ludendorff could rid themselves of the overshadowing anxiety concerning Rennenkampf's movements. 'According to Hoyle', the greater the German success and the more imminent and overwhelming the Russian defeat, the more certain it should have been that Rennenkampf would march south with all possible speed to the aid of his colleague. Only Hoffmann, sure in his inner knowledge and confident in his own belief, maintained his equanimity and observed, perhaps even with a tinge of secret enjoyment, the mental discomfiture of his chiefs. Moreover, his confidence was justified. Message after message was intercepted from Samsonov to Jilinsky and to Rennenkampf himself. Realizing the magnitude of the disaster that was about to overwhelm him, the wretched commander of the Second Army was filling the air with his demands, prayers and entreaties for assistance. But the First Army continued to skirmish outside Königsberg. That ten-year-old box on the ear still tingled. Rennenkampf did not move – nor would he.

However, the bogey was not completely laid. Towards evening on 26 August it was reported to German headquarters that a strong force of Russian cavalry from the south was threatening François on the right, and at the same time an aerial reconnaissance brought word that one of Rennenkampf's corps was in motion against the German left. It was this concatenation of ill-tidings that disclosed a flaw in Ludendorff's character as a soldier. He 'lost his cool'. His nerve cracked and he wished to recall François and abandon the encircling operation around Samsonov. It was at this moment of crisis that Hoffmann elected to disclose his knowledge of the existing relations between the opposing Russian commanders to Hindenburg, who at once grasped its vital significance. Supported by François himself, and of course by Hoffmann, he overcame Ludendorff's *crise des nerfs* and avoided the crowning blunder of a hasty and panicky action which would have cheated the Eighth Army of its final victory. In any event the report from the north turned out to be a figment of the airman's imagination and the movement on the south proved well within François's capacity to deal with.

The battle continued with great fierceness throughout 27 and 28 August, but the final issue was never again in doubt, except once more at the hands of Ludendorff. In every way the German generalship and staff work were superior to the Russian, who were 'out-thought' on all points; but the Russian army showed great gallantry. For Samsonov, deserted by his colleagues, fought with the fury of despair to break from the enveloping movement which, inexorable as the march of time, was slowly but surely encompassing his destruction. Again and again he drove like a bull against the ring, but to no purpose. No hope remained but in general retreat.

On the evening of 28 August the enveloping movement was well advanced when imperative orders came to François on the right from Ludendorff, once again a prey to *Angst*. The I Corps was to change its line of march to due north. Such an order implied the abandonment of the attempt to round up the vast force of the Russian centre and would, moreover, compel the I Corps to plunge into the Polish forests which had already entrapped and bewildered many of Samsonov's units. At this important juncture François deliberately disobeyed his orders. Ignoring Ludendorff's explicit command, he pursued his original course and by a series of forced marches along a road which skirted the forest area he drove his corps forward throughout the 29th. By the evening of that day, he had joined hands with Mackensen, and the encirclement of the Russian centre was completed. On the 30th fresh Russian forces attempted to break through from outside the circle, but without success. Hour by hour the ring of fire around the Russian masses, now crowded tightly together, swaying this way and that, milling against each other like cattle in an abbatoir and ceasing to have any military formation, became closer and narrower.

By the evening of the 30th all was over. The Russian dead, lying in heaps and swathes, numbered over 100,000; the number of prisoners taken was no less. Three whole army corps had been destroyed and the small body of troops that remained outside the German circle was in panic-stricken flight towards the frontier. Samsonov left the field with the remnants of his staff, and wandered almost aimlessly among the trackless forests. His asthma, accentuated by the agony of despair and the bitterness of heartbreak, rendered him practically helpless. At last he dismounted, walked off by himself, and a single shot told its own story. His officers made a hurried but fruitless search for his body and then made good their own escape.

The news of the disaster of the Battle of Soldau was broken to Maurice

Paléologue in Petersburg by a deeply depressed Sazonov. 'Samsonov's army has been destroyed,' said the Russian Foreign Minister and paused. Then he added, 'We owed this sacrifice to France as she has showed herself a perfect ally.' But when, little more than four years later, the Allied armies marched through Paris in a victory parade, there were no representatives of Russia among them. '*Les morts de Tannenberg*' had been forgotten.

Before turning northwards to repeat the process of annihilation against Rennenkampf at the Battle of the Masurian Lakes, Ludendorff prepared the report on the destruction of Samsonov's army for Hindenburg's signature and despatch to the Kaiser. The chief of staff had dated it from Frögenau, which had been their headquarters, and as such it would have gone down to history had it not been for Hoffmann's intervention. He suggested that the despatch be headed from the little village of Tannenberg, which had formed the focal point of the centre held by the XX Corps against the earlier attacks of Samsonov. Tannenberg was sacred to every Prussian as being the site of the battle where, five centuries before, the marshalled chivalry of the Order of Teutonic Knights, in which had fought both a Beneckendorff and a Hindenburg, had been annihilated almost to a man by an advancing host of Lithuanians and Slavs. Now the memory of that terrible defeat had been wiped out, and a Slav host had gone to destruction before a Teutonic force commanded by a descendant of the Teutonic Knights. The historic circle was complete, but it took the imagination of Hoffmann, a Hessian, to see this.

(ii)

In assessing the historic significance of the East Prussian campaign, which began with the engagement at Stallupönen on 18 August and ended a month later when the routed remnants of Rennenkampf's First Army regained Russian soil, leaving behind it 145,000 men in casualties and prisoners, it is clear that the Battle of Tannenberg was not of isolated importance. Mr Winston Churchill, as percipient and clear-minded an analyst of history as he was an inspirational wartime leader, attributes a special significance to the action at Gumbinnen:

> It induced Prittwitz to break off the battle and propose a retirement to the Vistula. It provoked Moltke to supersede Prittwitz. It inspired Moltke to appoint Hindenburg and Ludendorff, and thereby set in motion the measureless consequences that followed that decision. It procured from Hoffmann and the staff of the Eighth Army the swift and brilliant combination of movements which dictated the Battle of Tannenberg. It imparted to the Russian Command a confidence which was in no way justified. It gave them an utterly false conception of the character, condi-

tions and intentions of their enemy. It lured Jilinsky to spur on Samsonov's marching army. It lured Samsonov to deflect his advance more to the West and less to the North (i.e. further away from Rennenkampf), in the hopes of a greater scoop-up of the defeated Germans. It persuaded Rennenkampf to dawdle nearly three days on the battle-field in order to let Samsonov's more ambitious movement gain its greatest effect and it led Jilinski to acquiesce in his strategic inertia.

Truly a formidable array of consequences for the historian to weigh and consider, though with regard to the last of them – Rennenkampf's delay – there were additional and more personal causes than those which Mr Churchill cites. Moreover, as Mr Churchill goes on to explain, the long-term results of Gumbinnen were vital to the whole course of the war. For had Moltke not decided on 25 August to reinforce the Eighth Army with two veteran and battle-wise army corps, he could have used them a fortnight later to plug the fatal breach in the German line at the Battle of the Marne, where they were desperately needed.

It was Tannenberg, however, which set the seal upon the defeat of Russian arms. The destruction of Samsonov's army, whether it was sacrificed in the cause of the French alliance or not, had devastating results for the course of history. Here the magnificent flower of the Imperial Army perished in humiliating and irretrievable disaster; here the proud façade of Russian patriotism was wrecked; here the position of the monarchy, already weakened, began to crumble. These were the long-term repercussions of the East Prussian campaign of the summer of 1914, which lasted just twenty-eight days and in which Tannenberg was the crucial event.

Had fate nodded in the opposite direction and awarded victory to Russian arms at Tannenberg, the subsequent course of history might have been very different. Failure in the West and defeat in the East might well have induced Imperial Germany to conclude a negotiated peace and the Great War would have been among the shortest major conflicts on record. As it was, however, the Battle of Tannenberg led directly, though in due process of time, to the Bolshevik Revolution, to the Treaty of Brest-Litovsk, and ultimately to the downfall of the Hohenzollerns as well as the Romanoffs.

Note on Sources

The best study of Tannenberg is still, to my mind, that of Lord Ironside, being based on both German and Russian sources, but the most readable account of the campaign in East Prussia in August 1914 is, of course, Sir Winston Churchill's.

Some may be surprised to find three works of fiction included in the following list but Solzhenitsyn's *August 1914* has already become a classic and the novels of Dr Catherine

Gavin and Miss Stephanie Plowman contain very moving accounts from the Russian angle which are based on detailed historical research.

Churchill, Rt. Hon. Winston, *The Unknown War* (1931).
Cruttwell, Charles, *A History of the Great War, 1914–1918* (1934).
Edmonds, Major-General Sir James, *A Short History of World War I* (1951).
Gavin, Catherine, *The Snow Mountain* (1973).
Hindenburg, Field-Marshal von, *Out of my Life* (1920).
Hoffmann, Major-General Max, *War Diaries and other Papers* (1929).
Ironside, Field-Marshal Lord, *Tannenberg* (1925).
Knox, Major-General Sir Alfred, *With the Russian Army, 1914–1917* (1921).
Liddell Hart, B. H., *A History of the World War 1914–1918* (1934).
Ludendorff, General Erich, *My War Memories 1914–1918* (1919).
Plowman, Stephanie, *My Kingdom for a Grave* (1970).
Solzhenitsyn, Alexander, *August 1914* (1972).
Tuchman, Barbara, *Guns of August* (1962).
Wheeler-Bennett, Sir John, *Hindenburg, Wooden Titan* (1936).

Chapter Three

THE MARNE

Alan Palmer

THE RIVER MARNE winds its way across north-eastern France for some 325 miles. Like the Seine, into which it flows just short of Paris, the river rises on the Langres Plateau. But while the Seine turns westwards to cross a monotonous countryside until it reaches the Forest of Fontainebleau, the Marne meanders northwards in a broad arc, as if asserting its independence as a river of distinction. Its waters reflect the contrasts of the French landscape: thickly wooded hills south of Chaumont; the wide chalkland of the Champagne plain; Epernay and thirty miles of vine terraces; pastures and fields of grain on the Brie Plateau; and old townships held in the loops of the main river or nestling on promontories above its principal tributaries, the greater and lesser Morin and the Ourcq. The Marne is more than half as long again as either the Thames or the Severn and, like them, its banks are rich in history. Near Chalons, in the Battle of the Catalaunian Fields, Gaul was saved from Attila and his Huns. Henry V of England, Joan of Arc, the great Napoleon, Schwarzenberg, Blücher and Tsar Alexander I marched and fought over this rolling countryside. And it was by way of the Marne that the German columns advanced inexorably on Paris in the autumn of 1870. But it was in another September, forty-four years later, that the Marne was suddenly swept into the headlines of the world's press and ultimately into legend. For between 5 and 11 September 1914 the Allied armies of France and Britain gained a strategic victory on the Marne so decisive that it denied Germany the speedy triumph upon which the Kaiser and his generals had based their hopes in the war.

At the time it was fought, the Battle of the Marne was unique in the military history of Europe. Two million men were locked in combat along a front of over 125 miles; there had been nothing on this scale in previous campaigns. That in itself is sufficient to make the Marne memorable. But more remarkable still is the character of the week's fighting and its relationship to the cataclysmic events of the previous month of war. For the Marne was not so much a single battle as a series of interrelated engagements brought about by a massive military manoeuvre. It was the climax of a decade of staff planning; never before had there been so great a contest between rival high commands.

During the last tense years of peace neither the German nor the French General Staffs envisaged a decisive battle on the Marne. The operational plan prepared by General Count von Schlieffen in December 1905 did indeed assume that the war would be won by swift successes in the West rather than on the Eastern Front against Russia. But Schlieffen proposed a powerful enveloping movement through Flanders and Picardy which would cross the Seine between Rouen and Paris, invest the capital from the west and the south, and force the French armies eastwards against the rear of their own defences from Nancy to Belfort. Although the original Schlieffen Plan was modified extensively in the three years immediately preceding the war, it was still believed in 1914 that the final act of the campaign would be fought out

Fighting at the Marne. British front-line transport struck by shrapnel, 8 September 1914

against a backcloth of the Vosges or Jura mountains and not along the rivers of the central plain. The French, for their part, had no desire for bloody encounters on the sacred soil of the homeland. Plan XVII, as finally revised by the French General Staff early in 1913, provided for a frontal assault to iberate the lost provinces of Alsace-Lorraine and for an advance into the Ardennes, should the Germans enter Belgium or Luxembourg. It was confidently anticipated that the Ardennes offensive would 'cut the invader in two', paralysing the enemy right wing before it reached the French frontier. The generals in Paris believed the decisive theatre of operations would be between the Meuse and the Moselle or, better still, on the Rhine; but certainly not on the Marne, barely an hour's drive by staff car from the Ministry of War.

The French commander-in-chief was General Joseph Joffre, an engineer officer of sixty-two from the foothills of the Pyrenees and (like Marshal Ney before him) the son of a cooper. Joffre was not a strategist by training or experience, nor had a career of distinction in Tonkin, Madagascar and Timbuktu prepared him for war with the national enemy, against whom he had fought briefly as a cadet in 1870. But he possessed two great assets: the ability to move and mass armies; and a totally phlegmatic temperament, imperturbable in crisis. These qualities saved France in those first disastrous weeks of war in 1914.

The Chief of the German General Staff was a very different type of man. Colonel-General Helmuth von Moltke was four years older than Joffre, beyond the normal age of retirement from the army. But, as nephew and namesake to the victor of Sadowa and Sedan, he was retained on the active list, in part as a talisman of success. Certainly he possessed his uncle's intelligence and open-mindedness, his shrewd conviction that campaign plans become dangerously rigid instruments once contact is made with an enemy; but he lacked the elder Moltke's nerveless professionalism. Two days after the start of the Marne battles he confided his private fears in a letter to his wife: 'I would give my life for victory,' he wrote, 'as thousands of others have done. How much blood has been spilt and how much misery fallen on numberless people. . . ! Often terror sweeps over me when I think about this and I feel that I must answer for this horror, though I could not have acted in any other way.' Such humane sensitivity would hardly have troubled his uncle ('In war I have an iron hand,' he had once declared), nor did such reflections disturb the ruthlessly unimaginative Joffre.

Had Joffre's conscience been alive to these moral issues he could never have survived the strain of the earliest battles in the war. For the French the terrible casualties began in mid-August when the counter-offensives in the Ardennes and on the eastern frontier were launched against the Germans. Courageous charges inspired by patriotic zeal, as on the faded canvasses of battle panoramas, were no match for machine gun fire. In a fortnight the French suffered more than 300,000 casualties (dead, wounded or missing);

one in ten of the commissioned officers in the whole of the French army was killed or incapacitated. Joffre himself was amazed at the strength of the German forces and, in particular, at the efficiency shown by the reservist units as they followed crack regiments through Brabant and Hainaut. On 25 August the Germans crossed the Franco-Belgian frontier. Plan XVII had already become a historical relic.

Joffre had every intention of resuming the offensive once he could check the relentless pressure of thirty German army corps bearing down on the Allied left wing. For the moment, however, there was little enough he could do, except ensure that the retreat was orderly and controlled. The German First Army, under General von Kluck, wheeled southwards through Brussels, Mons and Le Cateau to the Somme between Amiens and St Quentin. The Second Army (General von Bülow), on its left, advanced south of Liège and down the Sambre. The Third Army, a predominantly Saxon force under General von Hausen, advanced through the wooded defiles of the Ardennes and ultimately headed for Rheims. These three armies, in the third week of August, could concentrate 760,000 men against an Allied force which comprised the badly mauled Belgian forces (still defending the western third of their homeland), a British Expeditionary Force of 110,000 men under Field-Marshal Sir John French, and the French Fifth Army of 250,000 men under General Lanrezac, supported by the smaller French Fourth Army (General de Langle de Cary) on the Meuse. For thirteen days of intensive heat and blazing sunshine, the B.E.F. and the Fifth Army fell wearily back, down the long and dusty roads of northern France. The actions of the B.E.F. at Le Cateau on 26 August and of the I Corps of the Fifth Army (General Franchet d'Espérey) at Guise three days later checked the advancing Germans and gave the Allies a respite. General Franchet d'Espérey, a commander of vigour and resolution inspired by a Bonapartist vision, astonished the German Second Army by mounting a flank attack with the regimental band playing the 'Sambre et Meuse' march and with colours flying in the wind. It was clear to General von Bülow that, with such resilience, the French were still far from defeat.

General von Kluck, on the other hand, was convinced that final victory lay within his grasp. He accelerated the momentum of the First Army's advance, effectively frustrating Joffre's hope of halting the long retreat along the line of the Rivers Somme and Aisne. On 30 August readers of *The Times* in England were startled by the grave report of a war correspondent from Amiens, which even suggested that 'the investment of Paris cannot be banished from the field of possibility'. That same Sunday Joffre, learning that Sir John French wished to withdraw the B.E.F. behind the Seine, proposed that the British might retire east of Paris, falling back on Meaux and the River Marne.

Characteristically this first mention of the coming battle zone was added almost as an afterthought. Joffre did not rate the Marne any higher than the

Aisne or the Seine as a defensive position. Had the politicians permitted him to do so, he would have fallen back deeper and deeper into France, tempting the Germans to overtax their front-line troops and outpace their supplies before he launched a counter-offensive. If Joffre had any strategic mentor from the past it was not a Frenchman but the Russian Marshal Kutuzov, who had encouraged Napoleon to ruin himself in Moscow before falling on the retreating Grand Army. When the French Minister of War asked Joffre where and when he intended to fight the decisive battle he replied 'Brienne-le-Chateau' and gave the date as 8 September. This may have been an inspiration of the moment, but it is significant that the three successive headquarters of Joffre in the first six weeks of the war were in an arc around Brienne: at Vitry-le-François until 2 September; at Bar-sur-Aube for three days; and thereafter at Chatillon-sur-Seine. On the other hand, Joffre's preference for this area may have sprung from its central position. From each of these headquarters he could be driven rapidly to any army in the field and he remained in personal contact with his commanders.

Moltke was further from the war zone: he had, after all, to take decisions about the Eastern Front as well as about operations in the West. From 16 to 30 August the German High Command was in Coblenz, a poor communications centre for troops advancing through Belgium and into France. The High Command then moved to the city of Luxembourg, establishing headquarters in an empty school, for no one had as yet summoned the children back from the summer holidays. The building had no gas and no electricity, and it was so cramped that the Operations Branch was housed in the girls' cloakroom. Moltke was still nearly 200 miles away from the battle zone in the West. A younger and fitter commander would have countered this disadvantage by making personal visits to the various army headquarters; but Moltke was convinced it was essential for him to remain with the High Command, closely in touch with the Kaiser (who had set up a miniature court at Luxembourg), and with representatives of the civil government. Unable to confer with his field commanders and dependent on telephones and primitive wireless transmitters, Moltke was left to study the maps on the classroom walls, assessing and questioning outdated information. Small wonder if doubt and anxiety began to torment his waking hours.

For though the Kaiser was convinced that Paris would soon fall, Moltke remained sceptical. He was worried by the continued Belgian resistance on the rear flank of the main invading force and, above all, by Russian pressure in East Prussia. On 25 August he had ordered two army corps to be withdrawn from the Western Front and transported eastwards, a diversion soon rendered unnecessary by the German victory at Tannenberg. By the end of August he had begun to suspect that the absence of these two corps, together with the loss of troops for operations against Antwerp and the old barrier-fortress of Maubeuge, was weakening the attacking power of the German right wing in northern France. Moreover, he was disappointed at the failure of the Bavarian Sixth Army to make any progress between Nancy and Epinal against the French Second Army (General de Castelnau) and the French First Army (General Dubail). On 1 September Moltke warned the Chief of the Kaiser's Naval Staff, 'We have driven the French back but they are not defeated yet. We still have to do that'.

There seemed no grounds for Moltke's gloom. On that same Tuesday Joffre himself decided he could no more stem the Germans on the Marne than on the Aisne, and he ordered the retreat to continue. Next day the French government left Paris for Bordeaux. But Joffre certainly had not abandoned hope of mounting a counter-offensive. His *Instruction Générale* No. 4 (issued on the afternoon of 1 September) explicitly declared that 'as soon as the Fifth Army has escaped the threat of envelopment pronounced against its left' it would join Langle's Fourth Army and the Third Army (which had been severely mauled in the Ardennes) in turning against the invader. Joffre's skill at improvisation, at creating new units, was now to serve France well. Already he had sought to strengthen his left wing by hurrying troops westwards from the Lorraine front and forming them into a Sixth Army under the command of General Maunoury. He had every intention of building up this embryonic force with regiments summoned northwards from the Alps when it became clear Italy would remain a non-belligerent. To bolster up the centre of his line Joffre assigned three corps to General Foch, the nucleus of what was to be known as the Ninth Army from the evening of 4 September onwards. On 30 August General Sarrail was appointed to command the Third Army in place of General Ruffey, whom Joffre considered to have lost his nerve. Sarrail was an ambitious political general, with powerful patrons in the Radical Socialist Party, but he was a good infantryman, more conscious of what footsloggers could and could not achieve than most of the corps commanders in the long retreat.

Joffre would at the same time have liked to dismiss General Lanrezac from command of the Fifth Army. Lanrezac was slow in carrying out Joffre's orders, and it was painfully clear that there was a lack of trust between the staff officers of the Fifth Army and their neighbours in the B.E.F. But Lanrezac's prestige was high in government circles and it was not until 3 September (after the politicians had scurried from Paris to Bordeaux) that Joffre ordered him to hand over the Fifth Army to the commander of his I Corps, Franchet d'Espérey, who had already proved his aggressive spirit. Joffre calculated that his armies would be reconstituted by the end of the first week in September. He would – at least on paper – be ready for a counter-offensive by 8 September.

But to one Frenchman of distinction this was not soon enough. General Galliéni, appointed Military Governor of Paris on 25 August, had been a senior commander in the army until a few months previously, when he had reached the age of sixty-five and been removed from the active list. Joffre had served under Galliéni in Madagascar, and it was indeed largely through the energetic support of Galliéni that he was appointed commander-in-chief. He respected Galliéni as an ascetic authoritarian with a healthy contempt for senseless routine; but Galliéni found it difficult to restrain his own inclinations so as to conform to the slower pace of his former subordinate's plans. Galliéni believed it his duty to save Paris and thus France, Joffre to save France and thus Paris. The distinction involved so great a difference in strategic reasoning that it opened the way for a controversy which outlived both protagonists, and in retrospect sadly sullied the lustre of their contributions to the common victory.

At the beginning of September it seemed questionable whether either Paris or France could be saved. Although Joffre had assigned Maunoury's Sixth Army to the capital, Galliéni was horrified to discover the weak state of the defensive works at the approaches to Paris; and it was becoming clear to Joffre's staff that, though the commander-in-chief might conjure up new armies, there was no guarantee that troop trains would be able to get them through to their assembly points. The far-ranging cavalry patrols of the German First Army threatened to disrupt a railway system which radiated from the capital. Yet there was one encouraging development for the French. On the afternoon of Monday 31 August, British airmen reported that General von Kluck had changed the direction of advance of his First Army from south-west to south-east, information verified by French cavalry patrols and by a map found on the body of a dead German officer the following day. If Kluck's columns advanced down the River Ourcq and the corridor between Meaux and Château-Thierry on the Marne, they would be exposed to the risk of a flank attack from the Paris garrison and Maunoury's Sixth Army. Galliéni was eager to strike, preferring to take the initiative rather than allow the Germans to discover the weak state of the Paris defences. But Joffre was puzzled. What really was the German line of advance? By Wednesday morning Kluck's columns had veered south again, as though heading for the capital. The prospects of a flank attack receded rapidly.

Yet if Joffre was puzzled at his headquarters on the Aube, so too was Moltke in Luxembourg. Poor wireless communications prevented him receiving any direct reports from General von Kluck between 30 August and the morning of 2 September. The delay was serious, for Moltke now wished to modify his plans. He was less interested in seizing Paris than in destroying the French armies in the field: and, since he thought his First and Second Armies weakened by the long enveloping movement (and the troop withdrawals he had ordered), he wished to make more use of the Fourth, Fifth and Sixth Armies in the centre, employing them to drive the French back westwards and against the German First and Second Armies in their rear. Kluck's movements alarmed him, for on the map there was a gap opening between the First and Second Armies. Hence on the evening of 2 September Moltke sent a fresh directive to both Kluck and Bülow: they were to cut the Allies off from Paris by driving Joffre and the B.E.F. south-eastwards, but it was essential for the First Army 'to follow behind the Second Army in echelon, thus covering the flank of the main body' from any sorties by the Paris garrison.

In General von Kluck's estimation this plan was no longer practicable. He was within twenty miles of Paris and more than a day's march ahead of General von Bülow. Moreover, he had already given orders for his advanced corps to cross the Marne. Whatever they might think in Luxembourg, Kluck personally discounted any threat from the defenders of Paris; it seemed sufficient to him to assign an under-strength reserve corps and a cavalry division to protect his western flank while the main army crossed the Marne between Château-Thierry and La Ferté on 3 September.

By noon on that Thursday both Joffre and Galliéni had received reports indicating that the Germans were resuming their advance south-eastwards. It became increasingly difficult for Joffre to hold Galliéni in check. Galliéni even resorted to telephoning the commander-in-chief personally, which Joffre found especially irritating, as he had always regarded the field telephone as an instrument of the devil intended to tempt commanders into hurried and rash decisions. He did not doubt Galliéni's right to advise him, but he had no intention of allowing him to draw up the final military plans.

Joffre was still committed to the idea of a general offensive, in which every Allied army between Paris and Verdun would participate. He recognized, however, that the crucial sector of the front was the area between the Seine and the Oise and that it was essential for there to be close collaboration between Franchet d'Espérey's Fifth Army and the British, who were falling back south of the Marne, from Meaux towards Melun on the Seine. The basic operational plan for this sector of the front was drawn up by Franchet d'Espérey at Bray-sur-Seine on the afternoon of 4 September after consultation with Major-General Henry Wilson, deputy chief of staff to Sir John French. The plan provided for concerted attacks on the morning of 6 September: Maunoury's Sixth Army was to advance south-eastwards from the River Ourcq on Château-Thierry and, ultimately, Montmirail; the B.E.F., having changed direction so as to face eastwards, was to march directly on Montmirail; and Franchet's Fifth Army would advance on Montmirail northwards from the Provins–Sezanne line. Joffre approved this plan in essentials that same evening, although he proposed that Foch's Ninth Army should hold the marshes of St Gond while at the same time supporting the Fifth Army by an advance north-westwards. He also proposed that Sarrail's Third Army should make a flank attack on the Germans in the Argonne and ordered Castelnau's Second Army to hold Nancy at all costs against the increasingly violent assaults of the German Sixth Army.

Unfortunately confusion arose over the precise role of the British. While Wilson was conferring with Franchet d'Espérey, the chief of staff of the B.E.F. (Sir Archibald Murray) was working out a more limited project in conference with Galliéni at Melun. Sir John French, returning from visits to his detachments in the field, was thus faced by two operational plans. Although Joffre was at pains to clarify the situation he feared a misunderstanding, and on the morning of 5 September he was so uncertain of British intentions that he ordered his chauffeur to drive him to Melun – a journey of more than 100 miles – so that he could appeal to Sir John French in person for close collaboration. That afternoon Joffre, speaking with rare passion, pleaded for effective British assistance 'in this supreme crisis' for France and for Europe. 'Then,' he wrote later in his *Memoirs*, 'carried away by my convictions and the gravity of the moment, I remember bringing down my fist on a table which stood at my elbow, and crying, "*Monsieur le Maréchal*, the honour of England is at stake!" ' Deeply moved, French replied, 'I will do all that is possible.' 'For me,' wrote Joffre later, 'these simple words were as good as an oath.' Franchet d'Espérey's cavalry would begin the advance on Montmirail at six on the following morning, the British moving eastwards on the River Grand Morin two hours later. Joffre calculated that within twelve hours of his return to headquarters from Melun the counter-offensive would have started.

In fact, although he did not know it until much later, the first of the series of actions which constituted the Battle of the Marne had begun while he was in conference with the British. At half past two on the afternoon of 5 September advance units of Maunoury's Sixth Army, moving into position on the River Ourcq, encountered Kluck's flank guard in the high ground to the north of Meaux. The French infantry – men from this very region of the Ile de France, together with Moroccans – were soon within range of German batteries located on the hills. Although they fought courageously they could not reach their objective. On this plateau between Meaux and Betz grim fighting continued for four days through fields of beetroots and unharvested grain. For though at first General von Kluck had ignored this sector, he realized once the battle had become general that what happened on the west bank of the Ourcq decided whether his own columns were to be cut off or whether he might redeem his strategic error in outpacing the Second Army by shifting the emphasis of his attack westwards so as to drive Maunoury's Sixth Army back on Paris and sweep into the enemy capital in full pursuit. For Kluck, and for Galliéni, the Ourcq rather than the Marne was the centre of the battle.

For Franchet d'Espérey, on the other hand, the key to the future lay on the historic battlefields of Montmirail and Vauchamps where his idol Napoleon had checked the advance of Blücher's Prussians in 1814. At first his troops made slower progress than he had anticipated. On 6 September both the X Corps on the right and the XVIII Corps on the left of his sector were able to press forward several miles and reach slopes down to the Grand Morin River before nightfall, but there was bitter fighting in the centre, with the Germans digging in at the approaches to Montceaux-les-Provins.

It was at St Bon, five miles east of Montceaux, that the newly promoted General Pétain personally led his wavering infantry forward to a ridge which was under heavy enemy fire, ensuring by his courage that they were able to enter Montceaux early the following morning. There was as yet no sign of the enemy pulling back, but at least it was clear that the long retreat was over.

Joffre was satisfied with the Fifth Army's progress but he was uncertain what was happening west of the Ourcq and was troubled by the slowness with which the British changed direction for their thrust along the deep valleys of the Grand and Petit Morin. The situation farther east also caused Joffre anxiety. Foch's Ninth Army had been forced on the defensive by the German Second Army; and in the marshy ground to its right it had even had to retreat. Farther east still Sarrail had kept the Third Army cautiously within touch of the great fortress of Verdun, although the accurate and persistent fire of his artillery prevented the German Fifth Army, under the Crown Prince, from making any effective contribution to the battle.

By midday on 7 September it had become apparent to Joffre that the Ourcq was the vital sector of the front. Reports coming in to the headquarters of both Joffre and Galliéni indicated that General von Kluck had now resolved to transfer two of his best equipped corps from south of the Marne to the west bank of the Ourcq. This was an extremely bold manoeuvre since it meant that Kluck was re-aligning his order of battle while the counter-offensive was still in progress, switching his forward troops on average thirty-five miles from south to west. He was thus turning away from the German Second Army on his left, opening up a gap exposed to the B.E.F. if only it could move forward rapidly.

The strengthening of the German forces on the Ourcq imposed a severe strain on Maunoury. He sought any reinforcements Galliéni could find for him in Paris, hoping that the Sixth Army might be able to envelop Kluck's right while the British were exploiting the gap between the two German armies. Throughout 7 September Galliéni made use of convoys of taxis requisitioned the previous evening from the streets of Paris in order to bring the 7th Infantry Division into the line. Legend has exaggerated the contribution to victory of the taxis of the Marne. Their significance was primarily psychological; they associated the citizens of Paris with the struggle being waged a mere thirty miles from the Eiffel Tower.

Meanwhile, in Luxembourg, Moltke's gloom had spread to his staff. They were depressed at the failure to break through on the eastern frontier of France and alarmed at the lack of coordination between their First and Second Armies. Disquieting reports came in from neutral capitals and from Belgium: a Russian expeditionary force was said to be on its way from Archangel, a rumour to which the landing of British marines at Ostend in an unfamiliar uniform momentarily seemed to give substance. Moltke's nerves were overtaxed. On 8 September he authorized a relatively junior staff officer, Lieutenant-Colonel von Hentsch, to visit each of the army headquarters in the West: if disaster appeared imminent on the Marne, he might order a retirement to the Aisne in Moltke's name. Hentsch (who had already made one journey to the French front) found the situation satisfactory at the headquarters of the Third, Fourth and Fifth Armies, but he spent the night with General von Bülow at Second Army headquarters and there found dismay at Kluck's movement westwards. Bülow felt the two armies should make a concerted retreat northwards, converging their lines of march so as to close the gap opened by Kluck's impetuosity.

Wednesday, 9 September, was the decisive day. On the previous evening Kluck had narrowly escaped capture by Franchet d'Espérey's cavalry at La Ferte, but that morning his troops launched a series of attacks on Maunoury's army, which suffered heavy casualties. So, too, did Foch's army on the edge of the St Gond marshes and around Mondemont Castle, sixty miles east of Maunoury's battle. Soon after midday Hentsch reached Kluck's headquarters, where Kluck's staff at first refused to believe there was any need for a retreat. While Hentsch was arguing with Kluck's chief of staff a report was received that the Second Army was already pulling back, since air reconnaissance had shown the British advancing in strength along the corridor between the First and Second Armies. It was the end of Kluck's hopes of entering Paris; it was virtually the end of the battle.

The French Fifth Army, which had entered Montmirail after heavy fighting on the Tuesday evening, sent cavalry out as far as Château-Thierry and was firmly established north of the Marne by nightfall on 9 September. By the next morning it was clear that the Germans were retreating, not only from the Ourcq and the western Marne but from the region south of Epernay where Foch had defended so resolutely. The fighting continued well north of the Marne until 11 September when Foch could report 'an incontestable victory' to the Ministry of War. The Germans retreated in good order until at last they halted north of Rheims and along the Aisne. The Allied armies were too exhausted to exploit their withdrawal and the material fruits of their triumph were therefore disappointing. But strategically there was no doubt what had been achieved. The rapid blow which had stunned France in 1870 – and which was to do so again in 1940 – had this time been parried. The war of movement was over; it remained to be seen which of the antagonists would first shape its military machine to the agonizing restraints of trench warfare.

Note on Sources

Azan, P., *Franchet d'Espérey* (1949).
Barnett, C., *The Swordbearers* (1963).
Bloem, W., *The Advance from Mons, 1914* (1930).
Blond, G., *The Marne* (1965).
Isserlin, H., *The Battle of the Marne* (1965).

THE MARNE

Joffre, J. J. C., *Memoirs* (1932).
Koeltz, L., *Documents allemands sur la bataille de la Marne* (1930).
Kluck, A. von, *The March on Paris and the Battle of the Marne 1914* (1920).
Les Armées Françaises dans la grande guerre, I, Vol. 2 and annexes (1925).
Moltke, H. von, *Erinnerrungen, Briefe, Dokumente, 1877–1916* (1922).
Müller, G. von, *The Kaiser and his Court* (1961).
Muller, V., *Joffre et la Marne* (1931).
Ritter, G., *The Schlieffen Plan* (1958).
Spears, E. L., *Liaison, 1914* (1930).
Tuchman, B. W., *The Guns of August* (1962).
Volkmann, E. O., *Am Tor der neuen Zeit* (1933).

Chapter Four

VERDUN

Alistair Horne

AT DAWN ON 21 February 1916, a Krupp naval gun in an emplacement nearly twenty miles away fired on the city of Verdun. The first note in the overture to what was to become known as the 'Year of Big Guns', its heavy shell knocked a corner off the cathedral. It was the signal for the opening of a ten-month battle, the longest in either world war and one of the most atrocious that all history can record. Immediately afterwards, German artillery massed along a narrow front brought down on the French lines the greatest concentration of fire ever seen since the invention of gunpowder.

Between the Battle of the Marne, which halted the German armies at the gates of Paris in 1914, and Ludendorff's last-gasp offensive of 1918, which momentarily seemed to come even closer to success, the Germans stood on the defensive in the West, while attacking in the East. The Allied forces spent themselves assaulting a brilliantly prepared and powerfully supported line, at a horrendous cost in human lives, so it was a policy that paid the defenders handsome dividends. During these three and a half years of bitter positional warfare, the Kaiser's high command only once deviated from its strategy in the West; at Verdun, in 1916. Compared with the seven German armies that marched into France in 1914, and the sixty-three divisions that struck at Haig in March 1918, the Crown Prince's nine-division offensive at Verdun began as a small affair – yet it was to grow into a monster which deeply influenced a whole generation of Frenchmen and Germans, and which had a profound bearing on the course of warfare beyond the armistice of 1918.

At the Marne in 1914, the Germans had failed to win the war by one sledge-hammer blow against a numerically superior enemy. They had suffered three quarters of a million casualties; but France, in attempting to repulse the invasion, had lost nearly a million men, of which 300,000 were killed. With her smaller population, she could ill afford these astronomic losses. Yet they had been further augmented by the useless *grignotage* (nibbling) offensives of 1915, in Artois and Champagne, so that by the beginning of 1916 the French army had lost half of its regular officer cadre, and the numbers killed already approached the total Britain was to lose in the whole war. Britain, though fighting hard on a small scale in 1915, would not be in a position to shoulder more of the burden on the Western Front until late in the coming year. At Gallipoli, British naval supremacy had proved impotent to open a 'second front'. Russia, isolated from her Western allies, staggered on from one defeat to another. But still the Central Powers could not achieve a decision in the limitless plains of the East. Meanwhile, by December 1915, deadlock had been reached in the West along a static front stretching from Switzerland to the Channel.

In that month both sets of opposing general staffs met to prepare their plans for 1916. France had just nominated Joffre, the 'victor of the Marne', to be her supreme commander. A 63-year-old engineer with a large paunch

The aftermath at Verdun. Remains of the forts around which the battle raged

and little experience of handling infantry, Joffre was now incomparably the most powerful figure on the Allied side; this enabled him to concentrate everything on the Western Front. At his G.H.Q. in Chantilly, Joffre held an historic conference of the Allied commanders which drafted plans for a coordinated offensive by all the Allies the following summer. Its principal component would be a joint Franco–British push, with forty French and twenty-five British divisions, astride the River Somme. For the first time there would be an abundance of heavy guns and ammunition; with Kitchener's army of conscripts about to replace the lost 'First Hundred Thousand', there should be no shortage of manpower either.

But Germany was to beat the Allies to the draw. In mid-December, the Chief of the German General Staff, General Erich von Falkenhayn, submitted his own plans to the Kaiser. A withdrawn, unpopular figure, Falkenhayn was a curious compound of ruthlessness and indecision, who helped bring Germany to ruin by his espousal of half-measures. He had performed a brilliant salvage job on the army after the defeat of the Marne, but had enraged the Hindenburg–Ludendorff team by calling off the 1915 offensive against the Russians just at the moment when a decisive victory seemed within reach. Falkenhayn began his memorandum to the Kaiser arguing that, as in Napoleonic times, the dynamo of the hostile coalition was Britain. As long as the war went on, Britain could create superior forces of men and arms to set against Germany. But, apart from U-boat warfare (which Falkenhayn emphatically espoused), no direct attack on Britain was possible. The only way Britain could be defeated was by knocking her 'best sword' out of her hand. This was the French army which Falkenhayn judged to have been 'weakened almost to the limits of endurance'. Yet, although at the close of 1915 military prospects for Germany would never again seem so bright, Falkenhayn ruled out any mass offensive in the West, on account of the limited reserves of German manpower. Instead, he argued ingeniously that the French army should be emasculated by luring it into the defence of an indefensible position.

Falkenhayn's choice fell upon Verdun. Rated the world's most powerful fortress, Verdun had been left in the aftermath of the Marne precariously perched at the tip of a long salient, just 150 miles due east of Paris. Its history as a fortified camp stretched back to Roman times, when Attila had found it worth burning. Louis XIV's great engineer Vauban had made Verdun the keystone in his cordon protecting France; and in 1870 it had been the last of the great French strongholds to fall to Moltke. After 1870 it had become the lynchpin in the chain of fortresses guarding the frontier, and in 1914 it had proved itself an unshakable pivot for the French line, without which Joffre might not have been able to stand on the Marne. Its psychological importance to the French nation was inestimable. Thus Falkenhayn reckoned that France would be forced to defend Verdun to the last man. By menacing it with only a limited infantry force, he hoped to draw the main weight of the French army into the narrow salient, where the vastly superior German heavy artillery would grind it to pieces from three sides at a relatively low cost in German lives. In Falkenhayn's own words, France was to be 'bled white'. It was a conception totally novel to military history, and symptomatic of a war where soldiers' lives tended to be rated as little more than corpuscles.

The operation was to be conducted by the Fifth Army, commanded by the German Crown Prince. From the beginning there was a rift of opinion between the Crown Prince and his tough chief of staff, Knobelsdorf, and Falkenhayn. The Fifth Army command wanted to attack simultaneously along both sides of the River Meuse, while Falkenhayn insisted on limiting the offensive to the right bank only. The Crown Prince regarded his objective as being nothing less than the capture of Verdun; but this was not Falkenhayn's. Moreover, with curious and cynical disingenuousness, Falkenhayn never revealed to him the true face of his 'bleeding white' strategy.

Aided by their interior lines of communication, plus the national genius for organization, the German preparations moved with amazing speed and security. D-day was set for 12 February, and by the beginning of that month 1,220 guns were in position – on a frontage of barely eight miles. More than 500 were heavy weapons, including thirteen of the 420-mm 'Big Bertha' mortars, the 'secret weapon' that had smashed in the supposedly impenetrable Belgian forts in 1914. There were also 210-mm howitzers, detailed to pulverize the French trench system, and long-range 150-mms with the task of knocking out the French artillery and raking all roads leading up to the front. To feed them, $2\frac{1}{2}$ million shells were stockpiled: a mere six days' supply.

Verdun itself, emptied of civilians, lay less than ten miles up the loopy, winding Meuse from the German lines. In contrast to the featureless, flat country of boggy Flanders and the Somme, it was surrounded by interlocking patterns of steep hills and ridges which offered immensely strong lines of defence. Three concentric rings of underground forts crowned the key heights, containing some twenty major and forty intermediary works. These were so well sited that the guns of each could dislodge any hostile infantry that might appear on the superstructure of its neighbours. Some of the major forts, such as Douaumont, had carapaces of concrete eight feet thick that were strong enough to resist even the one-ton shells of the German 'Big Berthas'. They mounted heavy artillery and machine guns firing from retractable steel turrets and linked by subterranean passages; while in their shellproof cellars each could house as much as a battalion of infantry. Between these forts guarding Verdun, five to ten miles away, and the front lines stretched the usual protective network of trenches, redoubts and barbed wire to be found elsewhere on the Western Front.

On paper, Verdun deserved its reputation as the world's most powerful fortress. But like other 'unassailable' fixed strongpoints throughout history – the Maginot Line, Singapore, the Bar Lev Line – its mere reputation made it vulnerable, insofar as it exerted a standing challenge to the ingenuity of an attacker. Also, like all the rest, Verdun had its Achilles' Heel: its imposing defences were not properly manned. Having seen the fate of the Belgian forts, Joffre had decided to remove the infantry garrisons from the Verdun forts, as well as many of their guns, to feed his 1915 offensives. Although on both sides the fighting men were the best the war was to produce – no longer the green enthusiasts of 1914, nor yet the battle-weary veterans of 1917–18 – those holding the front at Verdun had become slack, a consequence of many months spent in so quiet and 'safe' a sector. The *poilu* was never over-fond of digging in, and the forward trench system at Verdun compared poorly with the deep, concreted dug-outs the Germans had already constructed at their key points on the Western Front. 'Between the forts and beyond them there was nothing but dilapidation; countless trenches which had largely fallen in,' writes General Pétain. Moreover, in contrast to the seventy-two battalions of high-quality troops with which the Crown Prince was to launch the attack, the French defenders had only thirty-four, some of them second-class units.

The Germans had reinforced the admirable secrecy of Operation *Gericht* (or 'Judgement Place'), as it was named, by massing their aircraft to fly an aerial barrage through which no French 'spy' plane could penetrate. It was the first time that the air weapon was utilized as a coordinated force. Joffre, however, had received at least one warning of the impending attack and the poor state of the Verdun defences from the distinguished commander of a *chasseurs* regiment, Lieutenant-Colonel Driant, who was holding the very tip of the salient. Driant was told to mind his own business, and the imperturbable 'Papa' Joffre paid little attention.

Thus, in fact, the French weakness at Verdun was far greater than even Falkenhayn suspected. An early collapse there was probably only prevented by a last minute postponement of the German attack. Verdun has one of the nastiest, cold, rainy, foggy climates of all France, and day after day in early February the German artillery observers were blinded by blizzards and fog. The resultant nine-day respite caused even Joffre to wake up and set vital reinforcements on the road to Verdun. Nevertheless, the intensity of the dawn bombardment on 21 February took the French completely by surprise. Nothing like it had ever been experienced before, even on the shell-saturated Western Front. For nine dreadful hours it continued, obliterating the poorly prepared French trenches and burying alive many of their defenders. The brunt of it was borne by Driant's *chasseurs* in the Bois des Caures, which seemed as if it were being swept by 'a storm, a hurricane, a tempest growing ever stronger, where it was raining nothing but paving stones'.

The first German assault troops went in as the bombardment lifted at 4 p.m. It seemed impossible that any human being could have survived in that methodically devastated soil. Yet, with a heroic tenacity that was to immortalize the French defence during the months ahead, the survivors hung on to what remained of their trenches. The Germans were in fact cautiously carrying out what was but a strong patrol action, testing like a dentist's probe for the soft areas in the French front. Here excessive caution perhaps led to their first mistake; a massive infantry follow-up on that first day might well have carried the first French line. But then, as has already been noted, a swift capture of Verdun was not Falkenhayn's intention.

The brutal bombardment began again at dawn on the 22nd, and that afternoon the Germans threw in their main infantry attack, equipped with a deadly and terrible new weapon: flamethrowers. The French line buckled, and Driant was killed while withdrawing the remnants of his regiment. Of his two battalions, totalling 1,200 men, only a handful of officers and about 500 men straggled back to the rear. But the defence had been stubborn enough to force the German storm troops back once again, to await a third softening up bombardment the following morning. By the 23rd, signs of mounting confusion were reaching the various field H.Q.s before Verdun. Whole units were disappearing from the sight of their commanders; communications were breaking down under the shelling, and runners were not getting through. One by one the French gun batteries were being knocked out by the long-range German 150-mms. On at least one disastrous occasion, a French counter-attack was broken up after the assembled infantry had been shelled by their own guns, in the belief that their position had already been abandoned. Order and counter-order were followed by the inevitable consequences.

The twenty-fourth of February was the day the dam burst. A reserve division of North African troops, unacclimatized to the harsh Verdun weather and flung in piecemeal, broke under the bombardment. The whole of the second line of the French defences fell within a matter of hours. Between the attackers and Verdun, however, there still stood the line of forts. Above all, Douaumont, the strongest of them all, a great tortoise-like dome dominating the whole battlefield, was a solid bulwark of comfort behind the backs of the retreating *poilus*. But on 25 February, without planning it, the Germans pulled off one of the greatest coups of the entire war. Acting on their own initiative and taking advantage of the prevailing confusion, several small packets of the 24th Brandenburg Regiment worked their way into Douaumont without losing a man. One actually penetrated into the fort's heavy gun turret, which was still firing on distant fixed targets, blissfully unaware that the war had come so close. To their astonishment, the Germans discovered that (thanks to Joffre's policy of de-activating the forts) the world's strongest bastion was virtually defenceless.

In Germany, church bells acclaimed the capture of Douaumont; in France its surrender was regarded as a disaster of the first magnitude, comparable to the fall of Singapore in 1942 – except that it had taken place just 150 miles from Paris. Its loss was reckoned, after the battle, to have cost France the equivalent of 100,000 men. Through the streets of Verdun itself some panic-stricken survivors from broken units ran shouting '*sauve qui peut*'! After four days of battle, the way to Verdun was open, and it looked as if the war had again become one of movement – for the first time since the Marne.

The urgency of events had at last impressed even Joffre, back in Chantilly, and he immediately despatched General Philippe Pétain to take over the threatened sector. Already sixty, Pétain had had a slow rise through the army, largely on account of the unorthodoxy of his views, which opposed the Foch school of *attaque à outrance*, and by 1914 he was still no more than a colonel. Since then, however, his career had been meteoric: with the eclipse of the *attaque à outrance* gospel in the bloody shambles of the 1914 'Battle of the Frontiers', Pétain's axiom that 'firepower kills' and his brilliance on the defensive had achieved due recognition. In human terms, no general possessed the confidence of the *poilu* more than Pétain: because of a simple faith that he at least would not squander their lives in futile offensives. Now – in tragic irony – he was called upon to subject his men of the Second Army to the most inhuman experience of the whole war. Pétain's first orders were to hold Verdun 'whatever the cost', and although he spent the first days of his new command in bed with double pneumonia (a secret carefully guarded from the French public), the defence reacted with extraordinary speed to his presence. New lines of resistance were established, and powerful artillery reinforcements brought up, often to be sited by Pétain, the expert, himself. Above all, the impact of Pétain's presence on morale was magical.

As a result of his intervention, the German attack began to slow down. Guns became bogged in the heavy mire when crews tried to move them forward to keep pace with the infantry advance. Losses, too, had already been far heavier than Falkenhayn anticipated, many of them caused by flanking fire from Pétain's guns on the left bank of the Meuse. It was the tragic story of the whole Western Front, so often repeated and never to be resolved; on the flanks of every successful thrust there would always turn out to be one more lethal machine gun, one more battery of guns to massacre the attackers and halt the advance. Determined to keep his own commitment down to the barest minimum, Falkenhayn when drafting Operation *Gericht* had refused the Crown Prince's entreaties to attack on both sides of the river simultaneously. But now, to clear the menace of the French artillery, Falkenhayn reluctantly agreed to extend the offensive, releasing another army corps from his tightly hoarded reserves. But he had missed his best opportunity, and now the deadly escalation of Verdun, which he had been so determined to avoid, was under way.

The respite before the next phase of the German offensive gave Pétain a heaven-sent opportunity to stabilize his front. The railway links to the Verdun salient having been cut by German long-range guns, Pétain established a road artery later immortalized as the *Voie Sacrée*. To contain demoralization, Pétain introduced the *noria* system (named after the perpetually rotating water wheels found in French North Africa), whereby units sent into this particularly atrocious battle would relieve each other after the shortest possible time. Thus, while only a relatively small proportion of the German army went through Verdun, almost the whole French army was to be affected by its horrors, which were, in any event, constantly worse for the defenders. During the critical first week of March alone, 190,000 troops marched up the *Voie Sacrée*, which was to accord Verdun the precedent of being the first major battle to be supplied almost exclusively by motor transport.

On 14 March the Crown Prince launched his new all-out attack along the left bank towards a small ridge called the Mort-Homme, which, with its sinister name acquired from some long forgotten tragedy of another age, became the focus of the most bitter, see-saw fighting for the better part of the next three months. This one tiny sector established a monotonous, deadly pattern that continued virtually without let-up, and which was to characterize the whole Battle of Verdun. After hours of saturating bombardment, the German infantry would push forward to carry what remained of the French front line. There were no longer any trenches, so what they occupied were generally clusters of shell holes, defended by isolated groups of men sacrificing themselves for an obscure tactical purpose. On both sides most fell without ever having seen the opposing infantry, under the non-stop artillery bombardment which continued to be more intense at Verdun than on any other First World War battlefield.

'Verdun is terrible,' wrote Sergeant-Major Méléra, killed a fortnight before the Armistice, 'because man is fighting against material, with the sensation of striking out at empty air. . . .' Death became the constant companion: 'One eats, one drinks beside the dead, one sleeps in the midst of the dying, one laughs and sings in the company of corpses,' wrote Georges Duhamel, the poet and dramatist, who was serving as a French army doctor. The highly compressed area of the battlefield was turning it into a nauseous open cemetery, where often the dead had to remain unburied because of the murderous shelling, or were repeatedly disinterred by it. As the Germans gradually lost their initial advantage in big gun superiority, so conditions for their troops came to compare with what the defenders were suffering. By April, as was later admitted by the German official history, 'Water in the trenches came above the knees. The men had not a dry thread on their bodies. . . . The numbers of sick rose alarmingly.' About the same time a soldier wrote home that, under the French counter-bombardment, 'many would rather endure starvation than make dangerous expeditions for food'. On both sides it was the endlessly repeated story of ration parties and stretcher-bearers setting out but never arriving.

Despite the heroic defence put up by Pétain's men, each day brought the Germans a few yards closer to Verdun. By the beginning of April French losses totalled 90,000; but the Germans had also lost 82,000 men. Even after they had taken the Mort-Homme, the Germans found themselves under savage fire from Côte 304, yet another ridge out on their right flank. Like a surgeon treating galloping cancer, Falkenhayn's knife had to cut yet further from the original point of application. To seize Côte 304, still more fresh German divisions had to be thrown into the battle. It was not until May that the German 'clearing action' on the left bank of the Meuse was completed; by the end of that month, French casualties equalled the total German losses at Stalingrad in the Second World War, and still the battle ground on. The Crown Prince was in favour of calling off the offensive, and Falkenhayn, prey to his habitual indecision, was already wavering; only Knobelsdorf was determined to continue, whatever the cost. The strategic significance of the battle had long since passed out of sight; yet it had somehow achieved a demonic existence of its own, beyond the control of generals on either side. Honour, and *machismo*, had become involved to such an extent as to make disengagement all but impossible. On the French side, Pétain (according to Joffre) had become too deeply affected by the slaughter, so he was promoted to make way for two more ruthless generals, Nivelle and Mangin, nicknamed 'the Butcher'. On 22 May an abortive and costly attempt by Mangin to recapture Fort Douaumont encouraged the Germans to attack once again, this time on the right bank, directly towards Verdun. Four days later, a 'very excited' Joffre appealed to Haig to advance the date of the Somme offensive. Haig's target was 15 August, but (according to the British commander-in-chief) Joffre shouted that 'the French army would cease to exist if we did nothing by then'. So Haig finally agreed to help by attacking on 1 July instead.

A torrid June brought the deadliest phase in the battle so far, with Knobelsdorf throwing in a weight of attack comparable to that of February – but this time concentrated along a front only three, instead of eight, miles wide. It lapped over Fort Vaux, where – resisting grenades, flamethrowers and gas in its subterranean passages – Major Raynal and 600 men held up the main German thrust in an epic defence lasting a whole week, until thirst forced them to surrender. Then, just as Vaux was falling, the Russians unleashed the first of the coordinated Allied offensives planned the previous December. Striking with forty divisions, General Brusilov achieved a spectacular initial success against the Austrians, forcing Falkenhayn to transfer troops badly needed at Verdun by Knobelsdorf to bolster up his sagging ally. Yet still the Germans attacked again, though now on an even narrower front. Using, for the first time, a deadly new gas called phosgene, they nearly reached Fort Souville, located on the last ridge before Verdun. The crisis had been reached, and still the French held; but there were ominous signs that morale was cracking, with units refusing to return to the line. The next day, however, the rumble of British guns was heard at Verdun. Haig had begun his preliminary bombardment on the Somme. On 11 July a leaderless party of German troops actually reached the glacis of Fort Souville and could see the promised city lying below them – until they were either killed or captured.

This was the high-water mark of the German offensive, and with the swift ebbing of the tide Verdun was finally and definitively reprieved. Throughout the summer static warfare continued at Verdun, and the murderous fugue of the heavy cannon was never silenced; but the focus of the fighting had now shifted to the Somme.

In August, the Kaiser replaced Falkenhayn by the joint team of Hindenburg and Ludendorff who, horrified by the slaughter at Verdun, promptly ordered the army onto the defensive. Then, in the autumn, Nivelle and Mangin retook Douaumont and Vaux in a series of brilliant counter-strokes. By Christmas 1916 most of the territory so painfully acquired by the Crown Prince's army had been regained, and after ten terrible months Verdun was saved. But at what a cost! The French admitted to losing 377,231 men, of whom 162,308 were listed as dead or missing; while German losses amounted to 337,000. In fact, however, combined losses may have totalled well over 800,000 – most of them in an area no larger than a small city. 'The German unwisdom in attacking Verdun,' wrote Churchill, 'was more than cancelled in French casualties.' Among those casualties was also Joffre, replaced by a triumphant Nivelle who would lead the French army – too deeply affected by what it had suffered at Verdun – to the brink of catastrophe in the mutinies of the following year.

Verdun was the Pyrrhic victory par excellence; the battle in which, although it was to become a moral glory of transcending significance for the French nation, there were only losers. In this strictest sense, it was the indecisive battle in an indecisive war. Yet it marked 1916 as the watershed year of the war; the year beyond which all rivers changed directions. Even though Verdun may be rated as a military defeat for Germany, the grimly macabre 'bleeding white' strategy of Falkenhayn did succeed to the extent that, by the end of 1916, it became plain that Britain would henceforth have to assume the main burden on the Western Front; and that, even so, victory could still not be achieved there without the arrival of fresh, American troops. In the East, by trying so bravely to relieve Verdun, Brusilov had broken the heart of the Russian army, which now reeled ineluctably towards revolution. Verdun also saw the death of Germany's last hopes of outright victory. On both sides the fighting men themselves underwent a marked change. One German divisional history records that, in 1916, 'there was a spirit of heroism which was never again found in the division . . . the men in 1918 had not the temper, the hard bitterness and spirit of sacrifice of their predecessors'. For the French army it was the excessive sacrifices at Verdun that germinated the seeds of the 1917 mutinies.

Within the context of the First World War, Verdun strikes a parallel with Vicksburg or the grinding battles fought at such heavy cost by Grant in 1864 in Virginia, without which the spirit of Lee's Confederate army would never have been broken in the American Civil War. But, for France, with the cost of Verdun too great to bear, the true decisiveness of the battle lies outside the confines of 1914–18. A young French ensign, Raymond Jubert, wrote in prophetic despair before he was killed at Verdun: 'They will not be able to make us do it again another day; that would be to misconstrue the price of our effort. . . .' Almost an entire generation of Frenchmen – more than three quarters of the whole army – had passed through the nightmare of Verdun, and nobody knew better than Pétain how haunted it remained. Years after the war he wrote that at Verdun 'the constant vision of death had penetrated him [the French soldier] with a resignation which bordered on fatalism'. By 1940 that spirit of 'fatalism' was to be renamed 'defeatism'.

Verdun and 1916 introduced a number of 'firsts' into the history of land warfare. Among them were numbered flamethrowers, phosgene gas, and the 'creeping barrage', the use of an air force as a coordinated weapon and the use of road transport to supply a battle. That same year, on the Somme, the tank made its first half-hearted appearance – the weapon that, one war later, was to provide the antidote to positional warfare of which Verdun will always be the enduring, ghastly symbol. After 1918, both France and Germany studied the lessons of Verdun methodically and each came to different conclusions. From the successful role of Douaumont and the other forts at Verdun, France's military leaders (headed by Pétain) derived the wrong lessons. As a result the Maginot Line, with its impenetrable and interlinked underground bastions, was born. But its astronomic cost made it impossible for an economically weak France to extend it all the way to the sea, or to provide the armoured covering force without which the Maginot Line became little more than an elaborate, but unguarded anti-tank ditch. In Germany Guderian (who also fought at Verdun) concluded that this was the kind of battle that Germany must never again accept, and devoted his energy to devising the panzer weapon, which would bring back a war of movement by sweeping round the flank of France's line of super-Douaumonts.

The lessons of Verdun have their point even today, now that – with the 'Ramadan War' of 1973 – the argument of positional versus tank warfare seems to have described at least a half-circle. In the early days after their 1967 victory, the Israeli General Staff studied 1916 minutely to discover how, while holding a line on the east bank of the Suez Canal, they could avoid getting dragged into a war of attrition, and diminish the casualties which the constant Egyptian bombardments were inflicting. Their decision was to go for the Hindenburg Line style of deep fortifications in depth, held by only thin garrisons, as opposed to the Verdun technique of holding everywhere strongly – the cause of the appalling casualties suffered by France. When the big attack came in 1973, had the Bar Lev Line not been held so lightly the manpower losses consequent on its fall might well have proved fatal to Israel. Meanwhile, for the Egyptians – as with the Belgian forts, Verdun, and the Maginot Line in 1940 – the 'unassailability' of the Bar Lev Line itself exerted an irresistible magnetism; this time it was not 'Big Berthas' or flamethrowers but the humble fire-hose that sought out its Achilles' Heel. The principles, however, were the same: like Falkenhayn's, the manifest aim of the Egyptian General Staff was to entice the Israelis into a protracted 'bleeding white' battle, which, with their inferiority in numbers, the Israelis could not survive. The ghosts of Verdun die hard.

Note on Sources

Boasson, M., *Au Soir d'un monde* (1926).
Bordeaux, Henry, *The Last Days of Fort Vaux* (1917).
Chapman, Guy, *Vain Glory* (1937).
Chastenet, Jacques, *Jours inquiets et jours sanglants 1906–18* (1957).
Churchill, W. S., *The World Crisis* (1931).
Cru, Jean Norton, *Temoins* (1929).
Delvert, Charles L., *Histoire d'une compagnie* (1918).
Duhamel, Georges, *Civilisation* (1921).
Falkenhayn, E. von, *General Headquarters, 1914–16, and its Critical Decisions* (1919).
Falls, Cyril, *The First World War* (1960).
Hoffmann, Max, *The War of Lost Opportunities* (1924).
Horne, Alistair, *The Price of Glory* (1962).
Joffre, Marshal, *The Memoirs of Marshal Joffre* (1932).
Jubert, Raymond, *Verdun* (1918).
Klüfer, Kurt von, *Seelenkräfte im Kampf um Douaumont* (1938).
Laure, General, *Pétain* (1941).
Liddell Hart, B. H., *Reputations Ten Years After* (1928).
Liddell Hart, B. H., *History of the World War, 1914–18* (1934).
Méléra, César, *Verdun* (1925).
Ministère de la Guerre, Etat-Major de l'Armée, Service Historique, *Les Armées françaises dans la grande guerre*, Tome IV and annexes (1931–5).
Palat, General B. E., *La Grande Guerre sur le front occidental*, Vols X–XII (1925).
Pétain, Marshal, *La Bataille de Verdun* (1929).
Radtke, E., *Douaumont – Wie es Wirklich war* (1934).
Reichkriegsministerium, *Der Weltkrieg, 1914–1918*, Vol. X (1936).
Reichsarchiven: Beumelburg, W., Vol. 1, *Douaumont* (1925).
Taylor, A. J. P., *The First World War, an Illustrated History* (1963).
Wendt, Hermann, *Verdun 1916* (1931).
Wilhelm, Crown Prince of Germany, *The Memoirs of the Crown Prince of Germany* (1922).

Chapter Five

JUTLAND

Peter Kemp

BY 8.30 p.m. on 30 May 1916 the British Grand Fleet at Scapa, with Sir John Jellicoe flying his flag in the *Iron Duke*, had cleared the entrance of the Flow. Half an hour later the battle squadron at Cromarty was also at sea, and by 11.30 these two forces had joined and were steaming eastwards to a rendezvous beyond the 'Long Forties', some sixty miles east of Aberdeen. They formed a fleet of twenty-four dreadnoughts, three battlecruisers, eight armoured cruisers, twelve light cruisers, five flotilla leaders, forty-six destroyers and one minelayer.

Sir David Beatty, commanding the Battlecruiser Fleet with his flag in H.M.S. *Lion*, sailed from Rosyth at 11.30 p.m. bound for the same rendezvous, where he would take station sixty miles ahead of the battle fleet. His total force consisted of six battlecruisers, four dreadnoughts, fourteen light cruisers, twenty-seven destroyers and one seaplane carrier. As the British fleet put to sea, and for some hours afterwards, the High Seas Fleet of Germany still lay in its harbours.

The events which had led to the British fleet being ordered to sea were strong indications in the Admiralty that the German commander-in-chief, Admiral Reinhard Scheer, was planning a major operation with the High Seas Fleet. Many of the German code signals were decipherable in the Naval Intelligence Division, and the volume of German wireless traffic in the week up to 30 May had shown that something big was in the wind. At 5.40 p.m. on 30 May a high-priority operational signal, which was not decipherable, was made to the High Seas Fleet, and an Admiralty order to Jellicoe to concentrate the fleet east of the 'Long Forties' and to be 'ready for eventualities' set the British ships in motion.

Scheer's plan was relatively simple. He knew that his High Seas Fleet was no match for the Grand Fleet, and the last thing he wanted was a pitched battle between them. He aimed at drawing the British ships out to sea over a force of sixteen U-boats, which he stationed off the British bases, expecting that a reported movement of his fleet would inevitably tempt the British ships out. Once at sea with his fleet he hoped to encounter isolated squadrons of British ships which he could annihilate, thus redressing to some extent the adverse balance between the two main fleets. His plan required the High Seas Fleet to sail north up the western coast of Denmark as far as the Skagerrak; this was the fleet movement which was to bring squadrons of the Grand Fleet to sea. He sailed from the Jade at 1 a.m. on the 31st with his battle fleet, flying his flag in the dreadnought *Friedrich der Grosse*. One and a half hours later Vice-Admiral Franz von Hipper, commanding the scouting groups and with his flag in the battlecruiser *Lützow*, sailed from the Jade and Elbe, taking station about sixty miles ahead of the battle fleet. The combined forces amounted to sixteen dreadnoughts, six pre-dreadnoughts, five battlecruisers, eleven light cruisers and sixty-one destroyers.

The first part of Scheer's plan failed to materialize. One of the sixteen U-boats was sunk by an armed trawler, one managed to fire two torpedoes,

Admiral Jellicoe's flagship Iron Duke *opening fire at the Battle of Jutland, 31 May 1916. The battleships* Royal Oak *and* Superb *are astern, the* Thunderer *ahead*

which both missed, at the light cruiser *Galatea* when she was seventy miles out from the Scottish coast, and the remainder did nothing. There were a few scattered sighting reports, but they were of little value to Scheer and gave him no impression that the whole of the Grand Fleet had put to sea.

Jellicoe and Beatty similarly had no knowledge that the High Seas Fleet was at sea. It was nothing new for the fleet to receive orders from the Admiralty to sail on the suspicion of a German fleet movement: it had happened on at least five previous occasions and the fleet had swept down the North Sea to find the ocean empty of German ships. There was nothing to indicate to Jellicoe or Beatty that this time it would be different, however much they hoped to find the German fleet at sea.

Indeed, during the morning of 31 May they both received a signal from the Admiralty which dashed any hopes they may have entertained. It was a stupid mistake which arose out of the suspicions and lack of cooperation which existed in the Admiralty between the Operations and Intelligence Divisions. During the morning Rear-Admiral Thomas Jackson, director of the Operations Division, went to Room 40, where the German code signals were deciphered, and asked where the directional wireless put the German call sign D.K., which was the German commander-in-chief's harbour call sign. He was informed that it was in Wilhelmshafen, and without asking any other question left Room 40 and sent a signal to the fleet to the effect that the German flagship was still in the Jade. What everyone in Room 40 knew was that when Scheer put to sea he transferred his harbour call sign to the Wilhelmshafen wireless telegraphy station and used a different one to conceal the fact that the High Seas Fleet had put to sea, but Jackson waited for no such explanation, hurrying out of the room to get off his signal to the fleet.

Jellicoe and Beatty both received the signal at about 12.30 p.m. Any urgency they may have felt about the whole operation was effectively destroyed, and Jellicoe reduced the speed of the fleet to fifteen knots in order to conserve fuel. But a much more distressing effect of the signal was to undermine Jellicoe's confidence in the accuracy of the Admiralty's later intelligence reports when, less than three hours after the receipt of the signal, Beatty sighted the High Seas Fleet well out to sea.

Beatty had been ordered to turn northwards at 2 p.m. to close the battle fleet if by then he had sighted no enemy ships, but he held on until 2.15 as he had not quite reached the southern limit of his sweep. The alteration of course to the north was made at 2.15, but as his light cruiser screen was taking up the new disposition, the easternmost ship of the screen, H.M.S. *Galatea*, sighted a Danish steamer stopped and blowing off steam. She closed to investigate the cause and discovered that two German destroyers had stopped the ship to investigate her. The *Galatea*, accompanied by H.M.S. *Phaeton*, opened fire, and at 2.28 made the general signal 'Enemy in sight'. She followed it up with an urgent signal reporting the enemy as two light cruisers.

The two destroyers were the westernmost ships of Hipper's screen. The sighting was simultaneous and they made a similar signal to Hipper. The two battlecruiser forces at once altered course towards each other. Beatty sighted the German battlecruisers at 3.30 at a distance of fourteen miles; Hipper's sighting of Beatty's ships was a few minutes earlier and at 3.33 he swung his ships round to the south-east with the object of drawing the British ships down to Scheer's battleships, which were some sixty miles to the south. Beatty also altered course to E.S.E., similar to Hipper's course but closing the enemy line. At 3.49 the *Lützow* opened fire, the *Lion* a minute or two later. The range was 15,000 yards. The Battle of Jutland had begun.

Beatty had with him six battlecruisers and the four battleships of the 5th Battle Squadron, the *Barham*, *Warspite*, *Valiant* and *Malaya*. These were the latest battleships to join the fleet, capable of a speed of twenty-one knots and armed with eight 15-inch guns. Unfortunately, when Beatty made the signal to alter course towards the enemy it was not repeated to the *Barham*, and for some minutes the 5th Battle Squadron remained on its northerly course while the battlecruisers which the squadron was supporting were working up to their maximum speed towards the enemy. The five miles which separated the battleships and battlecruisers in their normal cruising formation had opened to ten miles before Rear-Admiral Evan-Thomas in the *Barham* altered course to conform with Beatty's movements. This gap of ten miles delayed the 5th Battle Squadron for twenty minutes in coming into action with the enemy, and even then they had to engage at maximum range.

As the battlecruisers, with both forces in line ahead, settled down in their run to the south, the German gunnery proved remarkably accurate. Beatty's ships were visible in clear outline to the German gunlayers against the bright western sky. Their stereoscopic rangefinders provided the range with remarkable accuracy, and within twenty minutes of fire being opened they had hit the British ships fourteen times. One hit on Q-turret of the *Lion* almost proved fatal, the ship only being saved by the quick action of the turret officer, Major Harvey of the Royal Marines, who though mortally wounded ordered the magazine to be flooded. A minute or so later a salvo of three shells landed on the deck of H.M.S. *Indefatigable* and she hauled out of the line with her stern submerged. The next salvo hit her near the fore turret and she disappeared in an enormous explosion.

Four minutes later the 5th Battle Squadron, coming up from astern at full speed, opened fire. They opened at a range of 19,000 yards, but as the range closed their accurate fire began to tell on the rear of the German line, both the *Moltke* and the *Von der Tann* being heavily hit. Beatty took the opportunity, now that the 5th Battle Squadron was at last in action, of turning his battlecruisers to close the range and at the same time ordered his destroyer flotillas to attack the enemy line with torpedoes. The closing range gave the German battlecruisers *Derfflinger*, which because of a mistaken concentration signal from the *Lion* was not being engaged, and *Seydlitz* the opportunity to bring the *Queen Mary* under a devastating concentrated fire. At 4.26 she was hit by a salvo and, like the *Indefatigable* before her, blew up and sank.

When Hipper saw the British destroyers coming in for their torpedo attack on his line, he ordered his own destroyers out to meet them. There was a confused mêlée between the two lines of battlecruisers, with the destroyers firing at each other at ranges down at times to as low as 600 yards and with both sides intent at the same time on making their torpedo attacks. The British torpedoes forced Hipper to turn away three times and the *Seydlitz* was hit, though not with very damaging results. The German torpedoes forced the 5th Battle Squadron to turn away once, but no torpedoes hit any ship in the line. Both sides lost two destroyers in the exchange.

But in spite of the British loss of two battlecruisers, Hipper was now in dire straits. There were eight British capital ships still in action against his five, and the accurate shooting of the 5th Battle Squadron was beginning to make an impact. He was forced to break off the action and by 4.36 was steering due east, away from Beatty.

It was at this moment that H.M.S. *Southampton*, one of the cruisers in Beatty's light cruiser screen, sighted smoke to the south-eastward. Then, through the smoke, there appeared masts, and a few moments later ships were visible. To Arthur Peters, Commodore Goodenough's signal officer who was standing with his chief on the bridge of the *Southampton*, it seemed 'the day of a light cruiser's lifetime. The whole of the High Seas Fleet is before you [Commodore Goodenough].' And so it was. Scheer's twenty-two battleships were in sight in line ahead, with their attendant destroyers about them. Within minutes of receiving the *Southampton*'s sighting signal, the High Seas Fleet was also in sight from the bridge of the *Lion*, at a distance of twelve miles, steering north.

At this sudden change in the shape of the battlecruiser action, Beatty had but one thought in his mind. Some fifty miles to the north was Sir John Jellicoe with the Grand Fleet, steering south at twenty knots, and Beatty's task was now to draw the High Seas Fleet up into its arms. At 4.40 a flag signal was hoisted on the *Lion* ordering an alteration of course sixteen points to starboard, that is, from south-east to north-west. The flag signal was not seen in the *Barham*, and was not repeated by searchlight as it should have been, with the result that the 5th Battle Squadron, which had not received the *Southampton*'s sighting report, continued on its southerly course. As the squadron passed the battlecruisers, now steering north-west, Beatty made another flag signal to them, ordering them to turn sixteen points in succession to starboard, but for some reason the signal was not hauled down (the executive order to start the turn) until the battleships had passed. This delay not only once again opened up a gap between the battlecruisers and the 5th Battle Squadron, but also gave Scheer a useful point at which to concentrate his gunfire, since when turning in succession each ship makes her turn in the same water as her predecessor. This was the patch of water which later became known as 'Windy Corner', and in which the *Barham* received several damaging hits.

So began the run to the north, on Beatty's side to draw the High Seas Fleet within range of the Grand Fleet's guns, and on Scheer's, who still had no intimation that the Grand Fleet was even at sea, to realize his dream of finding a detached British squadron which he could annihilate, so reducing the numerical odds against him. Leaving out of account his cruisers and destroyers, and even his pre-dreadnoughts, he still had sixteen dreadnoughts and five battlecruisers against four dreadnoughts and four battlecruisers. It would have been a substantial victory.

Up in the north, with his battleships disposed in six divisions in line abreast, Jellicoe was anxiously awaiting information on the enemy's position, course and speed. Since Beatty's signal reporting that he had sighted the German battlecruisers, he had received no information until the *Iron Duke* read the *Southampton*'s signal reporting the High Seas Fleet. At 4.45 a signal from Beatty ('Have sighted enemy's battlefleet bearing S.E.') was mutilated in transmission and was decoded in the *Iron Duke* as '26–30 battleships, probably hostile, bearing S.S.E., steering S.E.' Jellicoe, of course, realized at once that the signal was garbled but saw no reason to disbelieve the '26–30 battleships', since this was the available German battleship strength at the time (eighteen dreadnoughts, ten pre-dreadnoughts).

Even when visual touch was established between the two forces, the *Falmouth* in Beatty's cruiser screen sighting the *Black Prince* of Jellicoe's cruiser screen, the commander-in-chief received no information of any value. Even when the *Iron Duke* sighted the *Lion* herself at 6.01 p.m. there was no immediate information. 'Where is the enemy's battle fleet?' signalled Jellicoe, to receive the reply from Beatty, who had in fact not seen Scheer's battleships since he began the run to the north, 'Enemy battlecruisers bearing S.E.' It was very little on which to act, but it was all Jellicoe had, and on it he had to make his decision on the Grand Fleet's deployment for battle.

Meanwhile, what of Hipper and Scheer? They had settled down in the chase to the north, with Hipper in action intermittently against the British battlecruisers and the 5th Battle Squadron and the head of Scheer's line firing against the 5th Battle Squadron. During the run to the north the gunnery of Beatty's ships was a good deal better than it had been during the previous chase to the south, but the ships were only engaged part of the time. The shooting of the battleships was excellent, and although bearing the brunt of the battle against both battlecruisers and battleships they hit four of the former and two of the latter and inflicted far more damage than they received.

Nevertheless, there was nothing in the shooting of the 5th Battle Squadron to discourage Scheer or to make him any less confident that he had an annihilating victory within his grasp. Suddenly Hipper, who had turned away to the eastward under a hot fire from Beatty's ships and the 5th Battle Squadron, found heavy shells pitching alongside from the opposite direction. They came from the battlecruiser squadron with Jellicoe's fleet which, on receipt of Beatty's first sighting signal, had been steaming south at full speed to join him. They forced Hipper to turn down to the south to search for protection from the main High Seas Fleet, where he took station immediately ahead of the German battle line. The time was 6.10 p.m., and the dramatic appearance of this new British battlecruiser squadron, by forcing Hipper to the south, also concealed from him any view of the approaching Grand Fleet. Neither German admiral yet knew of its presence, although it was now no more than seven miles away.

The time had come when Jellicoe had to make up his mind on deploying the Grand Fleet for battle. He had still had no sight of the enemy, and no one had told him where Scheer's ships were. He had two choices, deployment either on the starboard or on the port column of the fleet. If he deployed on the starboard column he would be about five miles nearer where he thought the German ships were and thus would have another ten minutes of action before daylight faded. But against this advantage had to be placed the possible disadvantage that such a deployment might well enable Scheer to 'cross the T', to bring his battle line across the head of the British line where every German gun would bear with the British ships powerless to reply until they had made an eight-point turn. There was a risk, too, of the German destroyer flotillas making a massed torpedo attack against the point of deployment as the British battleships made their turn into the line of battle, and there was a further disadvantage in that a deployment to starboard would not provide the best conditions of visibility for the Grand Fleet gunlayers. The disadvantages of deploying to port were the greater distance from the enemy and the ten minutes' delay in opening fire, but against those were the virtual certainty of 'crossing the German T', of getting the Grand Fleet between Scheer's fleet and its bases in Germany, and of providing the British gunlayers with the most favourable conditions of visibility, with the German battleships silhouetted against the western horizon and the British battleships almost invisible, except for their gun flashes, to the High Seas Fleet. After a few moments of thought (about twenty seconds, according to Jellicoe's flag captain) the commander-in-chief ordered deployment on the port-wing column. The time was 6.15.

It proved a tactical masterstroke. Scheer's first view of the Grand Fleet was of a long line of ships, or of the flashes of their guns, stretching right across his line of advance. He had had one piece of good fortune a minute or two earlier when the 3rd Battlecruiser Squadron (the *Invincible*, *Indomitable* and *Inflexible*), steering westwards to join up with Beatty's battlecruisers and thus ahead of the German line, came into sight. The shooting of the 3rd Battlecruiser Squadron had been magnificently accurate, and Hipper's battlecruisers, already considerably mauled, had been hit frequently, particularly the *Derfflinger* and the *Lützow*. But as the British ships steamed into view of Scheer's battleships, the *König* and the battlecruisers concentrated their fire on the *Invincible* and a salvo of shells landed on Q-turret to repeat the tragic chain of events which had earlier sent the *Indefatigable* and the *Queen Mary* to the bottom. The explosion of the German shells ignited the cordite in the turret loading trays and the flame penetrated to the magazine down the loading trunk. Like her sisters before her, the *Invincible* blew up in a tremendous explosion, breaking into two halves.

Yet Scheer was now in deep trouble. The ships of the Grand Fleet were shooting steadily and accurately, with the range down to about 12,000 yards, which was also about the maximum visibility in the patchy mist. Hipper's battlecruisers and the leading battleships in Scheer's line took the brunt of the punishment, and the *Lützow*, with a heavy list and her bows nearly awash, had to turn away out of the line. Of the other four battlecruisers, the *Derfflinger* was taking in water through a large hole in her bows, the *Seydlitz* was low in the water and almost awash, and all the gun turrets of the *Von der Tann* had been put out of action. Hipper, in search of a new flagship now that the *Lützow* was virtually out of action and likely to sink, embarked in a destroyer and made for the *Moltke*, which was the only battlecruiser still serviceable, but it was not until over two hours later that he was able to get aboard her, rehoist his flag, and resume command.

In order to extricate his ships from their impossible situation, Scheer put into operation a tactical manoeuvre known as the *Gefechtskehrtwendung*, or 'battle turn-about', in which all ships turned simultaneously sixteen points (180 degrees) to starboard, thus reversing the line. This had been practised in manoeuvres but had never yet been used in action. At the same time he ordered a flotilla of destroyers to cover the movement with a smoke screen and a torpedo attack on the Grand Fleet. His 'turn-about' was completed by 6.45 and the High Seas Fleet was lost to sight in the smoke and the thickening mist. Some of the British ships saw the German turn but none of them saw fit to report it to the commander-in-chief.

There was little that Jellicoe could do in the low visibility and with no reports of the enemy's movements, beyond bringing his ships round to a more southerly course to make certain of remaining between the High Seas Fleet and its bases in Germany. There was still a little more than two hours of daylight remaining, but with the visibility closing in the chances of a sustained fleet action were now dwindling. Smoke, too, was interfering with accurate observation, and this added to the difficulties both of finding the enemy again and, when found, of holding him in sustained action.

It was Scheer himself who solved Jellicoe's immediate problem for him. Once again he ordered a sixteen-point turn to starboard, again reversing his course and the order of sailing, his new course bringing him straight back into the centre of the British line. The only reasonable explanation must be that Scheer thought he could get round to the north of the British fleet and thus gain both access to his bases and the advantage of the light for his gunlayers. He himself gave a different reason, wanting 'to deal the enemy a second blow by again advancing regardless of consequences. . . . This manoeuvre would necessarily have the effect of surprising the enemy, upsetting his plans for the rest of the day and, if the attack was powerful enough, of facilitating our extricating ourselves for the night.' Placing his already battered battlecruisers in the van, he steered east through the mist.

At 7.10 the two divisions of battleships in the rear of the British line sighted the German fleet to the south-west and opened fire at a range of 10,000 yards. Five minutes later the German ships were visible to the whole of the British line and brought under a heavy fire. The leading German battleships slowed down under the intensity of fire and caused the rear of the line to bunch. Once again it was the battlecruisers which took the main weight of the British firing, and by now they were in a sorry state.

It was at that moment that Scheer made his controversial 'charge the enemy' signal to his battlecruisers. The literal translation of the signal is 'Battlecruisers, at the enemy. Give it everything!' With the *Lützow* out of action, the four remaining battlecruisers set off on their 'death-ride' towards the British line, and the range decreased to 7,700 yards before they altered course to the southward, parallel to the British line. At the same time Scheer ordered his destroyer flotillas to attack the line with torpedoes and to make smoke, and for the third time in the battle executed a sixteen-point turn to starboard to extricate his battleships from the impossible position into which he had led them.

Two of the German destroyer flotillas answered Scheer's call and went in to the attack, firing thirty-one torpedoes. Twenty-one of them reached the British line, but none hit a ship; one German destroyer was blown out of the water by a 12-inch shell and two more were badly damaged by gunfire. Jellicoe, who saw the German destroyers attacking, ordered one light cruiser squadron to engage the destroyers (the British destroyers did so automatically under the standing battle orders) and turned the fleet away by two turns of two points each, or a total of forty-five degrees. This was the normal procedure in any fleet in the face of a torpedo attack and was also in the standing battle orders. Both Hipper (three times) and Evan-Thomas, commanding the 5th Battle Squadron, had done so in similar circumstances during the first battlecruiser action. Yet Jellicoe's action at this juncture in turning the fleet away shocked many officers in the fleet and has been widely criticized ever since, mainly on the grounds that if he had turned towards the enemy, accepting the risk of having six or eight of his battleships hit by torpedoes, he might have caused the High Seas Fleet very serious loss and even perhaps have turned the battle into a rout. This argument supposed that Jellicoe knew that Scheer had made his third sixteen-point turn, that his battle line was in some disarray at the time, and that he was virtually in headlong flight. But Jellicoe knew none of these things, and it would have been accepting too great a risk to take the fleet blindly through the smoke and mist patches, to say nothing of the other German destroyer flotillas which had not yet made their attacks, in the hope of finding a disorganized enemy on the other side of the smoke screen. In fact, at least six British ships had seen Scheer's third about-turn but, inexplicably, again none had reported it to the commander-in-chief. Certainly, Jellicoe's turn away came at an unfortunate time in the course of the battle but, without the use of hindsight, it was his only sensible course at the time.

By now the time was 7.30 and about one and a half hours of daylight remained. After the Grand Fleet's turn away from the torpedo attack, Jellicoe brought the fleet back into line ahead and ordered a course of south-west, towards the enemy. A sighting report from the *Lion*, received in the *Iron Duke* a minute or two before 8 p.m., brought a further alteration of course to due west and an increase in speed to eighteen knots. In the mean-time Scheer had, at 7.48, altered course to south to avoid being driven still further to the west and, consequently, still further from his base. This was a course which would bring him ahead of the Grand Fleet but which would also lead him into contact with the British battlecruisers. This in fact occurred at about 8.15, and Beatty opened fire, hitting the *Seydlitz* and the *Derfflinger*. The action once again forced Scheer to turn away to the west, and in fact deprived Jellicoe of his last chance of bringing the High Seas Fleet within range of his guns. Although steering for the sound of Beatty's guns, Scheer's alteration of course to the westward took the German fleet beyond the reach of Jellicoe's battleships until darkness had fallen. Beatty's brief action against the German battlecruisers was in fact the last time that capital ships engaged each other during the war.

Neither commander-in-chief could feel fully satisfied at the outcome of the day's action. Jellicoe, who at the start of the main battle must have thought he had the High Seas Fleet in the hollow of his hand, had twice seen it disappear in the mist and smoke of the evening before his greatly superior tactics could reap their proper reward. He had been hampered not only by mist and smoke but equally by the lack of reports which should have been signalled to him by his cruisers. The overriding importance of such reports was laid down in the battle orders, but few of the cruiser admirals had kept him properly informed of the enemy's movements. Yet he was still between the High Seas Fleet and its bases, his fleet was virtually intact and undamaged, and he could justifiably look forward to a convincing defeat of the enemy when daylight arrived on the morning of 1 June.

Scheer, perhaps, could feel some satisfaction in the fact that he had twice succeeded in extricating his fleet from a desperately dangerous situation. But he knew too, as he had always known, that the High Seas Fleet could never engage in a full-scale action against the Grand Fleet without a risk of substantial defeat, and he had been led into a situation where the very thing had happened that he had always most wanted to avoid. The sinking of three

British battlecruisers was perhaps something of a feather in his cap, though he knew that it was a loss that the British could well afford and would make no real difference to the overall British superiority. His own battlecruisers were in no shape for further battle, for the *Lützow* was sinking and it was doubtful whether the *Seydlitz* could keep herself afloat through the night. Of the other three, only the *Moltke*, and to a lesser extent the *Von der Tann*, were in anything like fighting trim. But above all, the British Grand Fleet was still to the eastward of him, between him and his bases, and it was imperative that somehow he should get past it in the night. He knew that if the High Seas Fleet were still at sea in the morning, nothing could save him.

As darkness fell, both Jellicoe and Scheer reformed their fleets into night cruising formation and altered course to the southward. Jellicoe was of the opinion that Scheer would make for the Ems passage back to his base, taking his fleet outside the British mined areas in the Heligoland Bight and steering along the north German coast to his base at Wilhelmshafen. To ensure remaining between Scheer and his bases he set a course a little east of south, and maintained a speed which would at daylight leave him in a position where he would be able to intercept the enemy whether he took the Ems route or a more northerly route through the minefield, where a swept passage existed near the Amrun Bank. He must also have considered the most northerly of all routes, the Horns Reef channel, since he detached the minelayer *Abdiel* with orders to strengthen the existing British minefield there.

Scheer had in fact decided to use the Horns Reef channel, since it was the nearest, and at 9.10 had ordered a course of S.S.E., adding to the signal the injunction that this course was to be maintained at all costs. It led direct to Horns Reef. Scheer was determined to force his way through the Grand Fleet should he meet it, regardless of whatever losses in ships it would entail.

With the Grand Fleet in its night cruising formation of three divisions disposed abeam, Jellicoe ordered the destroyer flotillas to take station five miles astern, so that should they encounter the High Seas Fleet trying to pass astern of the fleet they could drive it back to the westward by massed torpedo attacks. So, in his opinion, all was set for the decisive action on the morrow.

The two fleets steamed southwards through the night, their respective lines of advance making a long narrow V. Jellicoe was steaming at seventeen knots, Scheer at sixteen, and the difference in speed ensured that the point of convergence of the two lines of advance would occur about five miles astern of the Grand Fleet. This, in fact, is what happened, and the High Seas Fleet had to fight its way through the destroyers. About seven individual actions were fought as the German fleet met each destroyer flotilla in turn, and though they lost the pre-dreadnought *Pommern*, the light cruisers *Rostock* and *Elbing*, and one or two destroyers, it was a small price to pay for the escape of the fleet. By 2.30 a.m. on 1 June the High Seas Fleet was through with clear water between it and the Horns Reef channel. The only hazard left was a British minefield laid several days earlier, and though the battleship *Ostfriesland* hit one mine the damage was not enough to sink her.

During these seven night encounters, no reports were made to the commander-in-chief indicating that the High Seas Fleet was breaking through. Had Jellicoe received even one report up to midnight, or a few minutes later, to this effect, he could still have cut the German fleet off and forced an action at daylight. The night battles had been clearly visible to the Grand Fleet but were thought to be no more than engagements between the light forces of both fleets. What was more extraordinary was that enemy battleships were sighted by the two rear divisions of the Grand Fleet, the 5th Battle Squadron and part of the 1st, and were neither engaged nor reported. There can be little doubt that the commander-in-chief was badly served in this respect.

It was not only by some of his ships at sea that Jellicoe was badly served: the Admiralty was equally blameworthy. At 9.06 p.m. Scheer had sent a signal to the airship detachment urgently requesting early morning Zeppelin reconnaissance at Horns Reef. The signal had been decoded in Room 40 and sent to the Operations Division at 10.10. Another signal sent at 10.32, decoded and passed to the Operations Division at 11.15, ordered all flotillas to be assembled at Horns Reef by 2 a.m. on 1 June. Neither of these vital signals, both of which would have given Jellicoe the exact information he required in sufficient time to make proper use of it, was sent out by the Admiralty. It was little wonder that Scheer's bold, and potentially suicidal, course of action succeeded.

Both sides claimed the victory, and if victory lies in a comparison of the number of ships sunk and casualties inflicted then Scheer's claim was certainly valid. The Grand Fleet had lost fourteen ships (111,000 tons) in the battle, and its casualties totalled 6,784, while the German loss in ships was eleven (62,000 tons), and their total casualties amounted to 3,058. But in the wider context of the sea campaign as a whole the material losses and the casualties in one battle matter little; it is the long-term result that tips the final balance between victory and defeat.

When Jellicoe brought the Grand Fleet home to Scapa Flow in the afternoon of 2 June, he was able to send a signal to the Admiralty that evening reporting the fleet ready for sea at four hours' notice. When Scheer reached Wilhelmshafen shortly after noon on 1 June, the best estimate he could give of the High Seas Fleet's readiness for battle was mid-August. And there was more to it than that. In his confidential report to the Kaiser, which he wrote on 4 July, Scheer admitted that the High Seas Fleet could never break the British blockade of Germany, even if the entire U-boat strength was used in conjunction with the fleet, in purely naval operations. In this same document Scheer advised a full and unrestricted submarine campaign against British trade as the only way of breaking the British stranglehold. Strange words from the self-acclaimed victor of the Battle of Jutland!

The result of the battle brought convincing proof to the German naval command that the prospects of using the High Seas Fleet to force a decision in the North Sea were hopeless. From the start of the war the grey ships based at Scapa Flow and Rosyth had controlled the sea communications of the North Sea; after Jutland that control not only remained unimpaired but was absolute. So, too, was the moral ascendancy which the Grand Fleet enjoyed over the High Seas Fleet. Even the most ebullient of German officers who had envisaged a fight to the finish between the two fleets came to realize after Jutland that such a prospect was madness.

The longer-term result of the battle was the switch of German naval opinion: the U-boat came to be seen as the decisive weapon, provided that it was used not in naval warfare but in unrestricted warfare against trade. From its proud position as the pinnacle of German naval hope the High Seas Fleet was reduced to the role of supporting the U-boats. Between Jutland and the end of the war two and a half years later the High Seas Fleet put to sea on only three occasions, in August and October 1916 and in April 1918, and on each of those occasions considerable precautions were taken against any fortuitous meeting with the Grand Fleet. Its relative inactivity was responsible for the marked drop in morale which became apparent within a very few months of the battle and which continued throughout the remainder of the war. Some writers have attempted to relate the mutinies in the High Seas Fleet at the end of the war to the battle fought at the end of May 1916, and though this is obviously going too far it is undeniable that the deterioration of morale in the German fleet which set in after Jutland accelerated throughout the two remaining years of the war and ultimately led to the mutinies.

In its physical aspect Jutland was a groping, indecisive action fought in the mists of a North Sea evening amid the smoke of ships which had not yet learned how to control the black, sooty masses which poured out of their funnels. In its strategical, and even more its moral, aspect it was a battle which proved convincingly, to British and Germans alike, that the Grand Fleet controlled the North Sea and its communications, and that in its hands the blockade of Germany was unbreakable at sea. It was the weapon of blockade which in the end brought Germany down to defeat.

Note on Sources

The literature on Jutland is immense, engendered in large part by the unhappy internecine warfare which broke out between protagonists of the two British leaders in the battle, Jellicoe and Beatty. Long after the First World War was over, this strange feuding between the rival camps continued, and the modern reader needs to be careful in his choice if he is not to be led astray in his final evaluation of the battle by the writings of one camp or the other. Of British books listed below, some are from one camp, some from the other; it is difficult to find a book on Jutland which is entirely objective and neutral. One such is Professor Marder's study (see below); most of the others, including even some of the official accounts, are suspect from one side or the other.

German books which describe the battle are not subject to any such caveat, and most of them are reasonably factual and objective, though perhaps in some cases strangely uncritical of Scheer's odd tactics during the battle fleet stage of the action.

Official Publications

Admiralty, *Narrative of the Battle of Jutland* (1924).
Cmd. 1068/20, *Battle of Jutland, Official Despatches.*
Corbett, Sir Julian, and Sir Henry Newbolt, *Naval Operations*, 5 Vols (1920–31).
German Ministry of Marine, *Der Krieg zur See, 1914–1918*, a massive series of official histories, of which *Der Krieg in der Nordsee*, 7 Vols (1920–68), includes the Battle of Jutland.

Published Books

Alboldt, E., *Die Tragödie der alten Deutschen Marine* (1928).
Bacon, Admiral Sir R., *The Jutland Scandal* (1925).
Bacon, Admiral Sir R., *Life of John Rushworth, Earl Jellicoe* (1936).
Chalmers, Rear-Admiral W., *Life and Letters of David, Earl Beatty* (1951).
Dewar; Vice-Admiral K., *The Navy from Within* (1939).
Dreyer, Admiral Sir F., *The Sea Heritage* (1955).
Harper, Rear-Admiral J., *The Truth about Jutland* (1927).
Hase, Commander Georg von, *Kiel and Jutland* (1927).
Jellicoe, Admiral of the Fleet, Earl, *The Grand Fleet 1914–16* (1919).
Legg, Stuart, *Jutland* (1966).
Macintyre, Captain D., *Jutland* (1957).
Marder, A. J., *From the Dreadnought to Scapa Flow*, 5 vols (1961–70).
Scheer, Admiral R., *Germany's High Seas Fleet* (1920).

Chapter Six

OFFENSIVE 1918

Correlli Barnett

THROUGHOUT the Great War the fundamental German grand strategic problem lay in that while Germany was by a large margin the most powerful single state in Europe, ill-judged German diplomacy had raised up in her face a coalition of potentially overwhelming strength. German strategy therefore consisted of a succession of military expedients or short-cuts – gambles – designed to solve this problem. The original Schlieffen Plan was one such expedient: France was to be smashed in a six-week campaign, then in turn her slow-mobilizing ally Russia. Unfortunately the Schlieffen Plan miscarried militarily in the Battle of the Marne, while politically its consequence was to add to Germany's enemies by bringing Britain into the war because of the German violation of Belgian neutrality. By late 1916, and despite German–Austrian victories against Russia and successful defensives against Britain and France on the Western Front, the strain of fighting such odds – and especially such economic odds – was beginning to tell. A war of long endurance in the face of the Allied blockade, Allied superiority in manpower and the now mobilized Allied war economies spelt ultimate defeat. So at the beginning of February 1917 Germany resorted to her second gamble on a short-cut to victory: unrestricted submarine warfare. The German naval staff were certain from their calculations that Britain would be starved into making peace, her industries halted for want of raw materials, within a few months. German leaders recognized that unrestricted use of the U-boat must provoke America into joining the conflict. Nevertheless they were sure that Britain would be brought down and the war ended long before America could mobilize her colossal industrial strength and turn her reservoir of fresh manpower into an army; that in any case the U-boat would make it impossible for American armies to be transported across the Atlantic.

Unfortunately for Germany this gamble too failed, thanks to the British introduction of the convoy system and the consequent defeat of the U-boat. By the autumn of 1917 the German leadership therefore faced the prospect of the steady advent of a great American army on the Western Front during 1918, at the very time when their own army, worn down by four years of war, would be reaching the end of its reserves of manpower. Although Germany had finally succeeded in defeating Russia during 1917, and so removed one of her original enemies, she still faced her perennial problem: war against a potentially overwhelming coalition. So in the autumn of 1917 Germany's leaders once again sought a solution, and they sought it in yet another military short-cut – another gamble.

On 11 November 1917 a conference was held to decide German strategy for 1918. It was eloquent of Imperial Germany's political and constitutional weakness, the abdication of civilian authority since the war began, that this crucial conference was a purely military occasion and took place at the Mons headquarters of the army group commanded by Crown Prince Rupprecht of Bavaria. It was presided over by the First Quartermaster-General (and

German troops advancing during the 1918 offensive

de facto supreme commander), General Erich Ludendorff. Also present were General von Kuhl (Chief of Staff, Army Group Prince Rupprecht), Colonel von der Schulenberg (Chief of Staff, Army Group Imperial Crown Prince) and Lieutenant-Colonel Wetzell, head of Operations Section of the General Staff. The narrowly military nature of the conference's deliberations was emphasized by Ludendorff's own limitations, for he altogether lacked the reflective intellect and the broad grasp of grand strategic issues which had characterized, say, the elder Moltke. Rather he was a man of action, restless and impatient, happiest when immersed in the detail of military organization and technique.

The Eastern Front had ceased to exist with the final defeat of the Russian armies and the dissolution of Russia into revolution. On 16 December a Russo-German armistice at Brest-Litovsk was formally to close down operations in the East. From early summer 1918 onwards, however, the American army would intervene decisively on the Western Front. It seemed to Ludendorff, therefore, that Germany could take no other course but to transfer divisions from Russia to the West and, by exploiting her temporary superiority in the field, achieve a decisive victory over Britain and France before the Americans began to arrive *en masse*. Like the Schlieffen Plan of 1914, Ludendorff's strategy attempted to answer the immensely superior combined strength of Germany's enemies by beating them in detail. Ludendorff and his titular superior, Field-Marshal Paul von Hindenburg, ruled out the alternative strategy of seeking to wear the Allies down into a compromise peace by a prolonged defensive fed by the fresh troops from the East. In the first place, only outright victory in the field could secure Germany's grossly annexationist war aims. Secondly, it was highly doubtful whether the morale of either the army or the nation could sustain a defensive war much longer. On the home front the hunger and acute shortage caused by the Allied blockade had been compounded by the confusions of German administration, which had failed to distribute fairly and efficiently the food and goods actually available. Moreover, the German economy itself could not sustain the war indefinitely, thanks largely to yet another crucial misjudgement on the part of Germany's military leadership. At the end of 1916, and in response to lobbyings by big industrialists, they had adopted the so-called 'Hindenburg Programme', under which the German economy was turned over almost entirely to munitions production. The consequence was an immense short-term increase in such production, at the price of certain ultimate economic collapse. Finally, Germany's allies – Austria, Bulgaria and Turkey – were increasingly tottery.

Everything seemed to point to the necessity, the inevitability, of gambling Germany's fate on a great offensive on the Western Front. In their Mons conference on 11 November 1917, Ludendorff and his colleagues had therefore to begin planning Germany's last hope of winning the greatest conflict in history. Just how risky the gamble would be emerged in the course of the meeting. As Ludendorff summed it up, 'The strength of the two sides will be approximately equal. About thirty-five divisions and one thousand heavy guns can be made available for an offensive. That will suffice for *one* offensive; a second great simultaneous offensive, say as a diversion, will not be possible.'

Since from Verdun to the Swiss frontier the terrain was unsuitable for a grand offensive, Ludendorff had the 300 miles of front between Verdun and the North Sea from which to select a point, or points, of attack. There were two apparent areas of Allied weakness: the British in Flanders, where the mass of Haig's army, with its base areas and communications, was cramped in between Ypres and the coast; and the French in the Verdun salient. Kuhl argued for an attack on the British: if the German army struck through the vital rail junction of Hazebrouck towards the sea, Haig would be taken in flank without room for manoeuvre. Schulenberg disagreed: only France could be broken by a military catastrophe, whereas Britain could survive a defeat in Flanders. Therefore, argued Schulenberg, they should aim at bringing about a wide collapse on the French front by a double attack on both sides of Verdun. Verdun would provide an immediate prize with immense psychological impact. Once the French were smashed, the German mass of manoeuvre could be shifted to deal with the British.

Ludendorff himself favoured attacking the British, and, like Kuhl, by taking them in their right flank. However, his preference lay in a sector further south than the River Lys (the marshy valley of which would only be certainly free of flooding by April, which was at least a month too late). In his own words: 'In particular an attack near St Quentin appeared promising. After gaining the Somme line, Ham–Péronne, operations could be carried further in a north-westerly direction, with the left flank resting on the Somme, and lead to the rolling up of the British front.'

On 27 December Ludendorff conferred again with his subordinates. In the meantime Kuhl had sent him a paper strongly arguing in favour of the attack across the Lys on Hazebrouck. In Kuhl's view the Arras sector (another under consideration) was too heavily defended. As for St Quentin, he judged that while a breakthrough would be feasible enough, decisive exploitation might be beyond German strength, in view of the need to hold off the French while rolling up the British. Wetzell too had sent in a study the keynote of which was cautious realism. He warned against selecting 'objectives which, in view of the character of our opponents, we are not likely to reach'. For this reason he, like Kuhl, was against the St Quentin operation as being over-ambitious. Verdun remained his first choice, Hazebrouck his second.

Nothing was decided at this conference. Instead Ludendorff ordered planning and physical preparations to go forward in respect of no fewer than five options: Hazebrouck (codename: George); a subsidiary attack near Ypres (George Two); Arras (Mars); St Quentin (St Michael), and attacks on both sides of Verdun and in the Vosges. He gave 10 March as the date for completion of this work. Thus he was still unable to make up his mind, although the grand offensive had to begin in only about ten weeks' time if, as he intended, they were to beat the British before the Americans arrived in force from early summer onwards. Here was an early sign of an intellectual instability which was to have a grave effect on his conduct of the battle. It was not until 21 January that he at last reached a decision – in favour of the Michael operation on the St Quentin sector which both Kuhl and Wetzell had argued to be beyond German strength. The axis of attack would lie between Péronne and Arras towards the coast. 'If this blow succeeded,' wrote Ludendorff later, 'the strategic result might indeed be enormous, as we should separate the bulk of the English army from the French and crowd it up with its back to the sea. . . .'

The preliminary orders for Michael were issued three days later, the final operation order on 10 March. The breakthrough forces – forty-seven special 'attack' divisions and 6,608 guns – were not placed under the command of a single army group, as might be expected, but divided between the army groups commanded by Crown Prince Rupprecht of Bavaria and the Imperial Crown Prince, an anomaly partly to be explained on dynastic grounds, partly because Ludendorff meant personally to intervene in the direction of the battle. The Seventeenth Army (Below) on the right flank and the Second (Marwitz) in the centre were to strike the main blow; the Eighteenth Army (Hutier) on the left was only to provide a flank guard to hold off the French.

The distribution of strength between the three armies revealed further anomalies. The Seventeenth Army, the pivot of the whole offensive, was allotted 2,336 guns and fourteen 'attack' divisions, while the Eighteenth, with a subsidiary role, received 2,448 guns and twenty-one 'attack' divisions. The imbalance in the Michael forces was the greater when considered in terms of the strength of the British armies opposite them. The fourteen 'attack' divisions of the Seventeenth Army mostly faced the British Third Army, also with fourteen divisions. Yet thirty-three 'attack' divisions in the Second and Eighteenth Armies lay mostly opposite only fourteen divisions of the British Fifth Army. Moreover, it was the Eighteenth Army commander, Hutier, and his artillery specialist, Colonel Bruchmuller, who had planned and executed the successful prototype breakthrough operation at Riga in September 1917. It would have seemed logical to give them the principal responsibility for breaking through the British front rather than the role of flank guard. For all the weight and power of the Michael forces, their strategic balance betrayed the lack of a clear and dominating theme.

The concentration of forty-seven 'attack' divisions and over 6,000 guns, with all their ammunition, transport and supplies, behind a front which already contained twenty-eight 'trench' or static divisions constituted, in the words of the British official history, 'a gigantic problem which was solved with complete success'. No less successfully solved was the tactical problem of the breakthrough, a problem which had baffled the British and French during three years of vain attacking. Throughout the winter troops had been rotated through intensive training in offensive tactics and formed into high-quality 'attack' divisions. Instead of the fixed objectives and largely linear formations so long clung to by the Allies, German tactics were based on rapid infiltration by storm groups of all arms: riflemen, light machine guns, flamethrowers, mortars, even field guns. They were not to worry about their flanks, not to preserve a continuous line, not to stop in order to overcome points of resistance. Like a tide coming in over a rocky shore, they were always to flow forward and round by the paths of least resistance. The training pamphlets drove home the lesson: 'The objective of the first day must be at least the enemy's artillery; the objective of the second day depends on what is achieved on the first; there must be no rigid adherence to plans made beforehand. . . . The reserves must be put in where the attack is progressing, not where it is held up.'

Instead of the week-long preliminary bombardment which had signalled the British offensives on the Somme and at Third Ypres and impeded the attackers themselves by smashing up the ground, there was to be a five-hour hurricane bombardment without preliminary registration. Gas was to be mixed with high explosive. The object was not to demolish the British defences, but to dislocate and paralyse the defenders.

The Allies for their part by no means solved the problems of meeting so formidable attack. In January and February 1918 the Allied Supreme War Council chewed over the question of creating a central inter-Allied reserve and appointing a generalissimo to command it. Finally on 2 February the Council adopted a proposal by Lloyd George, the British war premier, that such a central reserve for all fronts (Western, Italian and Balkan) should be set up, and its deployment placed in the hands of a committee chaired by Foch. This committee was not, however, to enjoy the power to give strategic directions to the two national commanders-in-chief on the Western Front, Sir Douglas Haig and Phillippe Pétain. Even the central reserve came to nothing when Haig and Pétain informed the committee that they could spare none of their troops for it.

As it was, Haig and Pétain each prepared for his own battle, each believing that his was the front about to be attacked. For although Allied intelligence penetrated German attempts at concealment and pieced together a remarkably accurate picture of the Michael forces, these forces, deliberately assembled well back from the front, were so placed as equally to threaten a blow south against the French, or west against the British. The lack of a single Allied command organization was mitigated by detailed arrangements reached by Haig and Pétain for mutual aid on either side of the junction point of their two armies. General Humbert (French Third Army), with six divisions, was to arrive in the area Montdidier–Péronne or Amiens (behind the British Fifth Army) on the evening of the fourth day after a request for help, or rather later round St Pol.

Under intense French pressure, Haig had agreed at the end of 1917 to take over some twenty-eight miles of French front, so enabling Pétain to form strong reserves while Haig now found himself with an over-extended front of 126 miles and only eight divisions available for his own G.H.Q. reserve. In fighting troops he was some three per cent weaker in January 1918 than in January 1917, for whereas he had asked for drafts of 605,000 men, the War Cabinet had only promised him 100,000, although there were 603,403 trained 'A' men in the United Kingdom alone. The withholding of these reinforcements was a devious manoeuvre by Lloyd George intended to prevent Haig himself from launching another offensive. Because of the shortage of manpower the British Army in France had to be reorganized into nine-battalion divisions like the French and German, instead of twelve-battalion; an unsettling process not completed until 8 March, less than a fortnight before the battle began.

Like his German opponents, Haig appreciated that on the northern part of his front, from Arras to the sea, a short German advance would place him in great peril. Further south, and especially on the front of the Fifth Army, the right of his line, there was space to absorb a German blow before it could reach vital objectives, room for retreat and manoeuvre. Therefore while he gave the Second Army (Plumer) twelve divisions to hold twenty-one miles of line across the base of Passchendaele salient, and the First (Horne) fourteen divisions and 1,450 guns to hold a front of thirty-three miles from Armentières to Gavrelle, the Third Army (Byng) and Fifth (Gough) were together allotted only twenty-six divisions and 2,686 guns to defend seventy miles of front. And whereas even Byng was given fourteen divisions and 1,120 guns to twenty-eight miles, Gough found himself with hardly greater strength with which to hold forty-two. Events were to demonstrate that Haig, counting on prompt and sufficient French aid, had carried the strengthening of his left at the expense of his right dangerously far.

Yet from 2 March onwards the weekly G.H.Q. intelligence summaries warned that the German onslaught was most likely to fall on the Third and Fifth Armies. Only four days before the battle opened the latest such summary asserted that 'there is no reason to alter the view already expressed that an offensive is intended in the Arras–St Quentin sector, combined with a subsidiary attack in the Bois Grenier–Neuve Chapelle sector'. Gough himself, the Fifth Army commander, was convinced from the known presence of Hutier, the victor of Riga, opposite him that the Germans planned to break through his front and make for Amiens.

The weakness of the Fifth Army front, and to a lesser extent that of the Third Army, was accentuated by other factors. Nineteen out of twenty-one divisions in the forward zone of these armies had been through the Third Battle of Ypres (Passchendaele) in 1917; they were men morally tired. Moreover, the Fifth Army's defences, especially along the sector recently taken over from the French, were highly incomplete. The British had abandoned the old linear conception of trench warfare, with a densely held front line, in favour of the German system of defence in depth: a forward zone to slow and dislocate an enemy attack, a battle zone in which to offer the main defence, and a rear zone, each belt supposed to be a network of mutually supporting defended localities and barbed wire. However, owing to shortage of time and labour, it was only the forward zone, which in the German system mattered least, whose construction had reached anywhere near completion. The battle zone, which was supposed to offer the main resistance, lacked any kind of dug-out in the Fifth Army area, and machine gun dug-outs in the Third Army area. In the Third Army area the rear zone had been wired but not dug; in the Fifth area it consisted merely of a line of turned turf, known as 'the Green Line'. And whereas according to German doctrine the forward zone was only to be lightly held, about a third of the strength of the Third and Fifth Armies was posted in it.

Finally there was ambiguity in G.H.Q.'s instructions to Gough, dated 9 February, on how he should fight his battle – ambiguity which was to lead to fateful misunderstandings between him and his commander-in-chief. He was 'to secure and protect at all costs the important centre of Péronne and the River Somme to the south of that place . . .' Nevertheless he was in the first place to meet a serious attack in his present positions, but 'it may well be desirable to fall back on the rearward defences of Péronne and the Somme, whilst linking up with the Third Army to the north, and preparing for counter-attack'. This was far from a firm and clear order to fortify the Péronne bridgehead and fight a main battle there after a fighting withdrawal from a lightly held forward line. Yet Haig henceforward wrongly believed that Gough was basing his army plan and work of field fortification on just such a stratagem.

Sir Hubert Gough was himself a controversial figure. A cavalryman, he had won an early reputation in the war for dynamic and aggressive attack, and was entrusted by Haig with the planning and conduct of his offensive at Third Ypres in 1917. However, after nearly two months of vain and costly fighting Haig had handed over the main responsibility for the battle from Gough to Plumer. At that time, too, there had been fateful misunderstandings between Gough and Haig. At the beginning of March 1918, Lord Derby, the Secretary for War, wrote to warn Haig that neither the government nor, from all Derby could glean, Gough's own army enjoyed confidence in Gough and his staff.

On 16 March the forty-seven attack divisions of Operation Michael began marching the final stages to the front, their bands playing them along as they sang '*Muss i denn, Muss i denn*'. On 20 March, the very eve of the offensive, the guns and mortars were slotted into their places. The superiority of German firepower was enormous: the three Michael armies had 4,010 field and 2,598 heavy guns against only 1,710 field and 976 heavy in the British Third and Fifth Armies; 3,534 trench mortars as against only 3,000 for the entire British army in France.

At 11 a.m. on the 20th Ludendorff's meteorologist reported that weather conditions, though 'not strikingly favourable', would suffice for the use of the gas shell on which a successful breakthrough so much depended. At noon, in a conference at his advanced headquarters at Avesnes with Hindenburg and his staff, Ludendorff took his decision and issued his orders: Michael, Germany's last hope, would begin next morning.

The evening was misty along the front of attack. By 9 p.m. the mist had thickened to a fog; after midnight it grew yet thicker, dampening sound, blinding the tense watchers in the British lines. At 4 a.m. the German army synchronized its watches three times for absolute accuracy. Exactly forty minutes later the German guns fired together.

The bombardment lasted five hours: long-range guns, field guns, mortars and howitzers, on targets fixed without registration and by means of air reconnaissance and exact mathematical calculations that included allowance for the flight of shot under differing atmospheric conditions. The fire switched from target to target, from one British defence zone to another, alternating between gas and high explosive shells, the orchestral pattern of instruments changing according to need. A British heavy artillery officer in the Third Army wrote later: 'I awoke with a tremendous start, conscious of noise, incessant and almost musical, so intense that it seemed as if a hundred devils were dancing in my brain. Everything seemed to be vibrating – the ground, my dugout, my bed. . . . It was still dark.'

After five hours of this moving, changing deluge of shells which homed on to key targets through the fog and dark with astonishing accuracy, the British command and communications organization from army headquarters downwards was in shreds, the Fifth Army and to a lesser extent the Third Army reduced to isolated, uncoordinated units of gassed and blasted troops. The climax of the German bombardment came with a smashing five-minute concentration on the British forward positions. Then, without a pause, the fire changed to a creeping barrage. Behind the barrage came the German infantry, moving on swiftly through the still dense fog, infiltrating up the re-entrants between the British defended localities, erupting suddenly out of the murk to swamp their dazed, blinded and cut-off garrisons.

By 11.30 a.m. the Fifth Army's forward zone, containing a third of its troops and much of its field artillery and machine guns, had everywhere given way, engulfed by the speed and power of the German tide. As the sun grew hotter, the fog dispersed; the battle mounted in savagery under a cloudless spring sky. At midday Gough was hopeful that he could hold his present front for two or three days without other reinforcement than the two G.H.Q. reserve divisions behind him, but by 2 p.m. the Germans were up to his (virtually non-existent) battle zone and already infiltrating deeply into it via east–west river valleys. By evening Gough, believing that he had no other course if he were to save his army, ordered a retreat to the line of the Somme and the Crozat Canal. In the southern part of his front the

Germans had broken clean through all three zones of the defence system into open country.

In the Third Army the day had not gone so badly. The Flesquières salient near Cambrai had held against violent converging attacks by the German Second and Seventeenth Armies. Further south, however, Byng's defence was already clinging to the rear fringes of the battle zone. The psychological impact of the unprecedented speed of the German advance on defenders conditioned by over three years of static warfare was colossal. Long fixed organizations – headquarters, depots, heavy artillery – packed up in haste and took to the choked roads westwards. As one Third Army heavy artillery officer recalled, '. . . when I looked back and saw the vivid flashes of the field guns firing away in the midst of our once spotless headquarters it seemed – as indeed it so nearly was – the beginning of the end of all things.'

Next day, although the Third Army continued to hold fast to the Flesquières salient, the pace of retreat and disintegration on the southern portion of the Third Army's front and the Fifth Army's front accelerated, as troops untrained in mobile warfare and weakened by loss of artillery and machine guns and much of their own fighting strength in the overrun forward zone, struggled back with the relentless German spearheads close on their heels. At 10.45 a.m. on 22 March Gough instructed his corps commanders: 'In the event of serious hostile attack corps will fight rearguard actions back to the forward line of Rear Zone, and if necessary to rear line of Rear Zone.' Gough's subordinates interpreted his instructions as, in the words of the official history, 'an executive order for retirement'. At 8 p.m. Haig was informed by Gough on the telephone that 'parties of all arms of the enemy are through our Reserve Line'. Haig therefore 'concurred on his falling back and defending the line of the Somme and to hold the Péronne Bridgehead'. In fact by the end of the day's fighting Hutier's troops were already solidly along the Somme and Crozat Canal. Haig had already begun to shift his own reserves towards Gough's sagging line; now he asked Pétain for his promised help. But Pétain had already ordered General Humbert to move with seven divisions (more than his original undertaking) to defend the Somme and the Crozat Canal.

It was on a visit to Gough's headquarters on the morning of 23 March that Haig first comprehended the magnitude and urgency of his danger. The Fifth Army, which he had expected to find conducting a steady fighting retreat to the Somme, was already behind it. Later in the day G.H.Q. ordered that the Fifth Army was 'to hold the line of the Somme River at all costs. . . . The Third and Fifth Armies must keep in closest touch . . . and must mutually assist each other in maintaining Péronne as a pivot.' At the time this order was issued Hutier's troops were already surging over the Somme by bridges unblown by French engineers, and Péronne was being evacuated. The Germans had now opened a complete breach forty miles wide in the Allied line; a breach across which was loosely strewn the exhausted wreckage of Gough's command. Although the Third Army had still given little ground on its left, elsewhere it lay along the Green Line, which was non-existent as a defensive system, while its right lay in open country, like the Fifth Army, in whose débâcle it had participated.

Haig's anxieties began to turn on the key rail junction of Amiens, and on the danger that the British and French armies might be sundered, and the British army driven back on its ports (as was to happen in 1940). When Pétain visited him at his advanced headquarters at Dury at 4 p.m. that day, he asked the French commander-in-chief for no fewer than twenty divisions to be concentrated astride Amiens with the utmost speed. Pétain gave no direct answer to this request. While assuring Haig that he wished to do all he could to support him, he averred that he was expecting to be attacked himself in Champagne at any moment. Nevertheless he agreed to take over the British line as far north as Péronne – an admission by both generals that the Fifth Army had ceased to exist as a coherent formation.

On 24 March the crisis in the Allied command worsened. The British everywhere lost the line of the Somme; Hutier thrust south-westwards towards Chaulnes-Noyon, driving before him the debris of the Fifth Army's XVIII and III Corps and the advanced elements of the French reserves. Behind the fighting line chaos, not to say panic, was widespread. Near Ypres, in the Third Army line, for example, 'Agitated staff officers . . . galloped wildly across country, vainly searching for troops for whom they had orders, but could not find. Roads and villages were packed with transport and units on the move . . .' At 11 p.m. Pétain again visited Haig at Dury. This time he struck the British commander-in-chief as 'very much upset, almost unbalanced and very anxious'. Pétain handed Haig a copy of an order to all French armies, the nub of which was that the maintenance of the link with the British army was placed second to keeping all the French armies together as a solid body. There would be no force of twenty French divisions placed astride Amiens. 'I at once asked Pétain,' wrote Haig in his diary that night, 'if he meant to abandon my right flank. He nodded assent and added, "it is the only thing possible, if the enemy compelled the Allies to fall back still further." ' In fact General Fayolle (commanding the French Reserve Army Group) had been instructed to retreat south-westwards on Beauvais if heavily attacked.

For Haig Pétain's visit opened a vista of catastrophe. In his own words, 'In my opinion, our Army's existence in France depends on keeping the British and French Armies united.' Yet it is possible that Pétain, for his part, believed that Haig was already abandoning *him* and falling back north-westwards. That very day he had asked the French government 'urgently to press the English to rally on him and not force him to extend himself indefinitely to reach them'. Moreover, Haig's own original deployment hardly gave overriding priority to preserving liaison between the two armies. It is clear from Pétain's orders and conversation that he believed that a situation had already arrived, like that of 18–19 May 1940, with all the Allied forces north of the Somme being herded away into the sea, and those south of it having to fight a later battle on their own to cover the heart of France. He wanted to make sure that the French army was preserved intact for this later battle.

Now Haig became really alarmed. That night and next morning he was in urgent touch with the Chief of the Imperial General Staff (Sir Henry Wilson) and the Secretary for War (now Lord Milner), imploring them to come to France in order to press the French government into appointing Foch or some other resolute soul as Allied supreme commander – someone who would rush twenty French divisions to Amiens. As he told Wilson on the morning of 25 March, 'everything depends on whether the French can and will support us *at once* with 20 Divisions of good quality north of the Somme . . .'

Between 23 and 25 March Ludendorff was therefore in reach of victory, and as much because of the impact of his offensive on the minds of Allied commanders as because of his unprecedented advances on the ground. But the nearness of the Allied front and Allied solidarity to final collapse was not apparent from the reports of his own armies. Above all, the pattern of success on the ground had failed to correspond with the strategic architecture of the Michael plan. On the right, Below's Seventeenth Army, the pivot of the whole wheeling movement to the north-west, had failed to break through the British Third Army's battle zone on the first day of the offensive, despite ferocious fighting and heavy loss, the consequence partly of a less effective preliminary bombardment than Bruchmuller's in the Eighteenth Army, partly of less whole-hearted adoption of the new infiltration tactics, and partly because their British opponents were defending a more complete defence system and in greater density than Gough's Fifth Army. On the second day of the offensive the Seventeenth Army again failed to bring about the collapse of the Flesquières salient and make the fast progress looked for. Partly because of Below's failure, Marwitz's Second Army, charged with the principal task of breaking through and rolling up the British front, similarly made only slow progress against fierce resistance, except on its left, where it participated in the sweeping successes achieved by Hutier's Eighteenth Army. Indeed, only Hutier had achieved the kind of swift, deep advance which Ludendorff had been counting on, standing now along the Somme and Crozat Canal. Yet under the original Michael strategy, Hutier's role was the subsidiary one of flank guard. The German success was all on the wrong wing.

On 23 March, therefore, Ludendorff was faced with the need to take new and fundamental strategic decisions. Had he chosen to concentrate all resources behind a single thrust by Hutier's Eighteenth Army and the left wing of Marwitz's Second towards Amiens, he might well have finally sundered the British from the French, so consummating the catastrophe which Pétain feared had all but occurred already. Such a strategy would also have been true to Ludendorff's own principle of reinforcing success rather than failure.

Instead he displayed the same inability to choose one clear strategic design which had characterized his original planning of the offensive. His orders of 23 March gave the Michael forces no fewer than three thrust-lines instead of one, and those divergent both in direction and purpose. The Seventeenth Army was to attack north-westwards towards St Pol in order to push the British back on their ports, and at the same time advance its left wing westwards through Doullens towards Abbeville. The Second Army was to advance westwards in a direct approach to Amiens. The Eighteenth Army was to wheel south-westwards (away from Amiens) on Montdidier and Noyon, in order to shoulder the French away from their allies. It was all a fatal dispersion of effort, a plan beyond the powers of his rapidly tiring troops.

By feeding the advance with reinforcements rather than relieving whole units by rotation, Ludendorff had succeeded where the Allies had so often failed – in maintaining the forward speed of the attack beyond the first day. It was, however, a crushing physical and moral strain to march and fight without relief under incessant air attack. Abandoned British canteens and supply depots were another factor which helped to slow the pace of advance and to weaken German morale. Lieutenant Sulzbach, a field gunner in the Eighteenth Army, noted in his diary on 23 March the lavish provisions they were finding: oats for the horses in abundance, jam, cheese, bacon. Others noted the excellence of captured British equipment. Suddenly the German soldier realized that the U-boat campaign, despite what he had been told, had failed; he realized on the contrary just how pinched and shabby an army he belonged to. What was more, those luxurious British stores offered a temptation to loot which diverted too many German soldiers from the less agreeable task of driving on.

For whereas in 1940 the internal combustion engine was to keep up the momentum of the German advance, in 1918 there was only the flagging muscle of man and beast. Although every available kind of transport had been pressed into service the problems of nourishing the offensive became every day more insuperable. Years of blockade had reduced the number of horses and rendered it impossible adequately to feed those that remained. British prisoners noted that even German cavalry mounts were like old cab horses. And cavalry too was short, so preventing rapid exploitation of the breakthrough. With every day the German impetus was fading, Ludendorff's opportunity fleeting.

On 24 March the Second and Seventeenth Armies gained some ground westwards north of the Somme in heavy fighting, as the British Third Army swung back its right to keep in touch with the Fifth. Yet though Bapaume was captured, the advance generally fell short of expectations by some seven miles. Hutier got across the Somme almost everywhere on the Fifth Army front and, on his left, drove on towards the line Chaulnes–Noyon. Yet he too fell between six and ten miles short of his objectives. Meanwhile the French divisions despatched by Pétain were steadily arriving opposite him. As the German impetus faded, Allied resistance was hardening.

On 25 March Ludendorff changed his mind yet again. The directive of 23 March, although only two days old, was drastically modified. Despite the fact that the Second and Seventeenth Armies had so far failed to achieve the decisive success called for under the Michael plan, Ludendorff now returned to them the principal task of breaking through to Amiens and rolling the British up. Hutier's army was once again relegated to the role of flank guard. Moreover, Ludendorff opted for fresh offensives elsewhere against the British: both sides of the British bastion of Arras (Mars), and an emasculated George (Georgette) between the La Bassée Canal and Armentières. These he believed would bring about the final collapse of the whole British front. However, owing to the time needed for preparation, Mars, the first of the two new attacks, could not take place before 28 March – a dangerous delay when the German opportunity was slipping away hour by hour.

Instead of belatedly placing all German resources behind Hutier and a single thrust on Amiens, Ludendorff had elected further to fragment his effort by starting up fresh smaller-scale operations. In the meantime the Michael offensive itself was to run even more out of steam. As Ludendorff himself wrote later: 'On the 25th March the 17th and 2nd Armies had passed far beyond the line Bapaume–Combles, fighting hard all the way; the 18th Army had taken Nesle and met with but little resistance. The 17th Army was already exhausted. . . . The 2nd Army was fresher but was already complaining of the old shell-holes [of the 1916 Somme battlefield, which the advance had now entered]. It could get no farther than Albert. . . . The 18th Army was still full of fight and confidence . . .'

On 26 March only the Eighteenth Army made further significant progress – some five miles towards Amiens and Montdidier. It too was now faced with a continuous and hardening line of resistance. In the words of the British official history, 'The battle was now becoming stabilized . . .'

Yet on the Allied as on the German side there was a time-lag between the High Command's appreciation of the situation and the actual state of the battle. At this very moment, when the crisis of the Michael offensive had already passed, the crisis in the Allied command came to a head. It centred round Haig's urgent desire to induce the French to place twenty divisions astride Amiens. This appeared to Haig the only means by which the link between the British and French armies could be preserved – given that the British remained fast in their present positions in the Pas de Calais and Flanders (and Haig seems never to have contemplated a general withdrawal south of the Somme in order to maintain touch with his ally). The locale of the resulting conference of politicians and soldiers was the *mairie* of Doullens.

Beforehand Haig conferred with his army commanders (Plumer, Byng and Horne; Gough was not invited, possibly because the Fifth Army had been placed under the command of General Fayolle, French Reserve Army Group). Haig, who was conducting his battle with remarkable coolness, told his hearers that '. . . my object is to gain time to enable the French to come and support us. To this end we must hold our ground, especially on the right of our Third Army [near Bray] on Somme, where *we must not give up any ground.*' Horne (First Army) would therefore yield three Canadian divisions, to be concentrated behind the Third Army, possibly for a counter-stroke against the northern flank of a German penetration to Amiens. The Third Army commander himself, Byng, had heartening news: in the south of his front, near the Somme, the Germans seemed to have exhausted their offensive power.

At twelve noon President Poincaré took the chair at the main conference. Present were the French Prime Minister, Clemenceau, Loucheur (French Minister of Armaments), Foch, Pétain, Haig, Wilson, Milner and Generals Lawrence (Haig's Chief of the General Staff) and Montgomery (for General Rawlinson, British military representative at Versailles). Pétain, Haig noted, 'had a terrible look. He had the appearance of a Commander who was in a funk and had lost his nerve.' This was only too true: before the meeting Pétain had told Clemenceau, 'The Germans will beat the English in the open field; after which they will beat us as well.' Here was manifested the defeatism of 1940. At Doullens in 1918 Pétain was out of step, whereas at Bordeaux in June 1940 only the fighters were out of step. Haig spoke first. North of the Somme he was confident of holding his ground; south of it he could do nothing. Pétain now defended his measures since 22 March, and added, 'It is evident everything possible must be done to defend Amiens.' At the mention of Amiens, Foch burst out: 'We must fight in front of Amiens, we must fight where we are now. As we have not been able to stop the Germans on the Somme, we must not now retire a single inch!'

This was Haig's opportunity. He took it: 'If General Foch will consent to give me his advice, I will gladly follow it.' After informal discussions Clemenceau read out a draft agreement charging Foch 'with the co-ordination of the action of the British and French Armies in front of Amiens'. This was not enough for Haig. As he wrote in his diary, 'This proposal seemed to me quite worthless as Foch would be in a subordinate position to Pétain and myself. In my opinion, it was essential to success that Foch should control Pétain.' At Haig's request the conference agreed that Foch's authority should extend to the entire Western Front and all national forces. At last, after three and a half years of war, there was an Allied generalissimo. Yet the advent of Foch to this position did not materially alter the course of the current battle; did not lead to those results most urgently hoped for by Haig. Instead of twenty divisions astride Amiens as soon as possible, Foch managed eight by early April – no more than Pétain had thought possible. And although Foch ordered Fayolle to defend, support and relieve the present British Fifth Army front, 'defending the ground foot by foot', in order to protect Amiens, Fayolle continued to fall back south-westwards and the British westwards so long as the Germans remained capable of advancing. Nevertheless the appointment of Foch, that fiery fighter, over the defeatist Pétain meant the end of the moral crisis within the Allied command. Moreover, by the time the Doullens conference met, it was already becoming clear that the moment of acutest danger was passing away on the ground.

And indeed 26 March, the day of the conference, saw the German effort further diminish. The Eighteenth Army, now again supposed to be merely a flank guard, once more made the best progress, advancing nine miles beyond Roye against the remnants of the Fifth Army and advanced elements of Fayolle's Reserve Army Group. The Second and Seventeenth Armies again failed to break the dour resistance of Byng's Third Army, a circumstance which enraged the unstable Ludendorff and provoked him into trying to drive them on by means of furious telephone calls to their headquarters. That evening Ludendorff changed his strategy yet again. Believing that the British were tottering on the verge of general collapse, he ordered his Second and Seventeenth Armies to keep on attacking, in conjunction with the fresh offensive (Mars) round Arras to be launched on the 28th; the Seventeenth was to attack towards St Pol, the Second's main effort was to be south of the Somme on Amiens, after the capture of which it was to swing south-west to the line Moreuil–Airaines. The Eighteenth Army was to advance south-west across the Avre and be ready for a further advance southward on Compiègne. So the more the attacking power of his armies faded away, the more Ludendorff enlarged their objectives.

But on 27 March the Second and Seventeenth Armies finally struck, and although Hutier's Eighteenth Army made another ten miles beyond Montdidier, it was only on a narrow twelve-mile front. Next day the German gains were limited to three miles towards Amiens, between the Somme and the Avre, and some small pockets near Montdidier. Moreover, the new offensive on the Arras sector against the junction of the British First and Third Armies was completely defeated in the course of that single day. The preliminary bombardment was neither so devastatingly accurate nor so brilliantly orchestrated as Bruchmuller's masterpiece at the opening of Michael; the assaulting troops and their officers were not so highly trained in rapid infiltration as the 'attack' divisions of 21 March; the British defence zone was here deep and strong, garrisoned by some of Haig's best troops – the Guards Division, two Regular divisions, the 3rd Canadian Division; the principles of defence in depth – local withdrawal followed by counter-attacks – had been better digested here than in the Fifth Army: in particular, the front line was only thinly held; there was no fog to cover the attackers. As a consequence of these factors, Mars turned out to be just another classic Western Front offensive, in which the attackers were soon held up on undestroyed defences manned by resolute machine gunners and mortar teams, their massed troops pounded in the open by British counter-bombardment. By the end of the day the Germans had failed to gain a single lodgement in the British battle zone.

Yet again Ludendorff altered his strategy, abandoning all his over-ambitious and divergent objectives, and finally – at least four days too late – fixing on Amiens alone. According to his orders that night, '. . . to secure that place all the efforts of this and the following days will be directed; the attacks near Montdidier and eastward of that town are only diversions designed to delay enemy forces.' At the same time preparations were to go forward for Georgette, the attack across the Lys on Hazebrouck. This was to be launched in eight to ten days' time as a second major offensive – itself an admission that Michael was failing in its main purpose. If 23 March was the turning point of the Michael offensive itself, 28 March therefore marked a turning point in the 1918 campaign.

Despite Ludendorff's orders, the Second and Seventeenth Armies remained at a standstill, all offensive power exhausted. Only Hutier's Eighteenth Army continued until the end of March to struggle forward on a narrow front between the Somme and the Avre; they were stopped some six miles short of Amiens by the remnants of the Fifth Army, including the stragglers, training personnel, tunnellers, field survey companies and Canadian and American engineers of 'Carey's Force', so named after its commander, Major-General G. G. S. Carey. On 4 and 5 April, after a pause for rest, reorganization and another opening bombardment, the Eighteenth Army made a last effort to reach Amiens. But they could get no further than Villers-Bretonneux. Operation Michael, the greatest single offensive launched on the Western Front in the whole of the Great War, was over, and it had failed.

The further German offensives which followed from April to July – one against the British in Flanders, two against the French in Champagne – were all smaller in scale. The Georgette offensive across the Lys on Hazebrouck, launched on 9 April, took place on a front of only twelve miles, compared with Michael's fifty; only twelve out of the twenty-six divisions allotted to the offensive were of the high-quality 'attack' variety, as against forty-seven in Michael. For two days the offensive made dangerous progress, partly because of the fortuitous collapse of three Portuguese brigades in the British line. By 18 April, however, Georgette too had exhausted itself against a resolute and well conducted defence. On 27 May Ludendorff struck at the French Sixth Army along the Chemin des Dames ridge. The army commander, Duchêne, played into the German hands by packing his troops into the front line instead of retiring behind the Aisne. Overwhelmed by another of Bruchmuller's masterpieces of ordnance and rushed under cover of fog, the defence collapsed. Once again the delusive prospect of decisive victory lured the opportunist Ludendorff on. The offensive rolled over the Vesle and the Aisne towards the Marne. But Pétain methodically installed his reserves, strong in guns, along the line of that river, the eastern ring of the Forest of Villers-Cotterets and the Montagne de Rheims. On this line the German impetus spent itself. Significantly two United States divisions fought alongside the French round Château-Thierry. For week by week the mathematics of manpower and reinforcement were demonstrating to Ludendorff with merciless clarity that his great gamble on winning the war before the Americans could arrive in force had failed. The average field strength of a German battalion had sunk from 807 men in February to 692 in May, while according to German information about fifteen American divisions reached France in the course of April, May and June. As Ludendorff himself put it, '. . . not only had our March superiority in the number of divisions been cancelled, but even the difference in gross numbers was now to our disadvantage, for an American division consisted of twelve strong battalions.'

Nevertheless, on 15 July he opened another offensive against the French, this time on both sides of Rheims, as a preliminary to what he still intended to be a final war-winning blow against the British. The attack was smashed after making only small gains. Three days later the French launched a powerful counter-stroke, led by tanks, from the Forest of Villers-Cotterets against the flank of the German bulge down to the Marne. Although the Germans were able to stabilize their front after withdrawal, the French stroke spelt the end of Ludendorff's hopes of mounting another offensive of his own. On 8 August a British counter-stroke on the Somme brought about a local collapse in the German line and, even more perturbing for Ludendorff, a collapse in German morale. Moreover, under the shock of the sudden Allied counter-blows, his own nerve and self-control broke. The events of 8 August 1918 – 'the black day of the German army in the history of this war,' as Ludendorff called it – marked the moment of Germany's strategic bankruptcy – a bankruptcy rendered inevitable by the failure of the great March offensive. Next day Ludendorff told the Kaiser that the war must be ended.

Note on Sources

Barnett, Correlli, *The Swordbearers: Studies in Supreme Command During The First World War* (1963).

Blake, Robert, ed., *The Private Papers of Douglas Haig 1914–1919* (1952).

Behrend, Arthur, *As From Kemmel Hill* (1963).

Cruttwell, C. R. M. F., *A History of the Great War 1914–1918* (1934).

Edmonds, J. E., *History of the Great War Military Operations France and Belgium 1918: The German March Offensive and its Preliminaries* (1935).

Edmonds, J. E., *March–April: Continuation of the German Offensives* (1937).

Gough, General Sir Hubert, *The Fifth Army* (1931).

Hindenburg, Field-Marshal Paul von, *Out of My Life* (1920).

Ludendorff, General Erich, *My War Memoirs 1914–18* (1919).

Moore, William, *See How They Ran: The British Retreat of 1918* (1970).
Read, Herbert, *In Retreat: A Journal of the Retreat of the Fifth Army From St Quentin, March, 1918* (1925).
Sulzbach, Herbert, *With the German Guns* (1973).
Terraine, John, *Douglas Haig: The Educated Soldier* (1963).
Wyrall, Everard, *The History of the 17th Battalion, Royal Fusiliers 1914–19* (1930).

Happy return. An Atlantic convoy, photographed from a Flying Fortress of Coastal Command, nears a British port

Chapter Seven

BATTLE OF THE ATLANTIC

Stephen Roskill

THE CAMPAIGN described in this chapter comprised the assault by the sea and air forces of Germany in the first place, reinforced by those of Italy after 10 June 1940 and by those of Japan after 7 December 1941, against the merchant shipping of Britain and France in the first period, of the British Commonwealth and Empire alone from the fall of France until Hitler attacked the U.S.S.R. on 22 June 1941, and of all the United Nations during the final phase, which opened with the Japanese attacks on American, British and Dutch bases and installations in the Pacific and South-East Asia on 7 December 1941.

In spite of the technical inaccuracy of the title by which the conflict, which covered all the seas and oceans of the world, has become known it is certainly not inappropriate: control of the Atlantic Ocean was vital not only to the survival of Britain but also, after that had been assured by the frustration of Hitler's invasion plan in the summer of 1940, to the successful execution of the top priority in the grand strategy of the United Nations: namely the defeat of the Axis forces in Europe.

Before we turn to the actual conduct of the Battle of the Atlantic it should perhaps be made clear that in the statistics used throughout this chapter no attempt is made to distinguish between the nationality of either the instruments and weapons used by the Axis powers or that of the merchant ships which they were endeavouring to destroy. This convention has been adopted partly for the sake of simplicity and partly because it is, even today, sometimes impossible to be certain as to the nationality of both the attacking and the defending forces. Nor does it greatly matter, in a brief account such as this one, whether a particular ship was of British or other registration, or whether she was sunk by a German or an Italian submarine.

On the Axis side the instruments used in the conflict comprised warships and specially selected merchant ships which were powerfully armed and skilfully disguised to act as commerce raiders; and these were very soon joined by aircraft, minelayers (both airborne and seaborne) and submarines – sometimes one instrument acting in conjunction with another and sometimes each acting independently. We will here follow the efforts and fortunes of the aforementioned Axis instruments in turn.

Well before the outbreak of war the Germans sent out into the Atlantic two of their powerful 'pocket battleships', the *Deutschland* (renamed *Lützow* in November 1939) and the *Graf Spee*, and they began their depredations as soon as Britain declared war on 3 September 1939. The *Deutschland*'s cruise accomplished little, and she was recalled in November after sinking only two ships. The *Graf Spee* ranged the oceans far more widely and captured or sank nine ships (50,000 tons) before she was trapped by three British cruisers off the River Plate on 13 December 1939 and scuttled herself four days later. The pocket battleship *Admiral Scheer* made a successful sortie in the Atlantic between October 1940 and April 1941 and got home safely after accounting for sixteen ships (99,059 tons). The heavy cruiser *Hipper*, a short endurance ship, made two comparatively brief cruises in 1940 and 1941, but found only nine victims (40,078 tons). By far the most successful of the warship raiders were the battleships *Scharnhorst* and *Gneisenau* (32,000 tons displacement) which cruised in the north and central Atlantic between January and March 1941, sank twenty-two ships (115,622 tons), seriously disrupted the entire convoy system and returned safely to Brest, which was then in German hands, where they presented a constant threat to Atlantic shipping. The peak of warship raiding came, however, with the sortie of the giant battleship *Bismarck* (42,345 tons displacement) and the heavy cruiser *Prinz Eugen* in May 1941, which resulted in the sinking of the British battlecruiser *Hood* in the Denmark Strait on the 24th. This was followed by a dramatic pursuit by the Home Fleet and other forces, which ended three days later when the *Bismarck* was sunk almost within reach of air cover from western France. This sortie, though in British eyes menacing in the extreme, achieved nothing against merchant shipping; and its outcome made the Germans unwilling to risk their heavy warships in further Atlantic operations. In February 1941 the *Scharnhorst*, *Gneisenau* and *Prinz Eugen* escaped home up-Channel from Brest in a skilfully planned and executed dash, and thereafter the large German warships were only employed occasionally against the Allied convoys to north Russia – whose protection was a British responsibility. The results achieved were not significant.

Turning to disguised raiders, the Germans sent out ten such ships, the Italians one and the Japanese two. The Italian raider accomplished nothing and the Japanese pair only accounted for three ships; but the German raiders were well handled and redoubtable, and proved extremely difficult to catch. The first one (the *Atlantis* or *Schiff* 16) sailed in March 1940, and it was not until May of the following year, when a British cruiser sank the *Pinguin* (or *Schiff* 33) in the Indian Ocean, that a success was achieved against these adversaries. They ranged far and wide, from the Antarctic, where the *Pinguin* captured three valuable whale oil factory ships and their attendant whale catchers, to the north Pacific. They used a wide variety of disguises and were so skilful in the employment of ruses to conceal their identity that on at least one occasion a disguised raider escaped from an inquisitive British warship encountered at sea. One raider sank a British liner converted to armed merchant cruiser, another seriously damaged and escaped from two similar ships, while a third (the *Kormoran* or *Schiff* 41) sank a Royal Australian Navy cruiser, though in doing so she was herself destroyed. Not until 17 October 1943 was the last disguised raider (the *Michel* or *Schiff* 28), which was on her second cruise, accounted for – off the south coast of Japan. In all they sank or captured 133 ships (829,644 tons); but they also forced on the Allies a very extensive dispersal of forces to search for them; and their presence, actual or presumed, caused frequent delays to the movements of merchant ships. The Germans organized their supply most efficiently from vessels sent to rendezvous in remote parts of the oceans such as the south Atlantic; and some raiders were even able to refit themselves in little islands, such as Kerguelen in the southern Indian Ocean. In sum, the German disguised raiders undoubtedly obtained an excellent return from a comparatively small investment; and with one exception (Captain von Rückteschell of the *Widder*, and later of the *Michel*) the captains of the disguised raiders, like those of their warship counterparts, generally took reasonably humane precautions to safeguard the crews of attacked ships – even if they did not adhere precisely to international law. It should also be remarked that some Allied merchantmen, especially those blessed with a good turn of speed and an alert, well trained and resolute crew, successfully escaped from such attackers, while others put up a gallant if fruitless resistance against heavy odds.

Success was finally achieved against the disguised raiders chiefly through two measures. The first was the introduction in October 1942 of the 'Checkmate system' whereby a patrolling warship, on sighting a suspicious vessel, signalled direct to the Admiralty giving her alleged name, nationality and position. If the Admiralty's shipping plot showed that a vessel of that description could not be in the position reported the reply 'Checkmate' was at once made by wireless, whereupon the intercepting warship was authorized to treat her as an enemy. The second, and perhaps the more important, counter-measure was the gradual collection in the Admiralty of intelligence concerning possible supply ships or captured vessels employed on the same service. As soon as enough was known about their movements warships were sent to intercept them. The first important successes in this field were achieved in June 1941, during which nine supply ships (six of them tankers) were sunk or captured in various positions from the far north to the deep south of the Atlantic. As such ships were often fitted out to supply warship raiders and U-boats as well as disguised raiders, their loss affected the operations of all three classes of vessel. The Germans sent out thirty-seven supply ships (eighteen of which were tankers), and in addition used twenty-two captured ships (eleven of them tankers) for the same purpose. Out of the total of fifty-nine ships so employed no less than fifty-two were ultimately sunk, captured or scuttled by their own crews. By the end of 1942 it was plain that the day of the disguised raider had, like that of the warship raider, passed. Thenceforth the Axis powers had to rely on aircraft, mines and submarines – or on a combination of all three – and it is to them that we must now turn.

The Germans had organized and trained their air force primarily for close support of the army, and had, relatively speaking, ignored both strategic bombing and cooperation with naval forces. Moreover, Reichsmarschall Goering's selfish insistence that 'everything that flies belongs to me' frustrated any possibility of the German navy creating its own air arm; while relations between the higher ranks in the Luftwaffe and the navy were notoriously bad, and remained so virtually throughout the war. In the early months

German aircraft were used occasionally to reconnoitre British naval bases, and to locate units of the Home Fleet at sea; and a few were employed on minelaying (to which we will turn shortly). Not until the opening of the Norwegian campaign in April 1940 did the Luftwaffe exercise substantial influence on the war at sea. That 'ramshackle campaign', as Churchill described it, did however prove that within the comparatively short range of the Ju 86 and 87 dive-bombers and the longer-range Ju 88, Do 17 and He 111 bombers British naval forces could not operate successfully in coastal waters without fighter cover; and off Norway that cover was almost completely lacking. The heavy losses inflicted on Allied troop and supply convoys and on their escorting and covering warships, though only indirectly part of the Atlantic battle, taught the British a harsh lesson, a lesson which was to be driven home even more harshly after the German conquest of the Low Countries and France, when the convoys passing through the English Channel, up and down the east coast, and even through the south-western approaches to these islands, all came within range of German shore-based bombers. The grievous shortage of escort vessels, which was much aggravated by the heavy losses suffered in the evacuations from Norway, Holland and France, and the vast deficiency in all forms of close-range anti-aircraft weapons from which the British suffered, combined with the preoccupation of Fighter Command of the R.A.F. with the defence of the homeland and the lack of fighter aircraft in Coastal Command, rendered such targets as the slow-moving coastal convoys invitingly easy, and it is not surprising that during the second half of 1940 the German dive-bombers inflicted heavy losses. Gradually, however, Fighter Command accepted the need to defend offshore shipping. Emergency measures such as the diversion of as much shipping as possible to the north of Ireland and to west coast ports, the creation of specially trained anti-aircraft crews to join ships during the most dangerous parts of their passages, the instruction of merchant seamen in the rudiments of self-defence against air attack, and the improvisation of the weapons which the Allies did not yet possess and needed time to produce, bore fruit. The losses inflicted by enemy aircraft in 1940 totalled 192 ships (580,074 tons), but a large proportion of them were suffered during the evacuations already mentioned. In 1941 the Focke-Wulf four-engined (F.W.200) bomber began to make sorties from western France much farther out into the Atlantic in order to report convoy movements to the U-boat command headquarters at Lorient, and to attack merchant ships themselves far outside the range of British shore-based aircraft. Thence arose the need for convoys to carry their own fighter defences along with them.

As the navy had no escort aircraft carriers improvisation was once again necessary. It took the form of converting a number of merchant ships (nineteen in all) to carry a few aircraft. These became known as merchant aircraft carriers (M.A.C.s). Others were fitted with a catapult from which a Hurricane fighter could be launched and called catapult aircraft merchantmen or C.A.M.s. A third type, known as fighter catapult ships (F.C.S.s), was also produced but, unlike the C.A.M.s, which remained merchantmen and carried normal cargoes, they were manned by the navy and carried no cargoes. The C.A.M.s and the F.C.S.s were of course 'one-shot weapons', and the pilots of their Hurricanes, once they had been catapulted, had to parachute into the sea or ditch on it and hope to be picked up by one of the surface escorts. Everyone realized, however, that these hazardous and demanding improvisations were no more than stop-gap measures, and that the real need was for small aircraft carriers which could provide continuous air escort throughout the convoys' voyages; but time was needed to build such vessels and train their aircrews, and in 1940–41 the pressure on the building yards was so heavy that the British had to rely chiefly on the United States to produce such vessels. Nonetheless the improvisations described above did check the depredations of the Focke-Wulfs. But the event which undoubtedly had the greatest influence on the air side of the Atlantic battle, and which brought about a sharp fall in the losses inflicted by German bombers, was Hitler's attack on Russia on 22 June 1941; for the opening of the gigantic land campaigns on the Eastern Front necessitated large-scale diversion of Luftwaffe squadrons from Western Europe.

The autumn of 1941 saw the first proper escort carrier (a fine German merchant ship which had been captured and converted) enter service. Though she was very soon sunk by a U-boat her performance wholly confirmed the view that such ships provided the required solution. However, the need to employ the first generation of escort carriers to cover the North African landings in November 1942 prevented them joining in the Atlantic battle until early in the following year. The success they then achieved fully justified the confidence placed in them.

The débâcle in the Far East in December 1941 and early 1942, however, together with the heavy losses suffered by some Arctic convoys – notably by P.Q.17 in July 1942 when the Admiralty unwisely ordered it to scatter and the escorts to withdraw in anticipation of attack by the very powerful German naval forces based in north Norway – accounted for a large proportion of the losses caused by bombers. By the end of 1942 such losses had dropped sharply. This improvement was attributable chiefly to the increasing number of escort vessels and of improved weapons entering service as American production got into its stride and the strength available to the Western Approaches and Coastal Commands steadily grew, and the training of the escort groups and aircrews improved. In 1943, despite the large number of merchant ships employed in hazardous combined operations in the Pacific and the Mediterranean, losses caused by enemy aircraft fell to seventy-six ships (424,411 tons), and in the following year, which saw the invasion of Normandy, the landings in the south of France and many American amphibious operations in the Pacific, losses amounted to no more than nineteen ships (120,656 tons). Those figures illustrate the dramatic reversal of the situation which had prevailed in 1940; for the Allied air forces now enjoyed almost undisputed command of the air, with the result that merchant ships were able to load and unload in safety even close off an enemy-held coast.

The German minelaying campaign started with the outbreak of war, when their magnetic mine found the Royal Navy unprepared – despite the fact that the British had themselves produced and laid mines of that type towards the end of the 1914–18 war. In 1939 British minesweepers were only equipped to deal with moored mines, and the magnetic mine thus inflicted substantial losses during the early months and produced a serious situation by forcing the temporary closure of many harbours and offshore channels. However, by October 1939 the necessary antidote in the form of magnetic minesweepers had been produced and all warships and merchantmen were demagnetized to give them a measure of self-contained immunity. In 1939 Allied losses to mines totalled seventy-eight ships (262,542 tons) and in the following year 201 ships (509,889 tons). Not long after the magnetic mine had been mastered the Germans began to lay a different variety, which was detonated by the sound waves produced by a passing ship; but the Admiralty had anticipated such a development and had designed the necessary countermeasure, with the result that the acoustic mine never achieved results commensurate with the magnetic mines of the early months. The production of many variations of the magnetic and acoustic mine, or of a combination of the two, initiated the struggle between enemy minelayers (which might be surface ships, U-boats or aircraft) and Allied minesweepers which was to last throughout the war. Although the ingenuity and persistence with which the Germans prosecuted their minelaying campaign forced on the Allies a very great minesweeping effort, and a large number of the little ships which toiled to keep the channels clear were destroyed by the mines they were endeavouring to sweep, after 1941 the actual merchant ship losses suffered were comparatively small: fifty-one ships (104,588 tons) in 1942, thirty-seven ships (108,658 tons) in 1943, twenty-eight ships (95,855 tons) in 1944 and the same number (93,663 tons) in the last year of the war. The most serious threat after the magnetic mine of 1939 actually arose in 1944, when the Germans produced a pressure-operated mine and laid it in the channels and harbours used by the ships supporting the invasion of Normandy. Though the Allies never managed to produce a sweep capable of exploding such mines harmlessly, precautionary measures, such as steaming at slow speed, and the complete air supremacy enjoyed by the R.A.F. and U.S.A.A.F. prevented this new type of mine from becoming a serious threat.

We must now turn to the U-boat campaign, which constituted by far the greatest threat to Allied control of the vital shipping routes and inflicted by far the greatest losses. Though the instruments already described were certainly not negligible in their influence, it is no exaggeration to say that the Battle of the Atlantic was chiefly fought between the U-boats and Allied (and in particular British) surface ship and air convoy escorts. One clear lesson of the 1914–18 war was that the convoy system was much the most effective strategy against submarine attacks; and the fact that it saved Britain from disaster in 1917 was not forgotten between the wars. The Admiralty always insisted that if another war broke out merchant ships not capable of steaming at a fairly high speed must be sailed in convoy – despite all the well-worn arguments against doing so. However, as the probable influence of air power became clearer in the 1930s the Air Ministry, in reviewing the part that the R.A.F. should play in war, argued that to mass ships into convoys would present enemy aircraft with easier targets and so opposed the introduction of the convoy system. Not until nearly the end of 1937 did the Air Staff accept that such a system should be introduced, and allocate a large proportion of the strength of Coastal Command (167 out of a total of 339 aircraft) to convoy escort duty. On the Admiralty's side the invention in the early 1920s of the Asdic submarine detection device (called Sonar by the U.S. navy) produced something approaching euphoria – because in the 1914–18 war the submarine had been virtually undetectable. Certainly the Asdic was a very valuable development; but it did not, as the Naval Staff argued as late as 1937, by itself mean that the submarine threat had been mastered. Furthermore, the Admiralty long held that as the various naval treaties signed between the wars had forbidden unrestricted submarine and air attacks on merchant ships, and Nazi Germany had become a party to those arrangements in 1935, a campaign such as had brought Britain to the verge of defeat in 1917 would not be repeated. Fortunately this illusion in naval circles was dissipated at about the same time as the adoption of the convoy system was agreed by the Air Ministry. In 1938 the Admiralty accordingly set about the difficult task of organizing the worldwide control of merchant shipping which would fall to its lot in war, and started to create the administrative machinery necessary to put shipping into convoy – initially only on the most important routes, namely those crossing the Atlantic. But the actual introduction of convoys, even on a limited number of routes, was bound to take time, and it thus came to pass that for some months after the outbreak of war many ships were still sailing independently, even in the most dangerous waters. Furthermore the Allies did not possess sufficient escort vessels and aircraft to give convoys the necessary protection – except at the very end of a homeward journey or the beginning of an outward one; and such strength in escort vessels as they did possess was too often wasted by sending ships and aircraft out to hunt for U-boats instead of using them to escort convoys. The conception that the convoy system was a 'defensive' strategy and therefore inferior to 'offensive' measures such as hunting was very long-lasting, and found a powerful supporter in Mr Churchill as First Lord of the Admiralty. In the Air Ministry the doctrine that strategic bombing was the primary function of an air force and the only answer to enemy bombing was equally enduring; and the Air Staff remained markedly reluctant to reduce its bombing effort in order to provide convoy air escorts. Taken together these false arguments and stubbornly held convictions resulted in the U-boats finding large numbers of comparatively easy targets in 1939–40 among ships sailing independently or in weakly escorted convoys.

By the Anglo–German Naval Agreement of 1935 Germany was allowed to build a tonnage of submarines equal to Britain's if she herself considered it necessary, and on the outbreak of war she actually possessed fifty-six U-boats. Thirty of them, however, were of a small coastal type suitable only for use in the North Sea. By the end of August 1939 thirty-nine U-boats had put to sea to take up their war stations; but only seventeen of them were of the ocean-going type. Their orders were to obey 'for the present' the rules laid down in international law governing attacks on merchant ships; but the sinking of the British liner *Athenia* on the day war was declared showed that unrestricted submarine warfare had begun and strengthened the Admiralty's conviction that the strategy of shipping defence had to be primarily based on the convoy system. In fact homeward-bound convoys from Halifax, Freetown (Sierra Leone), Bergen (Norway) and Gibraltar, and outward convoys from the Thames ports, Liverpool, and the Clyde, as well as coastal convoys between the Thames and Firth of Forth, were all started between September and October 1939. Though anti-submarine escorts based on British ports (including those in Northern Ireland) and on Halifax could only remain with their charges for about the first 400 miles of their trans-Atlantic voyages the results of the first phase of the struggle (September 1939 to May 1940) were not unfavourable to the Allies. After inflicting comparatively heavy losses in September and October 1939, when many ships were still sailing independently, the U-boats did much less well until the cataclysmic month of June 1940; and they themselves suffered quite heavily, losing no less than twenty-four of their number from one cause or another.

The German occupation of Norway in April and May 1940, followed quickly by the conquest of the Low Countries and France and the entry of Italy into the war, caused the pendulum of the Battle of the Atlantic to swing very strongly in favour of the Axis countries: not only had the Royal Navy suffered heavy losses of destroyers and smaller ships in the evacuations from Europe, but the U-boats were now able to use bases in north Norway and western France, so enabling them to reach much further out into the Atlantic and increase the duration of their patrols. Furthermore, new production, though not yet on the massive scale achieved later, had sufficed to replace losses. The U-boat captains called the period June to October 1940 their first 'happy time', and it was then that the so-called 'Aces' – Prien, Kretschmer, Endras, Frauenheim, Schepke, Lemp and others – made their names. They operated independently and generally attacked at night while on the surface. The graph representing Allied shipping losses rose steadily and steeply until in October 1940 the U-boats sank sixty-three ships (352,407 tons). The second winter of the war saw a slight improvement, which can confidently be attributed to the gradual increase in the number of surface escorts as ships damaged in the inshore operations of 1940 returned to service. Mr Churchill's 'destroyers for bases' deal with the Americans, whereby fifty of the oldest American destroyers (of First World War vintage) were transferred to the Royal Navy in exchange for the use of sea and air bases in the western hemisphere, helped to mitigate the shortage of escort vessels. Moreover, despite the heavy sinkings of merchant ships, there were several encouraging instances in which well trained escort vessels, sometimes working in conjunction with shore-based aircraft, struck back hard and successfully at the U-boats.

Between October 1940 and March 1941 Admiral Karl Dönitz, the commander of the U-boats, gradually introduced new tactics. The number of boats available to him enabled him to replace the single-handed work of the 'Aces' by coordinated attacks by a group of U-boats controlled from his own headquarters at Lorient. The system employed was that the first U-boat to sight a convoy would report its position, course and speed by wireless, whereupon the closest supporters would be ordered to join the sighting boat, whose duty it was to keep in touch with the convoy. When the group – or 'wolf pack' as the British called them – had assembled Dönitz would order it to begin attacks. But what made these new tactics, which had not been foreseen, so serious from the British point of view was that the Asdic detection device was useless against a surfaced U-boat – and attacks were usually made at night, operating on the surface. The British reply was therefore to try and turn night into day by the use of illuminants, so forcing the U-boats to submerge, break off their attacks, and perhaps offer a target to the escort vessels, which could now detect them. The fitting of searchlights (called Leigh lights after their inventor Squadron-Leader H. de V. Leigh) in Coastal Command aircraft was another development which helped to counter the wolf pack threat, and later became a vitally important instrument. But the most promising new counter-measure was the introduction of short-wave radar sets which could detect a surfaced U-boat and could be fitted in escort vessels and in aircraft. The fitting of these sets began early in 1941, and the British commands and authorities involved in the Atlantic battle at once gave their production high priority – because the new radars, used in conjunction with the Leigh light or illuminants sent up from surface ships, filled the yawning gulf produced by the uselessness of the Asdic against U-boats operating like torpedo boats on the surface.

At the time when the campaign by the wolf packs in the north-western approaches to the British Isles was at its height the Admiralty made an important change in the shore organization which controlled and directed the Atlantic battle, namely the Western Approaches Command. Its headquarters were shifted from Plymouth, where they had been situated since the beginning of the war, to Liverpool. There the naval authorities were in much closer touch with No. 15 Group of Coastal Command, the R.A.F.

authority chiefly responsible for that service's part in the struggle. In the same month of February 1941 Admiral Sir Percy Noble took over the Western Approaches Command, and it was he who extended the practice of forming groups of escort vessels, which would as far as possible always work together, invigorated the training of key officers and men serving in those ships, and created intimate coordination between the naval and R.A.F. headquarters and units involved in the struggle. In April 1941 operational control of Coastal Command aircraft was transferred to the Admiralty, thus establishing unified responsibility at the summit of the command organization, and in November of the following year Admiral Sir Max Horton, a former submarine specialist who had achieved great distinction in the 1914–18 war and thoroughly understood the capabilities and limitations of such vessels, took over the Western Approaches Command. Though he reaped much that his predecessor had sown he was the ideal opponent to pit against Dönitz, and he held that command until the end of the war.

Throughout the first half of 1941 Allied losses remained high, averaging forty-four ships (241,930 tons) per month; but the shorter nights of summer and the new developments already mentioned brought a substantial reduction during the second half, which produced average losses of only twenty-eight ships (120,027 tons) per month. Furthermore, the losses inflicted on the U-boats rose from twelve in the first six months to twenty-three in the second six months; and March 1941 produced the end of the dominance of the U-boat 'Aces' when the boats commanded by Prien, Schepke and Kretschmer were all destroyed. In May these successes were reinforced by the capture of Lemp's command U-110, and although she sank while being towed into port her captors' search of her after she had been abandoned by her crew produced material of priceless value to the Allied intelligence and cryptographic organizations.

The summer of 1941 also saw a great extension of the convoy and escort strategy both on the east–west routes in the north Atlantic and the north–south routes between Freetown and Gibraltar and British home ports. In May 1940, when the loss of the whole of Norway was plainly imminent, British forces were sent to occupy key points in Iceland, whose geographic position made it an ideal place to establish naval and air bases from which the central north Atlantic could be covered. Between that date and April 1941 the Allies developed the air and sea escort system which was, with only minor modifications, to last until the end of the war. Early in July 1941 American forces took over responsibility for the defence of Iceland – despite the fact that their country was still technically neutral. Once the bases in Iceland had been developed a homeward-bound convoy from the assembly ports of Halifax (for fast convoys) and Sydney, Cape Breton Island (for slow convoys), would be protected by the Newfoundland Escort Force, based on St John's, as far as a Mid Ocean Meeting Point (MOMP) at about thirty-five degrees west. There an Iceland-based force would meet the convoy and assume responsibility for its safety until it reached the Eastern Ocean Meeting Point (EASTOMP) at about eighteen degrees west. The convoy would then be met by a Western Approaches escort force sent out from the Clyde or Northern Ireland for the final stretch of its homeward journey. An outward convoy would of course be given similar protection by groups working in the opposite direction. Continuous escort across the North Atlantic in both directions and also on the north–south route thus became possible in July 1941, and was thereafter maintained until the end of the war.

Unfortunately there was in the middle of the north Atlantic an 'air gap' about 300 miles wide which could not be covered by shore-based aircraft working from Newfoundland, Iceland or Northern Ireland; and another, though less important, 'air gap' existed on the north–south route to the east of the Azores. It was, as will shortly be told, in the 'air gaps' that the U-boat packs concentrated their efforts in the next round of the struggle. The first campaign on the convoy routes, which may be taken as starting with the introduction of wolf packs towards the end of 1940 and ending with the disastrous events of December 1941 in the Far East, may reasonably be described as a stalemate. Although the U-boats inflicted heavy losses (432 ships totalling nearly 2.2 million tons in 1941) the British and Canadian navies had developed an efficient interlocking convoy system right across the north Atlantic; the training of escort groups and cooperation between them and shore-based aircraft had improved greatly; and technical developments such as the Leigh light, short-wave radar, heavier depth charges and ahead-throwing anti-submarine weapons promised well for the future. Yet these favourable trends did not prevent the U-boats achieving a second peak of success in the next phase.

Despite the fact that, ever since the crisis of 1940, American 'observers' had been serving in all the major British naval commands, and when a powerful American naval mission arrived in England in the autumn of that year it was given the benefit of virtually all the British war experience and technical developments, the Japanese attack and German declaration of war on the United States found the U.S. navy ill prepared in many respects – and perhaps especially in the defence of the merchant shipping which passed close off the American eastern seaboard. The U.S. navy was not convinced that the allegedly 'defensive' strategy of convoy and escort was the proper means both to defend the merchant ships and to create opportunities to counter-attack its assailants, and preferred to rely on hunting and patrolling – on which the British had in fact wasted considerable effort during the early months of the war. Nor was Dönitz slow to seize the opportunity to attack the stream of ships, which included a large proportion of precious oil tankers, passing between the Caribbean Sea or Gulf of Mexico and the terminal ports on the east coast of the U.S.A. on which a large proportion of the country's industries depended for raw materials and from which beleaguered Britain was receiving vital supplies. The result was to produce what the U-boat commanders described as their 'second happy time', and to encourage Dönitz and his staff to believe they could achieve the target of sinking 700,000 tons of shipping per month – which they had always estimated to be the figure necessary to bring Britain to her knees. Fortunately for the Allies other commitments, especially in the Mediterranean, severely restricted the number of boats Dönitz could send to the new battleground, and it was not until the beginning of 1942 that the first six sailed there from western France; but they were enough to produce a holocaust. In January U-boat sinkings rose to sixty-two ships (327,357 tons) and the U-boats, accomplishments rose steadily month by month until they reached their target of just over 700,000 tons (144 ships) in June. A large proportion of those sinkings took place in waters where the Admiralty's writ did not run, and they included many ships which had survived the perils of the Atlantic crossing. The Admiralty could do little except send out what reinforcements it could spare and urge the U.S. navy to adopt a convoy system and imitate the British system of shipping control and the collection and dissemination of intelligence regarding U-boat movements which had been so successfully developed in the Submarine Tracking Room deep down in the shelter beneath the main Admiralty building. But it was not until April that the Americans adopted even a partial convoy system.

Dönitz very naturally did his utmost to benefit from this state of affairs. He extended the time his boats could stay on patrol by sending out submarine tankers (or 'milch cows') to replenish them with fuel; and in February he extended his onslaught to the Caribbean, where the U-boats found many ships, and especially tankers, sailing unescorted. For the first half of 1942 Allied losses to U-boats averaged 97.3 ships (508,143 tons) per month and for the second half 95.5 ships (530,047 tons) per month – a rate of loss which, unless checked, spelt disaster to the entire Allied cause. However, by the middle of the year northbound and southbound convoys had begun to sail up and down the American eastern seaboard, and the U.S. navy thereafter steadily developed an interlocking convoy system until it covered the whole area from the St Lawrence River estuary to the coast of Brazil.

Dönitz's response was to send some of his long-range U-boats further afield to waters where they could still expect to find unescorted targets, and in October they appeared for the first time off the Cape of Good Hope and in the southern Indian Ocean. There they inflicted substantial losses on the vital troopships and supply traffic to the Middle East theatre. But he redeployed his main strength, still using wolf pack tactics, against the north Atlantic convoy routes, where the battle was renewed with rising intensity for the last four months of the year and heavy losses were inflicted. Not until December was there a substantial drop in the tonnage sunk; and that dawn was to prove a false one. Although eighty-seven U-boats were sunk by one means or another in 1942 the German rate of production far outstripped their losses; and the phases which may be called the 'Campaign in American Waters' and the 'Second Campaign on the Convoy Routes' had undoubtedly gone in favour of the Axis powers.

Despite the potentially disastrous developments in the Atlantic battle in 1942 the Allies did achieve one outstandingly important success: the safe transport from Britain and the U.S.A. of the huge military and supply convoys carrying the forces organized to launch the amphibious expeditions against Morocco and Algeria on 7 November. Though no losses were suffered while on passage, and complete strategic surprise was achieved, the necessary escorts could only be provided at the expense of the north Atlantic mercantile convoys. In some degree therefore the heavy losses suffered by the latter may reasonably be attributed to the priority given to the safety of the ships carrying the forces destined for the landings in North Africa.

The unfavourable trend in the Atlantic battle in 1942 brought to a head the clash between the Naval and Air Staffs over strategy and priorities. The former held that, as the Allies certainly could not launch a second front until control of the sea routes was reasonably secure, and would equally certainly be defeated if such control were decisively lost, the correct strategy must be to concentrate first on winning the Battle of the Atlantic – and that meant that Coastal Command must be given sufficient long-range reconnaissance bombers to enable it to provide air escorts throughout the convoys' voyages in both directions. The Air Staff, however, argued that as the bombing of Germany was the only possible 'offensive' strategy for the time being, as it assisted in the Atlantic battle by disrupting U-boat production, and as it made an important contribution to the support of the embattled Russian armies, nothing should be done to weaken the Allied bombing effort. When the new short-wave (ten-centimetre) radar sets became available for service at the end of 1942 the debate grew sharper, since the instruments which would make bombing far more accurate used many of the same components as those which would enable a surfaced U-boat to be detected from the air at night or in low visibility. The clash over priorities was repeatedly brought before the high-level service and ministerial committees responsible for British war strategy. The final decisions, taken by Mr Churchill in October, were that no large-scale diversion of aircraft from Bomber to Coastal Command should be made, that the need to close the Atlantic 'air gap', to which the Naval Staff rightly attached such great importance, should be met by obtaining long-range aircraft from the U.S.A., and that Bomber Command should have priority for the new radar sets. Not until March 1943 did Coastal Command receive any of those revolutionary instruments.

By the beginning of 1943 the number of escort vessels available to the Western Approaches Command had risen appreciably, and the Canadian navy was bearing an increasing share of the burden in the west Atlantic. In

March 1943 the Western Approaches Command was at last able to organize a number of support groups which could be diverted to reinforce the escorts of threatened convoys, and some of which included an escort carrier. On the other hand the Germans were still producing new and improved U-boats much faster than they were being sunk. Thus, all the signs were that, as the weather improved with the approach of spring, the battle on the convoy routes would be renewed with increased fury. On 1 April 1943 the Canadian navy assumed full responsibility for the routing and defence of shipping west of the Change of Operational Control (or CHOP) Line at forty-seven degrees west. The U.S. navy now withdrew entirely from the north Atlantic but took over responsibility for the important tanker convoys crossing the central Atlantic from the Caribbean oil ports.

The first two months of 1943, during which the weather was almost continuously stormy, produced something of a lull and losses on both sides were comparatively slight. Then in March Dönitz mounted a prolonged and vigorous onslaught by forty U-boats against a slow convoy from Sydney, Cape Breton Island, and a faster one from Halifax (respectively called S.C.122 and H.X.229*) which joined together in mid-Atlantic and totalled 100 ships. The main battle took place in the notorious 'air gap', and although reinforcements were sent out from Iceland and other bases the U-boats sank twenty-one ships (141,000 tons) for the loss of only one of their number. That month the total sinkings by U-boats shot up to 108 ships (627,377 tons), which was nearly as high as the worst months of 1942. Plainly a crisis was imminent.

It came in late April and early May when Dönitz concentrated about sixty U-boats working in four groups against a slow outward convoy, O.N.S.5.

Fortunately for the Allies a squadron of 'Very Long Range' Liberators had by that time joined the Coastal Command forces working from Iceland, and they and a support group sent out from St John's played a vital part in the battle which was fought throughout a week of very stormy weather. Though twelve of the convoy were sunk the sea and air escorts destroyed seven U-boats. In the next convoy battle the U-boats achieved only slight successes and again suffered heavily. Then in mid-May the wolf packs were decisively defeated in attacks on two homeward convoys (H.X.237 and S.C. 129), to which support groups including escort carriers were diverted. On 22 May Dönitz recalled the survivors and silence fell on the battle area. In fact, no fewer than thirty-three U-boats had been sunk since the first of the month; and by the end of it the total had risen to forty-one.

This victory was decisive. Never again did a comparable threat to the Atlantic life-line arise; and it is now plain that the victory was won by the escort and support groups sent out with the convoys, by the escort carriers'

* Self-evident letters were used to distinguish convoys. Thus S.C. stood for Sydney, Cape Breton Island, H.X. for Halifax and O.N.S. for Outward North Atlantic Slow.

aircraft and by Coastal Command's tiny force of Very Long Range aircraft; and of all the weapons and devices which they employed the ten-centimetre radar sets were without doubt the most important. A share of the credit for the victory must also be given to the Admiralty's Submarine Tracking Room, which successfully plotted the U-boats' movements and despatched sea and air reinforcements to the precise points at which they were needed. Between January and May 1943 Allied losses totalled 314 ships (1,782,628 tons), which was still too high for comfort; but no less than ninety-six U-boats were sunk in the same period – a rate of loss which simply could not be sustained. Such in brief outline was the result of the phase we may justly call the 'Triumph of the Escorts'.

The defeat suffered in May 1943 did not cause Dönitz to throw up the sponge, and he continued to send groups of U-boats from bases in Germany and western France to distant waters, where for a time they achieved some success. To counter these movements a joint Navy–Coastal Command offensive against the U-boats' transit routes through the Shetlands–Faröe Islands channel and across the Bay of Biscay was organized. The Coastal Command aircraft involved were by this time mostly equipped with ten-centimetre radar and Leigh lights. The combination of the two proved lethal on many occasions, since they enabled the aircraft to catch by surprise a U-boat which was surfaced and charging its batteries at night. The Biscay offensive proved far more rewarding than that against boats passing through the northern transit area. It reached a climax between 1 July and 2 August 1943 when twenty U-boats were sunk and many others forced to turn back. At about the same time American escort carriers struck hard and successfully against the 'milch cows' sent to refuel U-boats off the Azores. All in all the period from 1 June to 31 August 1943 was a very unhappy time for Dönitz and his crews. Their achievements averaged no more than twenty-seven ships (144,628 tons) a month, mostly sunk in distant waters, and no less than seventy-nine of their number were destroyed.

At the beginning of September Dönitz made an attempt to renew the struggle in the north Atlantic by sending out groups of boats equipped with the new acoustic homing torpedoes, improved radar search receivers to give warning of the approach of aircraft, and strengthened anti-aircraft armaments. The movement did not pass unnoticed in the Admiralty's Submarine Tracking Room, however, and preparations were made to deal with it. The expected attack took place against a slow and a faster outward convoy (O.N.S.18 and O.N.202) between 15 and 27 September. Six merchantmen (36,422 tons) and three of the escorts were sunk by acoustic torpedoes. As three U-boats were destroyed the result was fairly evenly balanced. Other convoy battles followed, but in none of them did the U-boats achieve substantial successes; and they were increasingly severely handled by the sea and air escorts. The phase 1 September to 31 December 1943 may be said to mark the final defeat of the wolf packs, since the losses they inflicted averaged no more than twenty-two ships (92,450 tons) per month, and sixty-two U-boats were accounted for in the same period.

Dönitz's next move was to attempt to repeat the great successes achieved in the north-western approaches to the British Isles at the beginning of the war. But in the early months of 1944 conditions were vastly different from those which had prevailed during the U-boat commanders' first 'happy time'. Not only were those waters now continuously patrolled and covered by the Coastal Command squadrons stationed in Northern Ireland and western Scotland, but the Allies possessed sufficient escort and support groups to send some of the best of them, reinforced by several escort carriers, against the new enemy concentration. This was the period when Captain F. J. Walker's famous 2nd Escort Group achieved its most outstanding successes. The outcome of this phase was therefore another severe defeat for the U-boats. Between January and May 1944 merchant ship losses averaged only 13.4 ships (82,944 tons) per month, and in return for those meagre accomplishments Dönitz lost no fewer than 103 U-boats from all causes.

While the second campaign in the north-western approaches was in progress the Allies were steadily building up in Britain the enormous forces required for the invasion of Normandy, and special measures were being put in hand to deal with the expected U-boat attacks on the cross-Channel troop and supply convoys. Most of the U-boats were by this time fitted with the 'Schnorkel' breathing device, which enabled them to charge their batteries while submerged and made their presence much harder to detect – even on the short-wave radar sets. However, so intensive was Allied air and sea patrolling of the routes from the bases in western France, and so powerful were the escorts provided to the invasion convoys, that the U-boats suffered constant harassment and very few of them succeeded in actually reaching the critical waters. The outcome of this phase (June–December 1944) was, from the German point of view, devastating. No fewer than 140 U-boats were sunk (including those scuttled in the bases of western France before they fell to the Allied armies), and in return they sank only sixty-five ships (358,609 tons) during the seven months which saw the launching, build-up and extension of the invasion of the Continent.

During the final phase of the battle what may be called the 'Campaign in Inshore Waters' continued, and the Germans brought into the struggle a large number of midget submarines of various types – called 'small battle units' – to try and rectify the plainly failing conventional U-boats. However, neither class achieved significant results, and the flow of reinforcements and supplies needed to support the Allied armies in their eastward advance was never severely threatened. Between 1 January 1945 and the German surrender on 8 May, U-boats sank only fifty-five merchant ships (270,277 tons); and no fewer than 151 of their number were destroyed. It was in this period that Bomber Command of the R.A.F., working closely with the heavy bombers of the U.S. Army Air Force, made a great contribution to victory in the Atlantic battle. Not only did the bombing raids delay the delivery of prefabricated parts to the assembly yards and destroy a number of U-boats on the stocks or in port, but the minelaying by long-range bombers completely disrupted the training of new U-boat crews in the Baltic. Furthermore, Allied bombing seriously delayed the production of U-boats of entirely new types (known as Types XXI and XXIII), whose much greater underwater speed might have restored the initiative to the Germans. There can be no doubt that the outcome of the final phase of the Atlantic battle was complete and final defeat for the Germans – as Dönitz himself has admitted.

To sum up the results of the five and a half year struggle for mastery of the seas and oceans, the Germans built and commissioned 1,162 U-boats, of which 784 were lost through one cause or another. By far the greatest proportion of the losses suffered *at sea* (500 out of 632) were inflicted by British warships and aircraft. It is also interesting that the final count shows that the Royal Navy and R.A.F. shared almost exactly equally in those successes. Apart from the U-boats sunk in combat or lost through other causes 156 surrendered when their country accepted the Allied terms for the cessation of hostilities, while 221 scuttled themselves in order to escape the indignity of surrender. The losses inflicted by German, Italian and Japanese submarines totalled 2,828 Allied merchant ships (14,687,231 tons), and by far the greatest share of that prodigous destruction was wrought by the German U-boats. In addition 175 Allied warships, the great majority of which were British, were sunk by Axis submarines; and many other warships and merchantmen were damaged by submarines' torpedoes but were repaired in time to re-enter the fray. Though enemy raiders, bombers and mines all at times caused substantial losses and considerable anxiety, the Battle of the Atlantic was in the main fought between the sea and air convoy escorts and the German submarines. And if in 1942 and early 1943 they came within measurable distance of victory it was the endurance and gallantry of the little warships and long-range aircrews, combined with the steadfastness of the merchant seamen, which combined to defeat the most serious challenge faced by this country after the Battle of Britain had been won in 1940.

APPENDIX I

Total Allied Merchant Shipping Losses by Causes

3 September 1939–15 August 1945

Cause	*Number of Ships Sunk*	*Tonnage*
Submarines (U-boats)	2,828	14,687,231
Aircraft	820	2,889,883
Mines	534	1,406,037
Warship raiders	104	498,447
Disguised merchant raiders	133	829,644
Fast torpedo boats (E-boats)	99	229,676
Unknown or other causes	632	1,029,802
Grand Total	5,150	21,570,720

APPENDIX II

U-boats Sunk or Captured

German	784
Italian	84
Japanese	154
Total	1,022

Note on Sources

The bibliography covering all aspects of the Battle of the Atlantic 1939–45, from the Axis as well as the Allied point of view, is vast. An attempt has here been made to list the most important and authoritative historical works and the biographies of the leading figures on both sides. The selection includes books describing the parts played by the Royal Air Force in the campaign as well as that of the Allied navies' warships and aircraft. Some which describe the vital role of the Allied merchant navies have also been included. Books by German, Italian and Japanese authors have only been included where they have been translated into English.

Bragadin, M. A., *The Italian Navy in World War II* (1957).
Busch, H., *U-boats at War* (Eng. trans. 1955).
Chalmers, W. S., *Max Horton and the Western Approaches* (1954).
Collier, Basil, *The Defence of the United Kingdom* (1957).
Cunningham of Hyndhope, Viscount, *A Sailor's Odyssey* (1950).
Dönitz, Karl, *Admiral Doenitz Memoirs* (Eng. trans. 1959).
Goodhart, Philip, *Fifty Ships that Saved the World* (1965).
Gretton, Sir Peter, *Convoy Escort Commander* (1964).
Grinnell-Milne, D., *The Silent Victory, September 1940* (1958).
Ito, M., with R. Pineau, *The End of the Imperial Japanese Navy* (Eng. trans. 1962).

Joubert de la Ferté, Sir Philip, *The Third Service: the Story behind the Royal Air Force* (1955).
Joubert de la Ferté, Sir Philip, *Birds and Little Fishes: the Story of Coastal Command* (1960).
Kemp, Peter, *Victory at Sea* (1967).
Kennedy, L., *Pursuit: The Chase and Sinking of the Bismarck* (1974).
Kerr, J. L., and W. Granville, *The R.N.V.R.* (1957).
Macintyre, Donald, *U-boat Killer* (1956).
Macintyre, Donald, *The Battle of the Atlantic* (1961).
Mars, Alistair, *British Submarines at War 1939–45* (1971).
Morison, Samuel E., *The History of United States Naval Operations in the Second World War*, Vol. I of 15 vols, *The Battle of the Atlantic, September 1939–May 1943*, and Vol. X, *The Atlantic Battle Won, May 1943–May 1945* (1947 and 1956). (*Note.* The attention of the student is drawn to the Errata List in Vol. 15, 1962.)
Okumiya, M., J. Horokishi and M. Cardin, *Zero. The Story of the Japanese Navy Air Force 1937–1945* (1957).
Peillard, L., *Sink the Tirpitz* (Eng. trans. 1968).
Pope, D., *73 North* (1958).
Porten, E. P. von der, *The German Navy in World War II* (1969).
Potter, E. B., and Chester W. Nimitz, *The Great Sea War* (1960).
Raeder, Erich, *Struggle for the Sea* (Eng. trans. 1954).
Rayner, D. (ed. S. W. Roskill), *Escort. The Battle of the Atlantic* (1955).
Robertson, T., *Channel Dash* (1960).
Roskill, S. W., *The War at Sea 1939–1945*, 3 vols. in 4 parts (1954–61). (*Note.* New editions with sources are in preparation.
Roskill, S. W., *The Secret Capture* (1959).
Roskill, S. W., *A Merchant Fleet in War 1939–1945* (1962).
Rutter, Owen, *Red Ensign. A History of Convoy* (1942).
Schofield, B. B., *The Russian Convoys* (1964).
Seth, R., *The Fiercest Battle. The Story of Convoy ONS.5* (1961).
Slessor, Sir John, *The Central Blue* (1956).
Webster, Sir Charles, and N. Frankland, *The Strategic Air Offensive against Germany 1939–1945*, 4 vols (1961).
Wemyss, D. E. G., *Walker's Groups in the Western Approaches* (*Liverpool Daily Post and Echo*, N.D.).
Werner, H. A., *Iron Coffins: German U-boat Battles in World War II* (Eng. trans. 1969).

German panzers, the steel tip of the Wehrmacht's offensive. A column of Mark III tanks on the move near the River Aisne

Chapter Eight

BATTLE OF FRANCE

Brian Bond

IN THE HISTORY of warfare few campaigns between great and approximately equal powers have been decided so swiftly and conclusively as the German conquest of Western Europe in May and June 1940. Within five days of the opening of the campaign on 10 May, Holland had surrendered, the French defences on and behind the Meuse had disintegrated and the French Prime Minister was already talking of defeat. By 20 May the British, French and Belgian armies north of the Somme had been cut off from the main French forces; and though a large proportion of the troops were to escape via Dunkirk, virtually all their weapons and equipment were lost. Thus weakened, deprived of all but token British assistance, and attacked in the rear by Italy, France – until recently widely regarded as the foremost military power – stumbled towards a humiliating capitulation.

Although that unhappy event was postponed until 22 June, and despite the fact that after an inglorious start the French army showed itself still capable of heroic resistance reminiscent of 1914–18, the campaign was truly won and lost in the first week or ten days. Thus the French Prime Minister, Paul Reynaud, though personally far from being a defeatist, was prophetic in his gloomy telephone message to Churchill on 15 May: 'We have lost the battle.' Few campaigns have been more frequently refought by armchair strategists, but there is broad agreement on the verdict that although France might, with better organization and sterner resistance, have delayed the outcome or rescued more from the débâcle, the basic outcome was irrevocably decided in the first few days. It therefore seems appropriate to focus attention on this decisive period rather than attempt to give equal weight to every aspect of the operations.

With the wisdom of hindsight it is tempting to overlook the hard fighting and simply ascribe the German victory to a superior strategic plan. Although this would be going too far, the significance of the German *Sichelschnitt* ('cut of the sickle') Plan was immense, for not only did it achieve strategic surprise, but by delivering the main thrust in an area thought to be impenetrable and then rapidly breaking through supposedly impregnable defences, it dealt the French High Command a psychological blow from which it never recovered.

In justice to the French commander-in-chief, General Gamelin, however, it must be pointed out that until the beginning of 1940 his analysis of German strategy was broadly correct and his defensive counter-measures stood a reasonable chance of success.

Even before Germany's first successful demonstration of *Blitzkrieg* against Poland, Anglo–French military planners had concluded that in the event of an attack in the West, Germany's comparative strength in air and ground forces (and the supposed weakness of her economy) would prompt her to seek a lightning victory. Furthermore, since the Maginot Line presented a formidable barrier along most of the vulnerable area of the Franco–German frontier, it seemed likely that Hitler would attempt to repeat the Schlieffen Plan of 1914 by an indirect approach through Belgium, and probably Holland too. The French had good cause to worry about their defence arrangements to the north of the Maginot Line (which ended just south of Sedan) because Belgium had proclaimed her neutrality in 1936, thus undermining the prospects of a successful Allied defence along her eastern frontiers. In the spring of 1939, then, Gamelin expected the main German attack to come through the Low Countries on the axis Brussels–Cambrai with the object of reaching the French position from Hirson to the North Sea.

Gamelin's outlook, in the short term at any rate, was essentially defensive. France's strategic doctrine, military organization and economy were all based on the assumption that the first long phase must be a holding operation to secure the territory of France to allow time for military and industrial mobilization. Only then could a major counter-offensive be contemplated. The key problem was not whether France and her allies could attack (despite the guarantee to Poland), but whether she should try to check a German advance beyond her own frontiers. This was considered so desirable as to warrant abandoning prepared positions. Anglo–French strategic planners concluded that Holland could not be effectively supported against a surprise attack, but that Belgium might be, particularly if she would cooperate before being invaded. Hence, in the course of the 'Phoney War' Gamelin formulated alternative plans D and E for an Anglo-French advance either to the Dyle or the Escaut (Scheldt) to be carried out by the B.E.F. and French First Army. To their right the Ninth Army would move up to the Meuse, while on their left – a bold and risky scheme – the highly mechanized Seventh Army would advance up the coast to secure the Scheldt estuary and, if possible, link up with the Dutch in south-east Holland. Only two defects in this plan need be mentioned at this stage: it assigned a large portion of the modern armoured units (three light mechanized divisions) to a dubious flank role, and it assumed that the major thrust would be made along the traditional route across the plains of Belgium.

Had the German offensive against the West, which was ordered and postponed on numerous occasions between October 1939 and January 1940, been put into execution, it could well have ended in a stalemate. The major role was assigned to Army Group B which was to eliminate Holland and thrust through central Belgium, while only a covering role was given to Army Group A on its southern flank, whose twenty-two divisions contained no mechanized units. Moreover, the territorial objective was limited to seizing the Low Countries and the Channel coast – presumably as bases for an attack on Britain; there was no notion that France might also be eliminated.

The credit for perceiving the defects of this plan and devising an alternative designed to secure a decisive victory belongs mainly to Army Group A's chief of staff, General Erich von Manstein. Essentially he proposed to transfer the principal role and the bulk of the armoured units (initially seven out of ten panzer divisions) to Army Group A, and to stake everything on a surprise attack through the Ardennes against what was known to be the weakest sector of the French defences (the Sedan–Dinant sector of the Meuse). Manstein's bold conception was at first opposed by the Army High Command (O.K.H.), but in mid-February 1940 he was sympathetically received by Hitler and his essential ideas were incorporated in the final operation order shortly afterwards. Army Group B still had the important task of drawing the Allied First Army Group into Belgium and holding it there, but the role of deep penetration – through the Ardennes, across the Meuse and then either sweeping south behind the Maginot Line or along the Somme valley towards the Channel coast – now fell to Army Group A.

Despite mounting evidence that the Germans were concentrating more heavily opposite the Ardennes area, Gamelin rigidly persevered with his plan for a rapid thrust forward of his left wing, and thus played into enemy hands when the crisis came.

One of the most persistent myths to emerge from the catastrophe was that the Allies had been beaten by overwhelming numerical and material odds. This was doubtless easier to swallow than the bitter fact that the Allies had been out-generalled and out-fought, but this was indeed the case, as a brief survey will show.

On 10 May 1940 Germany had 136 divisions in the West, of which ten were armoured (panzers), seven motorized, one cavalry and one airborne. The French and British together had 104 divisions (ninety-four and ten respectively) to which twenty-two Belgian divisions were added on 10 May. The French total included three armoured divisions, three light mechanized divisions (as powerfully equipped as any of the panzer divisions), and five cavalry divisions. The difference was thus not great, though it should be mentioned that the low-quality French reserve divisions made far less use of the 'Phoney War' period for training than their German counterparts. There has been much controversy on the question of total comparative tank strengths on the Western Front, but on R. H. S. Stolfi's careful reckoning the French by themselves had more tanks than the enemy – 3,254 against the Germans' 2,574. As for quality, the French tanks were certainly inferior to the Germans' in the mobile type of war they were called upon to fight because most of them were slower and had a more limited radius of action. Face to face, however, the French should have been more than a match for the enemy. Whereas all the modern French tanks had protective armour 40 mm thick, none of the panzer types had an all-round plating thicker than 20 mm. Again the French tanks clearly had the edge in armament. Many of the later types (H.39 and R.40) had a good 37-mm gun, while the medium Ds and SOMUAs (Société d'Outilage Mécanique et d'Usinage d'Artillerie) had an excellent 47-mm gun. The heavy B tank was probably then the best tank in the world, with armour proof against any German gun and itself mounting two guns of 47-mm (turret) and 75-mm (body). By comparison no less than a quarter of the German tanks had machine guns only, and another quarter only a small 20-mm gun. Stolfi's thorough analysis leads to the following conclusion: a larger number of more heavily armed and protected French tanks stood opposed on 10 May 1940 to a smaller number of faster and longer-ranged German and Czech (334) vehicles. The quantitative and qualitative balance in anti-tank guns was surprising also, with a larger number of comparatively ineffective German cannons (total 12,800) standing opposed to a smaller number (7,200) of highly refined French anti-tank guns of extraordinary penetrating power.

The striking contrast between the two tank forces lay in their differing organization, which in turn stemmed from a different conception of the role of armour. Even the four French armoured divisions (three existing and one formed during the campaign) had been hastily improvised and still lacked vital supporting elements such as motorized infantry. They were incapable of existing and fighting independently. By contrast the German armoured battalions constituted the spearheads of ten armoured divisions which in turn were organized in armoured corps forming an extremely strong assault force.

The only respect in which the Allies were markedly inferior was in the air, but even here the German superiority has sometimes been exaggerated. According to H. A. Jacobsen the German air strength in May 1940 was as follows: 1,016 fighters, 248 medium bombers, 1,120 bombers, 342 Stukas (dive-bombers) and 500 reconnaissance planes, a total of 3,226 aircraft. The French air force then possessed only some 1,120 modern aircraft, of which 700 were fighters, 140 bombers and 380 reconnaissance planes. To these of course must be added the British contribution, which initially consisted of the Air Component of the B.E.F. (four fighter squadrons, four bomber squadrons and five army cooperation squadrons) and the Advanced Air Striking Force (ten bomber squadrons and two fighter squadrons). In the first few days of the campaign a further ten fighter squadrons were sent to France, while others operated from south-eastern England.

Again the German air forces were better organized for their immediate purpose. The Stukas, as the Battle of Britain would show, had serious defects in slow speed and vulnerability, but they played a vital part in the crucial first days of the breakthrough. The Germans also enjoyed vastly superior anti-aircraft defences. Even so, it is noticeable that the effectiveness of the Luftwaffe declined sharply as the campaign progressed and it moved further from its bases. It proved incapable of dealing a knock-out blow to the beleaguered Allied forces at Dunkirk.

Thus, to sum up, Germany enjoyed a marked superiority only in bomber aircraft and anti-aircraft defences. In other respects, such as tanks and artillery, the opposing sides were either approximately equal or else the Allies held a slight advantage. The outcome of the campaign, however, depended much less on the quantity of men and weapons than on the style of operations which the attackers managed to impose on the defenders.

In the first few days of the battle the achievements of Army Group B seemed the more sensational, but meanwhile the decisive breakthrough was taking place, as planned, on Army Group A's front. As to the former, the Netherlands were quickly overrun by Kuechler's Eighteenth Army and the government capitulated on 15 May to avoid further devastation after the bombing of Rotterdam. The Belgian frontier defences were pierced on the first day when the principal fortress of Eben Emael, which commanded three vital bridges, was captured by a brilliant *coup de main*. Reichenau's Sixth Army pressed on to the Dyle Line where the leading French and British units were just assembling. Thereafter Army Group B made steady progress, assisted by the French collapse to the south, in pushing the Allies back to the Escaut by 21 May, but its main task had been accomplished when it drew the Allied left wing deep into Belgium. Bock's minor role was emphasized on 17 May when all his armoured forces (the XVI and XXXIX Corps) were ordered south to reinforce Rundstedt's drive to the Channel.

Meanwhile, on 10 and 11 May Army Group A was approaching the Meuse through the supposedly impenetrable Ardennes, led by the greatest concentration of tanks ever seen in war. This was Kleist's Panzer Group, composed of three panzer corps each arranged in three echelons with armoured divisions in the first two and motorized infantry in the third. This armoured array was more than 100 miles deep from head to tail so that at the start the rear of the column was still fifty miles east of the Rhine. On its right lay a separate panzer corps under Hoth (the 5th and 7th Panzer Divisions), whose initial objective was the Meuse between Givet and Dinant. Fortunately for the Germans, these densely packed formations met little serious resistance before reaching the Meuse. The Belgian *Chasseurs Ardennais* had mined or barricaded all the forest roads but did not stay to defend them, so that the delays were slight. Indeed, at this stage the Germans' main problem was administrative rather than tactical: meticulous staff work was necessary to coordinate the movement of some eighty-six divisions.

By the evening of 12 May the leading German armoured divisions had reached the Meuse in two places, and at least two days earlier than the defenders had thought possible. Sedan, on the east bank, had been captured by the 1st and 10th Panzer Divisions (from Guderian's XXIX Corps), while Rommel's 7th Panzer Division had reached Dinant. It was typical of the Germans' offensive spirit that they pressed straight on with the crossings on 13 May – again to the bewilderment of the enemy. All the bridges had been blown – though Rommel's leading motor cycle company was assisted by an intact footbridge over a weir – and French opposition was stiff, yet by the end of the day four precarious bridgeheads had been established on the west bank. At Sedan, especially, the French artillery was almost paralysed by perfectly coordinated Stuka and bomber raids. The concrete emplacements on the west bank were put out of action by anti-tank and anti-aircraft artillery and the French machine guns were also rendered ineffective. These initial crossings were made by infantry and motor cycle regiments without the support of either tanks or artillery. While Guderian personally supervised the construction of a pontoon bridge so that tanks could cross, his riflemen pressed on through the night and by the morning had reached Chemery, over ten miles south of the Meuse. This enterprise and dash by junior commanders probably made the vital difference at this critical stage.

There was still an opportunity for the Allies to launch a devastating counter-attack while the enemy was confined to congested bridgeheads and a makeshift pontoon bridge, but it was not taken. The Germans had deliberately struck at the junction of two French armies (the Second and the Ninth) which contained many poorly trained reserve units. On the evening of 14 May General Corap, commanding the Ninth Army, mistakenly ordered a general retreat to a new defensive position about ten miles to the west. He thereby eased the crossing of Reinhardt's XLI Corps at Monthermé, while Rommel breached the new line before it could be manned. Corap was dismissed and replaced by Giraud, who was captured a few days later. There had already been instances of panic flight. Now the Ninth Army's withdrawal turned into a rout, while to the south Huntziger's Second Army fared little better. By nightfall on 14 May Guderian's bridgehead was already some thirty miles wide and fifteen miles deep. That same day British and French bombers with French fighter cover made heroic but vain attempts to destroy the vital pontoon bridge at Sedan. Out of 170 bombers (the majority of them Blenheims) about eighty-five were shot down. As Guderian noted, 'Flak had its day of glory.'

The French had one other means of sealing off the hole in their defences which was opening up between Dinant and Sedan. On 10 May their three existing armoured divisions were in a central position in Champagne only about fifty miles from the Meuse, but they were tragically frittered away. The 1st Armoured Division, after a long journey north of the Sambre, ran out of fuel in the area of Ermeton and Flavion where it was annihilated. (Ironically, Guderian recalls that he had no fuel problem.) The 3rd Armoured Division was successfully concentrated south of Sedan but was then employed in a static role and split up along the defence line. The fate of the 2nd Armoured Division was perhaps most tragic of all. Its wheeled vehicles advanced towards the front by road whereas its tracked vehicles were entrained at Chalons. Losing patience with the slow rate of rail movement, General Georges ordered the tracked vehicles to be unloaded at Hirson. This unfortunately lay right in the course of the panzer advance and on 15 May the wheeled vehicles were cut off from the tracked vehicles. The division then ceased to exist as a fighting unit.

Thus by the evening of 15 May the Germans had already gained a decisive advantage. All three panzer corps (Hoth's, Reinhardt's and Guderian's) had broken clean through the Meuse bridgeheads and were thrusting westwards virtually unopposed in the chaotic rear areas behind the French Ninth Army. Guderian wrote that, considering the nature of the ground they had crossed, 'the success of our attack struck me almost as a miracle'. The breach was now sixty miles wide and the French had mishandled their armoured counter-offensive.

Although the dynamic panzer leaders, particularly Guderian and Rommel, were full of confidence and already thinking of driving on relentlessly to the Channel coast, some of their senior commanders and Hitler himself were astonished by the speed of the advance and became day by day more anxious about over-extension. They overrated Gamelin's ability to launch a counter-offensive and underrated the extent to which French morale had collapsed. Consequently, as the memoirs of Guderian and others wryly remark, in the days after 15 May checks and opposition derived more from their own high command than from the enemy.

Kleist first ordered Guderian to halt on 15 May, but after a heated argument the latter gained permission to continue for another twenty-four hours. Two days later, when his leading units were already more than fifty miles from Sedan, Guderian was again peremptorily halted by Kleist, whose manner this time was so hostile that Guderian asked to be relieved of his command. This *contretemps* brought up General List as mediator. He explained to Guderian that the order came from O.K.H. and must be obeyed. Wisely, however, he allowed Guderian to carry out a 'reconnaissance in force', provided his corps headquarters remained where it was. Guderian thereupon laid a wire to his advanced headquarters so that he need not use wireless with the risk of being monitored by O.K.H. or O.K.W. (Armed Forces High Command)!

On this and succeeding days Hitler gave Halder and Brauchitsch at O.K.H. an unpleasant time because he feared a major counter-attack from the south. Hitler found that his anxieties were shared by Rundstedt and his army group staff who expected 'a great surprise counter-offensive by strong French forces from the Verdun and Chalons-sur-Marne area, northward . . .' On the map the narrow panzer corridor north of the Somme did look exceedingly vulnerable, but Halder judged correctly that the tempo of the advance was too rapid for the French commanders to adjust to.

However, despite all the advantages of modern communications, these bitter disputes between Hitler, O.K.H. and the army group commanders had remarkably little effect on the battlefield – at this stage. As Telford Taylor sums up: 'While O.K.H. and O.K.W. argued, the Panzers rolled on west and reached the Channel almost before the high command knew what was happening.'

By the morning of 19 May Guderian's leading panzer division (the 2nd) had reached St Quentin only fifty miles from the Channel coast at Abbeville. Now, freed from all restraint by the army commander-in-chief, Guderian spurred his unit commanders on mercilessly, ignoring pleas that they were out of petrol, and by the evening of 20 May the 2nd Panzer Division was in Abbeville. Thus in only ten days' fighting Kleist's Panzer Group had cut a complete swathe through the French defences and in doing so had severed the supply lines of the French First Army Group, which was then still on the Escaut line.

With every passing day the Allies' prospects of launching an effective counter-attack diminished. Gamelin had been slow to see the need to pull back his forces from Belgium to avoid being cut off, and only on 19 May, the day of his supercession by Weygand, did he issue a directive for a combined counter-offensive from north and south of the Somme to pinch off the German corridor and so isolate the panzers from the infantry. Weygand's first action was to cancel this plan while he assessed the situation for himself, and by 21 May, when he drew up a similar scheme (the 'W' Plan), it was already too late. Communications were by now so bad that Weygand was unable to exercise proper control. The forces north and south of the Somme each expected the other to make the major effort and neither accomplished anything substantial. Weygand's optimism and brave rhetoric unfortunately created the impression with the British and French governments that the counter-offensive was succeeding. Consequently, when on 25 May Lord Gort, commanding the B.E.F., decided independently that his army was imperilled and that there was no alternative but to make for the coast, it seemed plausible for the French to argue that he had disrupted the plan.

The irony of this false accusation was that the one minor action which temporarily worried the enemy and had long-term effects on their high command was the British counter-stroke at Arras on 21 May. Improvising the attack under pressure, the British could only contribute two tank battalions (the 4th and 7th Royal Tank Regiments with seventy-four tanks in all) and two infantry regiments, supported on their right flank by part of the French 3rd Light Mechanized Division (seventy tanks). The British thrust caught Rommel's 7th Panzer Division and the S.S. *Totenkopf* Division by surprise, and for a few hours created havoc. Although outnumbered the British tanks' thick armour gave them a temporary advantage, to the extent that even Rommel was shaken and exaggerated the strength of the opposition. After the war Rundstedt also described this as a critical moment: 'For a short time it was feared that our armoured divisions would be cut off before the infantry divisions could come up to support them. None of the French counter-attacks carried any serious threat as this one did.' (De Gaulle had launched a valiant assault south of the Somme towards Montcornet on 17 May with the newly formed 4th Armoured Division – 'a ramshackle outfit' – but it had little effect on Guderian's progress.)

The wider significance of the Arras episode was that it reinforced the apprehension already displayed by Kluge, Kleist and Rundstedt that the armoured spearhead was running too many risks, and helped to influence the fateful decision to halt the panzers on 24 May.

But for this order the campaign would almost certainly have been even more 'decisive' in that Britain would have lost the whole of her organized army. The growing caution of the German High Command was already evident on 21 May. After taking Abbeville, Guderian intended to send the 2nd Panzer Division straight on to Boulogne, the 1st to Calais and the 10th to Dunkirk, but he was temporarily deprived of the 10th while detachments from the 1st and 2nd had to be left behind to hold the Somme crossings. Quite apart from the security of the southern flank, there was another factor, namely the imbalance of forces between the two army groups. Army Group B had dwindled to twenty-one infantry divisions whereas Army Group A had swollen to over seventy divisions (including all ten armoured divisions): there was simply not enough room in the bottleneck north of the Somme for so many units and headquarters.

The Allies' reprieve resulted from the fact that the German armoured forces were halted along the Canal Line from the evening of 24 to the morning of 27 May. In response to a plea from Kluge (Fourth Army), Rundstedt had ordered a temporary pause in the armoured advance for 24 May, but the halt order proper stemmed from a meeting between Rundstedt and Hitler at Charleville on the morning of 24 May. Hitler did not merely ratify the pause, but emphatically stated that the armour should be conserved for the coming offensive south of the Somme. The honour of destroying the besieged Allies in the Dunkirk perimeter would fall to the Luftwaffe.

It seems clear that it was not Hitler's intention that the B.E.F. should escape; rather he shared the widespread German belief that escape by sea was impossible. By the time this error was realized the defences of the perimeter had been organized and, thanks to the gallant efforts of all three services, more than 300,000 troops were evacuated before Dunkirk fell on 4 June.

Although Dunkirk was treated as something of a triumph in Britain, from the Continental viewpoint it marked the brilliant climax of the first phase of a whirlwind campaign. In three weeks the Germans had taken over a million prisoners at the cost to themselves of only 60,000 casualties. The Dutch and Belgian armies had been eliminated – the latter surrendering after a gallant resistance on 28 May. The French had lost thirty divisions, nearly a third of their total strength and including virtually all their armour. They had lost the support of twelve British divisions, for without equipment it would have been madness to send them straight back to France (two British divisions were still engaged south of the Somme and two more were sent out). Weygand was left with only sixty-six divisions (many of them already depleted) to defend an unprepared front longer than the original one, stretching from Abbeville to the Maginot Line.

When the second phase of the German offensive (codename Fall Rot) began on 5 June the French military situation was already hopeless. For some time the military leaders had been talking of 'saving their honour' rather than victory, and those who felt with Colonel de Gaulle, now Under-Secretary for War, that resistance must be continued even, if necessary, outside metropolitan France, found themselves in a small minority. The Cabinet had discussed the possibility of seeking an armistice independently of Britain even before Dunkirk, and thereafter Prime Minister Reynaud steadily lost ground to those, including Pétain and Weygand, who favoured an immediate ceasefire to save France from further losses. Reynaud's resignation in favour of Pétain on 16 June signalled the end of any surviving hopes that the struggle could be continued in Brittany or in North Africa.

Despite episodes of heroic defiance exemplified by the self-sacrifice of the Cavalry School Cadets at Saumur, all but the south of France was overrun in the period between 14 June when Paris fell and 22 June when unconditional surrender was accepted at Compiègne. Rommel's 7th Panzer Division swept through to Cherbourg and the 5th to Brest; the XVI Corps captured Lyon and Grenoble and Guderian's XIX Corps reached the Swiss border before swinging north-east to Belfort. The Maginot Line, which remained unbroken during the main battle, was taken from the rear in the mopping up operations.

France's defeat had come about so suddenly and completely that even dedicated students of war, such as Churchill, found it scarcely comprehensible – hence his quixotic offer of political union on 16 June. While the French and British continued to hope that the defenders would hold and rally – as in 1914 and 1918 – the situation that actually developed was more reminiscent of 1870. France had been worsted in the classic type of mobile war which seemed to have disappeared in 1914. Her smaller allies had been annihilated. Britain had been driven off the Continent and France herself overrun. How had such a disaster come about? Historians and polemicists from 1940 onwards have understandably been reluctant to accept as adequate the straightforward military explanation: namely that France and her allies were beaten by a superior war machine. Instead they have sought more profound explanations in French politics and society. Some of these analyses – placing their emphasis on treachery or the rot spread by communist propaganda – are rather crude, but others (as in the second part of Marc Bloch's classic study *Strange Defeat*) range so widely as to indict virtually every class in French society.

Nevertheless, despite the abundant evidence of low morale and outright defeatism in France, it still seems reasonable to locate the main and sufficient causes of defeat in faulty strategic doctrine and organization. As Telford Taylor neatly put it: 'The trouble was that those who fought were woefully hampered by those who did not, and fatally handicapped by those who had failed to prepare.'

The French forces were badly equipped for mobile operations, badly trained and badly led. As regards doctrine, there has been excessive criticism of the 'Maginot mentality'. As a defensive shield the Line was a worthwhile investment, but it proved inadequate in the crisis because France lacked an offensive sword. She had produced a large number of tanks and aircraft but her strategic thinking remained entrenched in the traditions of the First World War. This was most startlingly evident in her commanders' inability to adjust to the tempo of German movement. During the retreat the French commanders ordered places to be held which had already fallen, and repeatedly drew up new defensive lines which were overrun before they could be manned. Given such a degree of muddle and incompetence at the top, it seems unjust to place much of the blame on the troops or the civilians.

Finally, the basic question must be posed: in what sense was this a 'decisive' victory? The most immediate and important result of the French army's defeat was that it led directly to the demise of the Third Republic. On 10 July both houses of the legislature sitting together as the National Assembly voted by an overwhelming majority to give Pétain full powers to govern the country and to revise the constitution.

In strategic terms France's defeat meant that Hitler had secured the Reich against an attack on land from the West for the foreseeable future. German occupation of the Channel and Biscay coasts provided a springboard from which to launch submarine and air attacks designed to starve Britain into surrender. Britain had lost her Continental foothold and henceforth could only strike directly at Germany through the initially feeble means of long-range bombing.

Equally serious, with France beaten and Italy also hostile, it was extremely doubtful whether Britain could maintain her line of communications through the Mediterranean. Guderian was not alone in thinking that the best way to force Britain out of the war in the summer of 1940 would have been to thrust south against her Mediterranean bases, in combination with Italy. This opportunity, as we know, was missed, and Hitler's subsequent policy eventually resulted in a two-front war of attrition and total defeat.

The final outcome of the war, however, should not obscure the German achievement of 1940. As Peter Calvocoressi has written in *Total War*: 'The defeat of France was the high water mark of the German army – and something more. . . . It was a portentous distortion of history, all the more shattering because its completeness led nearly everybody to suppose that it was final and irreversible . . .' The German triumph was not primarily due to superior numbers or equipment, but rather to superior control of the means available and ruthless efficiency in exploiting the enemy's mistakes to the full. From a military viewpoint this, then, was a victory in the classic style: the strategic conquest of a near equal adversary achieved with economy of means and without excessive losses.

Note on Sources

Baudouin, P., *The Private Diaries of Paul Baudouin* (1948).
Beaufre, A., *1940: the Fall of France* (1967).
Benoist-Méchin, J., *Sixty Days that Shook the West* (1963).
Bloch, Marc, *Strange Defeat* (1968).
Bond, Brian, *France and Belgium 1939–1940* (1975).
Bond, Brian, ed., *Chief of Staff: the Diaries of Lt. Gen. Sir Henry Pownall, Vol. I* (1973).
Cairns, John C., 'Great Britain and the Fall of France – a Study in Allied Disunity', *Journal of Modern History* (December 1955).
Chapman, Guy, *Why France Collapsed* (1968).
Ellis, L. F., *The War in France and Flanders 1939–1940* (1953).
Goutard, A., *The Battle of France, 1940* (1958).
Guderian, H., *Panzer Leader* (1952).
Horne, A., *To Lose a Battle: France 1940* (1969).
Liddell Hart, B. H., *The German Generals Talk* (1948).
Liddell Hart, B. H., *History of the Second World War* (1970).
Liddell Hart, B. H., ed., *The Rommel Papers* (1953).
Manstein, E. von, *Lost Victories* (1958).
Reynaud, P., *In the Thick of the Fight* (1955).
Shirer, W. L., *The Collapse of the Third Republic* (1970).
Spears, Sir Edward, *Assignment to Catastrophe* (1954).
Stolfi, R. H. S., 'Equipment for Victory in France in 1940', *History* (February 1970).
Taylor, Telford, *The March of Conquest* (1959).
Weygand, M., *Recalled to Service* (1952).

Chapter Nine

BATTLE OF BRITAIN

Christopher Dowling

ON 30 JUNE 1940 Major-General Alfred Jodl, Hitler's closest military adviser, expressed the view that the final German victory over England was 'only a matter of time'. He had good reason to be confident. Thanks to a run of victories unparalleled since the days of Napoleon, Germany was master of Western Europe from the Arctic to the Bay of Biscay. The much-vaunted French army had been destroyed in a campaign lasting barely six weeks. The British, who had sent a token force to France and Belgium, had been bundled off the Continent. Although the greater part of the British Expeditionary Force had managed to escape, it had been compelled to abandon almost all its heavy equipment and, for the time being, was incapable of offensive action. With the fall of France Britain lost her only ally in Europe. Despite Churchill's defiant speeches, many, including President Roosevelt and his advisers, doubted whether Britain would be able to resist the expected German onslaught.

Paradoxically, the very magnitude of their triumph over France had created intractable strategic problems for the German High Command. No plans had been made for a direct attack on England because the possibility that the Wehrmacht would inflict a decisive defeat on the French army had scarcely been contemplated. At most, Hitler had hoped to occupy bases in the Low Countries and northern France from which a naval and air blockade could be mounted against the British Isles. On 21 May, after the German armour had reached the Channel coast, Hitler briefly discussed the idea of invading England with the commander-in-chief of the navy, Admiral Raeder, but he was too preoccupied with the Battle of France (which was far from over) and then with the armistice negotiations to give much thought to the matter. In any case he was convinced that the British, for whom he had a grudging respect, would recognize the hopelessness of their position and sue for peace. He was anxious to bring the war to a speedy conclusion so that he could fulfil the mission which had always been the ultimate aim of his policy: the carving out of a great land empire in the East.

Hitler's hopes of a settlement with Britain were not finally dispelled until the third week of July, when Churchill contemptuously rejected his ill-conceived 'peace offer'. In the meantime he and his advisers had begun, in a somewhat leisurely manner, to consider possible courses of action should the British refuse to see reason. Britain, with her insular position, her powerful navy and her rapidly expanding air force, was an awkward opponent for the Wehrmacht, which, as the relative size and strength of the three armed services demonstrated, had been designed for Continental warfare. Germany's naval weakness and her lack of long-range aircraft ruled out a strategy of blockade – even if the necessary forces had been available this was bound to be a lengthy process. An invasion seemed the quickest and surest method of bringing Britain to her knees. However, in view of the Royal Navy's overwhelming superiority in surface ships, it was clear that troops could only be landed after air supremacy had been achieved and that even then the

Scramble! Pilots of No. 601 (County of London) Squadron rush to their waiting Hurricane aircraft

operation would be fraught with risk. Unlike some of his generals, Hitler did not regard the voyage across the Channel as merely 'an extended river crossing'. As Raeder was at pains to point out, the navy, which had been decimated in the Norwegian campaign, could provide little or no protection for the invasion fleet. Hitler lent a sympathetic ear to Raeder's arguments and it was agreed that invasion should be a 'last resort', to be launched only when the British had been softened up by air bombardment. If, as its commander-in-chief Hermann Goering boasted, the Luftwaffe was capable of knocking Britain out single-handed, the government might capitulate before the first assault troops crossed the Channel.

On 16 July Hitler announced in a directive that he had decided 'to begin to prepare for, and if necessary to carry out, an invasion of England'. The operation was to be given the codename Sea Lion and preparations were to be completed by the middle of August. The planning for Sea Lion was not marked by the inter-service cooperation and consultation which characterized Operation Overlord, the Allied invasion of north-west Europe in 1944. Goering set little store by Sea Lion and did not attend a single planning session, yet the other two services were relying on the Luftwaffe to establish the conditions for the landing. Disputes between the army and navy over the number of divisions which could be put ashore and the width of the landing front led on 1 August to the postponement of Sea Lion until the middle of September. On the same day Hitler, who was becoming impatient at Goering's dilatoriness, ordered the Luftwaffe to begin intensified warfare against England on or after 5 August. The Royal Air Force was to be overcome as quickly as possible, after which attacks were to be directed against ports; those on the south coast which might be needed for Sea Lion were, however, to be spared. Goering issued his tactical instructions for the air offensive, which he christened Eagle, on 2 August. He had so poor an opinion of the R.A.F. that he allowed only four days for its elimination south of a line from Gloucester to London and four weeks for its total annihilation.

For the coming assault the Luftwaffe could muster some 2,500 serviceable aircraft, of which nearly 1,000 were He 111, Do 17 and Ju 88 medium bombers. In addition there were some 260 Ju 87 dive-bombers – the dreaded Stuka, which, with its menacing silhouette and blood-curdling scream, had come to symbolize the *Blitzkrieg*. The fighters comprised about 800 single-engined Me 109s and 220 twin-engined Me 110s. These aircraft were deployed in three *Luftflotten* (air fleets). *Luftflotte* 2, which was based in Holland, Belgium and northern France, was under the command of Field-Marshal Albert Kesselring, a former artillery officer who had transferred to the Luftwaffe in 1933. His genial manner had earned him the nickname 'Smiling Albert'. Further west lay *Luftflotte* 3 under Field-Marshal Hugo Sperrle, who had commanded the Condor Legion during the Spanish Civil War. It was intended that the 150 or so bombers of *Luftflotte* 5, under General Hans-Juergen Stumpff, should create a diversion by attacking targets in north-east England from their bases in Norway and Denmark. Of the three *Luftflotten* commanders, Sperrle was the only one who had flown in the First World War.

Although the Luftwaffe had officially been in existence for little more than five years it had already acquired a legendary reputation. It had played a spectacular and decisive part in the Polish, Norwegian and French campaigns; in the euphoria of victory the check it had suffered at the hands of the R.A.F. over Dunkirk in May 1940 was soon forgotten and its significance was overlooked. Yet, formidable though it was, the Luftwaffe was in many respects ill equipped for the task which it had been given and which its leaders had embraced so readily. It had been designed not for independent strategic bombing but rather for the tactical support of the army in the field, a role which it had performed with brilliant success. Its organization, the training of its crews and the weapons with which they were provided reflected this purpose. The Luftwaffe lacked the essential instrument for an effective air offensive, a long-range heavy bomber. The medium and dive-bombers which formed its striking force did not have the necessary range, armament or bomb-carrying capacity for strategic operations and were vulnerable to the latest fighters, the dive-bombers particularly so. Had the ambitions of the first chief of the Luftwaffe General Staff, the gifted and far-sighted General Walther Wever, been realized, Germany might by the summer of 1940 have possessed a fleet of heavy bombers capable of reaching every target in the United Kingdom. As early as 1936 – the year in which the British Air Staff first issued the specification for a four-engined bomber – prototypes of the Do 19 and Ju 89 were ready for testing. However, after Wever's death in an air crash both models were scrapped and the heavy bomber programme was given a low priority.

The Luftwaffe was also severely handicapped by the limited endurance (about eighty minutes) of its standard fighter, the Me 109, which in other respects was an outstanding aircraft. The return journey across the Channel took approximately an hour; this left only twenty minutes for combat over England. The longer-ranged Me 110, on which extravagant hopes had been placed, proved incapable of holding its own against the R.A.F.'s Hurricanes and Spitfires and had itself to be protected by the faster and more nimble Me 109. As the German bombers were too vulnerable to fly without escort in daylight, their operational zone was necessarily restricted to the Me 109's radius of action – that is to London and the south-east corner of England, where the British defences were concentrated. Moreover, owing to the comparative neglect of the fighter arm before the war, there were not enough Me 109s to provide adequate cover for the bombers, each of which needed an escort of at least two fighters. This, in effect, reduced the number of bombers that could be launched against Britain at any one time to a mere three or four hundred.

The Luftwaffe High Command was only vaguely aware of these deficiencies. Goering, who was more of a politician than an airman, greatly overestimated the strength of what he fondly regarded as 'his' Luftwaffe. He had been a dashing fighter pilot during the First World War, but he had resigned his commission in 1922 and since then had lost touch with the development of military aviation. Hitler took little interest in air warfare and was content to leave the management of the Luftwaffe entirely to his faithful party henchman. Though he was not without ability, Goering had neither the technical knowledge nor the professional experience to command a modern air force. He lacked the capacity for sustained work and concerned himself only spasmodically with Luftwaffe affairs, preferring to lead a life of self-indulgent ease on his country estate at Karinhall. His chief of staff, the youthful Hans Jeschonnek, was an ardent Nazi and was not disposed to challenge his overbearing superior. In any case, he, like the two field commanders Kesselring and Sperrle, shared many of Goering's illusions about the Luftwaffe's potential.

While the Battle of Britain was, from the Luftwaffe's point of view, an improvised operation hastily mounted with the resources to hand, the R.A.F. had been preparing for it over a period of more than four years. By the summer of 1940 a sophisticated system of air defence had been evolved under the direction of the commander-in-chief of Fighter Command, Air Chief Marshal Sir Hugh Dowding. The cornerstone of this system was the chain of fifty-two radar (originally called R.D.F. or radio direction-finding) stations which lined the coast from Pembrokeshire to the Shetlands. In the early 1930s the problem of intercepting enemy bombers before they reached their targets had seemed insoluble, since the defending fighters had to be alerted when the raiders were still well out to sea. In 1935, however, Robert Watson Watt demonstrated that radio waves might be used to detect and locate approaching aircraft. His ideas were taken up by another distinguished scientist, Sir Henry Tizard, who harnessed the new device of radar to operational requirements. Although the radar screen was not quite complete when the Battle of Britain began, it was able to provide accurate information on the distance and bearing of hostile aircraft at ranges of seventy miles or more and to give a rough indication of their height and numbers. Once the aircraft had crossed the coast their movements were tracked by the keen-eyed volunteers of the Observer Corps, whose methods Churchill rather tactlessly described as 'early Stone Age'. The Germans were aware of the existence of the radar stations – their towering masts made them an obvious landmark – but they underestimated their efficiency and did not realize how closely they had been integrated into the British defence system. Radar enabled the British fighters to be in the right place at the right time and obviated the need for standing patrols. Without its magic eye Fighter Command would have been at a hopeless disadvantage.

Information from the radar stations and Observer Corps posts was passed by means of an elaborate network of communications to the four groups into which Fighter Command was divided. The most important of these was No. 11 Group, which was responsible for the key area of London and the south-east of England. Its commander was Air Vice-Marshal Keith Park, a New Zealander, who, though very different in personality from Dowding, saw eye to eye with him on the handling of the fighter force. No. 12 Group, under Air Vice-Marshal Trafford Leigh-Mallory (brother of the famous mountaineer George Mallory), covered the Midlands; No. 13 Group, under Air Vice-Marshal R. E. Saul, Scotland and the north of England; and No. 10 Group, under Air Vice-Marshal Sir Quinton Brand, the south-west. Each group comprised a number of sectors. There were seven sector stations in No. 11 Group: Tangmere, Northolt, North Weald, Debden, Hornchurch, Biggin Hill and Kenley. The sector commander ordered aircraft into the air in accordance with the orders he received from group headquarters and directed their movements from the ground by the then advanced method of radio telephone. Although Fighter Command Headquarters at Bentley Priory near Stanmore had a general view of the situation as it developed from minute to minute, the actual conduct of the battle was left to the various groups and sectors. In addition to the radar stations, Observer Corps centres and fighter squadrons, Dowding had at his disposal the 1,500 barrage balloons of Balloon Command, and the 1,300 heavy and 700 light guns of Anti-Aircraft Command.

At the beginning of August the R.A.F. had a front-line strength of 1,200 aircraft, nearly 700 of which were fighters. (The 500 or so bombers were not directly involved in the battle.) All but a handful of the fifty-five fighter squadrons were equipped with Hurricanes or Spitfires, whose eight wing-mounted Browning machine guns were capable of destroying a bomber in a two-second burst of fire. The Hurricane has been overshadowed in the popular imagination by the more glamorous Spitfire, and it is not always recognized that it formed the backbone of the fighter defences. It was a steady, robust and highly manoeuvrable aircraft but it was inferior in performance to the Me 109. There was little to choose between the Me 109 and the Spitfire, though the system of direct fuel injection which enabled the German machine to go into a steep dive without any loss of power perhaps tipped the scales in its favour. In terms of the number and quality of their single-engined fighters and the skill and courage of the men who flew them the two sides were evenly matched. The British, however, had the greater reserves and, thanks to the forceful methods of Lord Beaverbrook, the Minister of Aircraft Production, were producing more than twice as many aircraft as the Germans. Between June and September 1940 deliveries of Me 109s averaged only 190 a month, compared with 470 Hurricanes and Spitfires.

The position as far as pilots were concerned was less encouraging. Nearly 300 fighter pilots had been lost during the Battle of France (a third of the total complement), and at the beginning of August Fighter Command was still 154 pilots below establishment, despite the welcome addition to its ranks of trained recruits from France, Belgium, Czechoslovakia, Poland, the United States and the Dominions. On the other hand the British enjoyed the advantage of fighting over their own territory: R.A.F. pilots who baled out or crash-landed could be in action again within a few hours, whereas their opponents were marched off to prisoner-of-war camps. Similarly, many of the British aircraft that were shot down could be salvaged.

Fighter Command was fortunate in being led by men of unrivalled professional ability and experience. Dowding, who but for the outbreak of the war would have been retired in 1939, was a career officer with a keen interest in the application of science to modern warfare. Just as the Grand Fleet of the First World War was moulded by Lord Fisher, so Fighter Command was largely Dowding's creation. Austere, reserved and dedicated, he presented a complete contrast to the flamboyant and vainglorious Goering. By his tenacious opposition to the War Cabinet's proposal to send additional fighter squadrons to France after the German breakthrough in May 1940, Dowding ensured that he had sufficient forces with which to fight the Battle of Britain. Unlike their German counterparts, many of whom had army backgrounds, Dowding and his senior officers had behind them a quarter of a century of continuous service in military aviation.

The Battle of Britain, like the Battle of the Atlantic and the Battle of France, was, strictly speaking, a campaign rather than a battle. In fact it was a campaign within a campaign, for it formed part of a major German air offensive against Britain which lasted from June 1940, when the first bombs fell on British soil, to May 1941, when the bulk of the Luftwaffe was transferred to the Eastern Front in preparation for the attack on Russia. Although there is no agreement about its exact time span, the Battle of Britain consisted in essence of a series of daylight engagements fought in the skies above south-east England between 12 August and 30 September 1940. During these critical weeks the Luftwaffe sought to destroy Fighter Command in order to pave the way for a landing or for the unopposed occupation of a country paralysed by bombing. As Fighter Command could only be engaged in daylight the night raids by unescorted bombers, which began to assume a regular pattern after 24 August, cannot properly be regarded as part of the Battle of Britain, except perhaps for those that supplemented the daylight attacks on London during the last three weeks of September. After September the daylight fighting gradually died down and the Battle of Britain merged imperceptibly into the Blitz.

The prelude to the battle was an attempt by Goering early in July to wear down Fighter Command by attacking ports and shipping in the Channel. Neither side was at full strength, for the Luftwaffe had not yet completed its redeployment after the French campaign, and Dowding prudently refused to commit more than a small number of squadrons in conditions which usually favoured the enemy. The *Kanalkampf*, as the Germans called it, continued with mounting intensity until well into August. The results of these preliminary skirmishes were inconclusive. The Germans sank 30,000 tons of shipping and succeeded in establishing air superiority over the Straits of Dover in daylight, but their losses in aircraft were twice those of the British.

The Battle of Britain proper can be said to have begun on 12 August, when the Luftwaffe struck its first real blows at the R.A.F.'s fighter airfields and radar stations. Of the six radar stations attacked, one, Ventnor on the Isle of Wight, was so badly damaged that it was out of action for ten days, though this was skilfully concealed from the Germans. The Luftwaffe, however, failed to follow up the limited success it had achieved. Owing to faulty planning and slipshod staff work the long awaited Eagle Day on 13 August, which was to herald the opening of the main air assault, proved to be a flop. No attempt was made to repeat the attacks on the radar stations, and the aerodromes at Eastchurch, Detling and Andover were heavily bombed in the mistaken belief that they were fighter stations.

On 15 August the Luftwaffe made its greatest effort of the battle, flying no fewer than 1,786 sorties. Every available fighter was thrown in and for the first and last time all three *Luftflotten* were committed. The outcome was a notable victory for Fighter Command, which shot down seventy-five German aircraft at a cost of thirty-four of its own. The weakly escorted bombers of *Luftflotte* 5 came in over the North Sea expecting to encounter little or no opposition. They were set upon by fighters from Nos 12 and 13 Groups when they were still some distance from land and suffered such crippling losses that they took no further part in the battle. There was heavy fighting on 16 and 18 August before a spell of cloudy weather brought the first phase of the struggle to an end.

Although Fighter Command was putting up stiff resistance, Goering, whose wishful thinking was reinforced by wildly inaccurate intelligence estimates, believed that Dowding had only about 300 fighters left – this was less than half the true figure. By concentrating his attacks on Fighter Command's vital airfields in south-east England he hoped to draw the British into an all-out fighter action in which Dowding's remaining squadrons would be wiped out. Hitherto, on Park's instructions, the British fighter pilots had engaged the bombers and avoided combat with the Me 109s. This had driven the Germans to employ their fighters in a close escort role rather than in the offensive sweeps for which they were best suited. In order to provide the strong escorts which Goering demanded for the bombers, almost all the Me 109s in Sperrle's area were transferred to Kesselring. The Ju 87s, which had been severely mauled, were withdrawn. Further attacks on the radar stations were discouraged by Goering, who considered them a poor investment, and after 18 August they were left unmolested.

The second and most crucial phase of the battle opened on 24 August with a devastating raid by *Luftflotte* 2 on No. 11 Group's forward aerodrome at Manston, which was so badly knocked about that it had to be evacuated.

During the next fortnight the Luftwaffe began for the first time to gain the upper hand. The new German tactics of maintaining continuous patrols over the Straits of Dover and of delivering feint attacks across the Channel confused the British defences. Park's fighters found it difficult to get to grips with the German bombers, which were now protected by swarms of Me 109s. The disparity in losses narrowed sharply. From 31 August to 6 September the Luftwaffe lost 225 bombers and fighters, the British 185 fighters. As bombers accounted for about half of the German figure the British losses in fighters were considerably higher. Of even greater concern than the dwindling reserves of aircraft was the wastage of trained pilots: weekly casualties were running at more than ten per cent of Fighter Command's total combat strength and the strain of almost daily action was beginning to tell. The Luftwaffe was also causing serious damage on the ground. At Biggin Hill, which was raided six times in three days, the operations room was wrecked, hangars, workshops and barracks destroyed and nearly seventy station staff killed or wounded. Early in September the Luftwaffe was close to winning some measure of air superiority over Kent and Sussex. This would have forced Park to withdraw his squadrons to airfields north of the Thames, from which an effective defence of south-east England would have been impossible.

But on 7 September Goering relaxed the pressure on Fighter Command's ground organization by switching the main weight of the offensive to London. Shortly after 5 p.m. over 300 bombers escorted by some 600 fighters converged on the capital and dropped a hail of bombs and incendiaries on the East End and the London docks, kindling numerous fires. Fighter Command was taken by surprise and the German bomber losses were comparatively light. The blazing warehouses and oil refineries acted as a beacon for a further 250 bombers, which continued the work of destruction during the night. When dawn rose over the smoke-laden city 306 civilians were dead and 1,337 seriously injured.

There were two reasons for what, in the event, proved a disastrous change of strategy: one military, the other political. The time of decision for Sea Lion was fast approaching. Already, in the first week of September, hundreds of barges and tugs had begun to creep round the North Sea coast to the ports of embarkation in the Channel, yet the Luftwaffe had still not achieved the necessary degree of air superiority to justify launching the invasion. Goering and Kesselring, though not the more realistic Sperrle, were convinced that Fighter Command was on its last legs and that mass daylight raids on a target as important as London would hasten their victory by forcing Dowding to expend his few remaining fighters. The possibility that ruthless bombing of the civilian population might break the British will to resist was an added inducement. The political reason for the assault on London was Hitler's demand that reprisals should be carried out for British raids on Berlin, which had themselves been ordered as reprisals for the accidental bombing of London by the Luftwaffe on the night of 24 August.

Because of unsettled weather and the growing fatigue of its aircrews the Luftwaffe was unable to sustain its daylight offensive against London. In the week that followed the big attack of 7 September there were only three days – 9, 11 and 14 September – when sizeable forces were sent over London, though it was heavily bombed every night. The raid on 9 September was a failure, but two days later the Luftwaffe inflicted greater losses than it incurred, while in the fighting on 14 September honours were even. The opposition was patchy and it seemed to the Germans that the British fighter defences were at last on the point of collapse. Encouraged by Goering's jubilant account of the Luftwaffe's recent achievements, Hitler determined to wait until 17 September before making a final decision about Sea Lion. In the meantime the raids on London were to continue.

The weather on the morning of 15 September was clear and sunny. Sensing that the day would not be devoid of incident, Winston Churchill paid one of his periodic visits to No. 11 Group's headquarters at Uxbridge. As Park accompanied the Prime Minister and his wife down to the operations room, fifty feet below the ground, he remarked: 'I don't know whether anything will happen today. At present all is quiet.' Shortly after 10.30 a.m. radar plots revealed that enemy aircraft were massing over the Pas de Calais, and it soon became apparent that a major attack was imminent. The Germans neglected to carry out their usual feints and Park was able to deploy his forces to the best advantage. When the German bombers crossed the English coast at about 11.30 a.m. they were engaged by successive squadrons of British fighters and harried all the way to London. Although a considerable amount of damage was done few of the bombers succeeded in reaching their targets. After a two-hour interval, which gave the British fighters an opportunity to rearm and refuel, a second and heavier attack was launched. It too was repulsed. One of the features of the day's fighting was the timely intervention of a wing of five squadrons from No. 12 Group, aggressively led by Squadron Leader Douglas Bader. Park, who believed in using his squadrons singly or in pairs rather than in the large formations advocated by Leigh-Mallory and Bader, had, on previous occasions, complained bitterly about the lack of support from No. 12 Group.

As the German bombers straggled back to their bases, many with their wings and fuselages riddled with bullets and with dead or wounded men on board, it became clear that the Luftwaffe had taken a severe beating. The British thought that they had shot down 185 German aircraft, and on the strength of this grossly inflated estimate 15 September has come to be celebrated as Battle of Britain Day. The actual German losses were about fifty – fewer than on 15 and 18 August. Even so, the two actions on 15 September, if not particularly significant from a tactical point of view, were strategically decisive. The German fighters had once again held their own but they had been unable to protect the bombers. There was no disguising the fact that Fighter Command, which had lost only twenty-six aircraft, was still very much in being and that air supremacy was as far away as ever. Furthermore, since 4 September Bomber Command had been mounting nightly attacks on the Channel ports and had sunk or damaged more than a hundred barges and transports. On 17 September Hitler postponed Sea Lion indefinitely. Two days later, after Bomber Command had struck further damaging blows, he ordered the invasion fleet to be dispersed.

The abandonment of Sea Lion (formally cancelled on 12 October) did not, as might have been expected, bring the Battle of Britain to an end, for Hitler was anxious to keep up the threat of a landing and Goering, who was not one to admit defeat, still nourished the hope that his stubborn adversary might yet be vanquished. After 15 September the Luftwaffe turned increasingly to night bombing – a tacit acknowledgement that it had failed to win the daylight battle – but daylight attacks on London and other targets by mass formations of bombers continued for another fortnight. The fighting did not go in the Luftwaffe's favour and at the beginning of October, in order to avoid further bomber losses, Goering resorted to the use of fighter-bombers, which relied on speed and altitude to evade the British defences. These raids were mere pinpricks compared with what had gone before and they served no real strategic purpose. Nevertheless the battle dragged on, its finale being the belated intervention of the Italian air force, which made two gallant but ineffectual raids on 29 October and 11 November. The crew of one of the antiquated Fiat B.R.20 bombers which was shot down over East Anglia presented an incongruous spectacle: they wore steel helmets and were armed with bayonets.

There were many reasons for the Luftwaffe's defeat in the Battle of Britain: Goering's muddled strategy and his boundless capacity for self-delusion; the failure of the Germans to destroy or neutralize the British radar screen; the shortage of Me 109s and their unsuitability as bomber escorts; the high courage and superb morale of Fighter Command's pilots and ground crews, whose belief in ultimate victory never wavered; and, not least, the resolute strategy and skilful tactics pursued by Dowding and Park. Ironically, their conduct of the battle, in particular their reluctance to employ their fighters in big wings, earned official disapproval, and both were removed from their commands before the year was out. Few battles of comparable importance in world history have been won at such a small cost in human life: between 10 July and 31 October 1940 (the official British dates for the Battle of Britain) Fighter Command's casualties were only 449, though these were nonetheless grievous losses. In the course of the battle Fighter Command lost 915 aircraft, the Luftwaffe 1,733. Tactically the fighting was inconclusive, since neither air force was able to do irreparable harm to the other. At the end of the battle Fighter Command's strength in aircraft was greater than it had been at the beginning. The Luftwaffe took longer to recover, largely because of Germany's low rate of aircraft production, but it had made good its losses both in aircraft and in personnel by the spring of 1941, and its operational efficiency was not noticeably impaired. Its leaders, however, failed to take action to remedy the shortcomings which the Battle of Britain had exposed. Little attempt was made, for example, to step up aircraft production, or to expand the woefully inadequate training programme, or to accelerate the development of a four-engined bomber. It is a remarkable fact that the only major new aircraft type introduced into service in Germany between 1939 and 1944 was the Focke-Wulf 190. In so far as the Luftwaffe never again enjoyed the prestige or the relative striking power that it had possessed in June 1940, the Battle of Britain marked the beginning of its decline.

Dowding's victory in the Battle of Britain was no less significant than Nelson's at Trafalgar, with which, indeed, it has sometimes been compared. Yet in many ways Lord Howard of Effingham's victory over the Spanish Armada in 1588 affords a closer parallel. The defeat of the Spanish Armada was the first great naval battle of modern times, the Battle of Britain the first (and almost certainly the last) great air battle. Like the Battle of Britain, the duel between the English fleet and the Armada was not a setpiece encounter but a string of engagements of varying size and intensity. Both were successful defensive battles, though neither decided the issue of the war. Nor was the disparity in strength between the respective fleets and air forces nearly as wide as was thought at the time: the two battles were more akin to the combat between Hector and Achilles than to that between David and Goliath. Like some of the German generals, notably Field-Marshal von Rundstedt, the Duke of Parma, whose troops were to carry out the landings, was indifferent to the invasion project. The antipathy which existed between Drake and Frobisher finds some echo in the clash between Park and Leigh-Mallory over tactics. Just as Howard was criticized for failing to annihilate the Spanish fleet, so it was argued in some quarters that Dowding and Park could have inflicted greater losses on the Luftwaffe by adopting a more aggressive policy. There, however, the parallel ends, for whereas the defeat of the Armada led to a revival of Spanish naval power, the defeat of the Luftwaffe, as we have seen, was one of the signposts on the road to its ultimate demise.

The failure of the Luftwaffe to destroy Fighter Command in the summer of 1940 had far-reaching strategic consequences. It was the first setback suffered by the Wehrmacht in the Second World War and it dented the myth of German invincibility in much the same way as Napoleon's repulse at Aspern-Essling in 1809 had shown a demoralized Europe that the all-conquering Grand Army could be mastered. Furthermore, it shattered Hitler's hopes of a swift victory and ensured that the struggle would be a protracted one; Germany, whose economy and armed forces were geared to a *Blitzkrieg* strategy, was ill-equipped to fight this kind of war. Hitler realized that in view of Britain's rapidly growing military strength an invasion in 1941 would not be feasible. Germany was thus forced to seek alternative avenues to victory, which involved her in costly campaigns in the Mediterranean. Although the frustration of the German attempt to conquer Britain had nothing to do with the attack on Russia, planning for which had started several weeks before Eagle Day, operations in the East seemed to offer a solution to the stalemate in the West. Hitler was obliged to embark on the invasion of Russia with an unsubdued enemy in his rear. The threat of British intervention on the Continent pinned down more than thirty-five divisions, thereby reducing the forces available for Operation Barbarossa. Perhaps the last word should be given to von Rundstedt. Shortly after the war he told a group of Russian officers that had the Luftwaffe won the Battle of Britain Germany would have defeated Russia in 1941. The Russians had come to ask him which he considered to be the decisive battle of the war, expecting him to name Stalingrad. When he replied, 'The Battle of Britain', they closed their notebooks and went away.

Note on Sources

The Battle of Britain has generated a considerable literature, much of it of high quality. The outstanding work is perhaps *The Breaking Wave* by Telford Taylor (1967), a brilliant and absorbing study of German strategy in the summer of 1940. Other works which throw light on various aspects of the battle are:

Churchill, Winston, *The Second World War*, Vol. II (1949).
Clarke, Ronald, *The Battle of Britain* (1965).
Collier, Basil, *The Defence of the United Kingdom* (1957).
Collier, Basil, *The Battle of Britain* (1962).
Collier, Richard, *Eagle Day: The Battle of Britain* (1966).
Galland, Adolf, *The First and the Last* (1955).
Johnson, John, *Wing Leader* (1956).
McKee, Alexander, *Strike from the Sky* (1960).
Middleton, Drew, *The Sky Suspended* (1960).
Richards, Denis, *Royal Air Force, 1939–1945*, Vol. I (1953).
Suchenwirth, Richard, *Historical Turning Points in the German Air Force War Effort* (1959).
Wheatley, Ronald, *Operation Sea Lion* (1958).
Wood, Derek, with Derek Dempster, *The Narrow Margin* (1969).
Wright, Robert, *Dowding and the Battle of Britain* (1969).
Wykeham, Peter, *Fighter Command* (1960).

Richard Hillary, who fought in the battle, described his experiences in *The Last Enemy* (1942), one of the few literary masterpieces to have emerged from the Second World War.

Winter, 1941, on the Eastern front. The terrible conditions under which the army had to fight

Chapter Ten

MOSCOW

Harrison E. Salisbury

AT DAWN ON 5 October 1941, a foggy overcast dawn, Major G. P. Karpenko and Major D. M. Gorshkov took off in their Pe 2 fighter from Luberets field just south-west of Moscow. They circled and then headed west, following the Warsaw chaussé, one of Moscow's main highways.

The flight of Karpenko and Gorshkov was a milk run. They made it daily at intervals of two hours. It was a precaution which had been ordered late in September by Lieutenant-General P. A. Artemov, commander of the Moscow Military District, as Hitler's armies began to approach closer and closer to the Soviet capital.

Every two hours fighter planes of the 6th Air Regiment took off from Luberets and flew along each of the main highways approaching Moscow from the west, observing conditions in the front areas 200 to 300 miles from the capital.

Karpenko and Gorshkov flew at a very low altitude, not more than 600 to 800 feet, carefully observing movements on the ground. In a month's fighting at the distant approaches to Moscow the Russians had come to understand that the German armoured and motorized forces inevitably and necessarily followed the main roads.

The weather rapidly improved – 5 October was to turn out a fine autumn day, sunny, dry and warm – and the fliers had no difficulty in making out every detail on the paved road. At first they encountered little movement. They flew over Maloyaroslavets, seventy miles west and slightly south of Moscow. Nothing abnormal. The same at Medyn, thirty miles further west. At Yukhnov, where the Warsaw chaussé crossed the Ugra River, they saw some activity, small military units and refugee carts moving east. This was 130 miles west of Moscow. Karpenko and Gorshkov flew on. Their objective was the Roslavl area 235 miles south-west of Moscow, where the front line had been yesterday and, so far as the aviators were informed, still was.

Just beyond Spas-Demensk, 185 miles west of Moscow, the airmen saw, only a few hundred feet below them, two great columns of tanks and armoured cars, followed by trucks and supply vehicles, moving eastwards. The columns extended for nearly twenty miles along the highway, one column on the pavement itself, the other moving parallel to it. The vehicles were marked with symbols clearly visible to the Soviet airmen: the Nazi swastika.

The Pe 2 swiftly flew over the column, then reversed its flight, drawing some scattered fire, and raced back to Luberets. In the minds of the airmen there could be no doubt about what had happened. The Germans had broken out of the positions around Roslavl and were now advancing nearly sixty-five miles east of where they had last been reported. The head of the column was already approaching the rail junction of Spas-Demensk.

It was ten o'clock before the report of Majors Karpenko and Gorshkov reached Colonel N. A. Sbytov, chief of the Moscow Military District Air

Force. He found it difficult to accept. The Germans only 125 miles from Moscow? And nearly sixty-five miles closer to the capital than previously reported? It was not believable.

Sbytov decided to consult Major-General K. F. Telegin, acting chief of the Moscow Defence District. Telegin's chief, General Artemov, was in Tula organizing the defence of this key city, 125 miles due south of Moscow. Tula had been threatened by the German capture of Orel, another 125 miles to the south-west.

It was the situation at Orel, Tula and Bryansk, sixty-five miles east of Orel, which was in the forefront of Soviet attention. Here Guderian's 2nd Armoured Group had smashed through General Yeremenko's Bryansk Front, exposing the whole south and south-west approach to the capital.

But so far as Sbytov knew, so far as Telegin knew and, as it emerged, so far as the Soviet High Command knew, nothing alarming, nothing of consequence, had occurred along the Warsaw highway, the main western approach to Moscow.

Telegin found himself in a delicate position. The Moscow Defence Command was a rear command. It was charged with the rear echelon defence of Moscow, the preparation of fortifications, the raising of forced labour and civilian military levies, the air defences of the capital and communications and supply functions. It was not the High Command. In fact it had only peripheral access to the High Command. The High Command was headed by Stalin, who was directing the overall defence of Moscow against the German Operation Typhoon, which had started with Guderian's assault on 30 September. On 2 October the main German forces had gone over to the offensive and the whole front – nearly 450 miles from north to south – along a profile that ranged from 200 to 300 miles from Moscow, was ablaze.

The Moscow Defence Command received briefings daily from a High Command representative but had no intelligence capability of its own – except the patrol of the western highways. The briefing which Telegin had received that morning contained no specifically alarming details. In part this was because the High Command had lost all communications with the Western and Reserve Fronts which, with the Bryansk Front, were the chief command sectors on Moscow's approaches. Communications with the Bryansk Front were very shaky, and it was known that Yeremenko was in grave difficulties. (That the commander himself had fallen into encirclement was not known.) The Tula position was being rapidly built up to provide a barrier to further German approaches towards Moscow from the south.

There was one curious fact which was in Telegin's mind that morning. A colleague had obtained a translation of a speech by Hitler the day before, 4 October, in which he spoke of the Germans having begun an operation on a 'gigantic scale'. Hitler declared that the Russians had already been defeated and 'never again would be able to recover their strength'.

Hitler's words did not seem to fit the intelligence reports Telegin had received from the High Command.

Around 10 a.m. General Telegin heard that some carts and trucks of the Forty-third Army, which was defending the Warsaw highway, had been halted by military policemen at Maloyaroslavets, only seventy miles from Moscow and far east of the Forty-third Army's defence zone around Roslavl. The soldiers claimed the Germans had started a huge offensive and that a number of divisions had been encircled.

This seemed impossible to Telegin. High Command data did not place the Germans within 125 miles of Maloyaroslavets. The reports obviously came from panic-mongers and deserters or possibly even from enemy agents. He ordered the Forty-third Army men to be turned over to the security forces. At the same time he suggested that scout cars be sent up the Warsaw highway to see what was happening.

It was against this background that Telegin and Sbytov discussed the report of the two airmen. Both were sceptical, and it was decided to send another patrol out to verify the findings of Karpenko and Gorshkov. Just before noon Telegin's phone rang. It was Sbytov in a state of excitement. Airmen Druzhkov and Serov had just landed at Luberets. They reported that the German armoured columns were well past Spas-Demensk and approaching Yukhnov.

Telegin was astonished and ordered Sbytov to come to his office. Sbytov hurried over. He told Telegin that his men had been fired on by machine guns and anti-aircraft guns and had clearly seen Nazi swastikas on the tanks.

But Telegin was reluctant to alarm the General Staff. First, he decided to find out what was known at G.H.Q. He called the duty officer who told him there was no news of anything unusual on the Western Front. He called Marshal Boris Shaposhnikov, the chief of staff, who agreed that 'all is quiet if you can call war quiet'.

Cautiously Telegin ordered Sbytov to send out another reconnaissance flight. In the meantime, he began drawing up a list of scratch forces he could send down the Warsaw highway: a couple of divisions of security troops, four rifle brigades, a few artillery units, some motor cycle troops, several infantry and artillery cadet schools. This was for use if the Yukhnov report proved correct.

At 2 p.m. Sbytov reported that three fighter planes had returned. They had been subjected to strong anti-aircraft fire. The Germans were now only seven to ten miles short of Yukhnov.

Telegin telephoned Shaposhnikov again. He got such a sharp response that he decided to send out yet another flight before reporting the German threat. At 3 p.m. Sbytov called again. The German column had reached Yukhnov. The fighter planes had again been fired on and some of the Soviet airmen wounded.

Telegin called Shaposhnikov a third time. The marshal was more than irritated but Telegin screwed up his courage and reported the air observations. Shaposhnikov was incredulous. The news contradicted his information. Then three or four minutes later Stalin's sinister secretary, Poskrebyshev, telephoned Telegin. Stalin came on the line. He ran over Telegin's report quickly then ordered him to put together a force capable of holding off the Germans for five to seven days along the so-called Mozhaisk defence line (which the Moscow Defence Command had constructed) fifty to sixty miles west of Moscow.

A few minutes later Telegin had another telephone call. Lavrenti P. Beria, Stalin's security chief, was on the line. He called Telegin's information 'nonsense' and said it came from panic-mongers and provocateurs. Beria asked who had given the information. He was told that it was the regional air commander, Colonel Sbytov.

A little later Telegin tried to locate Sbytov to find out why he was not organizing an air attack on the German armoured column at Yukhnov. Sbytov was nowhere to be found. Two hours later he entered Telegin's office and put his written resignation on the desk. Beria's deputy, Abakumov, had summoned him to his office, browbeaten him for accepting the evidence of 'cowards' and 'rumour-spreaders' and ordered him to resign his command.

Telegin managed to get Sbytov returned to his post and then continued amid more and more alarming reports his frantic efforts to muster troops to halt the Germans. He received a report that the Germans had advanced beyond Maloyaroslavets and were approaching Podolsk almost on the outskirts of Moscow, but this proved false (and brought him a violent reprimand from Stalin). It was only too clear, however, that the Germans had achieved a major tactical surprise and that Soviet defences west of the capital were tottering on the verge of collapse.

It was probably the most menacing moment of the war for the Russians – except for the days that lay immediately ahead.

That evening Marshal Zhukov got a call from Stalin. Zhukov was in Leningrad where in three weeks of incredibly difficult fighting he had brought the German assault to a halt at the very gates of the city. By 5 October the Germans had shifted important forces from Leningrad for the Moscow attack and the Russians themselves had diverted several divisions and many guns from Leningrad to the pivotal Moscow front.

Stalin and Zhukov talked over the Baudet telegraph line. Stalin wanted Zhukov to fly to Moscow. General Headquarters wanted to discuss with him the necessary measures to rectify the situation on the left wing of the Reserve Front in the vicinity of Yukhnov.

Zhukov agreed to fly to Moscow the next morning, but he was delayed a day by an emergency on the Leningrad Front. He took off on 7 October and his plane was met in Moscow by Stalin's personal bodyguard who escorted Zhukov directly to Stalin, who was working in his Blizhny *dacha*, just outside Moscow. He was in bed with the grippe.

The situation had grown even worse. Stalin could get no clear picture whatever of the Western Front. He ordered Zhukov to go to the front and find out what was happening.

It was mid-afternoon before Zhukov left Moscow, armed with a situation map from Marshal Shaposhnikov and bolstered by several glasses of strong tea. Zhukov drove straight west on the Mozhaisk highway, so sleepy that he periodically made his driver halt the car while he ran a few yards to wake himself up. He reached Western Front headquarters in the village of Krasnovidova, west of Mozhaisk and close to the famous Napoleonic battlefield of Borodino fifty-five miles west of Moscow, in the middle of the evening. He found Colonel-General Koniev, the Western Front commander, conferring with his chief of staff General (later Marshal) Vasily D. Sokolovsky, his political commissar Nikolai A. Bulganin (later Khrushchev's premier), and his operations officer, Lieutenant-General G. K. Malandin.

Malandin gave Zhukov a quick briefing. Russian strength on the three western fronts, the Western, the Reserve and the Bryansk, had totalled about 800,000 men, 782 tanks, 6,800 mortars and guns and 545 planes when the German offensive started. Most of the strength was concentrated in the Western Front under Koniev. Against the Russians Hitler had hurled a force which the Russians later estimated at more than 1 million men, grouped in seventy-seven divisions with a superiority of about 1·25 in men, 2·2 in tanks, 2·1 in artillery and 1·7 in planes.

The Germans had captured Orel on 3 October, splitting the Bryansk Front and surrounding large numbers of General Yeremenko's forces. On 6 October, partly because of the Yukhnov breakthrough, they had encircled even larger numbers of the Western and Reserve Front troops in the Vyazma area, less than fifty miles west of Koniev's headquarters. As Zhukov advised Stalin at 2.30 a.m. on the morning of 8 October, Koniev's Sixteenth, Nineteenth and Twentieth Armies and his Boldin attack group, as well as the Twenty-fourth and Thirty-second Armies of Marshal Budenny's Reserve Front, had fallen into encirclement. No one knew where Budenny was to be found. Zhukov set out to locate him.

Zhukov drove through a murky drizzle that produced a heavy fog when the sun rose and finally managed to locate Reserve Army headquarters at Obninskoye, about sixty-five miles west of Moscow. It had been moved there only two hours earlier. But Budenny was not at headquarters. He had last been seen with the shattered Forty-third Army the day before. Zhukov decided to drive on to Yukhnov, which seemed to be the critical spot. It was a region he knew very well. He had been born and raised in the village of Strelkovka only six miles from Obninskoye. Zhukov made his way south to the Warsaw highway and drove into Maloyaroslavets, thirty-five miles south of Mozhaisk. There he had the good luck to run into Budenny, who had no idea where his headquarters had moved. He had narrowly escaped capture with the Forty-third Army and thought the Germans now held Yukhnov. (He was wrong about this. Some Russians were still defending the Ugra River line.) So far as the Warsaw chaussé was concerned, Budenny said it was wide open to the Germans. The only Russian force he had encountered consisted of three policemen still on duty at Medyn, thirty miles to the west.

Zhukov ordered Budenny to get to Western Front headquarters as quickly as possible in order to take steps to guard the Warsaw highway. Then he started for Kaluga, twenty-five miles to the south. The next day a messenger caught up with him and told him to get back to Western Front H.Q. There Stalin was waiting on the telephone to name Zhukov commander of the combined western fronts with the responsibility of halting the Germans and preventing the fall of the Russian capital.

It could hardly have been clear to Zhukov on the morning of 10 October, when he was entrusted by Stalin with the defence of Moscow, precisely how he was going to accomplish his task. The German offensive had been extraordinarily successful. By mid-October the Germans would have nearly 600,000 prisoners in their hands, the cream of Koniev's forces and most of Yeremenko's. They were rapidly closing towards the Mozhaisk defence line, the last one before the outskirts of Moscow proper. They were threatening to envelop the capital from the north in the direction of Kalinin, which was taken on 14 October, and from the south from the unstable salient east of Tula. Hitler was confident that Moscow was within his grasp and Goebbels proclaimed to the Berlin correspondents that 'the annihilation of Timoshenko's Army group has definitely brought the war to a close'. Goebbels did not know that Timoshenko had been replaced by Koniev in mid-September and that Zhukov had just taken Koniev's place.

Zhukov's plan for the defence of Moscow was to try to hold the basic line Volokolamsk–Mozhaisk–Maloyaroslavets–Kaluga. The Kalinin sector was detached and given to Koniev. The remnants of the shattered Western, Reserve and Bryansk Fronts were pulled back into these prepared positions. Four broken armies were reformed and assigned: the Sixteenth under Rokossovsky to the Volokolamsk sector, the Fifth under Major-General D. D. Lelyshenko (and after he was wounded under L. A. Govorov) to Mozhaisk, the Forty-third under Major-General K. D. Golubev to the Maloyaroslavets sector, and the Forty-ninth under Lieutenant-General I. G. Zakharin to Kaluga.

Zhukov made one harsh decision. He would spare no force to try to relieve the huge number of encircled Soviet troops. If they were to escape it must be through their own efforts. Few succeeded, but the task of coping with the enormous pockets containing up to 200,000 troops radically slowed the German advance. So did the convergence closer to Moscow which limited German room for manoeuvre and road use. And the weather began to deteriorate. The first scattered snow was reported on 9 October. By 13 October heavy rains turning to sleet in many places turned the battlefields into mud. The paved highways like the Warsaw and Mozhaisk chaussés broke down under the heavy impact of the German armour.

But the German momentum was too great to be brought to an immediate halt. On 13 October Kaluga, eighty-five miles south of Moscow, fell, and the next day Kalinin, seventy-five miles north of the city, had to be abandoned. If these two spearheads could be pushed a bit further east the danger of encirclement of Moscow would prove as real as it had been in Leningrad just a month earlier.

Moscow seethed and bubbled with rumour and panic.

On 13 October all the Party leaders of the city were assembled by Moscow Party leader Aleksandr S. Shcherbakov, who warned them that the city was in the gravest danger. On the night of the 14th, probably after receiving news of the fall of Kalinin, Stalin decided to evacuate the government. Early in the morning of the 15th the word went out. Telegin was told by Shcherbakov that all the important defence organs, the basic components of the Party and government institutions and much of the local Moscow organization were to be evacuated. However, 'most of' the Politburo, the State Defence Council, the High Command and the General Staff would remain. All the ministries except for small liaison groups were to leave the capital.

The foreign diplomatic corps was advised that it was being evacuated to Kuibyshev. The Foreign Commissariat was going there as well. Marshal I. T. Peresypkin, Chief of Military Communications, was called to the Kremlin on the 15th. He had just finished setting up firm communications with the Western Front, whose headquarters were now only eleven miles west at Perkhushkovo almost at the city gates. At the Kremlin Peresypkin ran into a group of Party secretaries who had been called in by Stalin for a Party Central Committee meeting early in October. (The meeting was never held, probably because of the military crisis.) Peresypkin proposed to Stalin that new High Command headquarters be established at Kuibyshev because of excellent communications to that point on the Volga. Stalin turned that down, saying there would be too many foreigners there. Peresypkin then proposed Kazan, also on the Volga. Stalin turned that down and suggested a third city, the name of which Soviet censors have never revealed. Probably it was Gorky. The General Staff headed by Marshal Boris Shaposhnikov left on the 17th, the main staff going to the new headquarters and a small group headed by Marshal A. M. Vasilevsky remaining in Moscow.

In Moscow confusion was at its height. Railroad stations were besieged. Rumours circulated that the Jews were fleeing the city. The rumours may have been started by Nazi agents and leaflets, but they were energetically spread by the ordinary citizenry and, it was said, by the Party hierarchy. Ministries including the state security institutions were burning their records. The chimneys of the Lubyanka poured forth smoke and ashes (including half-consumed files and dossiers) day and night. Roads to the east of the city were jammed with fleeing citizens and evacuating ministries. The crowds on the Chaussé Entusiastov, the main highway east of Moscow leading to Gorky, grew so great that ten- and twenty-mile traffic jams ensued. Military police cleared the highway with great difficulty. Cars and trucks were simply tumbled off the sides of the road. Some persons evacuating without official papers were shot on the spot. But movement of traffic was delayed almost eighteen hours. Train after train roared out of Moscow carrying whole factories to the east. More than a hundred trains were despatched from Moscow in the twenty-four hours from the morning of 17 October to the morning of 18 October. On 16 October every official institution in Moscow was ordered to leave the capital. Small duty groups of six or seven officials were to remain at their posts.

What about Stalin himself – did he leave the capital? Official accounts insist that he did not. Rumour persists that he did – at least for a few days. He sent his two children, Vasily and Svetlana, to Kuibyshev. Admiral Nikolai Kuznetsov, Navy Commissar in that period, recalls that Stalin's Kremlin office was stripped of most of its furnishings. Even the pictures came down from the walls. The huge heaps of documents that usually covered his desk vanished. All that remained were Marshal Shaposhnikov's situation maps. Stalin was still in Moscow on the evening of 15–16 October when he visited the wounded General Yeremenko at the hospital in Serebryansky Pereulok near the Arbat in the heart of Moscow. V. P. Pronin speaks of visiting the 'dark and empty' Kremlin on the evening of 19 October. Certainly if Stalin did not leave his capital briefly every arrangement was made for him and his government to do so.

In any event, on the evening of 19 October Stalin in a sour and bitter mood met with the Politburo and the State Defence Council to determine whether to continue the defence of the capital or abandon it. In fact, the decision had already been taken to defend Moscow to the last. But the question was raised, nonetheless, pro forma. Not surprisingly all those present voted to continue the defence of Moscow. Georgy Malenkov, Stalin's Politburo protégé, was then instructed to draft a decree declaring Moscow in a state of siege. Malenkov took so long about it that Stalin finally took the paper away from him, gave it to Shcherbakov and dictated his own proclamation, which was posted on the city walls in the early morning of 20 October. More important, perhaps, than the proclamation of a state of siege was Stalin's approval, probably given before the Kremlin meeting, of a new withdrawal by Zhukov, to an inner defence line which at some points was only a few miles from Moscow. It ran from Novo-Zavidovsky through Klin, the Istra reservoir, the town of Istra, Zhavoronky, Krasynaya Pakhra, and Serpukhov to Aleksin. It was to be a fighting withdrawal, supported by air elements, and only in response to irresistible enemy pressure.

Zhukov's strategy and Stalin's gamble worked. By the end of October the Moscow front had become relatively stabilized. The ancient Russian gunmakers' city of Tula had held out against all assaults as an anchor of the southern approaches to Moscow. The line still ran from Turginovo, Volokolamsk, Dorokhovo, Naro-Fominsk and points west of Serpukhov and Aleksin. Even the very difficult situation north of Moscow around Kalinin and Klin seemed to have eased a little.

On 1 November Zhukov was called in by Stalin to the Kremlin – the first meeting, if his memoirs are to be credited, which he had had with the Soviet leader since assuming command of the Western Front. Indeed, his memoirs provide no accounts of interchange with Stalin during this period, although the two men must have been in very frequent communication.

Stalin wanted to hold the traditional 7 November parade in Red Square, and wanted to know if Zhukov could guarantee the front was stable enough for this? Zhukov correctly reported that the Germans were in no position for a major offensive in the next few days. In fact, the commander of the German Army Group Centre, Field-Marshal von Bock, had ordered a two weeks' pause while new guns, ammunition and supplies were brought up. Gasoline for trucks and tanks was in very short supply and Guderian's Second Panzer Army was on such short rations that only an improvised panzer brigade could be employed in an ineffective blow at Tula.

The 7 November parade was held in a light fall of snow. Marshal Budenny took the salute on Lenin's tomb. Many units marched right out of the square to the front. The night before, 6 November, Stalin delivered the traditional pre-November address at a Party meeting conducted in the Mayakovsky station of the Moscow subway.

But Moscow's peril was far from over. Zhukov knew that a new German assault was imminent. He had managed to pry another 100,000 men, 300 tanks and 2,000 guns (some of them flown from besieged Leningrad) out of Stalin – but that was all.

On 7 November Hitler decided to continue his attack on Moscow. Regardless of the fate of the city proper, he hoped to break into the Moscow–Vologda–Saratov triangle, thus destroying Russian communications with Siberia and southwards. If the triangle could be smashed any hope of Allied aid to Russia via Iran would be lost. On 13 November the German chief of staff, General Halder, convened a meeting at Orsha at which he outlined the long-range objectives of the new offensive which was to get under way on 15 November. He talked of advancing as far east as Gorky, 200 miles east of Moscow. None of the German commanders appear to have expressed any real opposition to these plans, though Guderian was getting somewhat nervous. He had heard that Siberian divisions were forming up in the area of Ryazan and Kolomna on his south-east flank.

Stalin's mood at this time is a subject of controversy. Zhukov complains of being compelled by Stalin to undertake an unsuccessful counter-attack by

Rokossovsky's Sixteenth and Zakharin's Forty-ninth Armies in the Volokolamsk area. He also tells a ridiculous story of Stalin insisting that Zhukov, Rokossovsky and General Govorov personally investigate the state of affairs at a tiny village called Dedovo which Stalin had confused with the strategic town of Dedovsk. However, General Belov, who participated in the unsuccessful counter-attack, had a different impression. He went with Zhukov to the Kremlin on 11 November where he saw Stalin. He thought the Soviet leader had aged twenty years and that Zhukov addressed Stalin in a self-confident manner while Stalin appeared uncertain and even bewildered. Belov testified that Zhukov submitted the plan for the counter-offensive and that Stalin accepted it with one minor change.

The new German offensive produced almost immediate results: a break-through at Klin against the Soviet Thirtieth Army and a retreat by Rokossovsky's Sixteenth Army towards the Istra reservoir and river. Rokossovsky's withdrawal produced a fearsome row involving Zhukov, Shaposhnikov, Stalin and Rokossovsky (who had wanted to withdraw more speedily), but with impressive leadership Rokossovsky managed to minimize his losses. On the southern Moscow flank trouble quickly developed around Tula. Tula did not fall but Guderian bypassed it and drove on to Kashira. Here his attack bogged down. He went over to the defensive on 5 and 6 December, noting in his journal, 'The offensive on Moscow has failed. All the sacrifices and efforts of our brilliant troops have failed. We have suffered a serious defeat.'

About 19 November Stalin telephoned Zhukov and asked for reassurance. Could Zhukov hold Moscow? Zhukov assured Stalin that Moscow would be held but insisted that he must have two more armies and 200 tanks. Stalin agreed to give him two armies, the First Shock Army under V. I. Kuznetsov and the Tenth under General F. I. Golikov. These were two armies of a very substantial force which Stalin was rapidly building up east of Moscow for use against a German breakthrough or, more hopefully, for a counter-offensive the moment the Germans were compelled to pause.

For a few days the Germans continued to progress, but north of Moscow the First Shock Army quickly showed its metal, as did the Tenth around Ryazan. Control of these armies passed into Zhukov's hands on 29 November, together with control of the new Twentieth Army led by General Vlasov, who six months later was to go over to the German side. Zhukov asked Stalin for permission to launch a general counter-offensive – permission being given almost immediately. Koniev's Kalinin Front and the South-west Front were ordered to open up offensive operations in order to pin down German forces.

The German attack had come to a halt in the first days of December. On 3 December Kluge, soon to replace Bock, ordered some of his forces to withdraw. On 4 December the Germans fell back to the Nara River, fearing encirclement. On 6 December Hitler was still talking of holding the ground before Moscow. This was the day on which Zhukov formally launched his counter-offensive, and by 8 December Hitler had abandoned his offensive, blaming the severe winter weather.

What was happening, however, was not a weather blitz. It was a fast-moving Soviet offensive which for the first time since Hitler had begun his career was compelling the Wehrmacht to reel back.

Exactly how many troops Stalin had held back for use in the counter-offensive is not known. There have been reports that it was as many as forty divisions. The bulk of the troops came from the Far Eastern Red Banner armies which for decades had been deployed against the Japanese in eastern Siberia and Mongolia. With the aid of these fresh, highly trained and well equipped troops the Russians made rapid progress. Guderian was badly over-expended and suffered a serious setback. He was compelled to pull back nearly 100 miles in ten days. Kaluga was regained. Klin was recaptured on 15 December. Soviet lines were pushed forward to the Istra reservoir and beyond. The Leningrad front went into action and recaptured Tikhvin, a key railroad junction without which it would have been difficult or impossible to supply Leningrad via Lake Ladoga. Rostov at the gates to the Caucasus was regained.

The first phase of the counter-offensive ended on about 18 December along the line Oreshky–Staritsa–the Lama and Ruza Rivers–Maloyaroslavets–Tikhonova–Pustyn–Kaluga–Mosalsk – Sukhinichy – Belev – Mtsensk–Novosil. The most limited gains had been made in the centre of the front where the Germans were still poised only forty miles from the Moscow city limits on the Mozhaisk chaussé.

Nonetheless, three things had occurred: the critical danger to Moscow had been lifted; the myth of German invincibility had been broken: for the first time under Hitler the German forces had been compelled to retreat; and Russian confidence in their ability to turn the tide of war had been born. In fact, Stalin himself became over-confident. Now he seemed to think that he might cripple the Wehrmacht so badly during the winter that spring and summer would bring him victory. It was an idle dream. Worse, it set the stage for new Russian defeats.

On the German side Bock resigned and was replaced by Kluge, commander of the Fourth Army, and Hitler assumed general command, relieving Brauchitsch.

But first, for the Russians, there was the question of continuing the Moscow counter-offensive. There was a virtual halt in operations for about three weeks while new forces were brought up and the Soviet troops were given a little breathing space. Then, on 5 January 1942, Stalin convened a meeting at the Kremlin to decide on the next phase. As usual, Zhukov found that Stalin had already decided what he wanted to do – and it did not accord with Zhukov's own opinion. Zhukov favoured a concentrated blow by the Western Front, delivered after a build-up of all available arms and reserves. He felt this would damage the Germans badly and compel a deep withdrawal before Moscow. Stalin was more ambitious. He proposed simultaneous winter offensives at Leningrad, at Moscow and in the south. The Leningrad assault would break the blockade of Leningrad; the southern offensive would recapture the Donets basin and the Crimea; the central offensive would carry out a vast double envelopment and destroy the main German forces in the area of Rzhev, Vyazma and Smolensk.

Stalin's ideas had the support of his police chief, Beria, and his protégé, Malenkov. Marshal Shaposhnikov, chief of staff, told Zhukov that orders for the attacks had gone out before the meeting was summoned. Zhukov wondered why, in that case, his opinion had been sought, but Shaposhnikov could not enlighten him.

Orders were orders, and Zhukov put his forces into motion. He managed to regain Mozhaisk, Ruza, Dorokhovo and Vereya by 20 January. The North-west and Kalinin Fronts made some gains and developed a threat to Vyazma, as did Zhukov, but when an effort to envelop Vyazma was put in train the Germans reacted sharply and managed to cut off and surround a substantial Russian force: General Belov's cavalry corps, two reinforced divisions of the Thirty-third Army and part of the IV Airborne Corps. The Thirty-third Army units were under the personal command of General M. G. Yefremov. The group was large and held an extensive battle zone which the Russians were able to supply by air, and the wounded were evacuated in the same way. But it proved impossible to continue the Vyazma offensive, and by the following May and June Belov and remnants of his cavalry had fought their way out but Yefremov and most of his force had been lost.

The net gains of the second phase of the counter-offensive were small in comparison with the price paid in destruction of divisions and material. The same was true of the efforts to break out of Leningrad and re-establish the positions in the south. The winter operations, most Russian military men concluded, were a failure and weakened the Red Army for the forthcoming trials of summer and autumn: Kharkov and Stalingrad.

But this could not take away the basic achievement at Moscow. The most deadly assault of the German opponent had been halted; the Germans had been defeated, pushed back; they had suffered serious losses. Never again would they come so close to Moscow. Hitler had failed in his effort to emulate Napoleon. And in the darkest days of Stalingrad the Soviet commanders, the Red Army troops and the Russian people were comforted by the conviction born at Moscow – that Hitler and his armies *could* be beaten.

Note on Sources

Bitva Za Moskvy (collective work) (1968).
Kondratyev, Z. I., *Dorogy Voiny* (1968).
Lelyshenko, D. D., *Moskva–Stalingrad–Berlin–Praga* (1973).
Na Strazhe Neba Stolitsay (collective work) (1969).
Perespykin, I. T., and A. V. Boyn, *Yeshche Vazhnei* (1970).
Samsonov, A. M., *Velikaya Bitva pod Moskovoi* (1958).
Sokolovsky, V. D., ed., *Razgrom Nemitsko-fashchistkiki Voisk Pod Moskvoi* (1964).
Telegin, K. F., article, *Vopros Istory*, December 1971.
Zhilin, P. A., ed., *Bezprimerny Podvig* (1968).
Zhukov, G. Z., *Vospominaniya i Razmyshleniya* (1969).

Pearl Harbor, 1941. A Japanese torpedo plane peels off after a direct hit on the U.S. battleship Oklahoma

Chapter Eleven

PEARL HARBOR

Alvin D. Coox

THE DISTINCTION between deterrence and incitement is fine. In May 1940, by directing that the Pacific Fleet be based at 'impregnable' Pearl Harbor and no longer on the U.S. west coast, President Franklin D. Roosevelt unwittingly sealed the doom of America's battleship force, pride of the navy. Long-range historical consequences were to prove even more decisive.

The key to Japanese naval thinking lay with Admiral Isoroku Yamamoto, who had taken command of the Combined Fleet in late August 1939. His hand could be felt in the new emphasis on air combat, training, unorthodox conceptions, and early decisions. Reacting to the presence of the U.S. Pacific Fleet at Oahu, Yamamoto advised the Naval High Command that, strategically speaking, the situation was 'tantamount to a dagger pointed at our throat'. But, Yamamoto added, America's naval threat to Japan could become Japan's threat to America.

Japanese naval policy towards the U.S.A., the major hypothetical enemy, had long been essentially defensive in the strategic sense. By 1940 it was anticipated that, in the case of war, the American battle fleet would steam promptly west from Hawaii and engage the Imperial Japanese Navy (I.J.N.) in decisive combat north of the Marshalls and east of the Marianas. The matter of initiative remained troublesome: destruction of the Americans' Asiatic Fleet, conquest of U.S. possessions in the Far East, and disruption of maritime trade – these actions could exert only indirect wartime effects. The most revolutionary scheme of the Japanese was to consider developing giant flying boats which could traverse 5,500 miles with a four-ton bomb load, strike Pearl Harbor from the Marshalls, and provoke the U.S. fleet into a sortie. The project never bore fruit. I.J.N. admirals still thought in terms of grand battles, but even their war games degenerated into a war of attrition, unacceptable to a navy of inferior quantitative strength.

The first realistic idea of an unconventional attack against the U.S. Pacific Fleet in Hawaii arose in Yamamoto's mind after successful I.J.N. fleet exercises in spring 1940. The admiral was particularly pleased by the progress of aerial torpedo assault tactics against battleship forces. Whereas his colleagues, however, could conceive only of submarine action and massive surface combat against targets in Hawaiian waters, Yamamoto was already thinking of decisive attack from the air. Major operations against bases in the mainland U.S.A. were out of the question, but not against targets farther west.

Impetus to rethink the whole situation occurred after the stunning German successes of late spring 1940, which led to a re-ordering of international forces and the appearance of a power vacuum east of Suez. Were Japan to grasp the resources of South-east Asia and seize the 'hostage' Philippines, urgent consideration would have to be given to the nature and speed of American reaction. After evaluation of map manoeuvres in November 1940, Yamamoto concluded that the oil-rich Dutch East Indies could not be subdued without provoking the U.S.A. and Britain into war. What if the Pacific Fleet counter-attacked while the main body of the Japanese navy was dispersed in the south?

By early January 1941, Yamamoto was recommending to the Navy Minister that, in the unhappy event of war with the U.S.A., the Japanese should strive to cripple the Americans' main battle flotilla in the Pacific by an air offensive concurrent with the initiation of a campaign against South-east Asia. The benefits would be multiple: enemy morale, civil and military, would be damaged, perhaps to the point of helplessness; and the U.S. fleet would be prevented from troubling the exposed flank of the Japanese and from unleashing psychologically disturbing air strikes against cities in the Japanese homeland. From what he knew of the Pacific Fleet commander, Admiral Husband Kimmel, and of recent U.S. navy doctrine, Yamamoto doubted that the Americans would limit themselves to conventional, frontal tactics.

Certainly, many serious questions vexed Yamamoto. He admitted privately that the Hawaii operation was spawned by desperation, by lack of confidence in classic surface battles such as those of the Russo-Japanese War, in which he had participated thirty-five years earlier. Divine assistance was a prerequisite, for annihilation by the enemy was a distinct possibility. Convinced of the need for empirical data, in January 1941 – entirely on his own initiative and known only to a few trusted navy associates – Yamamoto asked his friend Admiral Takijiro Onishi (a rare expert on naval aviation, then chief of staff of the land-based 11th Air Fleet) to conduct a top-secret feasibility study. Yamamoto also requested Japanese intelligence to supply detailed information about Hawaii.

Commander Minoru Genda had seen recent attaché duty in London, where he had learned of the successful raid in November 1940 by twenty-four British carrier-based planes against the Italian naval port of Taranto. At the cost of only two bombers, the raiders had sunk three battleships at anchor. Carefully studying the Pearl Harbor analogue, Genda concluded that the Japanese strike plan was dangerous but feasible. All of Japan's six fleet carriers (available or near completion) would be required, and the best pilots would have to be employed. The secret assembly base could be in the Ogasawara chain or Hokkaido. About 400 planes would be needed: reconnaissance aircraft, high-level bombers, dive-bombers, torpedo bombers, fighters. Armour-piercing bombs would be useful against the deck armour of battleships – the prime target – but torpedoes undoubtedly offered the best opportunity for horizontal attack if launched at very low altitude and slow speed. A small force of submarines should precede the task force.

Buttressed by the recommendations from Onishi's command, received in early April, Yamamoto could now order his own Combined Fleet staff, especially his excellent operations officer, Captain Kameto Kuroshima, to study the Hawaii project officially. The planning became less academic as Japan and the U.S.A. drifted toward hostilities. At an important Imperial Conference on 2 July 1941, the Japanese government and High Command agreed that 'our Empire will not be deterred by the possibility of being involved in a war with Great Britain and the United States' as the result of occupation of Indochina.

With a gnawing sense that Japan's natural resources were being depleted while those of her antagonists were improving, the Japanese navy pressed for an early governmental decision. The Chief of the Naval General Staff warned in early September, 'Although I am confident that at present we have a chance to win a war, I fear that this opportunity will disappear with the passage of time.' On the 6th, an Imperial Conference decreed that, in case Japanese demands could not be met by the first ten days of October, 'We will immediately decide to commence hostilities against the U.S.A., Britain, and the Netherlands.' Completion of preparations was targeted for the last ten days of October.

In mid-September, annual map exercises were conducted at the Japanese Naval War College amidst the darkening clouds of war. At the end of the games, a special study team of some thirty high-ranking officers was convened at the request of Yamamoto, who tried out his Hawaii scheme with inconclusive results. The draft, prepared in late August, was map-played twice. Once the raid proved successful: four enemy battleships presumed sunk and one damaged, two carriers sunk and one damaged, six cruisers sunk or damaged, 180 planes destroyed. A second time, the results were poor and the attackers lost two carriers sunk, two damaged, and 127 planes shot down. The participants questioned the possibility of secrecy and of refuelling in the wintry north Pacific. When the Chief of the Naval General Staff, who had not been present, learned of the special conference – and thus of the Hawaii idea – for the first time, he remarked that it seemed to be a very risky plan. In the strategic sense, the Naval General Staff also questioned, not without reason, the wisdom of subtracting carrier striking power from the South-east Asian thrust, especially if the U.S. Pacific Fleet did *not* make an early offensive sortie. Additionally, at the political level, the Japanese navy had not quite abandoned hope of success in diplomacy, especially since a cautious admiral, Nomura, was serving as ambassador in Washington.

While a number of I.J.N. 'hawks' liked the Yamamoto plan, its opponents included many senior officers: the unenthusiastic designated task force commander, a torpedo expert, Admiral Chuichi Nagumo, 1st Air Fleet commander; his chief of staff, an air officer, Admiral Ryunosuke Kusaka; the 11th Air Fleet commander, Tsukahara; and Admiral Onishi himself, whom Kusaka had 'converted'. The resistance was overcome by Yamamoto's reasoning, cajolery and, ultimately, his assertion that he would resign unless the Hawaii plan, as he saw it, were adopted. Not only was the operation approved, but all six fleet carriers were assigned to it. Nagumo revealed the scheme, under tight secrecy, to his air commanders in early October. Experts had constructed authentic mock-ups of Oahu Island and the Pearl Harbor facilities.

Since Japan's national course was set, whatever Yamamoto's innermost preferences, the Combined Fleet commander had to be sure that the chances of success in the initial phase were optimal. Training efforts were redoubled in the shallow roadstead at Kagoshima Bay, which bore a close resemblance to Pearl Harbor. One I.J.N. admiral unhappily called the effort 'last-minute' and 'patchwork'. Yamamoto himself was heard to say, 'If torpedo bombing is not possible, this operation will not be carried out.' The torpedo problem did prove to be very painful. Although the 1st Air Fleet was given everything it requested in the way of men and material, the last realistic manoeuvres of 4–6 November at Ariake proved disappointing. Six months of air torpedo training – a veritable 'aerial circus' – had been conducted by fine pilots but, since they did not learn what the stationary targets represented until late autumn, they had not comprehended the difficulty of their real task. Genda feared that torpedo attacks might even have to be struck from the plans, especially since the fleet was scheduled to sail in only ten days, on 17 November. All the planning would be unhinged, at this juncture, if the torpedo pilots lost confidence. None did.

After constant experimentation, the last technical problems were resolved on 10 or 11 November. Delivery of improved torpedoes (with wooden stabilizers on the fins) was still delayed; they would only arrive at the rendezvous point. The staff's last major apprehension was whether the task force would get to the launching site, little more than 200 miles from Oahu, undetected. Approach by a 'great circle' route, from the north instead of west, was expected to bypass the usual merchantman lanes while evading enemy reconnaissance. Various deceptive measures, particularly in the realm of signals traffic, were intended to cause U.S. intelligence to 'mislay' the Japanese carriers briefly – as indeed was the case.

In deference to the Emperor's pacific wishes, Hideki Tojo, Prime Minister since October when Prince Konoye's cabinet had fallen, had allowed negotiations to continue in Washington a month longer than the navy had desired. On 5 November an Imperial Conference confirmed the decision to fight the U.S.A. and Britain at the beginning of December, although offensive operations might still be called off if parleys had proved successful by midnight on 1 December. Two days later Yamamoto issued an operations order nominating 8 December, Japan time, as 'Y' Day. This would be Sunday 7 December in Honolulu – a day chosen not merely because it was the Americans' sabbath but because meteorological conditions would be good and the Pacific Fleet generally returned to port in full strength each weekend after training south-east of Oahu. If this 'Y' Day could not have been met, the Japanese would have had to wait until March 1942 for the next optimum combination of factors; by then, four months of precious oil stocks would have been depleted. This was unacceptable, since by October the Japanese navy was consuming 400 tons of oil per hour.

On 16 November, aboard the *Akagi* in the Inland Sea, Yamamoto delivered a moving address to the task force staff and attack pilots. The Americans were the most formidable foe in Japanese history, and Admiral Kimmel, who had been specially selected to become their fleet commander-in-chief, was extremely capable. Yamamoto also expressed concern lest a differentiation should not be made between the achievement of strategic surprise and making an attack without warning. Even in a night assault during feudal days, the Japanese *samurai* warrior would never have lopped off the head of a sleeping enemy; he would at least have woken him by kicking his pillow.

By 22 November the Japanese task force had concentrated at remote Hitokappu Bay in the murky Kuril Island chain lying north of Hokkaido, while the fleet submarines, in groups of three, headed for Oahu. Four days later, at Yamamoto's order, Nagumo's flotilla sailed for the Hawaiian islands. The last lingering prospect of a U.S.–Japanese settlement had vanished by the end of November, when Secretary of State Cordell Hull presented a statement of position which all senior officials in Tokyo regarded as extreme at best or as an ultimatum at worst. On 29 November, Foreign Minister Shigenori Togo finally learned his navy's zero hour, but the envoys in Washington were not told in advance. On 1 December a final Imperial Conference endorsed the resort to hostilities. Nagano, Chief of the Naval General Staff, called it the 'most serious crisis since the founding of our country'; Tojo said that 'our Empire stands at the threshold of glory or oblivion'. Next day Combined Fleet headquarters ordered Nagumo to proceed with the Pearl Harbor operation, by signalling him 'Climb Mount Niitaka!' When the Japanese crews were told their destination, at sea, one sailor exulted: 'An air attack on Hawaii! A dream come true!'

The thirty-one ships of Nagumo's command were well on the way towards their rendezvous. By 6 December (Hawaii time/date will now be used), the vessels were racing S.S.E. at twenty-four knots, blacked-out, silent, and refuelled for the last time: the large carriers *Akagi* (flag) and *Kaga*, the light carriers *Soryu* and *Hiryu*, the brand-new *Shokaku* and *Zuikaku*. Each carrier bore about seventy aircraft. The rest of the task force included the screening battleships *Hiei* and *Kirishima*, three cruisers (the heavy *Tone* and *Chikuma*, the light *Abukuma*), nine destroyers, and three submarines on patrol 200 miles ahead. The fleet train of eight precious tankers had been released by 7 December. Already en route to Hawaii were twenty-seven submarines, five of which carried midget subs and eleven launch-planes.

The waters were unexpectedly calm, and a light fog reduced visibility – 'divine grace', in Genda's words. Shortly before the launch, however – already in a state of grievous worry and suffering from insomnia – Nagumo received the latest intelligence regarding U.S. warships in Hawaii. Eight battleships lay in the Pearl Harbor roadstead, not in open Lahaina anchorage. But, unfortunately for the Japanese, all the vital U.S. carriers (and heavy cruisers) seemed to be absent: the *Lexington*, the *Enterprise*, the *Hornet*, the *Yorktown* (actually in the Atlantic) and the *Saratoga* (known to be on the U.S. west coast). Genda said he would have 'swapped' all eight U.S. battleships for two or three of the carriers.

Nagumo had been given permission to abandon the operation if he encountered an enemy fleet as late as X-2. Perhaps this was an eventuality he relished but, by 7 December, 400 miles from Pearl Harbor, it was too late to change plan. The U.S. battleship fleet was well worth the trip, and perhaps some of the carriers would be back in port too. Anyhow, as Kusaka said, 'We can't do anything about carriers that are not there.' No Japanese aircraft were diverted to look for the errant targets. Having received Yamamoto's Nelsonian exhortation for each man to do his duty to the empire, Nagumo ran up the 'Z' flag on the *Akagi* – the same pennon that was flown by Admiral Togo in the 1905 victory at the Straits of Tsushima.

At 5.30 a.m. on the 7th, float planes were launched by two Japanese cruisers for reconnaissance. Thirty-nine fighters were assigned to defensive patrol over the carriers; another forty planes, not entirely serviceable, were kept in reserve. At 6 a.m., in rather heavy seas 230 miles north of Oahu, the first wave of 183 planes began to take off, under the overall control of Commander Mitsuo Fuchida. These 183 consisted of:

Fuchida's forty-nine bombers, each carrying an 1,800-pound armour-piercing finned shell, against battleship targets.
Murata's forty attack planes, each carrying torpedoes, against battleships and cruisers.
Takahashi's fifty-one dive-bombers, each carrying an ordinary 550-pound bomb, against air base targets.
Itaya's forty-three Zero fighters, in three groups, armed with two 20-mm and two 7.7-mm machine guns each, for escort and attack against air bases.

The approach altitude was 3,250 yards, above cloud cover: time to target, about an hour and fifty minutes. Homing on Radio Station K.G.M.B. in Honolulu, Fuchida was heartened to hear that visibility was good over the city. At 7.49 a.m. he ordered the plain-code signal for surprise attack. Four minutes later, convinced of victory, he exuberantly radioed Nagumo's carriers of impending success: '*Tora! tora! tora!*' (Tiger, tiger, tiger). Miraculously, the message was picked up by I.J.N. receivers in Tokyo and Hiroshima.

Despite certain mistakes among the Japanese air formations, the Americans were taken completely by surprise. Only one of the ninety-four vessels in port was under way when, at 7.55 a.m., the dive-bombers hit Hickam and Wheeler fields. At 7.57 the torpedo planes struck Battleship Row; at 8 a.m.

the Zeros strafed air bases; at 8.05 the level bombers hit the battleships. Many American sailors could not comprehend why friendly planes should be attacking: 'very realistic manoeuvres', remarked a marine colonel. When the truth became apparent, one seaman reacted, 'Hell, I didn't even know they were sore at us!'

Although U.S. intelligence, by means of the MAGIC operation which had broken the Japanese diplomatic code, had been expecting an 'aggressive move' somewhere in the Far East, Pearl Harbor seemed far less likely a target than, for example, the Panama Canal locks. In Manila, General Douglas MacArthur reacted to the raid with incredulity: 'Pearl Harbor! It should be our strongest point.' Unaware of MAGIC, General Walter Short, the army commander in Hawaii, had been on his guard against subversion and sabotage, a decision unchallenged by Washington. Similarly bereft of knowledge from MAGIC, Admiral Kimmel had concentrated on training. Innumerable warnings and indicators had been missed, ignored, or pigeonholed by the many-layered U.S. intelligence and command community. Observing the disaster from his warplane aloft, Commander Fuchida was amazed by 'the shortsightedness of the United States in being so generally unprepared and in not using torpedo nets. . . . Had these Americans never heard of Port Arthur?'

The defenders were also plagued by bad luck. A destroyer's detection of a Japanese midget sub three hours before the air assaults, and destruction of the intruder in a restricted zone at 6.54 a.m., went virtually unnoticed. Two army enlisted men tinkering with a new radar installation detected the first large Japanese flights, but the crucial intelligence was dismissed, largely because unarmed B-17 Flying Fortresses were due from California that morning. A war alert message from Washington, transmitted by the army over commercial channels, arrived after the attacks had begun.

The first Japanese assault wave completed its mission in about an hour. At a trifling cost of one dive-bomber, five torpedo planes, and three fighters, the attackers had turned the port into chaos. Of the U.S. battleships, only the flagship *Pennsylvania*, in drydock, seemed unscathed. The *Arizona* was shattered and sinking; the *Maryland* and the *Tennessee* were on fire; the *West Virginia* had reportedly been hit nine times, the *Oklahoma* twelve (a complete loss), the *California* three. The only battleship to get under way, the *Nevada*, had been struck at least once before beaching herself to keep the channel open. The *Utah*, actually a defenceless target ship, had already capsized. The cruiser *Helena*, moored next to a minelayer, took five torpedoes. Japanese accuracy had equalled practice performance: fifty-five per cent of the torpedoes hit their targets, twenty-five per cent of the high-level bombs, nearly fifty per cent of the dive-bombs. The effectiveness of the aerial torpedoes struck the I.J.N. aviators as particularly remarkable. Significantly, the outboard battleship of each moored pair suffered the more grievously in each case.

At 8.54 a.m. a second wave of 167 Japanese planes, under Commander Shimazaki, thundered in; which consisted of:

Shimazaki's fifty-four level bombers, carrying 130-pound and 550-pound bombs, against Hickam, Ford and Kaneohe air bases.
Egusa's seventy-eight dive-bombers, each with one 550-pound ordinary bomb, against warships.
Shindo's thirty-five Zero fighters, to provide escort and to strafe airfields.

The second wave operated for another hour, concentrating against less damaged warships. Since the Americans were putting up heavier resistance by now, Shimazaki's planes suffered somewhat more severely: six fighters and fourteen dive-bombers were shot down. Total combat losses amounted to nine fighters, fifteen dive-bombers and five torpedo planes. Of all the Japanese planes which returned from the strikes, seventy-four had been holed. Fifty aircraft crashed on landing, of which twenty were destroyed; the winds and seas had worsened by now.

Although smoke veiled the target area, Fuchida circled over the carnage to observe and to photograph. He counted four battleships sunk, three 'knocked out for six months', one damaged slightly. All the airfields were in flames; at least half of the Americans' air strength must have been eliminated. Fuchida encountered not one enemy plane in three hours. (Two P-40B Tomahawk pilots claimed to have shot down eight bombers; five P-36 Mohawks shot down two Zeros and damaged two more, at the cost of two U.S. fighters.)

Of 231 army aircraft on Oahu, ninety-seven were written off as lost and eighty-eight considered repairable. U.S. navy plane losses totalled eighty, more than half of the inventory. The destruction was particularly severe because the planes were parked wingtip to wingtip as defence against saboteurs. A few U.S. naval fighters flying in from the *Enterprise*, later in the morning, were shot down by trigger-happy American gunners; the same fate befell an army P-36. U.S. personnel casualties totalled 4,575: navy/marine corps: 3,077 killed (including 960 missing, mainly trapped aboard the capsized *Arizona*, from which the haunting tap-tap of entombed men could long be heard) and 876 wounded; army: 226 killed and 396 wounded. I.J.N. airmen lost in action numbered fifty-five. In addition to the ruined battleships, three U.S. destroyers were crippled, three light cruisers damaged, and three auxiliaries sunk or damaged. It took nearly three years to remove the fuel which spilled into the harbour; the *Arizona*'s tanks seeped for decades.

By 10 a.m. on 7 December, all surviving Japanese aircraft from the two strikes had flown back to their carriers, now forty miles closer to Hawaii. There was discussion of further operations but Fuchida, the mission leader, was merely thanked for his fine work and told to take a rest, although he was prepared to sortie again. From the *Hiryu*, the aggressive Admiral Tamon Yamaguchi (whom some I.J.N. officers wished were commanding in

Nagumo's stead) signalled that he had completed preparations for a new air strike. But Genda, who was on the *Akagi*'s bridge, denies that there were heated arguments. The results of the day's operations had impressed Nagumo and Kusaka as being sufficient. Kusaka, indeed, told Genda later that both he and Nagumo had decided from the outset not to conduct follow-up air strikes. According to Kusaka, he unhesitatingly advised Nagumo to withdraw the task force. Nagumo agreed. Planes other than fighters were stowed in the carriers' hangars. Silently the great flotilla churned N.N.W. for refuelling and home waters. The *Akagi* hoisted the signal to retire at 1.30 p.m., little more than seven hours after the first attack planes had taken off for Pearl Harbor.

At Combined Fleet headquarters in Japan the staff were excited by the news of unexpected success and the disarray among the Americans. Although Nagumo's caution and reservations were well known, almost every officer wanted new orders sent to him, directing the task force to complete the slaughter of the Pacific Fleet, either that night or next morning. Yamamoto reportedly agreed that a new strike would be splendid but, since details of Japanese losses were still not known, he felt that it would be best to leave matters to Nagumo. Yamamoto admitted privately that 'Nagumo probably won't do it', but the Combined Fleet sent no follow-up orders to the task force commander.

Controversy has raged for decades concerning Nagumo's decision to quit Hawaiian waters after 'only' two air strikes. It is said that Nagano, Chief of the Naval General Staff, later expressed dissatisfaction personally to Nagumo. 'Hawks' have always argued that, despite obvious successes, Operation 'Z' could *not* be termed decisive. As Fuchida told Nagumo at the time, many worthwhile targets remained: the battleships mired in shallow water, dozens of other vessels, untouched hangars, shops, oil tanks. A new air attack, launched even closer to Oahu, might conceivably have lured back the U.S. carriers and heavy cruisers – to their doom. American and Japanese critics (including Genda) agree that the Japanese, beset by 'medal fever', lost sight of unglamorous logistical targets such as machine shops indispensable to the repair of the mauled U.S. fleet, and fragile fuel storage facilities containing $4\frac{1}{2}$ million barrels of oil. Captain Taussig reminds us that the U.S. navy possessed only three fleet tankers on the west coast in 1941. Regarding the fuel dumps, Admiral Tomioka claims the Japanese could not believe that other than dummies would be installed above ground. Some Japanese have argued that blazing oil fires would only have obscured the bombers' targets.

No one argues seriously that the Japanese should have landed an army on Oahu and seized Pearl Harbor in 1941. Yamamoto knew that the South-east Asian campaign took priority in amphibious resources and that a huge convoy of transports, moving for a month at eight knots, would have ruined the Nagumo force's element of surprise. As Fuchida says, the Japanese had been thinking of little more than 'pulling the eagle's tail feathers'. To which Tomioka would add, realistically, that I.J.N. intelligence overestimated the size of the American garrison in the Hawaiian islands.

Apart from the fact that Nagumo, a battleship admiral, was unenthusiastic at best and timid at worst, one must note that the I.J.N. submarine effort in Hawaiian waters, from which much was expected, proved to be a complete failure. The task force had other reasons for leaving the scene after the two great raids on 7 December:

As many as five aircraft carriers might be lurking in the region. Enemy heavy cruisers and submarines were also unlocated.

The results of the initial strikes had exceeded expectations; little more effect could be anticipated from additional assaults against the identical area. Enemy anti-aircraft fire had been surprisingly strong, even though surprise had been complete. Losses by the second wave had doubled those of the first, and could be expected to increase geometrically now that the element of surprise was gone.

Intelligence reported at least fifty large planes (presumably B–17s) still available to the defenders. It was unsound to hover within range of land-based enemy aircraft, especially since I.J.N. aerial reconnaissance was limited. The six aircraft carriers should be brought home safely; they represented the entire such force then available to the Japanese Navy.

The weather north of Hawaii had worsened, and the Japanese carriers were rolling at fifteen degrees. Attacks against ground targets would require refitting of ordnance loads, and any new strike would involve night flights and dangerous night landings. Illuminating the flight decks would invite enemy retaliation, especially if the missing U.S. carriers showed up; they had still not been located by Japanese reconnaissance on 8 December.

While deploring the insufficient I.J.N. scouting efforts, Admiral Fukudome suggests that Nagumo should be credited with a 'wise decision to terminate the attacks' instead of being criticized for not proceeding with them. It must be admitted that, at the time, the Japanese Naval General Staff were not unhappy with Nagumo's safe and skilful disengagement. Kusaka estimated the achieved success factor as eighty per cent. His outlook is summed up in a Zen saying: a lion attacks with every ounce of strength but, after the kill, he departs without regret. Genda adds that if the operation had turned out badly, Yamamoto would have been criticized for recklessness and Nagumo praised for caution.

In the larger sense Yamamoto and the Japanese leadership have been censured for the folly of uniting the Americans. Professor Samuel E. Morison, the official U.S. navy historian, goes so far as to charge that, 'One can search military history in vain for an operation more fatal to the aggressor. . . . On the high political level it was disastrous' to the Japanese. This contention is rendered poignant when one remembers that Yamamoto never thought Japan could win a protracted war. To a friend the admiral remarked in mid-

November 1941 that conflict with the U.S.A. was farthest from his personal wish, yet he had been compelled by circumstances to devise a diametrically opposed war plan. Was it not his tragic 'destiny', he mused.

Fukudome questions this assumption of Japanese 'folly'. While admitting that the Pearl Harbor raid infuriated the Americans, he deems it 'inconceivable that their fighting spirit depended upon the point on which the first attack was made, since Japan in any case would have . . . attacked US forces, and occupied enemy territory'. As Genda explained later, there was nothing mystical about the site of Pearl Harbor; if the U.S. Pacific Fleet had been deployed at Midway, for example, historians today would be speaking of a 'sneak attack' there.

Even at the target level there is controversy. Many have argued that the Japanese obsession with battleships was anachronistic and unintelligent. In a day when line-of-battle operations were passé, the ageing battlewagons whose superstructures were smashed at Pearl Harbor were of little immediate value; they lacked the speed to escort fast carriers. Even the newer, swifter U.S. battleships were of subsequent use only for supporting missions and bombardment of shore targets. Admiral Chester Nimitz later admitted it had been fortunate the Pacific Fleet battleship force had not been able to sail before the Japanese struck; without air cover and against a marauding task force at least two knots faster, the U.S. battlewagons would have been sunk in deep waters with perhaps 20,000 (mainly drowned) instead of 4,000 casualties. 'It was God's divine will,' Nimitz commented – although the event did not seem so providential at the time.

Most commentators on Operation 'Z' – the largest and most sensational such strike to date – call it a short-term operational masterpiece but a colossal long-range blunder. The luckless Admiral Kimmel admitted that the attack 'was a beautifully executed military maneuver'. Morison, however, calls it 'a strategic imbecility', 'idiotic'. Against such a vehement charge based on hindsight, it is instructive to consult authoritative U.S. military impressions from 1941. A week after the raid, Secretary of War Henry Stimson confided to his secret diary: '. . . the Navy has been rather shaken and panic-stricken after the catastrophe at Hawaii and the complete upset of their naval strategy which depended upon that fortress. They have been willing to think of nothing except Hawaii and the restoration of the defense of that island. They have opposed all our [army] efforts for a counter-attack, taking the defeatist attitude that it was impossible . . .' It has even been suggested that Admiral Thomas Hart, Asiatic Fleet commander, precipitously withdrew U.S. naval support from the beleaguered Philippines and fell back to the East Indies because he feared 'another Pearl Harbor' if he retained his forces near Luzon.

Fukudome sees invaluable benefits to the Japanese in the Second World War from the operation. 'It was not before 1944, three years after the war started,' he insists, 'that the US task forces could gain control of the sea.' Fukudome argues that the success of the raid on Pearl Harbor

> ... nullified the US Navy's *Rainbow No. 5* operational plan, and ... it took two full years to recover its strength; ... our forces, in the meantime, were able to complete without interruption the occupation of the Southern Resources Area. ... In the event that the Japanese Navy had not launched the Hawaii attack and had consequently encountered the US Fleet advancing on the Marshall and West Caroline Islands in pursuance to [*Rainbow 5*] ... it would have been impossible for the Japanese Navy to have inflicted greater damage ... than they did in the Pearl Harbor attack, however favorable our estimate ...

At the nub of the argument concerning the decisiveness of the raid is the conceptual difference between Yamamoto and the Naval General Staff. The latter were thinking in terms only of checking the U.S. Pacific Fleet, while proceeding with a campaign to develop a rich, invulnerable Southern Resources Area during a protracted war. But they were not convinced that the Pacific Fleet would have sortied in force as soon as the southern campaign began, and in this sense the Pearl Harbor raid was unnecessary from their point of view, or at least the scheme was pressed too hard. For his part Yamamoto intended to shatter, not merely check, the American battle fleet at the outset of the war, and thus free the entire western Pacific for Japan. Although reasonably satisfied with the immediate results of the raid, he was less happy than the Naval General Staff regarding the distant consequences, especially since he regarded a war of attrition as adverse to Japanese national interests. While the bloodied U.S. navy was in confusion, Yamamoto wanted to achieve decisive strategic results by retaining the initiative.

The Japanese Naval High Command decided to focus its efforts on the south, ignoring the intact U.S. carrier fleet to the east. Clearly the I.J.N. battleship admirals had not absorbed the lessons of Pearl Harbor – or of Malaya, where H.M.S. *Repulse* and H.M.S. *Prince of Wales* were sunk by air attack with ease. If only the myth of battleship supremacy could have been supplanted by Yamamoto's revolutionary task force concept, and Nagumo's six carriers had been joined by the seven battlewagons riding idly in the Inland Sea, Fuchida feels 'at the very least ... it seems reasonable to believe that the American carrier force, which had survived Pearl Harbor, could speedily have been crushed, and that the Japanese Fleet would not nearly so soon have lost its advantage to an enemy who was quicker to learn from defeat than our naval leaders were to learn from victory.'

The Pearl Harbor operation was no battle in the ordinary sense; it was a 'massacre' planned by the best I.J.N. thinker. That the attack was launched before delivery of the final diplomatic note is attributable only to the botching by the Japanese embassy staff in Washington, who engendered the unfair wartime castigation of the Japanese as 'sneaks'. Even Tojo could not believe that the Hawaii attack preceded his envoys' last visit to Hull. Perhaps they had been delayed deliberately by the Americans? For, despite Yamamoto's and the Emperor's sincere concern, the sleeping Americans' pillow-was not kicked beforehand by the sword-wielding *samurai*.

The true decisiveness of Pearl Harbor is to be found in the consequences of Franklin Roosevelt's astute use of semantics to describe the Japanese attack to the Congress and the American people – while the Japanese aggression went far to solve the President's personal problem of inflaming the American populace to wartime frenzy. ' "Infamy" was the note that struck home,' says Walter Lord, 'the word that welded the country together until the war was won.' Admiral Hara adds sardonically: 'President Roosevelt should have pinned medals on us.'

In classical fashion the Americans had preferred to estimate enemy intentions, not capabilities. Admiral King judged that an 'unwarranted feeling of immunity from attack . . . seems to have pervaded all ranks at Pearl Harbor, both Army and Navy'. Thus, Pearl Harbor's most chilling import concerns the decisiveness of the unexpected and the audacious. The lesson is as old as Sun Tzu – the originator of Chinese military thinking – but 'early warning' today must be reckoned in seconds and minutes, not the hours, days and weeks of 1941.

Note on Sources

A number of Japanese language books and articles were consulted in the preparation of this essay: *e.g.*, the Japan Defence Agency official histories and studies by H. Agawa, M. Fuchida, S. Fukudome, M. Genda, R. Kusaka, K. Matsushima, K. Sato, S. Tomioka, and H. Tsunoda. I also interviewed Admirals Kusaka and Tomioka in Japan.

From the very large literature in English, the following selected items were particularly useful:

Barker, A. J., *Pearl Harbor* (1969).

Fuchida, Mitsuo, and Masatake Okumiya, *Midway: The Battle That Doomed Japan* (1955).

Hayashi, Saburo, in collaboration with Alvin D. Coox, *Kōgun: The Japanese Army in the Pacific War* (1959).

Ike, Nobutaka, *The Japanese Decision for War* (1967).

Ito, Masanori, with Roger Pineau, *The End of the Imperial Japanese Navy* (1962).

Lord, Walter, *Day of Infamy* (1957).

Morison, Samuel Eliot, *The Rising Sun in the Pacific, 1931–April 1942*, Vol. III of *History of US Naval Operations in World War II* (1948).

Potter, John Deane, *Yamamoto: The Man Who Menaced America* (1965).

Taussig, Captain Joseph K., 'I Remember Pearl Harbor', U.S. Naval Institute *Proceedings*, December 1972.

Toland, John, *The Rising Sun* (1970).

Wohlstetter, Roberta, *Pearl Harbor: Warning and Decision* (1962).

Catastrophe for Britain in the Far East.
General Percival (extreme right) surrenders to the Japanese, 15 February 1942

Chapter Twelve

SINGAPORE

Louis Allen

IN TERMS OF political strategy, the Japanese capture of Malaya and Singapore was to guarantee that the oil they hoped to take from the Netherlands East Indies could be shipped back to Japan without hindrance. Ever since the invasion of China in 1937, the Americans had put pressure on the Japanese to withdraw. An economic embargo had been applied after Japan had occupied aerodromes in French Indo-China in July 1941, and the Dutch had agreed to cooperate with the Americans by refusing to supply Japan with oil. The strike against South-east Asia and the East Indies was intended to break this embargo and keep Japan's industries running.

But there was a deeper psychological motive. As the liberator of the oppressed colonial peoples of Asia, Japan had led the counter-attack against Europe in 1904–5, when she defeated the Russian empire. The capture of Singapore, the naval and commercial symbol of British power in the Far East, would complete her self-allotted role as the defender of Asia. The basic decision to move against the European powers and the U.S.A. was taken on 6 September 1941. The attack would begin in December, unless significant economic concessions could be negotiated first.

The operation was to last five months from start to finish, 100 days being required for the taking of Singapore. Malaya was to be invaded by the Twenty-fifth Army, using three divisions, the 5th (Lieutenant-General Matsui), the 18th (Lieutenant-General Mutaguchi), and the Imperial Guards (Lieutenant-General Nishimura), 62,200 men in all, with 183 guns and 228 tanks. The 3rd Air Division was attached to the Twenty-fifth Army, with 168 fighters, eighty-one light and ninety-nine heavy bombers, and forty-five reconnaissance aircraft. The Southern Expeditionary Fleet with the 22nd Air Flotilla (158 aircraft) was to protect the convoys. The 56th Division was also allotted to Malaya, but never entered the campaign. The Twenty-fifth Army was placed under the command of Lieutenant-General Iida until Lieutenant-General Yamashita took over from him on 6 November 1941, a month before operations were to begin. Troops were embarked from the China coast and Japan in the early days of December, and the Imperial Guards, then occupying part of Cambodia, were put in a state of readiness. Their first task was to seize Bangkok, the capital of Thailand, and so secure Japanese lines of communications overland to Burma and Malaya.

On the British side, Air Chief Marshal Sir Robert Brooke-Popham was appointed Commander-in-Chief, Far East, in November 1940. In 1941 Air Vice-Marshal Pulford became A.O.C. (Air Officer Commanding) Far East, and Lieutenant-General Percival G.O.C. (General Officer Commanding) Malaya. Five hundred and fifty-five first-line aircraft were needed to defend Malaya. When war broke out Pulford had 158, some of them obsolete. Percival had under his command the III Corps (Lieutenant-General Heath), consisting of the 11th and 9th Indian Divisions; and the 8th Australian Division (Major-General Gordon Bennett), with fortress troops and a reserve brigade, a total of 88,600 men. The Japanese estimated at the time that he had between 90,000 and 100,000. The III Corps was to defend northern and central Malaya and the Australians were to cover Johore.

British planes reconnoitring the approaches to the Gulf of Siam spotted Japanese convoys moving west on 6 December, but it was not clear whether they were making for Malaya, the Kra Isthmus or Bangkok. The first shot in the campaign – a whole day before Pearl Harbor – was fired by Japanese planes of the 22nd Air Flotilla at 10.10 a.m. on 7 December. They shot down a British Catalina flying boat which had been sighted tailing the convoy twenty-five miles west of the island of Panjang. The British suspected this had happened, but could not confirm it.

The British had planned a pre-emptive strike (Operation Matador) into Siam to deny the ports of Singora and Patani to the Japanese if war seemed likely. Matador required twenty-four hours' notice of a Japanese landing to be effective, otherwise the forestallers would be forestalled; and almost until the last minute – 5 December – the decision to move was reserved by Whitehall. The risk of appearing to be the aggressor was great. The British ambassador in Bangkok pleaded that no hostile act should be carried out against Siam. There was no guarantee that the U.S.A. would back such a move, and Brooke-Popham had been explicitly told that the basis of Far Eastern policy was to avoid war with Japan. In these circumstances, and given the uncertainty of his information, it is not surprising that he dithered about ordering Matador. By the time he was sure the Japanese had violated Siamese territory, it was too late. Shortly after midnight on 7 December, the Japanese 18th Division's Takumi Force began to land off Kota Barhu in north-east Malaya. The 5th Division landed at the Siamese ports of Singora and Patani a few hours later. They soon had over 26,000 men ashore.

The theory behind the Singapore naval base was that Royal Navy units could be in the Far East in forty-eight days if war broke out, assuming they were not involved elsewhere. In 1941 the navy was heavily engaged in the Atlantic and the government's wish to transfer important ships to the East – the old battlecruiser *Repulse* and the new battleship *Prince of Wales* – was not welcomed by the Admiralty. The First Sea Lord agreed to a compromise whereby the *Prince of Wales* was to sail for Cape Town, her onward destination remaining open. The very report of her presence there might deter the Japanese. Partly as a result of Australian pressure she was ordered on to Ceylon, and then to Singapore, on 11 November 1941.

When the Japanese attacked Pearl Harbor, they destroyed the naval balance in the Indian Ocean and the Pacific. There was some discussion as to whether to send the *Prince of Wales* and the *Repulse* on to Australia or to Hawaii to join what was left of the U.S. Pacific Fleet. In the event Admiral Sir Tom Phillips took neither course. He was reluctant to leave Malayan waters while British troops were engaged on the mainland and decided to go north to intercept the Japanese convoys. With surprise, and given fighter cover, he could wreak havoc among their transports. Phillips sailed north-east from

Singapore at 5.35 p.m. on 8 December. He should have had his own air cover but his aircraft carrier, the *Indomitable*, had run aground in Jamaica, which made him dependent on the airfields of northern Malaya. But Pulford could not provide air cover – the capture of airfields had been the first Japanese priority – and he lost the advantage of surprise when a Japanese submarine spotted the big ships on the afternoon of 9 December. Planes of the Japanese 22nd Air Flotilla made an unsuccessful sortie against them from airfields in French Indo-China; but Phillips was sure he had been sighted and decided to return to Singapore, changing course at 8.15 p.m. His chief of staff, Admiral Palliser, left behind in Singapore, signalled just before midnight: 'Enemy reported landing Kuantan, latitude 3° 50′ North.' If the Japanese seized the road running inland from Kuantan, Malaya would be cut in two. Phillips seems to have assumed that Palliser knew he would act on the report and that air cover would be arranged. So he did not signal his change of course to Singapore, possibly not wanting to reveal his position by breaking wireless silence.

The report was a false alarm, and Singapore did not provide fighter cover, having no reason to suppose any was needed. Another submarine sighted the ships and radioed Phillips's position to French Indo-China. The 22nd Air Flotilla set out again at 6 a.m. on the 10th, with thirty bombers and fifty torpedo bombers. They flew south, 150 miles beyond Kuantan, almost as far as Singapore, seeing nothing. Then, on the return flight, cloud broke over the British ships. High-level bombers came in first, just after 11 a.m., followed by the torpedo-bombers. A bomb hit the *Repulse*, but she managed to dodge the next attack, and went to help the *Prince of Wales*, severely damaged by two hits. The *Repulse* was hit again, then four torpedoes in rapid succession found the *Prince of Wales*. The *Repulse* rolled over at 12.33 p.m.; 796 men, including Captain Tennant, her commander, were rescued by destroyers, out of 1,309. The steering gear of the *Prince of Wales* was out of control before noon and at 1.20 p.m. the great ship finally turned turtle and sank, taking Admiral Sir Tom Phillips to the bottom with her.

Whether it was confidence in his own ships, or fear of breaking wireless silence for security reasons, that prevented him asking for fighter cover while at sea, and informing Singapore of his intentions, we shall never know. Brooke-Popham had no inkling of the attack until the *Repulse* radioed that she was being bombed. Fighters were then sent to Kuantan, but arrived too late.

Apart from the Japanese preponderance in aircraft carriers, the Allied fleets and the Japanese fleet had been roughly equally matched when hostilities began. By the afternoon of 10 December 1941, the Japanese fleet was mistress of the seas from Hawaii to Ceylon. The army in Malaya was on its own.

The British positions were dictated by a string of political reasons. The army was not there to defend territory, but to protect the airfields. The airfields were not there to protect Malaya, but to defend the naval base on Singapore Island. Percival's forward units were therefore to cover the airfields in the Kota Barhu area and around Alor Star, ten miles south of Jitra. The 11th Indian Division (Murray-Lyon) had been in readiness for two days – in pouring tropical rain – to carry out Operation Matador. When this was cancelled, they had to put up barbed wire barriers and lay anti-tank mines and telephone cables. Murray-Lyon told his forward brigade (the 15th) to hold the Japanese north of Jitra until 12 December. Then Japanese medium tanks and lorried infantry broke through. The anti-tank guns which should have stopped them were lying unmanned by the roadside while their gunners sheltered from the rain in the surrounding jungle. After the Japanese column rushed the bridge at Asun, the leading tank was hit and the road blocked. The Japanese cleared the road and their tanks rolled on. On the basis of an inaccurate patrol report that the British were not in position, the leading column put in a night attack. It was halted by British artillery, but when the Japanese began to use their guns the situation turned in their favour. The Japanese had captured a map showing the defence dispositions at Changlun and Jitra and knew the zone was heavily defended. Although their attack was reckless and based on inaccurate intelligence, it gathered its own momentum, and the tank assault carried them through. In fifteen hours the Jitra position was cut through by 500 Japanese, for a loss of fewer than thirty men. Three thousand Indian troops surrendered after taking to the jungle in despair. The British left behind fifty field guns, fifty heavy machine guns, 300 trucks and armoured vehicles, and enough ammunition and food to keep the Japanese going for the next three months.

The 5th Japanese Division had crossed over to the west coast. On this side were the best roads, leading south to Singapore. But the other entry from Siam (Patani–Betong–Kroh) was also soon in Japanese hands, and the 5th Division poured into northern Malaya along both roads. After a stiff British resistance at Kota Barhu, the landing column of the 18th Division pushed inland, taking the airfields in a few hours. In the first week of battle, the Japanese captured the airfields of northern Malaya, and neatly prevented reinforcement by air from India and Burma by seizing the airfield at Victoria Point in Tenasserim. Once the airfields at Alor Star and Kota Barhu had gone, Murray-Lyon asked to withdraw thirty miles south to a prepared position at Gurun. This was refused: the demoralization of troops and civilians by such a withdrawal made it unacceptable. But the request was made again when Murray-Lyon feared his rear communications might be cut by an advance from Kroh. After midnight on 12 December, his tired, rain-sodden men began to move south. Orders went astray, guns and equipment were abandoned, and the fear of enemy tanks made units take to the jungle, while others trying to escape by boat down the coast were shipwrecked. The collapse of the Jitra position, followed by the disaster at Gurun, where 6th Brigade H.Q. was annihilated, almost wrecked the 11th

Indian Division as a fighting force. Murray-Lyon withdrew beyond the Muda River on 16 December, and within four days was pushed further south on to Taiping, leaving Penang uncovered. The British had no tanks and no air cover. The Japanese were operating from forward airfields in northern Malaya, and the British fighters – out-of-date Buffaloes mostly – were no match for the Zeros. Penang completely lacked anti-aircraft defences. When it fell, its radio station and many small craft in the harbour were left to the Japanese.

The British command then had a facelift. Brooke-Popham was relieved as Commander-in-Chief, Far East, on 23 December by Lieutenant-General Sir Henry Pownall, who in turn became chief of staff on 3 January 1942, when the whole command structure was altered by the creation of ABDACOM (American–British–Dutch–Australian Command) under General Wavell. On 24 December, Murray-Lyon and all his three brigade commanders were replaced. The Japanese were in Taiping the day Pownall took over and five days later had taken Ipoh. The next serious attempt to stop them was planned for Kampar, roughly half-way between Penang and Kuala Lumpur.

The hill position of Kampar gave scope for artillery, an arm in which the British were still superior, even when continually harassed from the air. The road and railway south from Ipoh ran past a steep jungle-clad hill nine miles by six and 4,000 feet high, with a road looping round either side. The remnants of the 6th and 15th Brigades, merged together, were to hold this bastion, while the 12th and 28th Brigades fought delaying actions to the north. The new divisional commander (Paris) decided to fall back south of Ipoh on the night of 27–8 December. The 28th Brigade was to move into position at Kampar, and the 12th Brigade to delay the Japanese approach, then withdraw through Kampar to Bidor. The Japanese were on to them at once, and on 29 December kept close behind with tanks. The 12th Brigade was rescued by the armoured cars of the Argylls and managed to cross the Kampar River, but blowing the bridge did not stop the Japanese, and by the time the 12th Brigade was in its reserve position it had been totally beaten, losing almost all its armoured vehicles and 500 men.

Percival knew that reinforcements were on their way: an Indian infantry brigade, the British 18th Division and fifty Hurricane fighters with their pilots. It was vital to keep Japanese aircraft as far from Singapore as possible during the unloading period. If Percival could land the fifty Hurricanes, it might redress the balance in the air. The turn-round of the convoys was timed for 13–15 January and airfields in central Malaya had to be denied to the Japanese for this period.

A probe round the loop road was repulsed on 31 December. The next day the main Kampar position was attacked. Bitter fighting continued throughout New Year's Day and 2 January, until the 6th/15th Brigade started to pull back. But it was not the frontal assault which drove the British out. The

Japanese came down the Perak River in a flotilla of forty small boats and turned the coastal position at Telok Anson. Japanese planes prevented the navy from using its ships against other Japanese forces which had come down the coast, using the boats the British had left behind at Penang. The commander of the 12th Brigade estimated he was under attack at brigade strength and could not keep the road open for more than twenty-four hours. The withdrawal from Kampar was ordered as a result of his report. So a good defensive position was lost, and the 11th Indian Division withdrew to an inferior one at Slim River.

Here the 12th Brigade's area was a stretch of road between Songkai and Trolak, with rubber plantations on either side, and thick jungle behind that. The 28th Brigade covered the area from the eastward turn of the road at Slim River to the Slim River bridge. Battalions were down to company strength and poorly armed, none having more than two anti-tank rifles. Unlike Kampar, the country offered little prospect of effective artillery action.

On the afternoon of 5 January 1942, the Japanese came down the railway line, after blanket bombing of the 12th Brigade's position. They were repulsed, but advanced again down both rail and road corridors, and early on 6 January they put in a column of tanks. When these were 200 yards from the British positions, British artillery opened up and took out the sixth tank. Nineteen others came on, firing at lorries and petrol dumps which exploded in the darkness. A column of lorried British infantry broke up in disorder. The bridge over the Slim River should have been blown, but the Japanese took it intact. By the time a halt was called, the armoured thrust had taken the Japanese through nineteen miles of the 11th Division's area. Troops in the rear were not warned, and the Japanese tanks came as a total surprise. Yet their presence had been reported the afternoon before the attack, and the report was disbelieved at brigade H.Q.

Slim River was the mainland campaign's decisive engagement. When the Japanese broke through that position, central Malaya was lost to the British, and its largest city, Kuala Lumpur, was open to the enemy.

The Australians became involved in the battle once the decision was taken to cease piecemeal retreat and make an extensive withdrawal into Johore. This implied the abandonment without a fight of three provinces: Negri Sembilan, Selangor and Malacca. It also meant that the battle would be fought in open country, where the Japanese could make even better use of tanks. But the line Muar–Mount Ophir–Segamat, with a forward position at Gemas, was thought to offer the Australians the chance to hold the Japanese.

Gordon Bennett proposed that he command all the forces in Johore – he did not think highly of British leadership – or alternatively that the Australians on the east coast should be transferred to the west, leaving the east to the III Corps. Fearing administrative chaos, Percival refused. The decision was taken to stand at Muar, where no bridges crossed the Muar River's lower reaches. Wavell visited the front on 7 January and saw how badly the III Corps had been hammered by the Japanese onslaught. Gordon Bennett was ordered to assemble Westforce, which consisted of an Australian brigade round Segamat, with the 45th Indian Brigade under command, and the 9th Indian Division (the 8th and 22nd Brigades) as soon as it reached Johore. The III Corps would move into positions behind them on a line Endau–Kluang–Batu Pahat, with the 22nd Australian Brigade under command on the east coast.

In other words, Wavell's idea – a lateral division of the defence – was preferred to Percival's longitudinal division, with the Australians on the east and the III Corps on the west. The III Corps was in no state to resist a thrust from the two Japanese divisions (the 5th and the Imperial Guards) now coming down the trunk and coast roads. In the event, when Gordon Bennett could no longer control the widely separated areas of Muar and Segamat, Percival reverted to his original plan.

The 53rd Brigade of the 18th British Division landed at Singapore, with fifty Hurricanes but only twenty-five pilots, on 13 January. They had been three months on board ship, but Percival was by now convinced – wrongly – that five Japanese divisions were facing him, and the new arrivals were flung into the battle before they could become acclimatized.

By 5 January the Japanese were in Kuala Lumpur, where vast stocks of food and ordnance had been left behind. Yamashita then rested his 5th Division on Seremban, while the Guards concentrated in Malacca, the rest of the Japanese 18th Division being landed at Singora. On 14 January the Japanese moved into the Australian area. Gordon Bennett knew how to meet them. Seven hundred yards of trunk road west of Gemas were selected as an ambush site. There was a bridge over the river, with a company of the 2nd/30th Australian Battalion on either side of the road, and a field battery covering the road itself. The Japanese crossed the bridge, which was then blown. They sustained heavy casualties, which would have been heavier had the telephone cables to the Australian guns not been cut. Their attack on Gemas the next day was repulsed; but pressure increased, and the 2nd/30th Battalion was withdrawn that night.

On the west coast, the Japanese wrought havoc on the 45th Brigade at Muar. They landed by sea behind the British positions, crossed the river east of Muar on the night of 16 January, and blocked the Muar–Bakri road. This cut the 45th Brigade's links with its forward battalions, one of which was wiped out trying to break through. The way was open to Yong Peng, a vital junction with the road to Segamat: if Yong Peng fell to the Japanese, the Australians in the centre would be cut off. Bennett sent the 2nd/29th Australian Battalion to reinforce Muar, while the 53rd Brigade relieved an Australian battalion on the east coast, which was promptly switched to Westforce. But further Japanese landings were made between Muar and Batu Pahat, and units of the 53rd Brigade were driven from a crucial defile between Bakri and Yong Peng. The 45th Brigade was ordered to recapture Muar to allow the Australians the four nights they would need to move south, out of Segamat, before they were trapped. Japanese mastery of the air made daytime movement impossible. One prong of the 45th Brigade's three-pronged attack from Bakri was cut to pieces, and the counter-attack was cancelled. The 45th Brigade withdrew, through one road block after another, and its commander (Brigadier Duncan) was killed during the fighting. The force was taken over by Anderson, the commander of the 2nd/29th Australian Battalion, who had to destroy his vehicles and guns and take to the jungle. Of the 4,000 men of the Muar force, less than 1,000 finally rejoined. The Japanese massacred the wounded. The 45th Indian Brigade had been sacrificed, but not pointlessly: its fight had held up the Imperial Guards Division for a week, during which Westforce had managed to escape encirclement.

The next defence line was ninety miles further south, crossing Malaya from Mersing to Batu Pahat, via Kluang and Ayer Hitam. This was the III Corps' area, and Heath took command. No unit was to retreat without Percival's permission. Men's lives sacrificed to protect incoming reinforcements were in vain this time: the 44th Indian Brigade landed, 7,000 strong, nearly all raw and untrained troops; together with 2,000 Australian replacements described later by Sir John Smyth as 'a liability to their own side'.

Challen, who was at Batu Pahat in command of the 6th/15th Brigade, reported on 25 January that he could hold the town no longer. His withdrawal uncovered Westforce at Kluang and Ayer Hitam, which then had to pull out. Split into two, one half of the 6th/15th Brigade was captured, the other half – about 2,700 – escaped by sea.

In east Johore, the Australians repeated their successful ambush technique on the night of 26–7 January. A Japanese force moving through the Nithsdale Estate ten miles out of Mersing entered a 'fire box' of rifle companies, blocked by field guns firing down the centre, and was almost wiped out. But such actions did not reverse the general trend of the British retreat, and Wavell authorized Percival to withdraw on to Singapore Island on 30 January. The 9th Indian Division, on the west, withdrew down the railway line, and the 22nd Australian Brigade down the trunk road. But the road and railway ran separately for twenty miles, and the 9th Division's guns and vehicles, using the road, were cut off from the men. A railway bridge was blown, taking the telegraph with it. Units on the railway lost contact, as their wireless sets were sent by road. The Japanese slipped in between the 8th Indian Brigade and the 22nd Indian Brigade without the divisional commander (Barstow) being aware of this. He was killed trying to reach his forward brigade. Painter, in command of the 22nd Brigade, took to the jungle with his wounded. After four nights' bitter slog in unspeakable conditions, he failed to reach the causeway and was forced to surrender on 1 February.

In the last phase of the mainland campaign, the 45th Indian Brigade had been smashed to pieces, and the 22nd Indian Brigade's troops captured or killed. The III Corps was piped into Singapore Island at the end of January, several thousands of men fewer than it had expected to be. As the strains of 'Jennie's Black E'en' died away, the causeway was blown. A hole seventy yards long appeared in the structure. The Japanese would not be able to cross on foot. At any rate, not at high tide. At low tide, the break turned out to be only four foot deep. . . .

The population of Singapore was 500,000, but it had swollen with refugees and reinforcements to close on a million by the end of January 1942. To defend it, Percival had 85,000 men, including an administrative 'tail' of 15,000: seventeen Indian battalions, thirteen British, six Australian and two Malay. But numbers were deceptive. A large proportion were battered after the mainland campaign or fresh and raw from the convoys. There was enough food for three months, and 17 million gallons of water a day were available from the reservoirs. There was ample ammunition, save for the field guns, limited to 1,500 rounds apiece.

Percival divided the island into four areas: one round the city extending to Changi on the east, held by the 1st and 2nd Malaya Brigades, and the Straits Settlements Volunteers, with the Fortress Troops; a northern area including Seletar airfield and the naval base, defended by the III Corps (the 11th Indian Division, strengthened with the 8th Indian Brigade, and the 18th British Division, minus much of its weapons and equipment, lost in the *Empress of Britain*); a western area defended by the 8th Australian Division (the 22nd and 27th Australian Brigades, with the 44th Indian Brigade on their southern flank). The 12th Indian Brigade, the command reserve, held the reservoirs.

Percival gave Wavell the impression that he expected the Japanese to attack from the north-east, and sent him a telegram just after midnight on the night of 7–8 February to say that the main Japanese strength seemed to be on that side, north of Pulau Ubin, which was what the Japanese wanted him to believe. On the other hand, he had told the G.S.O.1. of the 11th Division on 28 January that he was convinced the Japanese would land on the west coast. He failed to act on that conviction. He parcelled out his forces, as he had done on the mainland, hoping to cover all possible shore landings, and defeat the Japanese on the beaches. It was almost the perfect formula for failure and produced the same result as at Jitra: out of an overall numerical inferiority – they were three divisions strong – the Japanese contrived to have local superiority at their point of assault.

Rifts grew between civil and military authorities. Given supreme authority to organize civil defence by Duff Cooper, who presided over the War Council, Brigadier Simson found his instructions countermanded by Sir Shenton Thomas, the governor, and was told to refer disputes to the Legal Department. It was the perfect civil service answer, but not the best way to run a siege. When he returned to England, Duff Cooper recommended Thomas's removal, but neither Wavell nor Pownall would support this. Wavell had the added embarrassment of reporting to Churchill on the island's inadequate defences. The fortress cannon had all-round traverse, but their flat trajectory made them useless for counter-battery work against the mainland. Landward defences were nearly non-existent. 'The possibility of Singapore having no landward defences,' Churchill later wrote, 'no more entered my mind than that of a battleship being launched without a bottom.'

Churchill expected a battle in the streets: 'I want to make it absolutely clear,' he wired to Wavell, 'that I expect every inch of ground to be defended, every scrap of material or defences to be blown to pieces to prevent capture by the enemy, and no question of surrender to be entertained until after protracted fighting among the ruins of Singapore city.' He was to be denied his imperial romantic *Götterdämmerung*. The upshot would be less glamorous.

Yamashita had been warned by a German general that oil could be used to set water alight, so his guns destroyed the oil tanks on the north shores of the island. He also planned an elaborate deception. The Imperial Guards were to show considerable activity in east Johore, and to occupy Pulau Ubin to make Percival think the attack would come from the north-east. Percival did in fact retain two divisions on this side. On the night of 8 February, the 5th and 18th Japanese Divisions made for the water's edge. Their artillery opened fire at 11 p.m. all along the straits, 440 guns using 200 rounds per gun. The first wave, 4,000 men, crossed at midnight from the north-west. By dawn, the entire infantry of both divisions, and part of their artillery, were ashore. The crossing was on the 8th Australian Division's front. The 44th Indian Brigade was attacked but fought back successfully. The 22nd Australian Brigade, on the other hand, which bore the main brunt of the landings, had its beach lights, guns and machine guns destroyed by shellfire, and the cutting of lines to forward posts delayed requests for artillery support until it was too late.

Percival reinforced the Australians with his command reserve and then with the 6th/15th Brigade, but Japanese infiltration split the Australians up, and they fell back in small groups, heavily shelled and bombed from the air. That night, Yamashita set up his H.Q. in a rubber plantation just north of Tengah airfield.

The 29th Australian Battalion held the western sector between Kranji and the causeway. On the evening of 9 February the Imperial Guards came ashore on their front at 7.30 p.m., pushing the Australians inland and leaving the 11th Indian Division's flank exposed. From Tengah, Yamashita planned to take Bukit Timah, a 60-foot-high position which dominated the island. His divisional commanders wanted to capture Singapore City by *Kigensetsu* (the 11 February festival celebrating the foundation of the Japanese empire). Accordingly they decided to put in a night attack before their heavy guns could be brought across to the island. By dawn on the 11th they had taken

Bukit Timah. To hasten the British surrender, a message was dropped by air to Percival, urging him to give in. He ignored it.

Yamashita still needed his heavy guns and tanks for the final blow, and for this the causeway had to be reopened. The Imperial Guards had not yet done this. The 5th and 18th Divisions were running out of impetus, and the Guards were now his main strength, though he disliked both them and their commander. They were ordered to advance east of the reservoirs and hit the British on the left flank as they made their expected counter-attack on Bukit Timah. But the Guards refused to be hurried. The reservoir sector was attacked by the 5th Division on 12 February, and stubbornly defended. But by this time heavy guns and tanks were coming across the straits. The Guards moved round north of the reservoirs and cut into the British flank. Repairs to the causeway were completed on 14 February, and soon all the Twenty-Fifth Army's three divisions were concentrated on Singapore.

At this moment, the Japanese discovered that their ammunition was running out. Barely 100 rounds per field gun were left, nowhere near enough for counter-battery work, and the British gunners were devastating. An infantry attack was halted by a furious British artillery barrage.

That barrage made the Japanese revise their thinking: if the British gunners were shelling like this, they no doubt intended a street-by-street and house-by-house defence of Singapore City. The Japanese were nearing exhaustion. The prize, which seemed to be within their grasp, was now receding.

Then, at 2 p.m. on 15 February 1942, the phone rang in Army Tactical H.Q. at Bukit Panjang to report the appearance of a peace envoy, a brigadier with a white flag. At first the Japanese were worried that it might be a trick – but it was no trick. Later in the day, Percival himself came to treat for peace with Yamashita across a table in the Bukit Timah Ford factory.

At 8.30 p.m. on 15 February 1942 British troops on the island ceased fire.

Judgement by hindsight is a perennial hazard for writers on the campaign in Malaya and the fall of Singapore. Recriminations are easy, and there is no lack of targets. But historical writing since 1945 has not gone uniformly in that direction. Journalists have published lively accounts of the sequence of British errors which led to the catastrophe, but apart from a thickening of anecdote, the analysis is little further advanced than it was in 1942. The official Japanese histories offer rectification of detail, but little else. Percival's reputation has been ably defended by Sir John Smyth, who had himself suffered from the summary judgements of his superiors in the parallel campaign in Burma. He showed that Percival was aware of the needs of Malaya before war broke out, that Whitehall had refused to face the facts about reinforcement of a difficult position, and that lack of training and inexperience in juniors contributed largely to the collapse.

But the purely military narratives play down or blithely ignore other factors. The racial factor is one of these. Until almost the final moments of the battle, there was little attempt to enlist the support of the local population.

Certainly there were Malay battalions, but they were confined to garrison roles on the island and their fighting qualities were not rated highly. Otherwise the Malays were regarded as a source of civilian labour, which dried up once the bombing began. In peacetime, fear of arousing Japanese hostility, and other political motives, had made the British soft-pedal any organization of the Chinese for defence, though a belated attempt to use them was made by the creation of a guerilla unit of young Chinese.

Little was done to defend the towns of Malaya from air attack, and bitter resentment was caused by the evacuation of mainly European women and children from towns threatened by the Japanese. Disaffection was not unknown among Indian officers, who were to bear the brunt of the initial Japanese assault, and racial discrimination was again at its root. Indians who were expected to give their lives in defence of the Empire were not permitted to enter the clubs of its cities, and although they were serving away from home were not paid the overseas rates given to their European counterparts or allowed to travel in the same railway carriages.

The British official history does not even mention the name of the Japanese Major Fujiwara. Yet it was he who derived much of the political profit from the defeat. After the surrender he took charge of the Indian prisoners-of-war and formed thousands of them into the anti-British force known as the *Azad Hind Fauj*, or Indian National Army. Many prisoners refused to join it. But Fujiwara would not have had the success he did achieve – one which was to play a crucial role in India's struggle for independence – without a strong basis of disaffection to work on.

When Percival summed up the cause of the defeat, he put inferiority in the air and lack of tanks high on the list. Rightly so. But Yamashita did the same piece of homework, and in his notes racial disunity – friction between British, Chinese, Malays, Indians and Australians – is given as one of the reasons for the British surrender.

On the other hand, it is also true that Percival was concerned for the civilian population of Singapore. He was a humane man, and it was unthinkable that a million Chinese and Malays should die of thirst or plague, or be put to the sword, simply in order to prolong resistance by – at the most – a few days or weeks. Once the Japanese controlled the reservoirs and could cut off the city's water, surrender was inevitable if civilian lives were to be saved.

In the purely local sense, Percival was right. His staff were convinced that the Japanese were only hours away from a total onslaught which would lead them into the heart of Singapore. Cyril Wild, the G.S.O.2 of the III Indian Corps, who acted as Percival's interpreter in the parley with Yamashita, stole a glance at the Japanese maps. From the arrows scrawled on them he saw quite clearly the times and directions of the attack planned for the night of February 15. 'The Japanese would have broken right through to the sea,' he wrote later.

This may seem likely. Many of the British forces were disintegrating in and around the city. It may have been psychologically impossible to reverse the pattern of constant withdrawals and demolitions into a death-or-glory stand. What troops might have done on their home ground they would have done less willingly for a piece of Empire. Yet others were stunned by the surrender and were ready to fight on.

The artillery contrast between the two sides is striking. The gunners had fought back hard and had hundreds of rounds unspent. The Japanese were nearing the end of their stocks. The Japanese 5th Division, which had done most of the fighting, was played out. Yamashita was on tenterhooks lest the British should decide to fight on. This explains his hectoring summons to Percival over the conference table: 'Do you intend to surrender unconditionally, YES OR NO?' It was not the brutal arrogance of the conqueror, as it seemed to many at the time and since. Like his staff, Yamashita was unsure, almost to the last, whether or not the British overture was a trick to gain time, and, aware that his own offensive had run out, time was the thing he could least afford to be generous with.

What might have happened had Percival answered NO then, and decided to sacrifice the people of Singapore? Wavell expected that the Japanese could be fought to a standstill, held, and then driven back. The Japanese campaign in Burma would slow down because their rear would be insecure. Their landings in Java and the rest of the East Indies might be made difficult if not impossible. British or Australian reinforcements could then be brought into Singapore, and turn the scales. It might have been like this. But Japan's Burma campaign was proceeding on its own impetus, and nothing short of cutting its roads from Siam would have stopped it. The Dutch East Indies archipelago was so scattered and vulnerable that a determined force, even if repulsed from one island, might easily have succeeded in landing on another. And the Japanese had resources in manpower in China and Manchuria which could have replaced Yamashita's tired troops, whereas British possibilities of reinforcement were limited. The Japanese were already moving on to Sumatra and preparing to land in Java, and had footholds elsewhere in the Indies.

That being said, it remains a fascinating imponderable, whether a last-ditch resistance might have had a lasting strategic effect. What one of Yamashita's staff has recently written on this is therefore of great interest. In the magazine *Maru*, Major Kunitake says that when the white flag was hoisted on the 5th Division's front, and the news phoned in to the Twenty-fifth Army at 2 p.m. on the afternoon of 15 February, every man in Army H.Q. held his breath. At first there was disbelief. Then the Japanese became convinced that it was a British ruse to gain time. They felt that they had made little progress in the last day or two, their ammunition was nearly exhausted, and they had no more reserves to throw into the battle. Their men were in a state of extreme fatigue. So much so that the Japanese were beginning to feel that the appeal to Percival had been premature, and that they might be the ones to surrender.

Perhaps, then, Wavell was right after all? Had their leadership been less compassionate, the British might have held the Japanese in the ruins of Singapore, or made them pay so dearly for its possession that stalemate might have resulted, giving enough time to right the balance.

As it was, in seventy days, and at a cost of no more than 3,500 dead, the Japanese led nearly 100,000 British, Indian and Australian troops into captivity, and smashed for ever the British Empire in the East.

Note on Sources

1. DESPATCHES

Brooke-Popham, Air Chief Marshal Sir Robert, Commander-in-Chief Far East, *Operations in the Far East, from 17th October 1940 to 27th December 1941* (1948).

Maltby, Air Vice-Marshal Sir Paul, *Air operations during the campaign in Malaya and the Netherlands East Indies from 8th December 1941 to 12th March 1942* (1948).

Percival, Lieutenant-General A. E., *Operations of Malaya Command, from 8th December 1941 to 15th February 1942* (1948).

Wavell, General Sir Archibald, *Despatch by the Supreme Commander of the ABDA area to the Combined Chiefs of Staff on the Operations in the South-West Pacific 15th January 1942 to 25th February 1942* (1948).

2. OFFICIAL HISTORIES

(i) *British*

Gwyer, J. M. A. and J. R. M. Butler, *History of the Second World War. Grand Strategy III*, Parts 1 and 2 (1964).

Kirby, Major-General S. Woodburn, *The War Against Japan*, Vol. 1 (1957).

Roskill, Captain S. W., *The War at Sea, 1939–1945, Vol. 1: The Defensive* (1954).

(ii) *Indian*

Mackenzie, Compton, *Eastern Epic, Vol. 1, Defence* (1951).

Prasad, Bisheshwar, ed., *The Official History of the Indian Armed Forces in the Second World War (1939–1945). Campaigns in South-East Asia 1941–42* (1960).

(iii) *Australian*

Wigmore, Lionel, *Australia in the War of 1939–45 (Army): The Japanese Thrust* (1957).

(iv) *Japanese*

Hitō Marē hōmen kaigun shinkō sakusen (Naval Operations in the Philippines and Malaya Areas) (1969).

Marē Sakusen (The Campaign in Malaya), compiled by a group of professors of military history for the Society for the Diffusion of Military Historical Research (1969).

Marē Shinkō Sakusen (The Campaign in Malaya) (1966).

3. COMMANDERS' AND PARTICIPANTS' NARRATIVES

(i) *British*

Coombes, J. H. H., *Banpong Express. Malaya and After* (1949).

Percival, Lieutenant-General A. E., *The War in Malaya* (1949).

Simson, Brigadier Ivan, *Singapore – Too Little, Too Late* (1970).

Stewart, Brigadier I. MacA., *History of the Argyll and Sutherland Highlanders (The Thin Red Line) Malayan Campaign 1941–2* (1947).

(ii) *Indian*

Durrani, Lieutenant-Colonel M. K., *The Sixth Column* (1955).

Khan, Major-General Shahnawaz, *INA and its Netaji* (1946).

(iii) *Australian*

Bennett, Lieutenant-General H. Gordon, *Why Singapore Fell* (1944).

(iv) *Japanese*

Fujiwara, Lieutenant-General Iwaiichi, *F Kikan* (F Organization) (1966).

Itō, Masanori, *et al.*, ed., *Jitsuroku Taiheiyō Sensō* (Authentic Accounts of the War in the Pacific), Vol. 1 (1960).

Iwakuro, Major-General Takeo, *Seiki no shingun. Shingapōru sōkōgeki* (A Historic March. The Assault on Singapore) (1956).

Kunitake, Major Teruo, 'Watakushi wa ano hi, mosho Yamashita ni eikan wo sasageta' ('That day I offered the victor's laurels to the conquering General Yamashita'), MARU, No. 324, August 1973, pp. 80–85.

Tsuji, Colonel Masanobu, *Singapore. The Japanese Version* (1962).

4. CONTEMPORARY JOURNALISTS' ACCOUNTS

Brown, Cecil, *Suez to Singapore* (1943?).

Gallagher, O. D., *Retreat in the East* (1942).

Morrison, Ian, *Malayan Postscript* (1942).

5. LATER ACCOUNTS

Bryant, Sir Arthur, *The Turn of the Tide* (1957).

Caffrey, Kate, *Out in the Midday Sun* (1974).

Churchill, Sir Winston, *The Second World War, Vol. IV, The Hinge of Fate* (1951).

Coffey, Thomas M., *Imperial Tragedy* (1970).

Cooper, Duff, *Old Men Forget* (1953).

De Belot, Contre-Amiral R., (R), *La Guerre aéronavale du Pacifique (1941–1945)* (1957).

Firkins, Peter, *The Australians in Nine Wars* (Ch. 25, 'The Worst Disaster') (1972).

Ghosh, K. K., *The Indian National Army* (1969).

Kennedy, Major-General Sir John, *The Business of War* (1957).

La Bruyère, René, *La Guerre du Pacifique* (1945).

Leasor, James, *Singapore, the Battle that changed the World* (1968).

Lebra, Joyce C., *Jungle Alliance* (1971).

Louis, Wm. Roger, *British Strategy in the Far East 1919–1939* (1971).

Owen, Frank, *The Fall of Singapore* (1960).

Smyth, Sir John, *Percival and the Tragedy of Singapore* (1971).

Toland, John, *But Not in Shame* (1964).

6. MANUSCRIPT SOURCES

Wild, Captain Cyril, *Notes on the Malayan Campaign.*

Wild, Captain Cyril, *Notes on the Fall of Singapore.*

Air power dominated the naval war in the Pacific. A squadron of Douglas Devastator torpedo bombers aboard the U.S. carrier Enterprise *prepare for take-off, 4 June 1942*

Chapter Thirteen

MIDWAY

Peter Simkins

BY THE EARLY SPRING of 1942, those responsible for shaping Japanese strategy had been encouraged, by the succession of victories following Pearl Harbor, to consider expanding the ribbon defence perimeter they had originally conceived. However, the form and direction which this second phase of operations should take became the subject of a prolonged debate in the senior echelons of the Japanese Naval High Command.

In theory, Japanese strategic planning was the joint responsibility of the Army and Navy General Staffs, acting through Imperial General Headquarters. The Naval General Staff, under Admiral Osami Nagano, advocated either an advance westward against India or a thrust southward against Australia, but the army, with their eyes on the Asian mainland and Russia, objected to the large-scale troop requirements for such offensives. Nagano was therefore forced to produce a modified plan to isolate Australia by cutting her lines of communication with the United States. This involved moving from Japanese-held Rabaul and Truk into eastern New Guinea and down the Solomons and New Hebrides to New Caledonia, Fiji and Samoa. Accordingly, Lae and Salamaua were occupied in early March, and by April preparations for the capture of Port Moresby and Tulagi were in hand.

Admiral Isoruku Yamamoto, commander-in-chief of the Combined Fleet, favoured a different strategy. He had already demonstrated his powerful influence on Japanese planning by his insistence on the Pearl Harbor attack despite the opposition of the Naval General Staff, and the success of this and subsequent operations had reinforced his position. A former naval attaché in Washington, he recognized the huge industrial resources of the United States and was convinced that a long war would be fatal for Japan. Only by destroying the remainder of the U.S. Pacific Fleet, and particularly its aircraft carriers, whose hit-and-run tactics in the south Pacific were causing increasing concern, could Japan's security be maintained, her conquests consolidated, and satisfactory peace terms negotiated. Yamamoto's plan, therefore, was to lure the Pacific Fleet into a decisive battle and eliminate it as a fighting force.

To do this, he proposed to occupy the two islands on the tiny atoll of Midway, 1,135 miles W.N.W. of Pearl Harbor and the westernmost outpost of the Hawaiian chain. Claimed by America in 1867, this aptly named atoll was situated, like a giant aircraft carrier, midway across the Pacific. By 1942, its strategic importance as an air base was second only to that of Pearl Harbor, for Midway-based search aircraft could provide early warning of possible Japanese moves against Hawaii from the west. Yamamoto rightly calculated that the Americans could ill afford to lose this 'sentry to Hawaii', thereby leaving the Japanese perilously close to Pearl Harbor. By attacking Midway, he thus hoped to entice the American carriers to destruction at the hands of the Combined Fleet and open the way for a negotiated peace on Japan's terms. Simultaneous occupation of the western Aleutians might offer further bait. Even if the Americans failed to react to either move, the Japanese would, at worst. have gained excellent vantage points from which to detect any threats which the Pacific Fleet's carriers might mount against the Japanese homeland from the east.

The strategic debate dragged on until 18 April, when sixteen B-25 Mitchell bombers, led by Lieutenant-Colonel James Doolittle, took off from the aircraft carrier *Hornet* for a surprise attack on Tokyo. Actual damage was slight but Japan suffered a major psychological shock. The strength of Yamamoto's case was now clear, and opposition to the Combined Fleet's plan dissolved. Although preparations for the Port Moresby-Tulagi thrust had now gone too far to be abandoned, Imperial General Headquarters issued Navy Order 18 on 5 May, directing the Combined Fleet 'to carry out the occupation of Midway Island and key points in the Western Aleutians, in co-operation with the Army'. Operation M.I., as it was called, was to take place early in June. Of its two central objectives, the occupation of Midway and the Aleutians was, in fact, the more limited aim. The U.S. Pacific Fleet was Yamamoto's real target.

These objectives were to be achieved by five main naval forces, each subdivided into two or more groups. All the larger units would operate semi-independently but were theoretically capable of mutual support if the situation dictated it. An Advance Expeditionary Force of submarines was to reconnoitre ahead of the Combined Fleet. While some took station off the Aleutians and America's west coast and one submarine scouted Midway itself, four more would patrol a line 500 miles west of Oahu with another seven deployed across the route from Pearl Harbor to Midway. All were to be in position by 1 June, in the hope of giving Yamamoto ample warning of any sortie by the Pacific Fleet. The attack on the Aleutians was to be handled by Vice-Admiral Hosogaya's Northern Area Force. This included the transports and support ships of the Attu and Kiska Occupation Forces and also the Second Carrier Striking Force, under Rear-Admiral Kakuta, with the light carriers *Ryujo* and *Junyo*, two heavy cruisers and screening vessels. Kakuta's carriers, which would later cover the landings in the western Aleutians, would open the battle on 3 June with an air attack on Dutch Harbor. This, it was hoped, might deceive the Americans as to the direction of the main attack and draw part of the Pacific Fleet northwards.

The Midway Occupation Force, commanded by Vice-Admiral Kondo, was organized around Rear-Admiral Tanaka's Transport Group of twelve invasion transports, carrying 5,000 assault and construction troops, closely screened by a cruiser and ten destroyers. Having assembled at Saipan by 24 May, the transports would sail for Midway on 27 May, linking up with Rear-Admiral Kurita's Support Group of four heavy cruisers and two destroyers, which would arrive from Guam to cover the southern flank of the invasion force. Further support would be given by the powerful Second Fleet Covering Group, under Kondo's direct command, and including the light cruiser *Zuiho*, two battleships, five cruisers and eight destroyers.

The key role in Yamamoto's plan fell to Vice-Admiral Chuichi Nagumo's First Carrier Striking Force, the pride of the Combined Fleet after its successes at Pearl Harbor and in the Dutch East Indies and Indian Ocean. Nagumo himself led the 1st Carrier Division, comprising the *Akagi* (his flagship) and the *Kaga*; the 2nd Carrier Division, under the aggressive Rear-Admiral Yamaguchi, comprised the *Hiryu* and the *Soryu*. These four carriers would be covered by Rear-Admiral Abe's Support Group, with the battleships *Haruna* and *Kirishima* and the heavy cruisers *Tone* and *Chikuma*. A Screening Group, with the cruiser *Nagara* and eleven destroyers, would also accompany the carriers. Nagumo's first task was precisely defined: at dawn on 4 June he was to launch an air strike to soften up Midway and eliminate its air units prior to the actual landings by the Occupation Force after dusk on 5 June. His second, more important, task was to engage the U.S. Pacific Fleet if, as was almost inevitable, it tried to interfere. He was then to strike it a crippling blow.

Yamamoto, following up with the Main Body, would exercise overall command from his flagship *Yamato*, the largest battleship afloat. The *Yamato*, two other battleships, the light cruiser *Hosho*, a cruiser and twelve destroyers would position themselves 600 miles north-west of Midway and some 300 miles west of Nagumo's carriers, ready to close for the kill once Nagumo had mauled the Pacific Fleet. Finally, an Aleutian Screening Force, of four battleships and two cruisers, would be detached from the Main Body and would wait between the Aleutians and Midway to intercept enemy forces heading in either direction.

This complex and subtle plan, with its multiple objectives and diversionary tactics, called for precise timing if the junction of several forces was to be achieved at the crucial moment, and depended, above all, on the maintenance of absolute secrecy, at least until Nagumo had launched his initial strike on 4 June. Complete radio silence was therefore to be imposed on all units during the approach to Midway. Yamamoto and his staff had based their plan on the belief that the Americans would have no carriers in the vicinity of Midway between 4 and 6 June and that they would only react positively in this area after Nagumo had revealed his presence. It was thought unlikely that the Pacific Fleet could mount a real challenge until 7 or 8 June, by which time Midway would be secured and Nagumo free to deal with the threat. Everything, in fact, rested on the confident assumption that the Americans would react exactly as the Japanese predicted and hoped.

Unknown to the Japanese, however, their naval code had been broken, early in 1942, by the U.S. Navy's Combat Intelligence Unit at Pearl Harbor. By late April, these crypto-analysts had pieced together enough scraps of information to produce a remarkably accurate picture of Japanese plans and preparations. Armed with this knowledge, Admiral Chester W. Nimitz who, in his dual capacity as Commander-in-Chief Pacific Fleet and Pacific Ocean Areas, exercised strategic and broad tactical control over all American forces in the Pacific outside General MacArthur's South-west Pacific Area, was able to deploy his slender forces with at least some prospect of countering the Japanese offensives. His immediate priority was to send Rear-Admiral Frank I. Fletcher's Task Force 17, with the carriers *Yorktown* and *Lexington*, to block the Japanese attempt to capture Port Moresby in south-eastern New Guinea and Tulagi in the eastern Solomons, scheduled to begin on 3 May. The ensuing Battle of the Coral Sea (4–8 May) was the first ever carrier versus carrier action and the first naval battle in history in which the opposing ships never came within sight of each other. Tulagi fell to the Japanese but the occupation of Port Moresby was thwarted. In the battle, the *Lexington* was sunk and the *Yorktown* damaged, while the Japanese lost the light cruiser *Shoho*. Of the two bigger Japanese carriers involved, the *Shokaku* was damaged and the *Zuikaku* suffered heavy aircrew losses which would take weeks to replace. Consequently, neither would be available for Operation M.I.

By mid-May Nimitz knew for certain that Midway would be the target of a major amphibious assault and did everything possible to strengthen the atoll's defences. Colonel Harold Shannon's 6th Marine Defence Battalion was reinforced, and on 3 June Shannon's garrison numbered 2,138 marines. By this time, Captain Cyril Simard, commanding the shore-based air detachments, would also have had some 1,494 aircrew and ancillary troops, including 1,000 navy, 374 Marine Corps and 120 army personnel. More anti-aircraft guns were installed, bombproof shelters were constructed, and the beaches around Sand Island and Eastern Island, where the airstrip was located, were heavily mined and covered with barbed wire. Nineteen submarines were deployed to cover the western and northern approaches to Midway and Oahu. Equally important, the air units were reinforced. Until this time Simard had had only twenty-one obsolescent Marine Corps Buffalo fighters and sixteen old Vindicator dive-bombers available for combat. During the last few days in May these were augmented by eighteen marine Dauntless dive-bombers and seven Wildcat fighters, six navy Avenger torpedo planes and four army B-26 Marauder bombers, the latter rigged for torpedo attacks. Some fifteen to eighteen army B-17 Flying Fortress bombers, switching daily between Oahu and Midway, were also added, while the number of navy P.B.Y. Catalina flying boats for reconnaissance was increased to thirty-two, the total number of aircraft on the atoll being brought up to 121 by 4 June.

Despite these measures, Nimitz was aware that Midway's fate ultimately depended on naval support, and he could muster precious little of this, being particularly short of aircraft carriers. The *Enterprise* and the *Hornet*, of Vice-Admiral William F. Halsey's Task Force 16, were recalled from patrol in the south Pacific and entered Pearl Harbor on 26 May. The damaged *Yorktown*, the surviving carrier of Fletcher's Task Force 17, came in on 27 May and was promptly drydocked. Working day and night, the men of the

Pearl Harbor navy yard effected, in three days, repairs which would normally have taken weeks. Some repairs were makeshift and three damaged boilers remained untouched, reducing the *Yorktown*'s speed, but, incredibly, she was ready to put to sea by 30 May. To escort the *Enterprise* and the *Hornet* only five heavy cruisers, one light cruiser and nine destroyers were available, and the *Yorktown* could be provided only with a weak screen of two heavy cruisers and five destroyers. Having decided to concentrate on the defence of Midway, all Nimitz could spare for the Aleutians was a force of two heavy and three light cruisers and ten destroyers. Meanwhile, the impetuous, colourful 'Bull' Halsey had been taken ill and was replaced by the quiet, methodical Rear-Admiral Raymond A. Spruance, until now the commander of Task Force 16's cruisers and destroyers. Spruance was no aviator, but his brilliant mind and cool judgement would prove invaluable assets in the days ahead.

Knowing only too well that if his three carriers were lost Hawaii and the west coast of America would be open to the Japanese, Nimitz outlined his plan of operations on 27 May, ordering Fletcher and Spruance to 'inflict maximum damage on [the] enemy by employing strong attrition tactics'. In a special Letter of Instruction he added: 'In carrying out the task assigned . . . you will be governed by the principle of calculated risk, which you will interpret to mean the avoidance of exposure of your force to attack by superior enemy forces without good prospect of inflicting . . . greater damage on the enemy.' He shrewdly directed them to take up initial positions north-east of Midway, thus placing them on the flank of Nagumo's carriers and beyond the search range of the approaching enemy. As soon as Task Force 16 and 17 had linked up, Fletcher, as the senior officer, would assume tactical command but, because Spruance had the larger task force, the faster carriers and the more experienced air staff, it was inevitable that he would exert a powerful influence on tactical decisions in the coming battle.

Task Force 16 left Pearl Harbor on 28 May, followed, two days later, by the *Yorktown* force. Refuelling at sea, the two task forces met at 'Point Luck', about 325 miles north-east of Midway, just before noon on 2 June. Thus, even before the scouting Japanese submarines had reached their stations, Fletcher and Spruance were already beyond their patrol lines and in a favourable tactical position. In the meantime, between 20 and 28 May, the rest of the huge Japanese armada had sailed from Japan, Saipan and Guam, its various components advancing eastwards in a wide, multi-headed formation towards their respective objectives. Nagumo had, in fact, left Hashirajima anchorage on 26 May, two days before the Main Body, and his carriers would be some 600 miles ahead of Yamamoto during the early stages of the approach.

Yamamoto and Nagumo both had cause for concern over the next few days, particularly as they were still uncertain of the whereabouts of the American carriers. The Japanese believed they had sunk two carriers in the Coral Sea and had ruled out the *Yorktown*. Halsey's two carriers had last been spotted in the Solomons on 18 May, but it was thought highly probable that they were now at Pearl Harbor. To check this, two flying boats from the Marshall Islands had been detailed to refuel from a submarine at French Frigate Shoals, 500 miles north-west of Hawaii, and then fly over Pearl Harbor during the evening of 30 May, but when the submarine arrived to find the shoals already in use as an American seaplane base the mission was abandoned. Both the Japanese submarine cordon and the flying boats had therefore failed to locate the Pacific Fleet's carriers. Even so, reports from a variety of sources between 31 May and 1 June noted a considerable increase in radio traffic out of Hawaii, the establishment of an American submarine cordon south-west of Midway and the extension of air patrols from the atoll, all indicating that the Japanese plan was known. Yet, in the absence of confirmation that the American carriers were at sea, Yamamoto remained confident that all was well.

Because of the *Akagi*'s limited radio-receiving capacity, Nagumo had not received much of this important information and, feeling it advisable to continue radio silence, Yamamoto and his staff had chosen not to relay it to him. Nagumo was soon in the dark in more than one sense for, on 1 June, he ran into a front of heavy cloud and fog which extended to within 340 miles of Midway. Indeed, by 1.30 p.m. on 2 June, when he reached the point where it was necessary to change course for the final approach, he had lost visual contact with his own ships and was obliged to break radio silence to give the order. However, the weather conditions also protected him from American search planes. Beginning on 30 May, twenty Midway-based Catalinas had daily been patrolling sectors from the south-west to the north-east to a range of 700–800 miles, while another P.B.Y. took off in the early hours to be at the expected launching position of the Japanese carriers by dawn. The army B-17s had also begun to conduct search and attack missions to the west but, in spite of all this activity, none of the Japanese forces had been sighted by nightfall on 2 June.

Both sides made their first tentative thrusts and parries on 3 June, as Yamamoto's forces approached their objectives. At dawn, Kakuta launched his air strike on Dutch Harbor, inflicting considerable damage on oil storage tanks and other installations, but Nimitz refused to be drawn off-balance by these events far away to the north. Then, shortly before 9 a.m., a Catalina, on its morning patrol some 700 miles west of Midway, spotted a large body of ships on course for the atoll. The American commanders, expecting Nagumo's attack to come from the north-west, correctly identified these as the transports of the Occupation Force and again declined the bait offered to their carriers. Nine B-17s took off from Midway at noon and bombed the transports from between 8,000 and 12,000 feet at 4.24 p.m., but their attack was ineffective. Four radar-equipped Catalinas also made a torpedo attack by moonlight at 1.43 a.m. on 4 June, but although they damaged the oiler *Akebono Maru*, the ship remained in formation. By this time, Fletcher and Spruance were steaming south-west, heading for a point 200 miles north of Midway which would place them within scouting range of Nagumo at dawn. Nagumo's carriers, now emerging from the adverse weather, but still covered by broken clouds, were approaching the point, 240 miles north-west of the atoll, from which the scheduled air strike was to be launched. At daybreak on 4 June the opposing carrier forces were therefore some 250 miles apart on an east–west axis.

At 4.30 a.m., the *Yorktown* despatched ten Dauntless aircraft to search a 100-mile arc to the north. Meanwhile, on Nagumo's carriers, a force of 108 strike aircraft and fighters took off to attack Midway. Led by Lieutenant Joichi Tomonaga, this force comprised thirty-six 'Kate' torpedo-bombers from the *Hiryu* and the *Soryu*, thirty-six 'Val' dive-bombers from the *Akagi* and the *Kaga* and nine escorting Zeros from each carrier. The Kates and Vals were armed with bombs suitable for land targets. Nagumo also launched seven scouting aircraft, including two seaplanes each from the *Tone* and the *Chikuma*. These scouts were to fan out from the north-east to the south-east, each covering a wedge-shaped search sector to a radius of 300 miles. Normally a second wave of scout planes would have taken off an hour later but Nagumo, who still did not suspect the presence of enemy naval forces in the area, failed to take the routine precaution of mounting a two-phase search. Moreover, one of the *Tone*'s seaplanes, delayed by catapult trouble, left thirty minutes late, at 5 a.m., an apparently minor setback which was to have far-reaching consequences.

Nagumo did, however, prepare a second attack wave to deal with any American naval forces which might be located. This wave included thirty-six torpedo aircraft from the *Akagi* and the *Kaga*, thirty-six dive-bombers from the *Hiryu* and the *Soryu* and a further thirty-six fighters. This time the Kates were to carry torpedoes and the Vals armour-piercing bombs.

At about 5.10, a Midway-based P.B.Y., flown by Lieutenant Howard Ady, who was searching the vital sector to the north-west, spotted a Japanese seaplane heading towards Midway. Following the opposite course, Ady sighted the Japanese carriers at 5.30, reporting their presence to Midway at 5.34. Twenty minutes later he signalled: 'Two carriers and main body of ships, carrier in front, bearing 320°, distant 180 [miles from Midway], course 135°, speed 25.' Another P.B.Y. pilot, further to the south, saw Tomonaga's strike aircraft, and at 5.45 radioed the warning: 'Many planes heading Midway. Bearing 320°, distant 150.'

Although only two Japanese carriers had been sighted, and Ady's report of their position was inaccurate by about forty miles, Fletcher now at least had some idea of Nagumo's whereabouts. Accordingly, Fletcher recalled his scouts and, at 6.07, ordered Spruance to 'proceed south-westerly and attack enemy carriers when definitely located.' Task Force 16 turned away and increased speed to twenty-five knots, Fletcher promising to follow as soon as his Dauntlesses were recovered. Nagumo's own search aircraft were meanwhile being beset by bad luck. One of the *Chikuma*'s seaplanes was forced to return early with engine trouble and the other, which according to its flight plan must have flown directly over the American carriers, failed to sight anything.

On Midway itself all serviceable aircraft had been sent aloft between 6 and 6.15, the marine fighters taking off first to intercept Tomonaga while the remainder headed for Nagumo's position. Fifteen B-17s which had left before dawn to attack the invasion transports, were also diverted to the Japanese carriers. The Buffaloes and Wildcats met Tomonaga's force less than thirty miles from the atoll and scored several victories, but they were soon outclassed by the escorting Zeros. Seventeen of the defending fighters were lost and another seven badly damaged. Tomonaga's bombers pressed on, the Kates dropping their first bombs at about 6.30 with the dive-bombers attacking next through vicious anti-aircraft fire. By 6.50 the marine command post and mess hall on Eastern Island had been destroyed and the powerhouse and fuel system badly hit; on Sand Island the oil tanks and seaplane hangar were destroyed and the hospital and storehouses set on fire. Casualties, however, were light, only eleven being killed. Later estimates put Japanese losses at about one third of the attacking force. Despite the damage, it was clear to Tomonaga that Midway's air strength had escaped destruction, and at 7 a.m. he therefore radioed to Nagumo: 'There is need for a second attack wave.'

While Nagumo considered the implications of this message, the six Avengers and four B-26 Marauders from Midway were fast approaching the Japanese carriers. They were spotted some miles out, giving the carriers time to augment their combat air patrols. The Avengers began their attack at 7.10, attracting a storm of anti-aircraft fire and the attention of the defending Zeros. Half the Avengers were shot down before they could launch their torpedoes and only one returned, severely damaged, to Midway. The B-26s fared little better: racing in at 200 feet, they released their torpedoes at 800 yards, but the attack was unsuccessful. Two Marauders were destroyed, one barely missing the *Akagi* before plunging into the sea. In both attacks, the unreliable American torpedoes were all easily avoided by the Japanese carriers.

For Nagumo, ignorant of the real danger, these attacks removed any remaining doubts about the need for a second strike at the atoll, as Midway-based aircraft obviously posed an immediate threat. Thus, at 7.15 he ordered the second wave of aircraft to stand by to attack Midway. For this mission, all torpedo planes and dive-bombers were to be rearmed with bombs of a type appropriate to land targets. This was a comparatively easy task with the dive-bombers, but on the *Akagi* and the *Kaga* it involved taking the Kates down from the flight deck to the hangar deck below so that the torpedoes could be replaced, a time-consuming operation. The rearming was still in progress when Nagumo received a message which altered the whole situation. Ironically, the *Tone*'s seaplane which had taken off late was searching the very sector where the American carriers were to be found, and at 7.28 her pilot reported: 'Sight what appears to be ten enemy surface ships in position bearing 10°, distance 240 miles from Midway. Course 150°, speed over 20 knots.' Even though the seaplane pilot had not identified carriers, Nagumo now knew, thirty minutes too late, that he faced a major new problem. At 7.45, he suspended the rearming and ordered his carriers to prepare 'to carry out attacks on enemy fleet units'. Torpedoes were to be left on those attack planes which had not as yet changed over to bombs.

As he waited anxiously for more precise information, the Japanese carriers came under attack from the sixteen Midway-based Dauntlesses, led by Major Lofton Henderson. Opting for a shallow, glide-bombing approach because of his squadron's inexperience, Henderson thereby rendered his dive-bombers doubly vulnerable to the Zeros and several, including his own, were shot down as they came in. The others attacked from 300 to 500 feet, concentrating on the *Hiryu*, but of some ten bombs dropped none registered a hit. Only half the force, with six aircraft seriously damaged, returned to Midway.

At 8.09, the *Tone*'s seaplane signalled: 'Enemy is composed of five cruisers and five destroyers.' This message brought considerable relief to Nagumo. He could now, apparently, forget the possible danger from American carriers and again prepare to attack Midway. However, between 8.14 and 8.20 his carriers once more came under attack, this time from the fifteen B-17s and eleven of the Vindicators from Midway. The B-17s, bombing from 20,000 feet, concentrated on the *Hiryu* and the *Soryu* while the slower Vindicators, quickly outnumbered by Zeros, were forced to shift their attack to the nearest target, the battleship *Haruna*. All the B-17s returned safely and only two Vindicators were lost, but none achieved better than a near-miss. The U.S. submarine *Nautilus*, which had hastened to the scene, also unsuccessfully fired a torpedo at a Japanese battleship around 8.25, but survived the intensive depth-charging which followed.

Nagumo's force had emerged unscathed from five separate air attacks, but at 8.20 had come the message that he feared most, the *Tone*'s seaplane pilot cautiously and belatedly reporting: 'The enemy is accompanied by what appears to be a carrier bringing up the rear.' The *Hiryu* and the *Soryu* were now almost ready to launch their dive-bombers and Yamaguchi advocated an immediate strike. Yet, although nearly four hours had elapsed since the first wave had left for Midway, Nagumo was in no position to send off a second, full-strength attack force, for many of the torpedo planes on the *Akagi* and the *Kaga* were still fitted with the bombs intended for Midway. To launch a strike now would also mean despatching the bombers without an adequate escort, as the fighter reserves had been used up defending the carriers and the Zeros were nearly out of fuel. Moreover, Tomonaga's aircraft were returning from Midway and, with some damaged and all low on fuel, their recovery aircraft still had to be brought up from the hangar decks, the launch would occupy an hour, during which the first planes to take off would wait overhead.

By 7.45, with some of his aircraft still on deck, Spruance knew he had been sighted by a Japanese seaplane and decided to wait no longer. Ordering McClusky to proceed on his mission, he thus reduced the chances of achieving a coordinated attack. All units were airborne by 8.06, but Fighting 6's Wildcats, detailed to cover Lieutenant-Commander Eugene Lindsey's Torpedo 6, mistakenly took station instead above the *Hornet*'s Torpedo 8, led by Lieutenant-Commander John Waldron. During the coming battle they were to wait in vain for Lindsey's prearranged signal for help while both Torpedo 6 and Torpedo 8 attacked unescorted. In fact, Task Force 16's air strike flew off in four distinct groups: McClusky's dive-bombers; the *Hornet*'s fighters and dive-bombers; Waldron's Torpedo 8 covered by the Wildcats of Fighting 6; and, finally, Lindsey's Torpedo 6.

Fletcher, aboard the slower *Yorktown*, had initially withheld his air group in the absence of firm reports about the two remaining Japanese carriers which were believed to exist but which were as yet unlocated. At 8.38 he too decided against further delay. Wisely keeping some aircraft in reserve, he launched seventeen Dauntlesses of Lieutenant-Commander Maxwell Leslie's Bombing 3; twelve Devastators of Lieutenant-Commander Lance Massey's Torpedo 3; and six Wildcats from Fighting 3, led by Lieutenant-Commander John Thach. All these aircraft had taken off by 9.06.

Largely owing to Nagumo's change of course, the air groups from the *Enterprise* and the *Hornet* failed to find the enemy where they expected. The *Hornet*'s dive-bombers and fighters, above the clouds, continued to search fruitlessly to the south-east. The fighters were forced to 'ditch' as their tanks ran dry while, of the dive-bombers, with their longer range, twenty-one returned to the *Hornet* and fourteen headed for Midway, where three crashed. However, Torpedo 8's aircraft, flying lower, became separated from their top cover by the intervening clouds and followed a more westerly course. At about 9.20 Waldron spotted enemy ships to the north-west and, although he lacked fighter protection, immediately began his approach. Met by anti-aircraft fire and fighters while still some miles from the target, the slow Devastators had little hope and, in the resulting slaughter, few managed to release their torpedoes. All fifteen of Waldron's aircraft were shot down without scoring a hit.

Lindsey's Torpedo 6, also lacking fighter cover, arrived next, having sighted the carriers just after 9.30. Lindsey split his squadron to come in on both sides of the *Kaga* but, as the Devastators circled widely to make their beam attack, Zeros swarmed in for the kill. Ten Devastators, including Lindsey's, were destroyed, and none of those which succeeded in launching torpedoes hit the target. This attack was all over shortly after 10 a.m., about the time that Massey, with the *Yorktown*'s Torpedo 3, first spotted the was becoming urgent. Nagumo therefore decided to defer the launching of the attack until he had brought in the Midway strike planes and fighters which had been diverted to combat air patrol. He would then reorganize his forces while temporarily retiring northwards to avoid further attack and, finally, when all was ready, he would despatch a single massive attack force to destroy the enemy fleet. Meanwhile, he ordered that all aircraft on the flight decks should be struck below while Tomonaga's planes were landed and that the bombers for the second wave should once again be fitted with torpedoes and armour-piercing bombs.

As Tomonaga's aircraft began coming in at 8.37, the hangar deck crews, with time running out, sweated to rearm the strike aircraft for the second time that morning. In their haste, they carelessly stacked the bombs being removed on the deck beside them, instead of returning them to the magazines. Nevertheless, by 9 a.m., all seemed to be going well as the recovery operations neared completion. Signalling his intentions to Yamamoto, over 500 miles to his rear, at 9.18, Nagumo ordered a ninety-degree change of course to E.N.E., not only to lessen the danger from Midway's air units but also to achieve a position of advantage over the enemy task force. He now hoped to launch his strike at about 10.30, with at least thirty-six dive-bombers and fifty-four torpedo-bombers in the attack force. Unfortunately, the *Akagi* now began receiving reports that several groups of American aircraft were heading towards Nagumo's ships and, as these appeared to be too numerous to have come from one carrier, *Soryu* sent off a search plane to establish the exact strength of the American surface force.

All this time, Fletcher and Spruance had been making their own preparations. Spruance, with Task Force 16, originally intended to launch his attack planes at 9 a.m. when, if Nagumo remained on course for Midway, there would be less than 100 miles to cover. However, as news of Tomonaga's strike came in, Spruance decided to launch two hours earlier, at 7 a.m., when the range would be 155 miles. His chief of staff, Captain Miles Browning, calculated that Tomonaga's aircraft would be landing on their carriers around 9 a.m. and might thereby be caught on deck while preparing for another attack on Midway. As the American fighters and torpedo aircraft had a combat radius of about 175 miles there would be little room for error, but Spruance felt the risk was worth taking. Although only two enemy carriers had been sighted, he boldly planned a full-strength strike, retaining only a few fighters for defence. The *Enterprise*'s air group, led by Lieutenant-Commander Clarence McClusky, would launch thirty-three Dauntless dive-bombers from the squadrons Bombing 6 and Scouting 6; fourteen Devastator torpedo planes from Torpedo 6; and ten Wildcat fighters from Fighting 6. The *Hornet*'s air group, under Lieutenant-Commander Stanhope Ring, would send thirty-five Dauntlesses from Bombing 8 and Scouting 8; fifteen Devastators from Torpedo 8; and ten Wildcats from Fighting 8. The fighters were to cover the slower torpedo aircraft, which would take off last. As some

Japanese. Before take-off, the *Yorktown*'s pilots had been told that if they found nothing at the predicted interception point they were to fly north-west along the reverse of Nagumo's course for Midway. Thus, although they were launched one hour after Task Force 16's air groups, they flew a more direct route and found Nagumo with relative ease. Massey too had lost his fighter cover en route, so he attacked independently at 10.15, making for the *Soryu*. Only a handful of Torpedo 3's Devastators reached a good launching position and ten aircraft were destroyed. The American carriers had now lost thirty-five torpedo planes in these three attacks and not a single hit had been achieved. Even so, the sacrifice of the torpedo squadrons was not in vain. The defending Zeros had been drawn down to low altitudes and, in their preoccupation with these attacks, the Japanese carriers, lacking radar, had not observed the approach of American dive-bombers high above. The latter were therefore able to strike almost unopposed, dropping their bombs on flight decks full of aircraft which were being prepared for take-off.

McClusky, having failed to find Nagumo where he anticipated, was soon dangerously low on fuel but, making one of the most significant decisions of the battle, had chosen to continue his search to the north-west rather than to the south-east. At 9.55 he was rewarded by the sight of a Japanese destroyer returning from the depth-charge attack on the *Nautilus*. Following her course, McClusky found the carriers at 10.05 and began his dive at 10.22. Nagumo's carriers were now in a rough diamond formation, with the *Akagi* to the west, the *Soryu* on her starboard beam, the *Kaga* astern and the *Hiryu* some way ahead to the north. Five Dauntlesses from Bombing 6 swooped down on the *Akagi* while McClusky, with the remainder of the *Enterprise*'s dive-bombers, attacked the *Kaga*. One bomb hit the *Akagi* amidships, detonating the bombs which had been carelessly stacked in the hangar deck. The flight deck was torn up and the midships aircraft lift destroyed. A second bomb exploded aft, among the aircraft on the flight deck, starting fires which soon reduced Nagumo's flagship to a blazing shambles. By 10.47 she had been abandoned, Nagumo transferring to the cruiser *Nagara*. The *Kaga* had simultaneously suffered four direct hits which also started uncontrollable fires; she too was abandoned later in the day. Meanwhile, unknown to McClusky, the *Yorktown*'s dive-bombers had arrived, thirteen of Leslie's Dauntlesses diving on the *Soryu*, from 14,500 feet, at 10.25. The *Soryu* was hit three times near the forward and midships aircraft lifts, wrecking the flight deck and spreading fire to petrol tanks and munitions storage compartments. Within twenty minutes she was a raging inferno and had been left for dead by her crew. The apparent coordination of these attacks owed more to good fortune and individual initiative than to careful planning but, in less than six minutes, three of Nagumo's carriers had been eliminated.

While Nagumo shifted his flag to the *Nagara*, Rear-Admiral Abe assumed tactical command. Yamaguchi, whose carrier, standing off to the north, had so far escaped, was now ordered to launch an immediate strike. The Japanese still lacked precise knowledge of American carrier strength, for the *Soryu*'s scout plane had a faulty radio and could not report. However, Yamaguchi did not hesitate and by 10.58 the *Hiryu* had launched eighteen dive-bombers and six fighters, led by Lieutenant Michio Kobayashi. Flying at 18,000 feet, Kobayashi was led to the *Yorktown* by the Dauntlesses of Bombing 3, then returning to their carrier after their attack on *Soryu*. All of Leslie's aircraft had survived but McClusky, pursued by Zeros, lost eighteen, some having been forced to 'ditch' because the *Enterprise* failed to reach the prearranged rendezvous in time.

The *Yorktown* had already launched ten more Dauntlesses at 11.20, to search for 230 miles to the north-west. By noon she had a combat patrol of twelve Wildcats aloft and was refuelling others when her radar picked up Kobayashi's formation forty miles to the south-west. Refuelling was abandoned, the aircraft on the flight deck hastily launched, and Leslie's returning Dauntlesses waved away out of trouble. Fighters from the *Enterprise* and the *Hornet* flew to Fletcher's support, giving him twenty-eight Wildcats in all, while his supporting cruisers added weight to the defence. Only eight of Kobayashi's dive-bombers penetrated the fighter and anti-aircraft screen, but the *Yorktown* received three hits. The first bomb holed the flight deck, starting fires below; the second exploded near the forward fuel tanks and magazines, which promptly had to be flooded; and the third burst in the smokestack, rupturing three boiler uptakes and extinguishing five of the six boiler furnaces. The *Yorktown*'s speed dropped to six knots and, with the ship's radar knocked out and his flag plot and communications untenable, Fletcher had shifted his flag to the cruiser *Astoria* by 1.15 p.m. The carrier's aircraft were meanwhile transferred to the *Enterprise* and the *Hornet*.

By now, the *Soryu*'s search plane had reported the presence of three American carriers to Yamaguchi, who quickly scraped together ten torpedo aircraft and six fighters for another strike. The torpedo attack would be led by Tomonaga, whose aircraft, damaged over Midway, had a leaking fuel tank. This had not been repaired when he took off again at 12.45 and Tomonaga knew that, for him, this would be a one-way mission.

The *Yorktown*'s damage control parties had worked with such success that by 1.45 the hole in the flight deck had been patched and four of the boilers relit. With her speed back up to twenty knots, she was again refuelling fighters when, at 2.30, her radar picked up the *Hiryu*'s torpedo planes about forty miles out. This time the *Yorktown* had only twelve Wildcats for air cover and these were unable to block Tomonaga's attack. Selecting the seemingly undamaged *Yorktown* as their target, the fast Japanese torpedo bombers flew unhesitatingly through a massive curtain of anti-aircraft fire and four Kates managed to reach favourable launching positions. Two torpedoes struck the carrier amidships, breaching most of the port fuel tanks and severing all power connections. The pumps were now inoperable and counter-flooding impossible. Within twenty minutes the *Yorktown* was listing at an angle of twenty-six degrees, and at 2.58 the order was given to abandon ship.

Revenge was not long in coming. After a long search one of the Dauntless pilots who had taken off late that morning sighted the *Hiryu* just after 2.30. His contact report was received by the *Yorktown* but, owing to the power breakdown, it could not be relayed to Spruance until after 3 p.m. At about 3.30, the *Enterprise* launched twenty-four dive-bombers, including fourteen refugees from the *Yorktown*. The *Hornet* also despatched sixteen of her surviving Dauntlesses at 4.03, to support Spruance's attack on the *Hiryu*.

The survivors of Tomonaga's force – five torpedo planes and three fighters – got back to the *Hiryu* at 4.30, claiming one carrier severely damaged. Coupled with the reports from Kobayashi's earlier strike, this led Yamaguchi to believe that two American carriers were out of action. Not knowing that the *Yorktown* had in fact been attacked twice, he now judged that each side had one intact carrier, by no means impossible odds for the *Hiryu*. He had few strike aircraft left but decided to mount another attack at 6 p.m., when the failing light would give them a better chance of achieving surprise. While this small force was being ranged up, the *Hiryu* was sighted, at 5 p.m., by the *Enterprise*'s dive-bombers. Without radar, the Japanese had once again been unable to detect their approach. Although three Dauntlesses were shot down, others succeeded in scoring four hits. The *Hiryu* suffered the same fate as her sister ships. One bomb blew the forward lift against the bridge, putting it out of action, and the other three caused the inevitable fires and explosions on the flight and hangar decks. By the time the *Hornet*'s aircraft arrived half an hour later, the *Hiryu* was burning so fiercely that they shifted their attacks, albeit unsuccessfully, to the *Tone* and the *Chikuma*.

The four Japanese carriers all went to the bottom during the next sixteen hours. The *Soryu* blew up and sank at 7.13, followed at 7.26 by the *Kaga*. Both the *Akagi* and the *Hiryu* were scuttled by Japanese destroyers at dawn on 5 June, although the *Hiryu* did not sink until about 9 a.m., Admiral Yamaguchi going down with his ship.

Yamamoto himself had been slow to acknowledge defeat. During the early morning of 4 June all had appeared to be progressing favourably, and even the reports from the *Tone*'s seaplane left Yamamoto and his staff comparatively undisturbed, for Nagumo was judged to be equal to the tasks in hand. The first blow fell at 10.50 when Rear-Admiral Abe signalled that fires were raging aboard the *Kaga*, the *Akagi* and the *Soryu*. However, only one American carrier had so far been identified and Yamamoto saw no reason to shelve his plans. He decided personally to direct subsequent operations and to concentrate all available forces to attack the enemy in the Midway area. Kondo's powerful forces were already racing to Nagumo's aid and the Main Body was soon also proceeding at full speed towards the atoll. At 12.20, Yamamoto ordered Kakuta's carriers to hurry south from the Aleutians, although he wisely directed the Midway invasion transports to retire to the north-west until the situation became clearer. It was, of course, still imperative that the Midway air base should be destroyed, so at 1.10 Kondo was ordered to detach four heavy cruisers of Kurita's Support Group to bombard the atoll.

As the day wore on, Yamamoto's optimism began to wane. The Main Body was being delayed by dense fog, and at 4.30 Kakuta signalled that he could not be expected to join the Midway battle for at least two days. Then, at 5.55, Nagumo reported that the *Hiryu* had been crippled. Yamamoto's main hopes rested on the possibility of Kondo's ships being able to contact and destroy the enemy fleet in a night surface action. At night, the American carrier-borne aircraft would be almost impotent and the Japanese naval units, well trained for such operations, would enjoy a tremendous advantage. It had gradually become obvious, however, that the confused and dispirited Nagumo had no stomach for this type of engagement, so just after 9.30 Kondo was given effective tactical control of the night operations.

Spruance, who had meanwhile assumed tactical command of the American task forces, was not to be caught. At sunset, he retired eastwards to take up a position from which, on the following day, he could either pursue retreating enemy forces or break up an amphibious attack on Midway. By midnight, Yamamoto realized that his hopes for a night action were illusory and that his own forces, still widely separated, might instead be vulnerable to air attacks at dawn, particularly if they persisted on their present courses. At 2.25 a.m. he finally bowed to the inevitable, cancelling the attack on Midway and ordering a general withdrawal.

Two more scenes in the drama remained to be enacted. Early on 5 June the heavy cruisers *Mikuma* and *Mogami*, part of the force detailed to bombard Midway, collided while taking evasive action from the shadowing American submarine *Tambor*. Both were damaged and subjected to a series of attacks from carrier and land-based aircraft during 5 and 6 June. The *Mikuma* sank the following night although the *Mogami* managed to limp back to Truk. Meanwhile, the *Yorktown* was miraculously still afloat. She had been reboarded and taken in tow on 5 June and hopes of saving her grew. However, the *Yorktown* and the destroyer *Hamman*, which had come alongside, were torpedoed by the Japanese submarine I-168 on 6 June. The *Hamman*, broken in two, sank at once, the *Yorktown* going down at 5.01 a.m. the next day. The United States had now lost a carrier and a destroyer as well as some 150 aircraft, while 307 Americans had died in the battle. The Japanese had lost four carriers and a heavy cruiser, together with some 280 carrier-borne aircraft; 3,500 Japanese lost their lives, including over 100 experienced pilots.

The American victory at Midway illustrated, above all, the value of good intelligence work. The advance discovery of the Japanese plan was the main cause of Yamamoto's defeat, while Japanese intelligence had proved faulty and inadequate. The Combined Fleet's operational plan also contained several major weaknesses, the most serious of which was the unnecessary dispersal of forces, an error which Yamamoto had tried to correct too late. By sharing his available carriers between the various elements of the Combined Fleet, Yamamoto had deprived Nagumo of overwhelming striking power at the decisive point. Similarly, by keeping his battleships with the Main Body, Yamamoto had reduced the defensive anti-aircraft firepower available to the carriers. In contrast, the Americans had concentrated in the most strategically important area and remained tactically compact throughout the battle. In most respects, particularly with their aircraft and their efficient 'Long Lance' torpedoes, the Japanese had superior equipment, but, without radar, Nagumo's carriers had been easy prey for the American dive-bombers. Tied to the rigid Midway invasion schedule, Nagumo himself had been faced with two incompatible tasks on the morning of 4 June, yet his own series of disastrous decisions, stemming from inadequate and inept reconnaissance, had contributed largely to his downfall. On the American side, Fletcher and Spruance had carried out Nimitz's instructions with skill and initiative, and Spruance in particular emerged as a naval tactician of the highest order.

Midway, like the Battle of Britain and Stalingrad, was essentially a defensive victory. Although the Japanese had suffered a severe defeat and their offensive strategy had been blunted, they had not yet lost the war, and indeed the struggle in the Pacific would go on for more than three years before Japan surrendered. Moreover, despite a temporary postponement on 4 June, their occupation of the western Aleutians had proceeded more or less according to plan, even if, without Midway, this operation lost much of its strategic significance. For Nimitz, like Jellicoe at Jutland, success in the battle could not, by itself, win the war, yet failure could have made America's defeat in the Pacific a real possibility. However, Midway was, in every sense, a major turning point in the war. It did much to restore the balance of naval power in the Pacific and robbed the Japanese of the margin of superiority which had enabled them to strike at will. The Allies had thus won precious time to build up their strength. As Winston Churchill later wrote in his book *The Second World War:* 'From this moment all our thoughts turned with sober confidence to the offensive.'

Note on Sources

Of the many studies of Midway published over the last thirty years, few equal the succinct and perceptive analysis of the battle contained in Vol. IV of Admiral Samuel E. Morison's monumental work *History of United States Naval Operations in World War II.* (1949). *The Great Sea War,* by E. B. Potter and Admiral Chester W. Nimitz (1961) also includes a valuable and concise summary. Walter Lord's highly readable book *Incredible Victory: The Battle of Midway* (1968) is the product of long and thorough research and contains much previously unpublished information, being particularly strong on the details of the battle as seen by its participants, both American and Japanese. For the Japanese side, *Midway – The Battle That Doomed Japan* by Mitsuo Fuchida and Masatake Okumiya (1955) has long been a standard reference work. Fuchida was a senior air commander aboard the *Akagi* during the battle while Okumiya was serving on the light carrier *Ryujo*. Other good general accounts are contained in *Midway: The Turning Point* by A. J. Barker (1971) and *Carrier Operations in World War II: Vol. II: The Pacific Navies* by David Brown (1974).

Useful, if subjective, histories of the three American carriers involved are: for the *Yorktown*, Pat Frank and Joseph D. Harrington's *Rendezvous at Midway* (1967); for the *Enterprise*, Edward P. Stafford's *The Big E* (1962); and for the *Hornet*, Alexander Griffith's *A Ship to Remember* (1943). Two informative biographical studies of major participants are John Deane Potter's *Admiral of the Pacific: the Life of Yamamoto* (1965) and *Admiral Raymond A. Spruance: A Study in Command* by Vice-Admiral E. P. Forrestel (1966).

The hero of El Alamein. Montgomery with (right) Lieutenant-General Leese, GOC 30 Corps and Lieutenant-General Lumsden, GOC 10 Corps, 6 November 1942

Chapter Fourteen

EL ALAMEIN

Sir William Jackson

It will be a decisive battle, a hard and bloody battle and there must be only one result. Success will mean the end of the war in Africa and an end to this running backward and forward between here and Benghazi . . .

Extract of notes made by Major-General (later Lieutenant-General Sir Leslie) Morshead for briefing officers of the 9th Australian Division before the Battle of El Alamein.

THE FINAL Battle of El Alamein, which was fought under the strategic direction of General Sir Harold Alexander and under the tactical command of Lieutenant-General Bernard Montgomery, will rank in British mythology with Nelson's Trafalgar and Wellington's Waterloo. It was the decisive battle which turned the tide of British fortunes in the Middle East in October 1942 before the Battle of Stalingrad had shown the finite limits of German military power. Nevertheless, it was a battle which need never have been fought. Five months earlier, the British Eighth Army had stood at Gazala, forty-five miles west of Tobruk, under General Sir Claude Auchinleck and Lieutenant-General Neil Ritchie in a strong defensive position awaiting attack by General Erwin Rommel's Panzer Army, Africa. Inaccurate German intelligence assessments led Rommel to underestimate British strength and make a faulty plan. He mismanaged his attack and was trapped with the Africa Korps behind the British minefields in the 'Cauldron', where he should have been severely penalized for his mistakes. But inept British generalship resulted in German instead of British victories in the hard fought tank battles of the 'Cauldron' and 'Knightsbridge'. The Eighth Army was routed; Tobruk was lost with its garrison of 32,000 British, South African and Indian troops; and Rommel advanced into Egypt, reaching the narrow forty-mile-wide defile between the Mediterranean coast at El Alamein station and the Qattara Depression on 1 July 1942. There he was brought to a halt by the over-extension of his supply lines; by the resilience of the Royal Air Force; and by the regenerated stubbornness of the remnants of the Eighth Army under Auchinleck's personal leadership. Auchinleck and Ritchie should have been remembered as the victors of the decisive Battle of Gazala; instead Alexander and Montgomery stand in their place, the nation revering Montgomery as the victor of El Alamein. And rightly so because the same officers and men who survived the Gazala defeats won El Alamein with a comparable balance of men and material on the two sides. The difference between defeat at Gazala and victory at El Alamein lay in generalship – Montgomery's generalship.

Montgomery's Battle of El Alamein was won by three critical pre-battle decisions taken long before the British artillery opened fire on 23 October 1942, and by four equally important decisions taken during the battle itself. Hitler took the first of the pre-battle decisions in April 1942 when he reversed the agreed Axis Mediterranean strategy for the summer campaign. Malta was to have been seized to protect Axis supply lines across the central Mediterranean before Rommel opened his Gazala offensive. Hitler disliked the proposed plan for a combined Italo-German parachute and amphibious assault on Malta, because he feared a costly repetition of the German invasion of Crete in 1941, so Rommel had little difficulty in persuading him that his Panzer Army's attack on the British at Gazala should be given priority. Malta could be taken later if it proved an embarrassment to the Axis quartermasters. Rommel won his field-marshal's baton for smashing the Gazala Line and taking Tobruk; Hitler lost Africa when he compounded his original strategic error by allowing Rommel to plunge onward into Egypt with Malta still unsubdued behind him. The battle of supply turned against the Axis, and by the third week of October, just four months after the fall of Tobruk, the Eighth Army had regained quantitative and qualitative superiority over the Panzer Army, Africa. The comparative strengths were:

	Eighth Army	*Panzer Army, Africa*
Men	195,000	104,000
Infantry battalions	85	71
Medium tanks	1,029	496
Field artillery	908	500
Anti-tank guns	1,451	850
Petrol	Unlimited	11 days
Ammunition	Unlimited	9 days

The second critical pre-battle decision stemmed from General Sir Alan Brooke's request to Churchill for permission to fly from London to Cairo to assess for himself what was wrong with the British forces in the Middle East. Churchill decided to accompany his Chief of the Imperial General Staff and then fly on to Moscow to explain to Stalin the reasons for not mounting a second front in 1943. Their tour of 'the vast but baffled and somewhat unhinged organisation' in Egypt convinced them that there must be a change of command. They decided to replace Auchinleck with Alexander as Commander-in-Chief, Middle East, and to appoint Lieutenant-General 'Strafer' Gott to command the Eighth Army. Their decisions were, however, of less moment than the chance action of two Luftwaffe fighter pilots who shot down the transport aircraft carrying Gott back to Cairo. Gott's death robbed the Eighth Army of its most experienced and respected desert hand who had fought in all the major battles in the Western Desert. And yet it was sadly fortunate that fate compelled the selection of Montgomery – the second choice – to command the Eighth Army at this critical moment in British affairs. Montgomery was the right man, in the right place, at the right time. He had the depth of military professionalism and the egocentric force of personality to master in a remarkably short time the strengths and weaknesses of his new command and of the many strong personalities who led the British and, more importantly, the Commonwealth contingents: Major-General Bernard Freyberg of the New Zealanders, Major-General Leslie Morshead of the Australians, and Major-General Dan Pienaar of the South Africans. He had the extrovert flare for contrived publicity which enabled him to impress his presence and policies on the Eighth Army, which soon became *his* army. And he believed in the type of military policy needed by the British army at that time. All his generation of British commanders had been junior officers in the First World War, which had etched deep prejudices on their minds. Men like Alexander and Gott, who had fought principally as regimental officers, were determined not to emulate methods which had led to debilitating loss of life in battles such as the Somme and Passchendaele. They, like Rommel, chose the indirect approach, hoping to avoid the horrors of attrition. Montgomery had been badly wounded in 1914 and spent the rest of the war on the staff. It was waste caused by inefficiencies in organization and planning which appalled him rather than the casualties. The British and German positions at El Alamein had much in common with those on the Western Front of 1914–18. There was no way round; the defences had been developed in great depth; the garrisons were securely entrenched; mines laid in profusion replaced barbed wire entanglements; and the men on both sides were too battle-experienced to give up easily. Only a man who was psychologically prepared to fight a ruthless battle of attrition could hope to defeat the Panzer Army at El Alamein in defences which it had strengthened and elaborated for four months. Montgomery was well cast for this role; Gott was not. But, first, Montgomery had to prove himself to the tired, cynical men of the Eighth Army. They had seen too many failures in the desert to do more than 'Give him a try', as the Australians expressed it.

And the third critical pre-battle decision was taken by Montgomery himself at a very late stage in the planning of Operation 'Lightfoot' – the Battle of El Alamein – which Churchill and the British chiefs of staff in London insisted should be mounted at the earliest possible moment. In his initial tours of the Eighth Army he emphasized ten points as he talked to officers and men. First, and most important, the Eighth Army was to get out of the habit of having one foot in the stirrup: all withdrawal plans were to be scrapped; forward defences would be strengthened with more troops brought up from the Nile Delta; transport held ready for further withdrawal would be moved to the rear; and all defensive positions would be stocked with ammunition, food and water for a protracted defence. Second, the days of employing small 'ad hoc' columns of all arms ('Jock' columns) were over: divisions would be fought as divisions under proper control by corps H.Q.s with artillery, engineer and logistic policy centralized at the highest practical level. Third, there were to be no more failures due to taking unnecessary operational or logistic risks: the Eighth Army would stay 'on balance' at all times; it would be deployed and handled in such a way that it need never react to Axis moves to its own disadvantage. Fourth, he was forming a '*Corps de Chasse*' to rival Rommel's Africa Corps. It was to be composed of Lieutenant-General Herbert Lumsden's X Corps with the 1st, 8th and 10th Armoured Divisions and the 2nd New Zealand Division. Fifth, if Rommel attacked through the weak southern half of the El Alamein position in the full moon period towards the end of August, as British intelligence predicted, he would be confronted with the strongly held Alam Halfa Ridge on his northern flank which he could not ignore and upon which his panzer divisions would be allowed to blunt their enthusiasm, attacking dug-in British tanks and anti-tank guns. There was to be no 'loosing of the British armour' (allowing them to leave their dug-in positions) in cavalry style which had lost the British so many tank battles in the past. The Eighth Army would stay balanced and continue with its preparations 'to knock Rommel for six out of Africa'. Sixth, the Eighth Army was untrained by his standards, but, he said, 'time is short and we must so direct our training that we shall be successful *in this particular battle*, neglecting other forms of training'. Everything required of the troops was to be reduced to simple battle drills and so thoroughly rehearsed with such realism that men would say during the battle itself, 'It's just like an exercise.' Seventh, enthusiasm and a sense of involvement were to be inculcated by telling every officer and man, at the appropriate moment, what was afoot and what was expected of him. This was to be done by commanders at all levels briefing their subordinates much more fully than had been the custom hitherto. In his instructions for the battle Montgomery said, 'Morale is the big thing in war. We must raise the morale of our soldiery to the highest pitch; they must be made enthusiastic, and must enter this battle with their tails high in the air and with the will to win.' Eighth, his own army H.Q. was to move from its fly-blown location on the eastern end of Ruweisat Ridge down to the coast where it would be alongside the Desert Air Force H.Q., and where its staff would be able to work in greater comfort and hence with greater efficiency. Ninth, there was to be no more 'belly-aching': orders were orders and not a basis for discussion. He did not mention publicly, though all his listeners were aware, that he was removing the 'belly-achers' and all those commanders who did not measure up to his standards of professionalism. Few of the senior officers who fought at Gazala survived this purge. And tenth, and last, as was appropriate for a God-fearing man and son of a bishop, he did not neglect his Christian upbringing, ending his pre-battle order of the day: 'Let us pray that "the Lord mighty in battle" will give us the victory.'

Montgomery was given the opportunity to demonstrate his abilities just a fortnight after taking over command. Rommel did attack, where and when predicted, and was stopped as Montgomery planned by British tanks and anti-tank guns defending the Alam Halfa Ridge. In Rommel's enforced retreat the R.A.F. and the Eighth Army artillery inflicted heavy losses upon the Axis striking force. There was no 'loosing of the British armour' in counter-attack. The Eighth Army stood fast and went on with its preparations for Lightfoot with renewed confidence in itself and a growing enthusiasm for Montgomery's leadership.

Montgomery's first concept for Lightfoot was based upon the orthodox belief, which had been held by successive British commanders in the Western Desert, that the Axis armoured forces – the Africa Corps' 15th and 21st Panzer Divisions and the Italian XX Corps' Ariete and Littorio Armoured Divisions – must be destroyed first, then the rest of the Panzer Army would collapse. He envisaged blasting two breaches in the Axis defences through which he would pass his *Corps de Chasse* to place itself on ground of its own choosing astride Rommel's lateral communications. The Axis armoured divisions would be compelled to attack at a disadvantage, as at Alam Halfa, to prize the British tanks off their life-line. The two breaches would not be equal in size or importance. The main breach would be made in the north by Lieutenant-General Oliver Leese's XXX Corps, using four infantry divisions: the 9th Australian in the north, the 51st Highland and 2nd New Zealand in the centre, and the 1st South African at the southern end of the breach. The breach was to be about ten miles wide and would involve a three to five mile advance from the British front line to the infantry objective, Report Line 'Oxalic', which was drawn along the rear of the known Axis defences. A specially organized minefield task force would be assigned to each armoured division to clear a minefree corridor for the advance of its tanks. Major-General Briggs's 1st Armoured Division would pass through the 'Northern Corridor', heading for the Kidney Ridge area; and Major-General Gatehouse's 10th Armoured Division would use the 'Southern Corridor' to cross Miteirya Ridge. Their objective was to be Report Line 'Skinflint' on the rising ground beyond the Rahman track running north and south through Tel el Aqqaqir, on which Rommel's armour was to be destroyed. The secondary breach would be made in the south by Lieutenant-General Brian Horrocks's XIII Corps, using Major-General Harding's 7th Armoured Division supported by Major-General Hugh's 44th Division. This was to be a diversionary effort designed to pin down the Axis reserves in the south. Horrocks was not to incur heavy casualties but was to make sure that his operations were realistic enough to hold Axis attention.

As detailed preparations and training went ahead doubts began to arise in the minds of several of the senior commanders. Montgomery claims that he came to the conclusion that his plan was too ambitious for the relatively poor standard of training of most of his units. The British armoured commanders doubted whether the infantry divisions would be able to reach Oxalic in one night, and whether the artillery would be able to neutralize the German anti-tank guns when their tanks tried to fight their way out from Oxalic to Skinflint on the first morning, as Montgomery was insisting.

All their experience of past desert operations had taught them not to rush anti-tank guns and minefields in broad daylight with inadequate infantry and artillery support. The Commonwealth infantry commanders, with equally bitter memories of the failure of British tanks to give them adequate support, doubted whether the British armoured divisions, in their current frame of mind, would try to break out at all. They were quite satisfied that their own infantry could reach Oxalic with the tanks which had been placed directly under their command. The New Zealanders, who had felt particularly badly let down in the August battles of Ruweisat Ridge, had the whole of the 9th Armoured Brigade under command. The other three assaulting infantry divisions had a regiment each from the 23rd Armoured Brigade.

After pondering these views and adding them to his own growing misgivings on training, Montgomery took the third critical pre-battle decision. He reversed the orthodox concept: 'My modified plan now was to hold off, or contain, the enemy armour, while we carried out a methodical destruction of the infantry divisions holding the defensive system.'

This was a radical change of policy, but fortunately necessitated only a change in emphasis rather than a major change of plan. The X Corps' armoured divisions would be given a more modest objective: Report Line 'Pierson', about two miles beyond Oxalic, upon which they were to fend off Axis counter-attacks while the British infantry dealt with their Axis opponents.

Montgomery put his new plan to his army using colourfully expressive phrases which have since entered the British army's military vocabulary. There would be a quick 'break-in' by the infantry to Oxalic and an equally quick passage of the armour through to Pierson. Then there would be a prolonged 'dogfight' lasting ten to twelve days during which the British infantry and their supporting tanks would 'crumble' away the Axis static defences, using carefully prepared but limited attacks supported by heavy artillery and air bombardments. And finally, when Axis endurance had been brought to the point of collapse, the 'break-out' phase would come with the British armoured divisions delivering the '*coup de grâce*'.

Montgomery's new plan did not entirely satisfy his critics. Intelligence began to accumulate suggesting that the Axis defensive zone was much deeper than originally thought. This made the armoured commanders more anxious than ever about their ability to reach even Pierson; and led the infantry commanders to suggest a two-phase attack on successive nights. Montgomery would not change plan again. There was to be no more 'belly-aching'.

On the Axis side, the adverse effects of Hitler's mistaken change of strategy were becoming increasingly apparent. Rommel found himself so short of fuel and spare parts for his tanks and vehicles that he was forced to adopt a defensive posture alien to his instincts. Instead of keeping his German and Italian tank formations concentrated for decisive counter-attacks of the type that had so often won him the advantage in the past, he deployed them in six mixed German and Italian armoured groups evenly spaced and close behind his static defences so that they could intervene quickly to seal off any British penetration before it became a major breach. This would save fuel, and it would reduce the distances his tanks would have to move in daylight and hence lessen their vulnerability to R.A.F. attack. In the northern sector, the 15th Panzer and the Littorio Divisions provided three mixed Italo–German groups, and in the south the 21st Panzer combined with the Ariete Division to provide three more. The German and Italian infantry divisions, which were not mechanized, were deployed within the main defensive line with German and Italian units alternated along the front to enable the Germans to corset their Italian colleagues and to stop the British singling out Italian sectors for attack. Rommel's static defences consisted of two deep belts of about half a million anti-tank and anti-personnel mines, running from north to south across the front some one to two miles apart with irregularly spaced and angled lateral belts between them producing a honeycomb effect. The belt nearest the British was held by outposts only, while the main Axis defence was based upon the rearward belt. In the spaces of the honeycomb Rommel ordered the creation of what he called 'Devil's Gardens' of random patches of mines and whatever ingenious booby traps the local garrisons could devise. But, strong though his positions became, Rommel had no illusions about the battle which he knew was coming and which (in his *Papers*) he refers to as the 'battle without hope'. His only reserve was his faithful 90th Light Division, grouped with the Trieste Mechanized Division, on the coast near Daba ready to repel a possible British attempt to land an amphibious force behind him.

In all great setpiece battles the attacker tries to deceive the defender about the exact point and time of the assault. Montgomery's deception plan was worked out and executed with meticulous attention to detail. Its aim was to suggest to the Axis High Command that the southern sector was under greatest threat; and that the full moon period at the end of November was the most likely date for the next British offensive. Vehicle densities in the desert were adjusted constantly by prolific use of dummy vehicles and tanks to maintain this illusion; bogus radio traffic was propagated to reinforce visual evidence; and the rate of construction of a dummy water pipe-line into the southern sector was timed for completion in mid-November. Some of these measures had their desired effect. Rommel was allowed to return to Germany for medical treatment and much needed sick leave, and was replaced by Panzer General Stumme from the Russian front. The Panzer Army War Diaries show that Stumme and his staff were deceived into thinking that the British offensive would strike the southern sector, but they gradually revised their earlier mistaken views on timing. On 20 October Stumme warned his corps commanders that a British offensive was imminent.

The stage had been set for the decisive Battle of El Alamein by the three critical pre-battle decisions; by Hitler losing the preliminary battle of supply through not taking Malta; by Churchill selecting the right British command team; and by Montgomery changing tactical policy at the last moment. The battle itself was to be won, as far as any great battle of attrition can be won by one man, by four further critical decisions taken by Montgomery during the battle: first, a psychological decision during the break-in gave him mastery of his army; then two tactical decisions during the dogfight prevented stalemate; and, finally, a change of plan during the break-out phase gave him the victory. Montgomery himself has belittled his own achievements by claiming that all went according to plan. It did not. His claim to fame rests more upon his single-mindedness of purpose and refusal to accept failure than upon the prescience of his planning.

The 'Break-in', 23–25 October

The break-in started at 9.40 p.m. on 23 October 1942 with a fifteen-minute air and artillery bombardment of all identified Axis gun positions. The assault infantry crawled out of their slit trenches where they had lain cramped but hidden all day and assembled on their start-lines. For five minutes there was silence; then the guns reopened at 10 p.m. on the Axis outpost line as a signal for the advance to begin. The night was fine and the moon clear, but the dust thrown up by bursting shells and by the movement of tanks, armoured carriers and other vehicles created a haze which made direction-keeping difficult, in spite of the help given by Bofors light anti-aircraft guns firing tracer overhead on known compass bearings.

The four assault divisions of the XXX Corps made rapid initial progress through the first minefield belt and the Axis outpost line. Delays thereafter accumulated as the infantry fought their way forward through the 'Devil's Gardens'. By dawn most of the assaulting brigades were on or approaching Oxalic. The XIII Corps, in the south, breached the first minefield, which was an old British field incorporated in the Axis positions after Alam Halfa, but dawn broke before they could tackle the second. The special minefield task forces of the X Corps were not so successful. The pace of clearing lanes for the armoured divisions proved slower than expected. The improvised 'Scorpion' Flail tanks were mechanically unreliable, and the electronic mine detectors failed in a number of lanes, reducing the Sappers to the slow and hazardous business of prodding for mines by hand. When daylight came the 1st Armoured Division was only half-way through the Northern Corridor, with its tank regiments still entangled in the partially cleared gaps in the first minefield belt. The 10th Armoured Division's Sappers in the Southern Corridor had been more successful and had four routes cleared up to but not over Miteirya Ridge. When its tanks tried to nose their way over the ridge they found another minefield on the forward slope and were forced by Axis anti-tank guns to pull back into the shelter of the ridge where they created unhealthy congestion amongst the New Zealand forward positions. Pierson lay out of reach to both armoured divisions of the X Corps on 24 October. The infantry divisions of the XXX Corps had to rely for protection on tanks within instead of in front of their positions.

Reviewing the situation as the first light reports came in, Montgomery decided to continue the break-in phase for another twenty-four hours before starting the crumbling process of the dogfight. The X Corps was to prepare further operations for the latter half of the day to reach Pierson at the end of both corridors; and the XIII Corps was to persist in its breaching operations in the south. The daylight hours of 24 October belonged to the R.A.F. who flew over a thousand sorties, and to the U.S. Army Air Force, who intervened for the first time in a British army battle with 170 sorties. The 15th Panzer/Littorio Groups had a very uncomfortable day.

On the Axis side, the command structure was temporarily upset by the disappearance of Stumme, who went forward to see for himself what was happening. His body was not found until the following day. General von Thoma, commander of the Afrika Korps, took over, and that evening reported to Berlin that he had contained the British penetration with an anti-tank screen which had been established fortuitously on the British armour's objective Pierson. Thoma's confidence confirmed what Montgomery had refused to admit in pre-battle planning: that the Axis defences were too deep to be breached in a single night's work. Alexander's chief of staff, Major-General McCreery, said later: 'In my opinion Monty made a big tactical mistake over the conduct of the battle. When it was clear well before D-Day that Rommel would have too much depth to his defences for our infantry attack to reach beyond the mine-fields, it would have been far sounder to make two bites at the cherry.'

Montgomery's improvised, instead of pre-planned, second bite did not go well. The XIII Corps in the south failed to secure a breach of the second of the old British minefields and was told to desist to avoid further casualties. In the main X Corps effort, the 1st Armoured Division reopened its attack in the Northern Corridor in the late afternoon with the help of the Highlanders and Australians. When darkness fell it had only reached Oxalic with considerable loss of Sherman tanks and could go no further. In the Southern Corridor the 10th Armoured Division's Sappers went forward at dusk to gap the minefield on the forward slope of Miteirya Ridge. They found more mines and took far longer to clear passable gaps than they had hoped. In consequence, the leading armoured units were held up in their assembly areas, presenting attractively concentrated targets to any Axis airman who happened to detect them in the light of flares which were being dropped over the battlefield by both air forces. At about 10 p.m. one Luftwaffe aircraft unloaded its bombs, possibly by chance, on these crowded vehicles, setting some on fire. The conflagration attracted every Axis gun within range and dislocated the 10th Armoured Division's staff arrangements for the passage of the minefield gaps. The leading brigade commander advised Gatehouse that in his opinion the operation should be stopped as too much of the night had been lost. Gatehouse reported to Lumsden that he feared his division would be caught in daylight on the forward slope of Miteirya Ridge with its freedom of manoeuvre restricted by minefields covered by Axis tanks and anti-tank guns. Lumsden agreed and informed Major-General Francis de Guingand, Montgomery's chief of staff, who realized the gravity of the situation and summoned both Lumsden and Leese to Tactical H.Q., Eighth Army. He then took the unusual step of waking the army commander. Montgomery listened to what his corps commanders had to say. Both believed that the battle had gone so wrong that it should be broken off before heavier losses were sustained. Their pleas fell on determinedly deaf ears. Montgomery reaffirmed his earlier orders that the armour was to break out to Pierson. If his armoured commanders were not prepared to obey, he would find others who would. This was the psychological turning point in the British army's affairs and the first critical battle decision. Previous Eighth Army commanders would have flinched from giving such an order for fear of repeating the unreasoning obstinacy that First World War commanders had shown. Montgomery did not hesitate. He believed, like Churchill, that war was a battle of wills not only between opposing commanders but also between a commander and his subordinates. The leading elements of the 10th Armoured Division did manage to fight their way through the minefields, but, as Lumsden had feared, were driven back by unsubdued anti-tank guns into the lee of Miteirya Ridge when dawn broke on the second morning of the battle. This adverse tactical outcome of the night's work was irrelevant to the main issue: Montgomery had shown who was master. His corps and divisional generals knew where they stood. Lightfoot would be fought to the limits of endurance by the British as well as the Germans. The break-in had not gone according to plan. The dogfight would have to start with the armoured divisions amongst instead of in front of the infantry.

The 'Dogfight', 25–31 October

Montgomery intended to start the crumbling process with an attack southwestwards from the Miteirya Ridge, using Freyberg's New Zealanders, while Briggs's 1st Armoured Division probed forward from the Northern Corridor to engage Axis tanks around Kidney Ridge. During the morning a sense of frustration and stalemate settled over the congested Miteirya area. Tank crews, dog-tired, were sitting hull-down engaging enemy targets at long range; equally tired New Zealand infantry huddled lower in their slit trenches cursing the tanks for drawing retaliatory fire; and behind the ridge a confused jumble of artillery and logistic transport clogged the narrow tracks through the uncleared minefields. Montgomery conferred again with his principal commanders about midday and accepted that it would be operationally costly and organizationally difficult to renew the battle in the Southern Corridor. Fortunately, affairs in the Northern Corridor were less depressing. Morshead was well ahead with his own plans for crumbling northwards from his Australian sector to take the Point 29 spur which had been identified during Lightfoot planning as a key feature from which the Axis defences in the coastal sector could be threatened. Montgomery accepted the logic of the situation and took his second critical battle decision. He cancelled Freyberg's operations and instructed Leese to concentrate upon the Northern Corridor, using Morshead's Australians to take Point 29, while the 1st Armoured and Highland Divisions developed their operations towards Kidney Ridge.

Morshead had anticipated these instructions and so was able to agree to launch his attack that night. Fortune favoured the willing. During the evening Australian patrols captured the German regimental commander and one of the battalion commanders responsible for the defence of the Point 29 feature. The battalion commander was carrying a marked map showing the Axis minefield layout, enabling Morshead to take the justifiable risk of rushing Point 29 with some of his infantry mounted in armoured carriers. The Australian operation, which started just before midnight, was neat and effective. Point 29 was secured and consolidated before dawn. A friable patch seemed to have been found in the Axis defences where further crumbling might prove profitable.

The twenty-sixth of October, the third day of the battle and the first full day of Montgomery's crumbling operations, was also a day for second thoughts by both army commanders. Rommel had returned to Panzer Army H.Q. during the evening of 25 October, having been hastily summoned back by Hitler from his convalescence. Thoma reported that the Axis situation was deteriorating under the heavy artillery and air bombardments and the long-range shooting by British tanks, which were better armed than they had been in past desert engagements. The German 164th Division and the Italian Trento Division, whose sectors had been breached, had suffered severely, as had the 15th Panzer/Littorio Groups. Rommel's first reaction was to order the recapture of Point 29, from which he realized the Australians could clear the Axis defences of the main coast road. He also gave orders that Axis tanks were to be husbanded and anti-tank guns, particularly 88s, were to be used to contain the British offensive while he concentrated the Axis reserves for a major counter-offensive.

Montgomery, for his part, was taking his third critical battle decision with similar ideas in mind. Throughout the desert fighting British commanders had been remarkably bad at recreating reserves as they were expended. The X Corps, his *Corps de Chasse* and principal striking force, had been committed. It was time to assemble a new striking force, with which to launch the break-out. He decided that he must risk some relaxation of pressure in the dogfight to regroup the Eighth Army. The Australians would maintain some pressure by mounting a further crumbling attack northwards from Point 29 to clear the coast road, and the 1st Armoured and Highland Divisions would continue their operations from the Northern Corridor. The rest of the Eighth Army would adjust its sectors to release the New Zealand Division and the 7th and 10th Armoured Divisions to form the new striking force.

Rommel's hastily mounted attempts to retake Point 29 were broken up by Australian artillery fire and R.A.F. bombing, but he was quicker than Montgomery in creating a striking force of his own. The 21st Panzer was summoned northwards, leaving the Ariete Division to look after the southern sector; and the 90th Light and the Trieste Divisions were brought forward from Daba. With these troops Rommel planned to strike the British penetration around Point 29 and Kidney Ridge, the 90th Light attacking from the north-west and the 21st Panzer from the south-west. Field-Marshal Albert Kesselring, German Commander-in-Chief, South, agreed to concentrate every available Axis aircraft to support this counter-offensive, which would be launched with all the old violence of a *Blitzkreig* attack, which had snatched victory out of defeat for Rommel so often in the past. The violence was there, but the men upon whom the attack fell were in a different frame of mind from their predecessors in earlier desert battles. The 90th Light's attack came in first against Point 29 and was broken up by the Australian gunners. Towards evening, when the sun was low and in the eyes of the British tank and anti-tank gun crews, the 21st Panzer attacked in the wake of a series of heavy dive-bomber raids. The 1st Armoured Division stood its ground. The main weight of the attack fell upon Lieutenant-Colonel V. B. Turner's 2nd Battalion, Rifle Brigade, and its supporting 239th Anti-Tank Battery, Royal Artillery, with their 6-pounder anti-tank guns dug in south of Kidney Ridge in an area codenamed Snipe. Their guns did great execution, as did the tanks and guns of other British units on either flank. The 21st Panzer recoiled defeated – a far cry from the disastrous Battle of Tottensonntag in the First Battle of Sidi Rezegh, when the Africa Korps overran the 5th South African Brigade, or the Second Battle of Sidi Rezegh in 1941, when the New Zealanders suffered a similar fate.

But it was one thing to repulse the Africa Korps in attack, quite another to beat it in defence. Rommel was quick to read the omens and interpret them correctly. He knew he could not win, but he was equally determined not to lose. He could still enforce a stalemate as long as his fuel and ammunition lasted. As a prudent precaution he ordered a reconnaissance of a potential delaying position at Fuka, fifty miles to the west, to which he could retire if forced to do so. Since such a retirement would mean abandoning his non-mechanized infantry, this had to be a last resort. In the meantime he decided: 'We were, therefore, going to make one more attempt, by the tenacity and stubbornness of our defence, to persuade the enemy to call off his attack. It was a slim hope, but the petrol situation alone made a retreat, which would inevitably lead to mobile warfare, out of the question.'

Rommel might perhaps have imposed a stalemate on other British commanders. Morshead's Australians soon found how difficult it was to unseat the 90th Light when they launched their second crumbling attack northwards on the night 28–9 October. They had some initial success but were stopped well short of the coast road. Lightfoot had lasted almost a week and there seemed little to show for the enormous expenditure of ammunition and tanks, though fortunately not of lives. Anxiety began to show in London and Cairo as the inherent possibility of stalemate grew into an ominous reality. Churchill became restive as he noted Montgomery's withdrawal of divisions from the line, and began to minute the Chief of the Imperial General Staff, saying querulously: 'Why had he [Montgomery] told us he would be through in seven days if all he intended to do was to fight a half-hearted battle? Had we not a single general who could win a single battle?'

Churchill's understandable lack of confidence in the new and untried commander of the Eighth Army was mistaken. Montgomery was already planning to use the new striking force which he had been creating. His first idea was to start the break-out phase with a concentrated attack along the coast road, taking advantage of Morshead's progress north of Point 29. Alexander, Major-General Richard McCreery, and Mr Casey, the Minister of State in Cairo, visited Montgomery's headquarters during the morning of 29 October to review the situation before replying to Churchill's interrogatory cables. They were reassured by Montgomery's plans for the break-out, Operation Supercharge, but they were less happy about the axis of attack which he had chosen. It seemed to be directed too far north into one of the strongest sectors of Rommel's front. McCreery, in particular, believed that the thrust should be delivered further south. Alexander, while agreeing with McCreery, was not prepared to interfere with his army commander's tactical handling of the battle.

That evening Montgomery took his fourth and final critical decision of the battle. His intelligence staff confirmed McCreery's view that the coastal sector had been heavily reinforced to stop Morshead's Australians. They suggested, incorrectly as it proved, that there was a boundary between German and Italian formations just north of the Northern Corridor. On de Guingand's advice Montgomery decided to abandon the coastal thrust and ordered the axis for Supercharge to be moved southwards. Although he believed in maintaining a steady balanced course, he showed that he was prepared to make sensible changes provided there were strong enough reasons and adequate time to do so without causing confusion in the vast complex mechanism of the army he was commanding.

The plan for Supercharge was a scaled down replica of Lightfoot. A breach was to be torn in the Axis containing line by one instead of four infantry divisions, on a two-mile instead of ten-mile front. Freyberg, in whom Montgomery had great confidence, would make the breach with his New Zealand Division, reinforced by two British infantry brigades (the 151st from the 50th Division and the 152nd from the Highland Division). The infantry would advance some 5,000 yards during the night to clear a way through the crust of the Axis containing line. The 9th Armoured Brigade would then pass through and advance on another 2,000 yards to cut the Rahman track before dawn. The X Corps, led by the 1st Armoured Division, would pass through the breach to meet any counter-attacks launched by the remnants of the Africa Korps and, having defeated these, would swing north to cut the coast road behind the Panzer Army.

Freyberg found that he could not complete his preparations by 31 October because of the extraordinary congestion behind the northern sector of the front, and so Supercharge was postponed twenty-four hours. In order to keep up the pressure on the Axis forces and to draw more of their strength into the coastal sector, Morshead agreed to make a third northerly crumbling attack to cut the coast road and to exploit to the coast if possible. This last Australian attack went in on the night 30–31 October. It reached and cut the coast road and railway, but Australian efforts to exploit to the coast were stopped by German reinforcements. Rommel assumed that this was the start of Montgomery's break-out, and counter-attacked strongly, giving Morshead's Australians the toughest twenty-four hours since they had resisted his attacks in the first siege of Tobruk in the summer of 1941. Their losses were heavy and their gallantry rivalled that of Turner's men on Snipe.

The 'Break-out', 1–4 November

Supercharge started well. A preparatory air raid by 100 bombers disrupted the Africa Korps' communications. By midnight the two British infantry brigades, leading the New Zealand Division's attack, were on their objectives. But there were delays in passing the 9th Armoured Brigade through and it was caught by daylight short of its objective. Some of its tanks did reach the Rahman track, which they found strongly held by German anti-tank gunners. Supercharge had run into the main Africa Korps concentration and not, as British intelligence had hoped, into weaker Italian units. The 15th Panzer fought back with the 21st Panzer in close support. The Australian official historians pay a well deserved tribute to the courage and endurance of the 9th Armoured Brigade as it fought to clear a way for the X Corps:

> If the British armour owed any battle debts to the New Zealand infantry, 9th Armoured Brigade paid them dearly and liberally that morning in heroism and blood. Directed by Eighth Army's plan and exhorted by their own resolute commander to proceed along a course which (to snatch

another's phrase soon to be quoted) led only to victory or death, they strove for a victory that was not to be theirs.

The X Corps' advance was delayed by continued traffic congestion in the New Zealand rear. Freyberg tried to hurry Briggs's 1st Armoured Division forward to support the 9th Armoured Brigade, but warnings were already being received from XXX Corps H.Q. that the Africa Korps was assembling to make one last bid to force a stalemate. Briggs prepared to meet it as his brigades took up battle positions amongst and on either flank of the remnants of the 9th Armoured Brigade.

During the night Rommel had misjudged the direction of Supercharge and had ordered Thoma to counter-attack towards Point 29, believing Montgomery was intent on breaking through in the Australian sector. At dawn he realized his mistake in time to stop Thoma's attack. He redirected him to deal with the New Zealand Division's breach in the Tel el Aqqaqir area of the Rahman track. Thoma attacked twice, at 11 a.m. and at 2 p.m., without decisive success. Briggs's 1st Armoured Division rode the crisis, destroying 117 Axis tanks. During the armoured mêlée two armoured car squadrons of the Royal Dragoons found a gap in the south-west corner of the British salient and slipped through to do as much damage as they could amongst Axis supply units. But although armoured cars had penetrated the Axis front there was no real breach in the Axis anti-tank screen and containing line. Supercharge, like Lightfoot, was only partially successful. Montgomery was forced to resume the crumbling process. The X Corps was ordered to develop its thrust due west through Tel el Aqqaqir, while the XXX Corps, using the Highland Division reinforced by the 5th Indian Brigade from the 4th Indian Division, was to 'crumble' south-westwards to exploit the potential crack found by the armoured cars.

The XXX Corps started its thrust during the latter half of 2 November and was increasingly successful, capturing its first objectives and taking substantial numbers of Italian prisoners from the tiring Trieste and Ariete Divisions. The X Corps still met with resolute resistance. The stubbornness of the Axis defence of the Rahman track, however, was deceptive. At nightfall Thoma reported to Rommel that, though he had checked the British attack, he could not do so much longer. He was down to thirty-five fit tanks; he was grossly outnumbered; he was out-gunned by the new American Sherman tanks; and his units had lost two thirds of their established strength. Withdrawal to Fuka was imperative, if they were to save the nucleus of their mobile troops on which to rebuild the Panzer Army. Rommel agreed and lost no time in ordering the preliminary moves to make a methodical withdrawal possible. He had just heard of the loss of two more tankers: one sunk by the R.A.F. at sea and the other by American bombers in Tobruk harbour. He reported his intentions to Berlin.

Operations started slowly on 3 November. At Thoma's suggestion Rommel decided to take advantage of the lull to thin out his front by sending as many of his non-mobile units back to Fuka as his available transport would allow. His mobile units were ordered to concentrate in the northern sector from which they could cover the withdrawal along the coast road. The Australians detected some thinning out in the coastal sector, and the XIII Corps reported Italian withdrawals in the south. British hopes rose as the X and XXX Corps reported a slackening of Axis opposition, but towards evening resistance stiffened again and the chances of an Axis collapse seemed to fade. A drama was being enacted on the Axis side.

During the afternoon, just as Rommel and Thoma were beginning to hope that they might yet extract the Panzer Army successfully, a signal arrived from Hitler ordering Rommel to hold on as help was being rushed to him. It ended with the words: 'Despite his superiority the enemy must also have exhausted his strength. It would not be the first time in history that the stronger will has triumphed over the enemy's stronger battalions. You can show your troops no other road to victory or death. Adolf Hitler.'

Rommel hesitated, but tried to obey. He cancelled all rearward moves and ordered the re-establishment of a front some six miles west of the Rahman track. But even his great powers of improvisation could not reverse the momentum of the withdrawal process. The Italians were beyond caring; and his staunch German 'Africans' were nearing the end of their endurance. Montgomery sensed that the crisis had come and ordered the X and XXX Corps to increase pressure west and south-westwards next day.

The fourth of November saw the end of the Battle of El Alamein. About midday the over-strained Axis defence snapped. Cohesion was lost and the containing line fell apart. Thoma was captured fighting with his *Kampfstaffel* (battle escort) to check the X Corps advance. At 5.30 p.m. Rommel realized the end had come and ordered a general withdrawal to Fuka to save the mobile elements of the Panzer Army. He was forced by circumstances to abandon most of his Italian infantry.

The immediate British pursuit was not a success. Field-Marshal Carver, who was present at the time, has described the first night:

> It would have been hard enough if all had been under the command of the same Corps; with two different Corps, who were not on the best of terms anyway, both trying to carry out the same task in the same area, it was chaotic. There is no other word to describe the incredible confusion of that dark night in a sea of dust. Vehicles of every formation were travelling in every direction on every conceivable track, looming up in front of each other from unexpected directions out of the thick, stifling pall of dust.

During 5 and 6 November indifferent British staff work caused by psychological exhaustion, shortage of fuel (due to difficulties in switching supply from large quantities of ammunition to equally large quantities of fuel), and the resolute action of the German rearguards, all conspired to delay the British advance. The official British historians comment, 'The magic of Rommel's name undoubtedly conjured up extra wariness.' Any chance Montgomery might have had of trapping Rommel disappeared during the evening of 6 November when heavy rain stopped all cross-desert movement. By then, Rommel had regained control of the remnants of his Panzer Army and had started his long 1,500-mile withdrawal to Tunisia. He stood twice: at Mersa Brega on the Tripolitanian frontier in December; and at Buerat, covering Tripoli, in January. On neither occasion did Montgomery trap a significant part of Rommel's force. He refused to be diverted from his avowed intention of staying 'on balance' at all times, avoiding any risk of failure and ensuring that his formidable opponent could never again turn the tables on the Eighth Army.

El Alamein in Retrospect

There are four reasons for numbering Montgomery's Battle of El Alamein amongst the decisive battles of the twentieth century. First, it was a major victory in material terms. Rommel lost half his Panzer Army and nearly all his tanks. He left 30,000 prisoners in British hands and suffered about 20,000 battle casualties. He abandoned over 1,000 guns of all types, and saved only twenty of his 500 tanks. Second, in strategic terms, El Alamein secured the British position in the Middle East for the rest of the war. There was no German riposte. Third, in psychological terms, the British mastered their fear of attritional battles which had been inherited from their bitter experiences in the First World War. El Alamein gave them back their military confidence. And fourth, the British at last found a command team in Alexander and Montgomery which could inspire and lead them to success.

Churchill summed up the decisive nature of Montgomery's victory with the words: 'It marked in fact the turning of "the Hinge of Fate". It may almost be said, "Before Alamein we never had a victory. After Alamein we never had a defeat." '

Note on Sources

This account of the Battle of El Alamein has been based upon the five official histories of the Commonwealth countries which took part:

United Kingdom:	*The History of the Second World War, The Mediterranean and the Middle East*, Vols III and IV (1960, 1966).
Australia:	*Australia in the War of 1939–45 (Army):* 'Tobruk and El Alamein' (1966).
New Zealand	*New Zealand in the Second World War:* 'Alam Halfa and Alamein' (1967).
South Africa:	*South African Forces in World War II, Vol. III: War in the Desert* (1952).

India: *Official History of Indian Armed Forces in the Second World War:* 'The North African Campaign, 1940–43' (1956).

It has been augmented by reference to:

Alexander of Tunis, *Despatches* (1948).
Alexander of Tunis, *Memoirs* (1962).
Barnett, C., *The Battle of El Alamein* (1964).
Barnett, C., *Desert Generals* (1960).
Bryant, A., *The Turn of the Tide* (1957).
Carver, R. M. P., *El Alamein* (1962).
Churchill, W. S., *The Hinge of Fate* (Vol. IV of *The Second World War*) (1951).
De Guingand, F., *Operation Victory* (1947).
Horrocks, B. G., *A Full Life* (1960).
Kippenberger, H. K., *Infantry Brigadier* (1949).
Liddell Hart, B. H., *The Rommel Papers* (1953).
McCreery, R. L., 'Recollections of a Chief of Staff', (XII *Royal Lancer Journal*, 1959).
Majdalany, F., *The Battle of El Alamein* (1965).
Mellenthin, von, *Panzer Battles, 1939–45* (1955).
Montgomery of Alamein, *El Alamein to the River Sangro* (1948).
Montgomery of Alamein, *Memoirs* (1958).
Phillips, C. E. L., *Alamein* (1962).

Chapter Fifteen

STALINGRAD

Malcolm Mackintosh

THE END OF the winter campaign on the Soviet–German front in the Second World War – a campaign which had brought the Russians their first major victory, the Battle of Moscow, over the Germans – found both sides in need of a pause in operations for relief and re-equipment of their forces. This pause coincided with the Russian spring thaw, the reign of mud which overtakes Russian roads and fields in March and makes organized movement on a large scale almost impossible. But the high commands of the two sides were full of activity, preparing for the summer campaigns, in which both sides hoped to seize the strategic initiative.

Generally speaking, the front line had been stabilized from the Arctic Ocean to the Leningrad enclave (held by the Soviet garrison in appalling conditions of starvation and cold, and under constant bombardment), then diagonally across northern Russia to a point 100–150 miles west of Moscow, southwards past Kursk into the Ukraine, from there to the River Donets east of Kharkov, and so to the Sea of Azov near Rostov-on-Don. Sevastopol in the Crimea was still in Russian hands, but it was isolated and under siege. The last major action of the Soviet–German war had been in front of Moscow, where the Russians' winter offensive had driven the Germans back from the capital, but it had not led to a strategic breakthrough, nor had it seriously affected German morale. While fierce local battles had taken place round Leningrad and in the far south, the line south of Moscow to the Sea of Azov had been generally quiet since November 1941. It may have been partly for this reason that both high commands looked to the south as the area of their strategic offensives for the summer of 1942.

German plans for 1942 were contained in Hitler's Directive 41, of 5 April 1942, which ordered the concentration of all available forces on this southern sector of the front from the city of Kursk to the Crimea in preparation for a major breakthrough to the Don and Volga Rivers, leading to the seizure of the whole of the Caucasus, including the Baku oilfields and the northern gateway to the Middle East. Of the 217 German and Axis divisions operating on the Soviet–German front in April 1942, seventy-four, including seven panzer divisions, were allocated to the offensive, to be led by Field-Marshal von Bock, the commander of Army Group South. This army group was to include the First and Fourth German Panzer Armies, the Sixth, Eleventh and Seventeenth Armies, and two Rumanian, one Italian and one Hungarian army: a total strength of about 1 million men, with the support of 1,600 planes of the powerful air formations of the 4th Air Fleet, under Richthofen.

The Soviet High Command, which consisted of a political committee for the overall direction of the war effort, the State Defence Committee, and a general headquarters, often known by its Russian title of Stavka, both headed by Stalin, had also decided to seize the strategic initiative in the southern sector, and had prepared plans for an offensive from the Donets River to Kharkov and the line of the River Dnieper. According to the Soviet command structure, the Soviet armies, which were much smaller than their

Desperate house-to-house fighting in the ruins of the shattered city

German counterparts, were grouped together in fronts (or army groups), which were themselves subordinated to two sector headquarters: the South-western, which controlled the front from the Kursk area to the Black Sea, under Marshal Timoshenko, and the North Caucasus, which was responsible for the defence of Sevastopol, parts of the Crimea, and the Caucasus, under General Kozlov. Together these sector commands disposed of seventy-eight rifle (infantry) divisions and seventeen tank brigades. Most of these formations were under-strength (a Soviet rifle division numbered about 5,000 men in 1942), and the Germans, whose infantry divisions approached 14,000 men, had superiority on this part of the front in men, tanks and aircraft over their Soviet opponents.

As April passed into May, both high commands struggled feverishly to seize the military initiative, and, in the event, it was the German army which struck first – though not on their main axis of intended advance. On 8 May 1942, the Germans attacked and destroyed the Russian bridgehead in the east of the Crimea, and then turned on the isolated fortress of Sevastopol, which they finally took by storm, in the face of a heroic Russian defence, on 3 July. Meanwhile, a Soviet offensive was launched, somewhat prematurely, on 12 May, which took the form of heavy attacks against the German Sixth Army north and south of Kharkov, with a deep penetration by three armies in the direction of the industrial area of the Donets basin. The Soviet offensive, however, was badly planned and executed: differences of opinion existed between the Stavka and sector H.Q. on its aims and limitations, and the flanks of the main penetration were left unprotected. On 17 May the Germans counter-attacked and, in a masterly operation, trapped and destroyed three to four Russian armies south of Kharkov. Marshal Timoshenko's deputy and two army commanders were killed in the disaster, and the Russians lost many thousands in dead and prisoners even before the main German offensive in the south got under way. Indeed, the real significance of the ill-fated Kharkov offensive of May 1942 was that the Russians faced the main German onslaught with weakened front-line armies and air units and with virtually no reserves, many of which had been thrown in to halt the German counter-attack near Kharkov: the battle was, therefore, an important factor in the Soviet collapse in the Ukraine when the Germans finally attacked at the end of June.

As the victorious German formations moved up to their chosen point of attack in the northern part of the line (between Kharkov and Kursk), the Russians carried through a hurried reorganization of their command structure and redeployments of forces which at this late stage certainly did not help their command and control in the critical defensive battles which were imminent. The sector H.Q.s were abolished as being too unwieldy, and four fronts were established: the Bryansk, under General Golikov; the South-western, under Marshal Timoshenko; the Southern, under General Malinovsky (the future Minister of Defence); and the North Caucasus, under the old Civil War cavalry veteran, Marshal Budenny. Meanwhile the Germans had divided their command into two groups: Army Group A, under Field-Marshal List, in the south, and Army Group B under Field-Marshal von Bock in the north. At the moment of attack the German forces amounted to sixty-nine infantry divisions of 14,000 men each, and ten panzer, eight motorized and three cavalry divisions. Comparable figures on the Soviet side are hard to come by because of the losses in the Kharkov offensive, but it seems unlikely that they were able to muster more than sixty under-strength divisions and tank brigades, a force which was particularly weak in tanks, artillery and air support.

On 28 June 1942 Army Group B went over to the offensive against the Bryansk Front and achieved an immediate breakthrough. By 2 July the Germans had penetrated up to fifty miles and were approaching the key city of Voronezh, whose capture would have allowed them either to advance down the Don valley or to threaten to outflank the Soviet position defending Moscow. Soviet reinforcements, subordinated to a new front H.Q., the Voronezh Front, under General Vatutin, were rushed to the city, where the operations were placed under the personal direction of the Chief of the General Staff, General Vasilevsky, himself. After hard fighting in which the Germans penetrated into Voronezh city, the Russians stabilized the situation near Voronezh. By this time, however, the main German effort was gathering momentum further to the south.

Although the initial German breakthrough came in the Voronezh sector, the main offensive was launched by the armies east of Kharkov, and then by Army Group A in the Donets basin. The German attacks were successful everywhere, and by early July the whole Russian line in the eastern Ukraine was in full retreat. The terrain was open and particularly good for tanks, which swept forward through the small Cossack villages of the Don country in whirling clouds of dust and smoke. In the dry heat of a Russian summer, water was at a premium; however, meticulous German planning ensured that their supplies were on time to keep pace with the advance. But for the Russians the losses incurred in the May and June battles had fallen heavily not only on the armoured forces, but also on the supply, repair and equipment services. Armies, often cut off from the front command and isolated by the German spearheads from their neighbouring formations, were trying to carry out an organized and coherent withdrawal towards the great bend of the Don River and Stalingrad. But the speed of the German advance scattered many Soviet units, and both commanders and men appeared to lose the sense of purpose and vitality which had brought them victory during the winter. Morale fell, commanders at the highest level quarrelled, and no one seemed able to stop the slide towards collapse. Newspaper correspondents in Moscow felt the dismay and anger in the capital at the failure of the southern armies, and there were those who talked in private about incompetence and even treachery among the retreating generals in the eastern Ukraine.

Perhaps in answer to these doubts, Stalin and the Stavka pushed through a hurried reorganization of the local command structure. The luckless Marshal Timoshenko, against whom much of the popular anger was directed, was dismissed, and a new front created to cover the bend of the Don, the Stalingrad Front, which was given three armies of the High Command's Strategic Reserve: the 62nd Army (General Kolpakchy), the 63rd Army (General Kuznetsov) and the 64th Army (General Shumilov). This front absorbed the battered formations of the South-western Front, and stretched in a vast arc from the upper Don round to the west of Stalingrad to the steppes bordering on the Caspian Sea. Its commander was Lieutenant-General Gordov, an experienced veteran of the old school, who had served in the First World War, the Civil War and the Soviet–Finnish campaign of 1939–40, and had emerged with some credit from the defensive operations in 1941 and early 1942. Gordov later fell foul of the Soviet regime, and his role in the Battle of Stalingrad has until recently been belittled or ignored, but there is now enough evidence (particularly from the memoirs of Marshals Zhukov and Rokossovsky) to suggest that this highly professional, if temperamental, soldier played an important part in the critical defensive battles on the Don, while the Stavka planned and executed the strategic counter-offensive which destroyed the German Sixth Army and its allies. Of considerable significance, as it later turned out, was the fact that Nikita Khrushchev, who had been Marshal Timoshenko's political commissar, assumed the same post at the headquarters of the Stalingrad Front, and almost at once quarrelled with General Gordov, whose authority, it now seems clear, Khrushchev was determined to undermine if he could. It is possible that when the Stavka decided to hive off the eastern part of the Stalingrad Front on 5 August and set up a new front H.Q. – the South-eastern Front – in Stalingrad city, it was Khrushchev's influence which led to the decision to give the commander of the South-eastern Front, Lieutenant-General Eremenko (an old associate of Khrushchev from before the war) authority over both the Stalingrad and the South-eastern Fronts: an obviously unworkable arrangement in the critical circumstances of the sweeping German victories of the summer of 1942.

While these high-level reorganizations were taking place, the situation at the front was going from bad to worse for the Russians. As July passed into August, the German armies of Army Group B swept down the valley of the Don towards its great bend, where it turns south-westwards past Stalingrad and the Volga to flow into the Sea of Azov at Rostov-on-Don. Army Group A, meanwhile, had broken the Russian line in the Donets basin and driven General Malinovsky's Southern Front out of Rostov and over the lower Don into the rolling plains of the North Caucasus. The Stavka relieved Malinovsky of his command, abolished the Southern Front, and incorporated the remnants of its armies into Marshal Budenny's North Caucasus Front. Budenny, however, was no more successful than Malinovsky had been in halting the German panzers as they drove through ideal tank country towards the Caucasus mountains and Baku, and he too was relieved of his command. By mid-August the Germans had reached the main passes through the Caucasus mountains, but stiffening Soviet resistance in the foothills and significant German withdrawal of armour and infantry for the main battle at Stalingrad put an end for the time being to the German drive for the Caucasian oilfields.

By mid-August, too, the battle for Stalingrad was really on. The strategic picture was dominated by the powerful thrust of the main German armies – primarily General Paulus's Sixth Army – down the middle Don and into the great bend of the river, and thence to Stalingrad itself and the River Volga. The first German spearheads reached the Volga north of Stalingrad on 23 August, the day on which the German 4th Air Fleet, flying up to 4,000 sorties a day, hurled itself against the city. The damage caused to Stalingrad in these early air raids meant that the Russian armies of the South-eastern Front retreated into a mass of ruins and rubble. But by this time the character of the fighting had changed: the Soviet troops were recovering their spirit and offering yard-by-yard resistance, both in the suburbs of Stalingrad and along the Don. It took the Germans from 21 August to 2 September to cover the last few miles from the bend of the Don at Kalach to the centre of Stalingrad itself. One reason for the serious slowing down of the German advance, in addition to stiffer Soviet resistance as they neared the city and the problems posed to the German command by the lengthening lines of communication, was the ceaseless pressure exerted on the Germans' left flank along the middle course of the Don by General Gordov's Stalingrad Front. Under General Zhukov's supervision, Gordov's under-strength armies (one of which had only four tanks left in the first week of September) threw themselves again and again at the German flank, forcing the Germans to detach units from the main axis of advance as reinforcements. The Stalingrad Front also seized and held bridgeheads on the south bank of the Don which were to be vital in the subsequent Soviet counter-offensive at Stalingrad.

The heavier and more successful Soviet resistance at Stalingrad led Hitler to order an all-out assault on the city by both the Sixth Army and the Fourth Panzer Army, which had been recalled from the Caucasus on 31 July to take over the southern wing of the advance on Stalingrad. So fierce were the German ground and air attacks that serious penetrations were made into the ruined centre of the city: it is not always realized how little of Stalingrad was actually left in Soviet hands by mid-September. The city was held by the weak and partly isolated Sixty-second Army, whose commander, from 12 September, was the General Chuikov who was to become so legendary a figure through his tenacious and heroic defence of Stalingrad. Chuikov, also a veteran of the First World War and of the Finnish war, had so far taken no part in the Soviet–German campaign: he had been Soviet military attaché in Nationalist China until mid-1942. But on his recall to Moscow the choice of this rugged, skilful and ruthless commander to hold on to a few square miles of rubble and shattered buildings on the western bank of the River Volga while the Fronts regrouped and reinforcements were brought up proved to be a stroke of genius on the part of the Soviet High Command.

By mid-September, Chuikov's Sixty-second Army had become the focus of the entire nation. Holding grimly on to every building, ruin and cellar in the city it could, the army fought bitterly against ferocious German assaults. The two armies, locked together, fought in small groups for days for a street corner or a basement; Russian and German soldiers stalked each other as shells and bombs reduced already damaged buildings to yet smaller rubble, and the heat and the brick dust caked the men of both sides in dry clay.

German tactics consisted of heavy air attacks followed by advances by tanks and infantry; the Russians, whose positions were often overrun during the day, counter-attacked at night, winning back key buildings or the ravines which criss-crossed the city. Chuikov himself was always in the thick of the fight. Snipers were often the most valuable soldiers, picking off enemy commanders and seeking out unexplored channels for movement through the ruined streets. The Sixty-second Army headquarters was frequently under direct fire, and it flitted from sewer to cellar, while divisional staffs were often to be found in corridors or slit trenches dug in parks or streets. Especially fierce were the struggles for the low hill known as Mamayev Kurgan in the centre of Stalingrad, for the salient where the Germans had broken through to the River Volga, and for the factory settlements Red October and the Barricades, which remained partly in Russian and partly in German hands until the end of the battle.

The climax to the defensive struggle came for the Russians in mid-October; General Chuikov says in his memoirs that 14–16 October were the most critical days for the Sixty-second Army. The strain of battle was telling on both sides; the German attacks, although pressed home with courage and perseverance, had begun to be shorter in duration and the pauses between them were lengthening. German and Rumanian morale was beginning to fail. The fierceness and bravery of the Russians was unequalled, but with the original six divisions of the Sixty-second Army reduced to regimental strength, and regiments reduced to companies, it was particularly hard to keep the army together as a cohesive force. It was especially difficult to combat the mental strain and battle exhaustion suffered by all ranks, and some officers – even senior ones – simply disappeared from the city to the imagined haven of the east bank of the Volga. On the other hand, those who did stay – commanders, soldiers, political commissars, doctors and nurses – found themselves hardening to the constant noise, smoke, casualties and destruction, and began to develop a new kind of determined ascendancy over the Germans which played a great part in enabling them to hold on until the tide of battle turned.

Meanwhile, on the east bank of the Volga, General Eremenko and the staff of the South-eastern Front were working night and day to organize reinforcements in men, weapons and supplies and ferry them across the Volga under fire. Eremenko, one of the toughest and most experienced of Soviet front commanders, spent much of his time in Stalingrad, where both he and Chuikov were wounded. He also saw it as his prime responsibility to keep the Sixty-second Army alive as a viable fighting force, and to this end he deployed almost all the front's artillery on the east bank of the river partly out of reach of the German dive-bombers, and sent the fresh divisions which arrived from the High Command's reserves straight into the battle for the city. The first and most famous division to arrive was General Rodimtsev's 13th Guards Division, which crossed the Volga on 14 September and went straight into action on the Mamayev Kurgan; within days it had been reduced almost to regimental strength. In the next two weeks it was followed by eight more fresh divisions, each of which was thrown into a desperate stand or counter-attack, hanging on grimly to a few buildings or a factory site until it too was reduced in strength. After a time no more reinforcements came; but the names of many of these divisional commanders who joined the Sixty-second Army in the city – Rodimtsev, Gorishny, Guriev, and Lyudnikov – became the legendary heroes of the 67-day defence of Stalingrad.

One of the reasons why reinforcements were not sent into Stalingrad after mid-October was that troops were being diverted to the strategic concentrations of forces to the north and south of Stalingrad in preparation for the massive counter-offensive being planned by the Stavka. There is a certain amount of argument in Soviet military-historical literature over the responsibility for the counter-offensive plan. General Eremenko claimed that the idea first came to him on 1 August, and that his staff, with Khrushchev's active participation, produced a draft plan and sent it to the Stavka on 6 October. However, other writers, including Marshals Zhukov and Malinovsky, credit the General Staff with the plan, along with the senior representatives of the Stavka who were sent by Stalin to supervise operations at Stalingrad, including Zhukov himself, General Vasilevsky, and the head of the Soviet artillery command, General Voronov.

Whoever was responsible, the strategic situation faced by the Soviet planners was this: Hitler's insistence on capturing Stalingrad at all costs had led to the concentration of some 330,000 men in the narrow Stalingrad salient, organized as Army Group Don: the German Sixth and Fourth Panzer Armies, and the Third and Fourth Rumanian Armies. Fourteen German divisions, two of them panzer, were locked in the city itself, and by October the long flanks of the German and Axis group along the middle Don and southward into the semi-desert towards the Caspian Sea were largely held by Rumanian and Italian formations. These were strung out thinly along the flanks, and very few formations were deployed in reserve in the centre of the Don bend.

The Soviet plan, whose aim was the encirclement and destruction of the German Sixth and Fourth Panzer Armies, envisaged two breakthroughs against the Rumanian and Italian-held flanks: one directed against the Third Rumanian Army north-west of Stalingrad at a point on the Don where General Gordov's Stalingrad Front held a small bridgehead at Serafimevich on the right bank of the river; the other against the Fourth Rumanian Army south of Stalingrad. When the two arms of the encircling pincers had met west of Stalingrad at Kalach on the Don, the Russians hoped to destroy the German forces cut off in the area of the city, to hold the external line of the encirclement against German counter-attack, and ultimately to advance from it westwards towards Rostov and the Donets basin, as the major part of the Soviet winter offensive of 1942–3.

In preparation for this offensive, the Stavka brought up tremendous reinforcements to the Stalingrad area; when these were added to the troops already in the front line the total amounted to a quarter of the Red Army's infantry and air strength and sixty per cent of its tank and mechanized formations. In the critical sectors on the Don and south of Stalingrad where shock troops were being concentrated, the Russians enjoyed a two to one superiority in men and machine guns, a three to one superiority in mortars, and a four to one superiority in anti-tank guns over the Third and Fourth Rumanian Armies guarding the area of the intended attack. The strictest conditions of secrecy were observed in the Soviet build-up: troops were moved into position only at night, radio silence was observed, and patrols from previous divisions were left behind to deceive the enemy over the build-up in case any Soviet prisoners were taken by the Rumanians.

One more major command reorganization took place before the Russian attack began on 19 November 1942. To control the operations of the northern pincer on the Don, the Stavka reconstituted the South-western Front under General Vatutin on the right flank of the Stalingrad Front. The latter was renamed the Don Front, and placed under the command of General Rokossovsky; General Gordov was relieved of his command and demoted; he served for the rest of the war as an army commander, and disappeared in 1946, apparently for having criticized the system of political control in the Soviet army. The name 'Stalingrad Front' was transferred to General Eremenko's South-eastern Front. The whole group of fronts was subordinated directly to the Stavka, whose representatives, Generals Zhukov, Vasilevsky and Voronov, directed operations from a forward general headquarters in the Stalingrad area.

The nineteenth of November 1942 dawned a bitterly cold day over the snow-bound steppes of the Don and the Volga, with fog clinging to the ravines and seriously hindering visibility for both sides. At 7.32 a.m. the guns of the South-western Front opened up on the Rumanian positions near Serafimovich on the Don, and eighteen minutes later the infantry of the Russian Fifth Tank and Twenty-first Armies went into the attack. To the

Rumanian defenders of the Third Army, wave upon wave of white-clad figures appeared through the swirling fog, and bitter fighting quickly flared up everywhere along the front. First came the Russian infantry, who broke into the Rumanian defences, and at midday the two army commanders, Generals Romanenko and Chistyakov, launched their armour into the battle. Three Soviet tank corps crashed through the IV and V Rumanian Army Corps; by early on the 20th, the Russians had penetrated to more than twenty miles south of the Don. Army Group Don headquarters brought up a German panzer division to counter-attack, and heavy fighting ensued – but the main Russian tank force wheeled eastwards and started its race for Kalach and the rendezvous with the southern pincer launched by the new Stalingrad Front.

This southern thrust had begun a day later than the northern one, and almost came to grief in the first hour when an over-hasty colonel misread a rocket signal and led his men into the attack before the artillery barrage was over, which brought the latter to an untidy halt on this sector. But the Russian infantry attacked fiercely through the fog, broke through the Fourth Rumanian Army's lines in three places, and cleared a passage for the Soviet armour. Severe damage was inflicted on the VI Rumanian Army Corps, after which one Soviet tank and one mechanized corps turned north and made for Kalach, clashing with outlying units of the German Fourth Panzer Army as they passed the outskirts of Stalingrad on their right. German and Rumanian counter-attacks proved unavailing, and at 4 p.m. on the afternoon of 23 November units of General Kravchenko's IV Tank Corps from the north, scouting warily but hopefully east of the bend of the Don, first saw white-clad tankmen coming towards them across the snowbound steppe. They turned out to be a patrol of the 36th Mechanized Brigade of General Volsky's IV Mechanized Corps of the Stalingrad Front. The initial encirclement had succeeded: twenty German divisions, an anti-aircraft corps, two mortar regiments, two Rumanian divisions and a Croat regiment were caught in the trap.

Although the South-western and Stalingrad Fronts had linked up at Kalach, the battlefield remained a vast landscape which the Russians were far from controlling. Soviet formations, on the move or refuelling, offered exposed flanks and maintained only intermittent communication with each other. Moreover, although two Rumanian armies had been defeated, the élite German divisions in Stalingrad had hardly been touched. Soviet intelligence knew that the Germans were already moving up reinforcements from the Ukraine and the Caucasus, and the encircled troops were quite capable of breaking through the slender ring drawn round them. It was essential for the Russians to strengthen the line round Stalingrad and to push the outer battle line further to the west and south-west as soon as possible.

For this purpose the Stavka ordered the Fifth Tank Army and another army of the South-western Front, General Kuznetsov's First Guards Army, to occupy and hold the line of the River Chir, which rises near the middle Don and flows roughly southwards to join the lower Don fifty miles south-west of Stalingrad. This move was designed to make the outer ring of the encirclement secure against attack from the west. At the same time, the Don Front was to step up its pressure from the north against the encircled Sixth Army. Because these armies were operating against German divisions their progress was much slower than the dramatic advances of 19–23 November, but by the end of the month they had pushed the XI German Army Corps further back towards Stalingrad and one Soviet army, the Sixty-sixth under General Zhadov, had linked up with the northern pocket of the Sixty-second Army still holding out in the city. A similar operation was carried out south of Stalingrad, where the left wing of the Stalingrad Front advanced towards the Don and pushed back units of the Fourth Panzer Army to strengthen and tighten the Russian hold on the encircled German forces in the Stalingrad pocket.

The Soviet High Command, represented by Zhukov, Vasilevsky and Voronov, then prepared a plan for a general assault on the encircled German forces, an operation which was to be entrusted to General Rokossovsky's Don Front, to which all the armies manning the inner line of the encirclement were subordinated, plus a new crack army from the strategic reserve, the Second Guards Army under General Malinovsky. As soon as this attack had begun, the remainder of the South-western, Voronezh and Stalingrad Fronts were to open up a major offensive from the outer ring of the encirclement westwards, which was aimed at Rostov-on-Don, the Sea of Azov, and ultimately the shores of the Black Sea, cutting off the German forces in the Caucasus.

The Germans, however, forestalled the Soviet offensive. First they threw back General Rokossovsky's first attack on Stalingrad on 27 November, and then they opened their own offensive from the south-west against what German intelligence had rightly identified as the weakest point in the ring round Stalingrad: the area of Kotelnikovo, about 110 miles from Stalingrad on the Stalingrad–Rostov railway. Here the newly constituted German Army Group Don (which included part of the Fourth Panzer Army) under Field-Marshal Manstein created a powerful force of 35,000 men and 300 tanks commanded by General Hoth. On 12 December Manstein sent Hoth into action with orders to drive straight through to Stalingrad and relieve the trapped divisions. The attack opened most auspiciously. On the first two days the 6th, 17th and 23rd German Panzer Divisions broke through the lines of the Soviet Fifty-first Army and a Central Asian Cavalry Corps and advanced rapidly along the railway towards the city. On the 18th, Germans in Stalingrad could hear the fire of Manstein's artillery, and General Hoth broadcast a message to the Sixth Army: 'Hold on – we are coming'; the relief of the garrison indeed seemed imminent.

The Russians, however, reacted quickly and effectively. Rokossovsky's assault on the Stalingrad grouping was postponed, and his best army, the Second Guards Army, was transferred (against Rokossovsky's strenuous protests) by General Vasilevsky to the Stalingrad Front, then organizing a more secure defence along the frozen course of the little River Myshkova. More and more Soviet reinforcements arrived on the battlefield, and slowly the German advance was brought to a halt. On Christmas Eve 1942 General Hoth ordered a withdrawal of his force from the Myshkova River, and the pursuit was quickly taken up by fresh forces from the Stalingrad Front. With this retreat, the only serious German attempt to save the trapped armies in Stalingrad failed.

Field-Marshal Manstein in fact needed Hoth's men to help to hold off another major Russian offensive which had opened up along the River Chir and northwards along the middle and upper Don. On 16 December the rest of the South-western and Voronezh Fronts had attacked in strength from Voronezh city to the Chir, and broken through into the eastern Ukraine against German, Italian and Rumanian formations; they then advanced towards the Donets and the Donets basin. The Stalingrad Front (renamed the Southern Front on 1 January 1943) advanced on Rostov at the mouth of the Don, and linked up with other Soviet troops arriving from the Caucasus, whose evacuation had been ordered by the Germans. After further heavy fighting the Russians recaptured Rostov on 14 February 1943, and occupied a line from there to the Donets which was so far west that Stalingrad city found itself over 200 miles behind the main front line.

Meanwhile the last act was already under way for the doomed German garrison of the Stalingrad area. The operation planned for December was rescheduled for 10 January 1943. For the destruction of the encircled troops General Rokossovsky's Don Front deployed seven armies (280,000 men, in thirty-nine divisions), and in addition ten infantry brigades, four tank brigades, fifty-five heavy artillery regiments and five 'katyusha' brigades (the Soviet rocket artillery weapons). The Russians also had almost total air superiority. The Germans in the pocket numbered 190,000 fighting men together with the remnant of the Rumanians and support troops. On the whole, the ground favoured the defenders, but the weather did not, for the full severity of the Russian winter had set in, and the Russian soldiers were much better prepared for it than were the Germans and their allies.

After General Paulus, the German commander in Stalingrad, had rejected a Soviet summons to surrender on 8 January 1943, the Soviet attack began on 10 January. The initial bombardment was carried out by more than 7,000 guns and mortars, and then the infantry went in. The Germans resisted furiously, and nowhere more than in Stalingrad against General Chuikov's Sixty-second Army; they seemed to have a special urge to hold on to the houses and streets which they had seized with such heavy losses during the summer and autumn, and now they fought bitterly for every yard.

Nevertheless, the Russians' élan, skill and weight carried them on, and by

15 January the outer German lines west and south-west of the city had caved in, and the defenders had fallen back into the city, having lost some 30,000 men in five days' fighting. Two days later the first serious sign of a crack in German morale appeared as the Russians began to find groups of exhausted, starving and frostbitten Germans ready to give themselves up. Lack of rations and medical care was helping to reduce the Sixth and part of the Fourth Panzer Armies to a herd of stumbling, frozen men with hardly the strength even to fire their weapons.

The Russians moved relentlessly on. On 22 January the Twenty-first Army advancing from the west met the Sixty-second Army in the centre of Stalingrad, cutting the German garrison in two. A Rumanian and two German divisions laid down their arms on the same day. On 31 January Soviet troops uncovered General Paulus's command post and took him and his staff prisoner. Two days later the southern group capitulated, and on 2 February 1943 the last shot of the Battle of Stalingrad was fired – inside one of the factories where men of the Sixty-second Army had fought it out with the Germans since the early days of the siege. The battle was over, and it proved to be one of the greatest and most crushing victories for Russian arms in the whole of Russian history.

There can be no doubt that the Battle of Stalingrad, for the first time in the Second World War, seriously shook the Germans' confidence in the outcome of the war and the invincibility of German arms. Stalingrad faced Germany with a situation which she had never met before: the total destruction of 330,000 men on the battlefield with all their weapons and equipment. Until the defeat at Stalingrad German soldiers had gone to the Russian front with a sense of participating in a crusade which they confidently expected would be fulfilled on time with German efficiency and power. After Stalingrad, the ancient fear of the Slav menace from the East descended on the Germans; a posting to the Russian front now became synonymous with death or capture – and capture meant for them Siberia. Most German leaders had gambled on the belief that the Soviet Union could be defeated in war if her armies could be destroyed before the country's vast resources could be mobilized; Stalingrad showed that the gamble had failed.

At the same time, Stalingrad was not an unalloyed victory for the Soviet Union. It had grown out of a series of bitter defeats in the summer of 1942, and the means of winning it, both material and in terms of morale, had been acquired at the cost of hundreds of thousands of lives and the long and bloody siege of Stalingrad itself. The counter-offensive was an experimental campaign for the Russians: the armies, corps, divisions and brigades which attacked on 19 November 1942 were experimental in armament and organization, and were led by men who were still developing the tactics which were later to carry them to Berlin and Vienna. Some of these were quickly adopted as standard tactics; others were as quickly abandoned. Cooperation between infantry and armour, reconnaissance methods, and recognition of the importance of mass artillery and rocket fire were good; but much had yet to be done to introduce better coordination between the higher staffs, and problems over devolution of responsibility were still serious. But these were the growing pains of an army which had been taken by surprise – in June 1941 and July 1942 – and had fought and won defensive battles at Moscow and Leningrad, and mounted a major counter-offensive at Stalingrad, and was now going on to win the greatest battle of all on the Eastern Front: at Kursk in the summer of 1943. For if Stalingrad was held and won after a long strategic retreat, at Kursk the Red Army fought it out where it stood, and its subsequent counter-offensive started the move which two years later led to the capture of Berlin.

Note on Sources

Most of the source material for the chapter on the Battle of Stalingrad comes from original Soviet military-historical books and articles, which have not been translated into English, French or German. Some has been drawn from original German sources.

Among the works which have been published in English are:

Chuikov, Marshal V. I., *The Beginning of the Road* (1963).
Garder, Michael, *A History of the Soviet Army* (1966).
Mackintosh, Malcolm, *Juggernaut: A History of the Soviet Armed Forces* (1967).
Schröter, Heinz, *Stalingrad* (1958).
Zhukov, Marshal G. K., *Reminiscences and Recollections* (1970).

Soviet sources in Russian only include:

Istoria Velikoi Otechestvennoi Voiny Sovetskogo Soyuza 1941–1945, Vols 3 and 4 (1961).
Samsonov, General A. M., *Stalingradskaya Bitva* (*The Battle of Stalingrad*) (1968).
Skorobogatkin, General K. F., and others, *50-let Vo-oruzhennykh Sil SSSR* (*50 Years of the Soviet Armed Forces*) (1968).

Reference may also be made to the relevant chapters in Purnell's *Illustrated History of the Second World War*, with particular attention to the chapter on Stalingrad by Geoffrey Jukes.

Chapter Sixteen

KURSK

John Erickson

TOWARDS THE END of March 1943 a lull which was to prove of unusual and unaccustomed duration settled over the Soviet–German battle front. Both sides were sorely in need of respite after the ferocious winter fighting. The entire southern wing of the German army in the East, increasingly marooned in the mud brought on by the spring thaw and stalled by indecision, had barely escaped destruction at the hands of the Red Army, whose winter counter-offensive, unleashed across the Don north of Stalingrad on 19 November 1942, had forced the capitulation of the powerful German Sixth Army in Stalingrad itself, mauled the Fourth Panzer Army, dispersed four armies of Germany's allies fighting with the Wehrmacht on the Eastern Front and then spilled over to the north against the German Second Army, as well as southwards and westwards over the Donets. In mid-February 1943 Kharkov fell to the Red Army. The German southern wing hung limp and well-nigh shattered, with Soviet armies striking into the Donbas and dreaming even now of the Dnieper, but on 18 February Field-Marshal Erich von Manstein, without waiting for all the Fuehrer's promised reinforcements, launched the hastily reformed Fourth Panzer Army on a limited but devastating counter-stroke. Manstein's 'backhand stroke' deflected the destruction of Army Group South, brought the Donets front once more under German control, won back Kharkov, and turned the sourness of defeat into the elation of victory (though this was the last time either in the East or the West that German troops were to savour triumph). On 14 March 1943 Kharkov fell to the S.S. Panzer Corps, while further to the north the *Gross-Deutschland* (a panzer-grenadier division) took Belgorod, thus bringing German divisions on to the southerly face of the Soviet salient extending to the west of Kursk. Manstein's plan to eliminate the entire Kursk salient came to nothing, however, since Army Group Centre was unable to mount an attack of any weight against the northern face of the salient, while the steadily encroaching thaw with its familiar mud and slush all too soon made the ground impassable.

Thus, after weeks of fluidity as the German lines buckled, sagged or collapsed, the front assumed a new configuration: German troops still held the Donets and Mius line and Kharkov was in German hands, but the substantial Soviet 'Kursk salient' obtruded westwards into the German lines and jutted into the flanks of two German army groups, South and Centre. For all the massive scale and ferocious intensity of the winter fighting, painfully obvious from the mangled Soviet divisions and badly worn German units, neither side had achieved a decisive operational success: the Red Army had not unhinged the southern wing of the *Ostheer* (Eastern Army) and even Manstein's formidable counter-stroke had not put paid to the fighting capacity of the Soviet armies. Faced with this unstable equilibrium, both sides were turning to tense considerations of the summer campaign and both inevitably fixed their gaze on that singular bulge formed

Russian T34 tanks and infantry counter-attacking in the Kursk salient

by the Kursk salient, which offered tempting opportunities to the Soviet and German commands alike.

Even in the wake of the German defeat at Stalingrad, which was consummated in the humiliating surrender of Field-Marshal von Paulus and the Sixth Army in February 1943, Hitler was determined to win back in the coming summer what had been lost during the grim winter: '*im Sommer wiederzuholen, was im Winter verlorengegangen war*', a resolve full of fateful implications. In these same February days Army Group South had already submitted its own appreciation of the situation on the Eastern Front, which pointed to that conspicuous bulge in the German front running south from Kharkov along the Donets and Mius, a protrusion which, in Manstein's own words, 'was just begging to be sliced off'. Moreover, any major Soviet breakthrough here might again imperil the German southern wing, as well as bringing the Soviet armies into the Donets and on to the Ukraine. In view of the vistas which could unfold here, it was sensible to assume that the Soviet command would mount a major effort in the southern theatre – as indeed they did – and for the same reason the anticipated Soviet attack should be met by a deliberate German withdrawal, enticing the enemy to the lower Dnieper and then confounding him utterly by smashing into his flank with powerful armoured forces assembled for this purpose in the area west of Kharkov.

Though reconciled momentarily to going over to the defensive, Hitler nonetheless made it clear and expressed the view unequivocally in Operations Order No. 5 of 13 March 1943 that a limited offensive in the East provided the most effective defence: the attack should be carried out immediately the ground dried out and before any assault on Europe could develop from the Anglo-American forces in the West. Manstein's own victory at Kharkov contributed powerfully to his belief in the utility of such an offensive design. The Red Army would be punished before it could recoup after the winter battles and the Kursk salient – the semi-circular bulge jutting westwards for some seventy-five miles into the German lines and with a base of not less than 100 miles from north to south – suggested itself as the main target for this *Materialschlacht* (battle of attrition); the Red Army's men and machines would be pounded in an attack which would emasculate Soviet striking power. Slicing off the Kursk salient by mounting an enveloping attack from the north and the south would immolate that vast bulk of Soviet manpower and armament which had piled into the area west of Kursk, thus not only deeply wounding the Red Army but also restoring lustre to German arms in a rapid and spectacular victory. The outlines of Operation Citadel (*Zitadelle*) thus loomed up in March, though in this form it was the least preferable of the solutions advanced by Manstein, but one favoured by Hitler, a 'forehand stroke' whose success depended crucially upon a certain speed of execution: the longer the German forces waited on the defensive, the greater was the possibility of the Red Army expanding their salient and rupturing the German front in its entirety.

It was mid-April before this design took any firm shape. Early in the month Colonel-General Zeitzler, chief of staff of O.K.H. (*Oberkommando des Heeres*, the Army High Command), convened a conference at Rastenburg to discuss the coming offensive operations. Here Manstein's subtle 'back-hand stroke', his own plan favoured by Southern Army Group was formally rejected: it was to be rather an all-out setpiece assault on the Kursk salient. The memorandum submitted to Hitler on 11 April by Zeitler proposed that Colonel-General Model's Ninth Army (Army Group Centre) would attack the salient from the north, out of the Orel salient held by German troops, while to the south Colonel-General Hoth's Fourth Panzer Army supported by the *Armee-Abteilung Kempf* (Operational Group Kempf) (both from Army Group South) would strike northwards from the Kharkov salient to join up with Model moving from the northern face.

Time was of the essence and yet vacillation hung heavy in the air. Operations Order No. 6 dated 15 April 1943 specified that Kursk must be a victory 'to shine out like a signal beacon to the world'. Though replete with operational detail and the delineation of the tasks of Army Groups South and Centre, as well as insisting on the need for surprise, this operations order signalled virtual postponement in that it fixed the earliest date for the attack on the Kursk salient at 3 May (or, in yet another complicated rubric, the attack should be ready to be launched as from 28 April and 'within six days of receipt of an order from O.K.H.'). Such studied vagueness at least gave Hitler the latitude he required to stiffen the assault armies with the new Tiger and Panther tanks, in which he placed so much faith, having already averred that one battalion of Tigers was worth a whole panzer division: the Mark VI Tiger tank (*Panzerkampfwagen VI Tiger Ausf. H*) produced by Henschel was already in service in small numbers and the Mark V Panther exemplified the German answer to the formidable Soviet medium tank, the T-34. Meanwhile, out of a belated recognition of the plight of the panzer troops Hitler had recalled Colonel-General Guderian to service as Inspector-General of Armoured Forces: he had to grapple with the consequences of the mayhem inflicted on the once invincible panzer divisions, reduced in January 1943 to a mere 495 tanks to do battle across the length and breadth of the Eastern Front. Needless to say, Guderian became almost from the outset a vehement opponent of the attack on the Kursk salient, a stance in which he was joined before very long by Manstein. Guderian feared for this sacrifice in tanks and Manstein for the meagreness of the infantry, who would have to be stripped from north and south of the salient to provide support for the armour.

The signs of Hitler's hesitation were already apparent, while the German High Command fell to feuding within itself. Internal lines of battle were clearly drawing up in an encounter which was complicated by conflicting professional advice. The dilemma was becoming cruelly plain: the proposed attack promised great risk and dangerous sacrifice, at least in the minds of Guderian and Manstein, yet not to attack could only expose the *Ostheer* to the threat of being assaulted in the south by the massed and replenished ranks of the Red Army. Meanwhile, on 'the other side of the hill' (though, strictly speaking, the Kursk salient itself consisted of low-lying farmland, stretching cornfields, scattered villages and hummocks of high ground) the Soviet command had at this same time come to concentrate its gaze on Kursk and, like Hitler, Stalin also nurtured grand designs. If somewhat earlier, in February, Hitler had refused to believe that Army Group South faced anything approaching mortal danger, Stalin for his part had rammed his armies forward in the belief that a German collapse was imminent, only to have Manstein's 'backhand stroke' smash into depleted Soviet divisions in his drive to recapture Kharkov. As Golikov and Vatutin struggled to control the situation the iron hand of Marshal Zhukov fell on this front, as Stalin hurriedly recalled him from the north-western theatre and the operations to pierce the blockade of Leningrad. Zhukov moved up all available reserves, including a tank army and this, in combination with the weather, stemmed Manstein's drive towards Kursk itself. Once Manstein's drive was halted, the Soviet defensive lines did not alter appreciably: Rokossovsky's Central Front held the northern face of the salient with the Bryansk Front (under M. M. Popov) and the Western Front (commanded by V. D. Sokolovsky) to the north, while the southern face was invested by Vatutin's Voronezh Front with the South-western Front running to the south. These main fronts – Central and Voronezh – mustered ten armies between them (with one rifle and one tank army in reserve with the Voronezh Front, making a grand total of twelve armies). In addition, the greatest strategic reserve ever assembled by the Red Army during the 1941–5 war was to take its place within this order of battle: the Reserve Front (finally designated the Steppe Front) which was soon emplaced within the salient.

Originally Stalin had contemplated using the Central and Voronezh Fronts in a major attack directed towards Gomel and Kharkov, forcing the Dnieper and laying the foundation for the recovery of both the Donbas and Belorussia – a grandiose design indeed. But with a formidable German force building up on either side of the Kursk salient, this plan was obviously unworkable in such a simple form: the vital question at this juncture was how the Red Army should respond to the growing threat: mount a spoiling attack, or fight defensively and then strike back in full force? There is much to suggest that Stalin wanted to pre-empt any German offensive and that he was only with difficulty dissuaded from this predilection, the root of which seemed to be apprehension over the Red Army's ability to fight a major and prolonged defensive action. Marshal Zhukov, however, had decided and solidly based views on this subject. Early in April both the Central and Voronezh Fronts were reinforced (on 1 April the two fronts mustered 1,200 tanks between them, a figure which was to triple within two months and thus justify Manstein's warning to Hitler over the dangers of undue delay). Zhukov made his own inspection of the front area, particularly

Vatutin's Voronezh Front, and on 8 April 1943, after consultation with the General Staff and front commanders, submitted a major strategic appreciation to Stalin. Marshal Zhukov predicted a German offensive on a much narrower front than in previous campaigns: 'The Germans will assemble "maximum forces" including up to 13–15 tank divisions supported by large numbers of aircraft. They will attack with their Orel–Kromy concentration to outflank Kursk from the north-east and with their Belgorod–Kharkov concentration will attempt to outflank Kursk from the south-east.' Zhukov concluded his detailed appreciation with the stipulation that 'an offensive on the part of our troops in the near future aimed at forestalling the enemy I consider to be pointless'. Shortly after the despatch of this document Marshal Vasilevsky (Chief of the General Staff) arrived at Voronezh Front H.Q. and both Soviet marshals worked on the draft Stavka (G.H.Q.) directive dealing with reserves and the creation of the new 'Reserve Front', the Steppe Front, which ultimately came under the command of Colonel-General I. S. Koniev.

There was much for Stalin to brood over. In addition to field intelligence and his senior officers' reports, he had also crucial intelligence from 'Lucy', the codename of Rudolf Rossler, the Soviet agent in Switzerland, who was in receipt of incredibly accurate high-level information on German plans and dispositions. Meanwhile, in Moscow Zhukov, Vasilevsky and General Antonov (Deputy C.G.S.) prepared for the key Stavka conference of 12 April; front commanders had also submitted their own estimates and appreciations for this comprehensive plan destined for Stalin. The Zhukov–Vasilevsky paper picked out Kursk as the most dangerous sector: the German command was prepared to break through 'at any price' to restore the balance in favour of the Wehrmacht. The attack at Kursk would be concentric and originate from Orel and Belgorod, while elsewhere on the Soviet–German front German troops would be on the defensive due to lack of strength for multiple offensive operations.

Stalin agreed with the view that the main German striking forces were gathering about the Kursk salient, but he showed much concern for 'the Moscow axis'; he decided, therefore, to embark on a series of deeply echeloned defences, giving priority to Kursk. The strategic objectives of the Red Army's own summer–autumn offensive had meanwhile been determined: German forces were to be pushed back to a line running from Smolensk to the River Sozh and the middle and lower reaches of the Dnieper, and the 'Eastern Wall' was to be breached and German forces in the Kuban eliminated, but the main Soviet thrust would be along a south-westerly axis to liberate the industrial region of the Donbas and the eastern Ukraine. A second offensive would also be aimed due west to liberate eastern Belorussia and annihilate Army Group Centre. But first the Red Army would stand and fight in the Kursk salient.

By mid-April the decision for a planned defensive action by Soviet troops, followed by a carefully timed offensive, had begun to take solid shape. The enemy would rely on massed air and tank attacks, so the Soviet air force and the Red Army had to be prepared to deal with these by means of offensive air action against German airfields and ground defence against massed tank blows; in addition, the setting up of a powerful reserve (two to three armies at least) east of Kursk would provide the defence with effective operational depth. Already Stavka reserves were on the move into the salient, a massive reinforcement dictated not only by the requirements of the defensive battle but also by those of the subsequent offensive aimed at 'the final destruction of German forces' and the crushing of the southern wing, thereby eliminating 'the most active section of the German Army'. As April drew to a close the Central and Voronezh Fronts completed their basic deployment for the defensive battle, following the early Stavka directives: within a short time almost half (forty per cent) of the available rifle formations of the Red Army, supplemented by Stavka reserve armies and every existing Soviet tank army, had moved or was on the move into the reaches of the salient. Stalin's doubts, however, were not stilled: his strict orders (embodied in the Stavka directive of 8 May) to the Central, Voronezh and South-western Front commands demanded a state of full readiness to meet a German attack. Yet he toyed almost simultaneously with the idea of a spoiling attack – and General Vatutin himself suggested in a report to Stalin that the Voronezh Front might attack to break up German concentrations in the Belgorod–Kharkov area. But Marshals Zhukov and Vasilevsky with General Antonov firmly squashed the idea and rejected it formally in a joint submission to Stalin, who abandoned the plan. The Red Army continued to mass in the salient, digging in on a gigantic scale and embarking on massive fortification work. Each front built three defensive lines, with the Steppe Front forces building two additional rear lines, providing in all eight major defence lines echeloned to a depth of some 100 miles. Artillery and armour rolled into position, while Red Army engineers laid 40,000 mines. Veteran commanders of Stalingrad – Batov, Chistyakov, Shumilov, Zhadov – took over their formations, while the rank and file was put through systematic tactical training.

After an initial tremor within the Soviet lines at the beginning of May, the ominous lull continued, though the air war rapidly intensified. On 4 May Hitler convened yet another conference to discuss Citadel: Manstein demurred cautiously, Guderian came out flatly against the folly of an offensive, and Model (in a letter) expressed some serious reservations, while Kluge favoured an attack but no further delay with it. Yet delay there was once more: in a talk with Guderian on 10 May Hitler insisted that his mind was by no means made up, that at the thought of Citadel 'my stomach turns over', though he did not take Guderian's advice to 'leave it alone'. Not until 18 June, when O.K.W. (Armed Forces High Command) operations staff submitted that Citadel should be definitely called off, did Hitler commit himself to a final decision, fixing early July as the date for the attack. At this juncture Keitel supported the proposed offensive, though Jodl came out against it with 'emphatic objection'. The die was all but cast.

On the ground the Russians dug in and the Germans proceeded with their meticulous preparation. Throughout June the forces on both sides swelled prodigiously, bringing together more than 2 million men, 30,000 guns, over 6,000 tanks and assault guns and a little over 5,000 aircraft. Whatever misgivings the German command felt were well concealed from the men, while the Soviet command persisted with its intensive training at a well tried pace. One Soviet officer commented that whereas before the Red Army had scrambled into action, this time the measured tread of due preparation was making itself felt, inducing greater self-confidence. The final array for Citadel was by any count immense, encouraging the attacker and giving the defender pause for thought: on a front of some thirty miles Model's Ninth Army (Army Group Centre), comprising the northern arm of the German pincer, deployed six panzer divisions, two panzer-grenadier divisions and twelve infantry divisions (eight of which were designated to take part in the attack), while to the south Manstein mustered an even more powerful force with twenty-two divisions, pride of place going to Hoth's Fourth Panzer Army with five panzer, one panzer-grenadier and three infantry divisions, supported by the subordinate shock group of the *Armee-Abteilung Kempf* with three panzer and three infantry divisions committed to a diversionary attack north-east of Belgorod while the Panzer Army smashed its way northwards at Oboyan. Air support in the north would be provided by *Luftflotte* VI (6th Air Fleet) with 730 aircraft, with *Luftflotte* IV in the south furnishing 1,100 aircraft through the VIII Air Corps. Citadel also consumed the bulk of the German armour: out of 2,700 tanks and 1,000 assault guns on the Eastern Front at the end of June 1943, 2,500 were assigned to the attack on the Kursk salient. There was every reason for Guderian to shudder at the extravagant commitment of precious armour, and even Hitler's faith in the new tanks could not be offset by the fact that the new models were relatively few in number – Manstein had ninety-four Tigers and 200 Panthers – and plagued with technical troubles which showed all too quickly on the battlefield. Finally, the western part of the Kursk bulge was held by Weichs's Second Army with seven infantry divisions, and Model's rear to the north of Orel was covered by the Second Panzer Army. The Germans no longer put their trust in Rumanian or Italian troops (as at Stalingrad) to hold supporting sectors.

Behind the minefields and the breastworks even greater masses of Soviet infantry, armour and artillery had been deployed. Rokossovsky's Central Front disposed of five rifle armies (the Thirteenth, Forty-eighth, Sixtieth, Sixty-fifth and Seventieth), one tank army (Second Tank) and one air army (Sixteenth Air), in all some 5,000 guns and 1,120 tanks lying across the main line of Model's assault. On the Voronezh Front Vatutin also deployed five rifle armies (the Thirty-eighth, Fortieth, Sixty-ninth, Sixth Guards and Seventh Guards), supported by the First Tank Army and the Second Air Army, amounting to almost 6,000 guns and 1,500 tanks. Behind Vatutin lay that massive reserve, the Steppe Front, under Colonel-General Koniev, consisting of another four rifle armies (Fifth Guards, Twenty-seventh, Forty-seventh and Fifty-third) and Rotmistrov's Fifth Guards Tank Army, with its own air army (Fifth Air). All fronts also had powerful reserves of their own, amounting to several corps, but the heaviest punch was packed by the Soviet artillery: no fewer than ninety-two High Command artillery regiments moved into the salient, bringing the total artillery strength on the Central and Voronezh Fronts to just under 20,000 guns (plus 900 and more 'Katyusha' rocket-launchers). Extra armour was also distributed on a lavish scale to strengthen the artillery during the defensive phase of the fighting.

The scene was now set completely for this saurian clash. It remained only to signal the final, irrevocable date (and time) for the German attack. After a final review of the attack plans between 1 and 2 July, Hitler revealed his great secret: Citadel would open on 5 July 1943. In a trice the Stavka informed Soviet front commanders that a German attack was imminent and could be expected between 3 and 6 July – a tribute to Stalin's intelligence apparatus, with 'Lucy' in the van, while local confirmation came through a Jugoslav deserter from the Wehrmacht who intimated that the German offensive would open at 3 a.m. on 5 July. The anguish for both side of weeks of waiting was almost over, and during the afternoon of 4 July the strained and sinister lull finally ended. Manstein's southern assault force moved off, with XLVIII Panzer Corps striking at the Soviet Sixth Guards Army west of Dragunskoye: at 10.30 p.m. Soviet artillery on the Voronezh Front belatedly fired off its *kontrpodgotovka* (counter-preparation fire) designed to frustrate the assembly of the attacking force. Rokossovsky on the Central Front was sharper off the mark: at 10 p.m. on 4 July his artillery opened fire, disrupting the German assembly on the northern face, but at 4.30 a.m. German artillery returned its own barrage. Both German army groups, Centre and South, were now committed to their main assaults, and the Soviet command was left in no further doubt: '*Nachalos*' – 'It's begun'.

* * *

On Monday morning, 5 July, General Model (Ninth Army), attacking the northern face of the salient held by Rokossovsky's Central Front, launched his first main assault supported by formidable infantry and tank strength against General N. P. Pukhov's Thirteenth Army, two of whose divisions (the 15th and 81st Rifle) took almost the full weight of this drive. After fighting off several mass attacks, they fell back to the second defensive line some five miles to the south. The power of the German blow also bludgeoned General I. V. Galanin's right flank (Seventieth Army deployed further to the west) into a limited withdrawal of three miles. At the junction of the Soviet Thirteenth and Forty-eighth Armies to the east, German assault troops also broke into the Soviet positions in a thrust aimed at Maloarkhangelsk, but they were finally checked. By nightfall large numbers of German tanks were marooned within the first line of Soviet defences, though assault infantry forced its way in hand-to-hand fighting through most of this defensive system, clearing mines and closing on the stranded armour, while Rokossovsky worked feverishly to ram in a powerful counter-attack. The Soviet front commander had already ordered up General A. G. Rodin's Second Tank Army to bolster the Thirteenth Army's left flank. The Soviet tanks reached their concentration area in time, but the brief hours of darkness allowed no chance to secure passages through the minefields or to reconnoitre, and what was meant to be an effective counter-blow ended only as desperate support for the Thirteenth Army within the second line of defences. Model attacked the Thirteenth Army at dawn on 6 July, but another day of murderous assault brought him only a few miles southwards, all at staggering cost: 25,000 men and some 200 armoured vehicles. The deepest penetration had come about on his right, but Model needed to break through to the left and thus crush through the Thirteenth Army's right flank towards Maloarkhangelsk in order to block a Soviet counter-attack on German armour.

The Soviet Second Tank Army failed to achieve any decisive success on 6 July, whereupon Rokossovsky ordered the tanks to be dug in and to fight German heavy tanks only from the hull-down position: charging Tiger tanks head-on had proved too costly, the Soviet armour had been flung back behind the infantry lines, and only guns firing over open sights had saved the day. A counter-attack by the Soviet XVII Rifle Corps failed to restore the situation, but it did block the German advance on Olkhovatka and thus (in Marshal Rokossovsky's own opinion) actually decided the fate of the German northern offensive, for the Soviet command gained time to concentrate on other threatened sectors. The greatest threat now loomed up further to the east, in the area of the village of Ponyri, as Model on 7 July switched his attack from the left flank and centre of the Thirteenth Army in order to smash down the Soviet defences at Ponyri, lying at the eastern edge of a ridge of high ground running between Molotychi and Ponyri itself. General Model attacked both the western and the eastern extremities of this ridge, both sides of which were held by Soviet troops, with Ponyri defended by the 307th Soviet Rifle Division, substantial artillery reinforcement and, above all, anti-tank guns.

At dawn on Wednesday (7 July) waves of German tanks, crashing through the Soviet minefields, opened a series of massed attacks on Ponyri, with German dive-bombers seeking out the Soviet artillery. Major-General Yenshin's 307th Division was finally pushed into the northern outskirts of Ponyri, which straggled untidily alongside the Orel–Kursk railway line, but during the short summer night he regrouped and went on to counter-attack. Although flayed with German firepower, Ponyri did not fall, even as the Germans advanced yard by yard and tried a final storming finish with their last reserves on the night of 10–11 July. Nor did the superhuman efforts of the German troops at the western extremity meet with any greater success. While trying to stave in the defences of Ponyri, Model committed a mass of infantry and armour at the junction of the Thirteenth and Seventieth Armies north-west of Olkhovatka: armour from three Panzer divisions supported by motorized infantry was hurled against the village of Teploye on 8 July, a wave of fire and steel which burned and blasted away the Soviet defenders. Dislodged from the village itself, Soviet troops withdrew to the top of the ridge, where only Colonel V. N. Rukosuyev's 3rd Anti-tank Artillery Brigade, rushed up at desperate speed, could hold off the German assault. Battered mercilessly, Rukosuyev held on with only a handful of guns, but his dwindling ammunition brought the 33rd Panzer-Grenadier Regiment onto the heights, only to be hurled off by a Soviet counter-attack. Three times this bloody grappling was repeated, and only the arrival of Soviet artillery and infantry reinforcement secured the ridge for the Red Army.

Neither to east nor west along this 25-mile front was there any significant German breakthrough: the maximum penetration reached only ten miles, all for the grim tally of 50,000 German dead, 400 tanks and S.P. (self-propelled) guns lying shattered and 500 aircraft destroyed. But, even more ominously, Model had now to look to his rear, for there were threatening signs from the Soviet Western and Bryansk Fronts. On 11 July Model's assault on the northern face ceased, only a matter of hours before five Soviet armies rolled over the German defences east and north-east of Orel in the massive counter-offensive stroke Operation 'Kutuzov' which opened on 12 July. On that same day the Soviet Thirteenth, Forty-eighth and Seventieth Armies of the Central Front recovered their original positions and sealed the northern face.

The southern face of the salient, however, saw no such speedy resolution of the struggle: on the contrary, here the coming of Monday (12 July) brought a hideous climax all its own in the shape of the mightiest tank battle in the history of modern war, following a week of ferocious fighting which introduced German armies deeper into the Soviet defences than in the north. The reasons for this were many and various, though prominent among them were Manstein's own formidable skill in the field, Hoth's proven ability as an armoured commander, the effectiveness of German tactics and, not least, the consequences of the Stavka's erroneous conviction that the weightiest German assault would fall on the northern face. Manstein's attack opened in all its intensity on 5 July, when Hoth's Fourth Panzer Army rammed the XLVIII Panzer and S.S. Panzer Corps against General I. M. Chistyakov's Sixth Guards Army, which was holding defensive positions south of the town of Oboyan. Though a sudden summer deluge brought fresh floods and delayed the German armour, the Luftwaffe – having beaten off a Soviet pre-emptive strike on German airfields in the Kharkov area – used its temporary air superiority to good effect, striking hard at the massed Soviet artillery. Meanwhile the *Armee-Abteilung Kempf*, with two infantry and one panzer corps, struck across the Donets, south of Belgorod and drove into General M. S. Shumilov's Seventh Guards Army. For all the steadily stiffening Soviet resistance and the mounting intensity of artillery fire, Chistyakov's front was split towards the end of the day, with the XLVIII Panzer heading north for Oboyan and the S.S. Panzer Corps aiming for Prokhorovka. With the Sixth Guards pressed back for some four miles, though Shumilov's front was still intact, General Vatutin (Voronezh Front commander) decided on the night of 5–6 July to move up substantial reserves: 'The Germans must not break through to Oboyan under any circumstances.' Already two regiments of assault guns ordered forward to help the Sixth Guards had been blown to pieces. Vatutin, together with Lieutenant-General N. S. Khrushchev (the 'political member' of the front military soviet), now supervised the deployment of General M. E. Katukov's First Tank Army, a reserve formation which was now ordered to dig in its tanks amidst the infantry positions (a decision which caused some acrimonious debate within the Soviet command). Katukov's tanks were nevertheless duly dug in to stiffen the Sixth Guards and hold off the German armour.

For all this movement of Soviet reserves, the German shock groups moved on relentlessly: unlike Model, Hoth (and Kempf) used the available armour in massive wedges rather than committing it piecemeal and using the infantry advance to clear a path for the tanks. These fearsome German panzer divisions struck out in the south virtually shoulder-to-shoulder, steadily crunching into the Soviet defences. The XLVIII Panzer Corps made good progress on 7–8 July, with the *Gross-Deutschland* Division forcing Soviet armour back to the River Pena and the last defensive line before Oboyan itself, while the III Panzer Corps of the *Armee-Abteilung Kempf* advanced in a north-easterly direction along the flank of Shumilov's Seventh Guards Army. Fortune at this juncture seemed to favour Army Group South, and at midday on 8 July the Soviet command came to realize that, in addition to the threat to Oboyan, a highly dangerous situation was building up in the area of Prokhorovka, a village some twenty miles to the south-east of Oboyan: here the flanks of the Sixth and Seventh Guards Armies joined, and it was on Prokhorovka that the S.S. Panzer Corps was now moving in its easterly drive for a major breakthrough and full freedom of movement. Even though Vatutin had dug in one tank army (the First) and thus could not deploy it for a counter-attack, there remained still the massed armoured reserve of the Steppe Front, General P. A. Rotmistrov's Fifth Guards Tank Army – whose way to the west lay through Prokhorovka. Vatutin had already stripped the artillery from two Soviet armies (the Thirty-eighth and

Fortieth) in less embattled sectors to stiffen the Sixth Guards yet again and cover Oboyan. One tank corps and a number of rifle divisions had then moved bodily from these quiescent armies to the fight for Oboyan, but more was needed.

On 10 July the main force of the XLVIII Panzer Corps forced its way closer to Oboyan, and by the afternoon German units had reached the high ground in front of Oboyan itself and the River Psel – the very last barrier before Kursk. In a desperately fought defensive action, even as the Sixth Guards appeared to be crumbling and its H.Q. was overrun, the Soviet command managed to hold off the German thrust some sixteen miles south of Oboyan. But on 11 July, the danger to Prokhorovka loomed ever larger. The S.S. Panzer Corps was coming in from the west and striking northwards, while the *Armee-Abteilung Kempf* mounted its own supporting attack with a strong force of armour – though Kempf's force could not accomplish its most vital task: to provide flank cover against approaching Soviet armour drawn from the Steppe Front, that massive reserve concentration destined for eventual use in the Soviet counter-offensive. Detaching two powerful armies could not but weaken Koniev's front command, yet not to stem a German breakthrough at Kursk could only mean mortal danger in the salient: the probability of any counter-offensive under these circumstances would be remote indeed. With the express and essential authorization of the two Stavka 'representatives' or coordinators (*predstavitelii*), Marshals Zhukov and Vasilevsky, Vatutin was hurriedly assigned two Steppe Front armies, General A. S. Zhadov's Fifth Guards Army and General P. A. Rotmistrov's Fifth Guards Tank Army with two tank and one Guards mechanized corps, in all 850 tanks and self-propelled guns. To move to the Prokhorovka battle area, however, meant a forced march of over 200 miles, an undertaking which Rotmistrov managed in masterly fashion, only to discover a rapidly deteriorating situation on his arrival in the front line: it was impossible to count on the beleaguered Sixth and Seventh Guards Armies (or the Sixty-ninth, itself moved in some time ago as an emergency reinforcement) for the forthcoming counter-blow at the S.S. Panzer Corps, which meant that the Fifth Guards Tank would have to go it alone.

On the morning of 12 July the Fourth Panzer Army and Fifth Guards Tank Army rode each other down in a sudden, frenzied armoured joust involving many hundreds of tanks fighting in the narrow reach of land between the River Psel and the railway embankment, ground intersected with fruit groves and orchards. Rotmistrov's counter-attack, planned without full knowledge of German deployments and intentions, now by sheer coincidence collided with the renewal of the German attack on Prokhorovka. As Hausser's S.S. Panzer Corps resumed its advance, Rotmistrov's tanks met it head-on in a furious high-speed charge, the T-34s rolling across the sloping ground and in a nightmarish mechanized re-enactment of the Light Brigade at Balaclava passing through the entire German first echelon and throwing the battle from the outset into milling confusion. Though outgunned by the awesome Tigers, the Soviet T-34s closed the range and used their 76-mm guns to devastating effect: tanks, literally locked together, blew up in mutual death or were separately blown apart, ripping entire tank turrets off and flinging them yards away from the mangled wrecks. Overhead Soviet and German aircraft battled among themselves for local superiority or tried to support the ground troops, though the swirling smoke from burning tanks and the inchoate battle made distinction between friend and foe difficult. Gradually, however, the Soviet air force gained the upper hand.

By midday these first Soviet tank charges had spent themselves: along some axes the tanks of the Fifth Guards were fighting offensive actions, elsewhere they were committed to tense defensive battles, setting up tank ambushes or putting in short, jabbing counter-strokes. Amidst this 'giant tangle of tanks' the Germans regrouped for a counter-attack, and in the afternoon Hoth himself arrived on the scene, but neither Hoth nor the Tigers could redress the balance. Only the arrival of the 6th Panzer Division from Kempf's command, driving on to Rzhavets, could restore the situation, but even if a skilful *ruse de guerre* had got one German division over the Donets the Russians were determined to hold more off and succeeded in doing so. The *Prokhorovskoe poboishche* (the slaughter at Prokhorovka) continued until the coming of the deep night, when thunderclouds piled over the battlefield, the gunfire slackened and the surviving tanks slewed to a halt. More than 300 German tanks (seventy of them Tigers), eighty-eight guns and 300 wrecked lorries littered the steppe, while more than half the tank strength of Rotmistrov's Fifth Guards lay shattered on the same ground. Though the Eastern Front had seen some appalling fighting, German troops insisted that there had been nothing like this: in the '*Blutmühle von Belgorod*' (the bloodbath of Belgorod) the arrogant, merciless S.S. troops, whose very emblem was so often their automatic death warrant once in Soviet hands, had taken a Valkyrie ride to death and destruction, the Tiger crews splayed out beside their tanks or interred in these steel tombs, no longer men but merely remnants of bodies amidst a ghastly litter of limbs, frying pans, shell cases, playing cards and stale bread.

Although the German armour withdrew from the field at Prokhorovka, for three more days (13–15 July) German troops stabbed at Soviet defences in the Prokhorovka area. Zhadov's riflemen were engaged in heavy fighting north-west of Prokhorovka, with S.S. units trying to get round the Soviet strongpoint, even if they could not get through it. Rotmistrov had to throw in his tanks to beat off attacks on his flank and rear, an unexpected emergency commitment which scarcely sweetened the relations between Zhadov, with the Fifth Guards Rifle Army, and the tank army commander. Not until 13 July did Zhadov eliminate the S.S. bridgehead on the eastern bank of the River Psel. The *Armee-Abteilung Kempf* continued to apply pressure on the

Seventh Guards and Sixty-ninth Armies, fighting now in heavy rain which ended the summer drought, but forcing the Sixty-ninth Army in particular into partial encirclement in the Rzhavets area. Panzer units pressed on to the north.

Citadel was, nonetheless, dying on its feet, if not actually dead. On 13 July Hitler had summoned Army Group Centre and South commanders (Kluge and Manstein) to a conference at his East Prussian H.Q., the *Wolfsschanze*: the mauling of the German armour at Prokhorovka was bad enough, but other dire events had already imperilled the German offensive in the Kursk salient. On 10 July an Anglo-American force had landed in Sicily, thus forcing upon Germany not merely the prospect but the reality of a two-front war in Europe, while two days later, on 12 July, the Soviet counter-offensive aimed at Orel had begun and put substantial forces of Army Group Centre at grave risk. Hitler proposed at once to take panzer divisions from the Kursk front for use in Italy and the Balkans; Citadel had to make way for this prior commitment to Germany's entire southern flank which could not be put in jeopardy. Kluge, less impressed with the turn of events in Italy, pointed in the first instance to the growing danger to the Second Panzer Army and the threat to Model if the Red Army succeeded in slicing off the Orel salient: a catastrophe was inevitable on a massive scale unless Model's Ninth Army pulled well away from the northern face of the Kursk salient. Field-Marshal von Manstein, however, took a wholly different point of view and argued that the attack in the south should continue: Model must stand firm while the Fourth Panzer and the *Armee-Abteilung Kempf* eliminated what little strength remained to the Red Army in the southern reaches of the salient. Persuaded over-optimistically, erroneously and even stubbornly that Soviet operational reserves were now almost wholly expended, Manstein won the limited concession that Army Group South might fight on in the Kursk salient alone, which accounted for the Fourth Panzer and Kempf's command battling against all the odds with the Seventh Guards, the Sixty-ninth Army and the further Soviet strength which steadily piled into the area. For all his agreement with Manstein, on 17 July Hitler personally ordered the removal of the S.S. Panzer Corps from Army Group South for eventual transfer to Italy and that date, 17 July, effectively marks the calling off of Citadel. The *Armee-Abteilung Kempf* fought on for a few days, pushing back Shumilov's right flank and inducing a state of panic within the command of the Sixty-ninth Army, but Koniev's Steppe Front once again provided reinforcement and Citadel had passed the point of no return: it officially flickered out for ever on 23 July. German troops had already begun pulling back in the direction of Belgorod, a withdrawal screened by powerful rearguards but a withdrawal nonetheless.

The remainder of July was taken up with furious Soviet preparations for the coming counter-offensive in the south and feverish German preparation to fight it off. Koniev's Steppe Front, which had been left after the major battles in the Kursk salient with only three out of the original eight armies assigned to it, was fitted out anew with fresh formations and swung into position for the great Soviet attack. To the astonishment of the German command, the Red Army launched a powerful blow from the northern segment of Army Group South's front, thus belying the notion that Soviet operational reserves about Kursk were depleted and enfeebled. Three weeks after the counter-offensive unleashed against Army Group Centre, the Red Army attacked Army Group South, on 3 August. Within two days Belgorod had fallen and a little more than two weeks later Kharkov had been recaptured. It was the Steppe Front, no frail phantom, that surrounded the city, and it was Koniev's men who finally stormed the ruins on the night of 22–3 August.

★ ★ ★

After the battle of the Kursk salient – Kursk itself was scarcely involved, for even at their closest in the southern thrust German divisions were still more than fifty miles from Kursk and almost 100 from Model in the north – the fighting on the Eastern Front became an unbroken catalogue of Soviet advances. Myths as well as men had been consumed in that massive collision: before Kursk, it had always been assumed that the Wehrmacht must advance in the summer, but that aura of overweening invincibility vanished for ever in the Kursk salient. The psychological effect was profound, though paradoxically the salient fighting lacked much of the drama of Moscow in 1941 and Stalingrad in 1942. Nevertheless, the monstrous scale of the clash impressed itself starkly upon the Russians, anxiously awaiting the outcome of a critical encounter taking place in the very heart of Russia, the battle Alexander Werth called 'a modern kind of Battle of Kulikovo' (it was at Kulikovo that Prince Dmitry Donskoi vanquished the Tartars in 1380). The Kursk salient killing ground aroused the same visceral reaction.

The scale of the Soviet preparations, above all that massive concentration of reserves, combined both to rob the Kursk salient operations of the high drama played out before Moscow in 1941, where the Soviet army had been bereft of major reserves, and to grind the German armies into the steppe. Some twenty panzer divisions had been mangled almost out of recognition, and while the Soviet armour had been ferociously mauled these were losses the Red Army could speedily make up. For Germany, as Guderian had gloomily predicted at the outset, such a loss could only be catastrophic, a profligate squandering of vital armour in an offensive badly conceived from the beginning. Strategic success totally eluded the Germans, because tactically the tasks were impossible of execution; thus were German divisions impaled before Ponyri, pinned down at Oboyan, or shattered at Prokhorovka. And as the bell tolled for the German armies in the East, so did Soviet confidence grow. It is this factor which invests the battle for the Kursk salient with its singular decisiveness: though defeat at the approaches to Moscow and at Stalingrad had wounded the Wehrmacht, neither had wrenched the strategic initiative in the East from the Germans. Kursk was the true turning point for the Soviet Union, and high, indeed inhuman, as the cost was, it was amply justified by that irreversible advance already begun in the late summer of 1943. Thereafter the German army was consigned to unrelieved retreat, to fight still, but with the certainty of losing in the end.

Note on Sources

BRITISH

Jukes, Geoffrey, *Kursk. The Clash of Armour* (1969).
Mackintosh, Malcolm, *Juggernaut. A History of the Soviet Armed Forces*, Ch. 10 (1967).
Seaton, Albert, *The Russo–German War 1941–45*, Ch. 22 (1971).

GERMAN

Carell, Paul, *Scorched Earth. Hitler's War on Russia*, Vol. 2. Chs 1–4 (1970).
General Staff (German): *Gen. St. d. H.* 'Kräftegegenüberstellung Stand: 20.7.43' (Comparison of German and Soviet strength).
General Staff (German): *Gen. St. d. H. Fremde Heere Ost* (Foreign Armies East. Intelligence). 'Zahlenmässige Zusammenstellung der bekannten Verbände . . . Stand 11.7.1943' (Soviet formations).
Guderian, Colonel-General H., *Panzer Leader*, Ch. 9 (1952).
Klink, E., *Das Gesetz des Handelns 'Zitadelle' 1943*, (1966).
Manstein, Field-Marshal Erich von, *Lost Victories*, Ch. 14 (1958). (Orig. *Verlorene Siege*, 1955.)
Philippi, Alfred, and Ferdinand Heim, *Der Feldzug gegen Sowjetrussland 1941–1945*, Pt II, Ch. II (1962).
Schramm, Percy E. (compiler), *Kriegstagebuch des Oberkommandos der Wehrmacht 1940–1945*, Vol. III, Pt 2, pp. 754–824 (1965).

SOVIET

Koltunov, G., 'Kurskaya bitva v tsifrakh', *Voenno-istorichesky Zhurnal* (1968), No. 6, pp. 58–68, and 1968, No. 7, pp. 77–92 (manpower, weapons statistics, command changes, order of battle).
Koltunov, G. A., and B. G. Solov'ev, *Kurskaya bitva* (1970), with map supplement.
Koniev, Marshal I. S., *Zapisky Komanduyushchego frontom 1943–1944*, Ch. 1 (1972).
Parotkin, Major-General I. V., *Kurskaya bitva* (1970).
Rokossovsky, Marshal K. K., *Soldatsky dolg* (1972 edn), under 'Kurskii vystup', pp. 192–202.
Rotmistrov, Marshal P. A., *Tankovoe srazhenie pod Prokhorovkoi* (1960).
Shtemenko, General S. M., *Generalny shtab v gody voiny*, Chs 8 and 9 (1968).
Solov'ev, B. G., *Vermakht na puti k gibely* (1973).
Vasilevsky, Marshal A. M., *Delo usei zhizni* (1974), under 'Na Kurskoi duge', pp. 298–325.
Zhukov, Marshal G. K., *Vospominaniya i razmyshleniya*, Ch. 15 (1970 edn).

Smoke from fires and bursting bombs blanketing Schweinfurt after the raid on the German ball-bearing factories by the U.S. Eighth Air Force, 14 October 1943

Chapter Seventeen

SCHWEINFURT

Noble Frankland

ON 14 OCTOBER 1943 the United States Eighth Air Force launched from its bases in England a major bombing attack upon the heart of the German ball bearing industry in Schweinfurt. Two hundred and ninety-one B-17 Flying Fortresses made up the attacking formations which, so far as their limited range made possible, were supported by P-47 Thunderbolts. This was the most ambitious daylight air attack yet seen, for the belief was that the destruction of the ball bearing plants in Schweinfurt might prove an insupportable blow to the German armaments industry in general and to aircraft production in particular.

In the battle which was fought that day, the Americans lost sixty of their four-engined bombers destroyed over Europe. Another seventeen Fortresses scraped home irreparably damaged, and more than a hundred came back with various degrees of lesser damage. This was the severest mauling to which a large-scale daylight operation had ever been subjected by the real measure of such things, namely the percentage of bombers engaged which were lost and damaged. This was a casualty rate of sixty-one per cent.

This destruction and damage to the American bomber force was a great victory for the Luftwaffe – a greater one it seemed than Fighter Command of the Royal Air Force had scored against the German bombers on 15 September 1940. And the cost to the Germans of this apparent reversal of the Battle of Britain was certainly not more than seventy-five fighters destroyed and damaged and probably it was less than that.

Such losses could well be sustained by the Germans, and so too, as it turned out, could the effects of what was nevertheless severe damage to the ball bearing plants. Despite this damage, despite some optimistic claims by the Americans, and despite some initial panic by the Germans, the effect on their armaments production and that of other war essentials was negligible.

On the morrow, the Americans curtailed their bombing programme, which had been designed to inflict critical damage by precision attack in daylight upon key German factories in 1943. They had no alternative, for losses on the Schweinfurt scale were far in excess of what any air force intending to remain in being could afford to sustain. But the Americans did not abandon their aim. In particular, they did not, as in like circumstances the British had done in December 1939 and the Germans in September 1940, look for salvation under the cover of darkness. Still less did they turn to altogether different strategies as the Germans had done in April 1941. They simply put off the day when the decision in battle would be reached.

The effect on the Germans was divided. By his own account Speer, the chief director of war production, was alarmed, while Goering, the Commander-in-Chief of the Luftwaffe, was jubilant. One, of course, was counting his dependence upon output from the Schweinfurt factories and the other the number of American bombers shot down. Of the two, Goering's, at least in the short run, was the sounder reaction, for the losses which caused his jubilation made it impossible, as Speer did not understand and apparently still does not, for the Americans to follow up with further similar attacks. Speer also discovered that he had 8 million more ball bearings than he thought and that some of the more specialized kinds were more in the nature of luxuries than necessities. He found too that he could, in spite of restrictions, cover gaps by Swedish imports. He and his able lieutenant, Kessler, who, after Schweinfurt, was charged with the rationalization of ball bearing production and distribution, weathered the storm.

This storm then, though it had been an air battle of unprecedented proportion in its aim, its severity and its bomber casualty rate, seemed to end inconclusively. Certainly it seemed to lack any of the characteristics of a decisive battle. But the appearance was misleading. In fact, the action on 14 October 1943 swiftly produced effects which changed the course, not only of the bomber offensive, but of the entire war, and did so decisively against the seeming victors of the battle: the Germans.

To understand the decisive character of the Schweinfurt operation we must first consider the strategic ideas which carried the Americans to that target, for it was from them that the operational facts of the battle itself were given the chance to establish themselves. We must then see how the Americans adjusted their plans to these operational facts, for it was from that adjustment that came the harnessing of the long-range fighter to strategic air warfare and the beginning of the struggle for command of the air by combat.

This idea of winning command of the air by combat had, though largely as an intellectual exercise, occupied the minds of the air staffs both in America and in Britain before the war. In the earliest days when the weights and sizes of 'bombers' and 'fighters' were the same or at least not much different, it was not difficult to envisage an air formation engaging the enemy air defences while on passage to or from its bombing targets. Bombers, after all, were initially no more than fighters with bombs on and fighters were simply bombers with guns installed. The development of performance, however, soon opened a gap of specialization between the types and already by 1917, when the Americans took their first steps to war in the air, there was a difference between a high-performance, light, aerobatic and short-range 'fighter' – say the S.E.5A – and the large, relatively cumbersome, long-range, load-bearing 'bomber' – say the Handley Page 0400.

The role of the latter – and the idea came long before the machine – was in the strategic air offensive: the attack by bombing upon the sources of the enemy war strength through the destruction of his armaments factories, his sources of power, his system of industrial communications, or even his industrial workers themselves. The role of the former, that is of the fighter, was air combat: the destruction in the air of enemy aircraft. The basic problem which this posed for the bomber was that a combat between an aircraft designed primarily for combat and another designed primarily for something else was not likely to end to the bomber's advantage. So it seemed that the bomber would need protection against enemy fighters in the form of what was to become known as fighter cover. But how could a fighter develop the range of a bomber, say East Anglia to East Prussia, and at the same time retain the performance of a fighter, say an S.E.5A or its later successor the Spitfire? This was the technical conundrum which discouraged the development of the tactics of fighter cover in Britain and America, though not to quite the same extent in Germany.

The Germans, indeed, and in this they were alone among the three strategic air powers, did enter the air war against Britain in 1940 with a reasonably formidable-looking long-range fighter: the Me 110. It did not, however, survive well in the face of the British short-range interceptors, the Spitfire and even the Hurricane, and it tended to confirm the British in their view that long-range fighters were of little utility and that bombers must seek protection not from friendly fighters, or to any great extent from their own gun turrets, but from the cover of darkness. In the autumn of 1940, the Germans came to much the same conclusion. So the night area bombing of Coventry, Manchester and London, of Mannheim, Cologne and Berlin began.

The Americans, from their still neutral vantage point, looked on. They were not impressed. They saw that London could take it and they saw too that a high proportion of the British night bombers, which had a much more formidable navigational challenge to reach Germany from England than the Germans had to reach England from France, failed to drop their loads on anything of much importance. Nor did American idealism readily take to the idea of spilling bombs over the centres of great cities crowded not merely with industrial workers but also with women and children. Their own women and children were, after all, immune from that sort of thing. In addition, while the German twin-engined Dorniers and Heinkels and the British twin-engined Wellingtons, Whitleys and Hampdens ground to and fro at 10,000 or 15,000 feet, the Americans were working up a so-called 'stratospheric' four-engined bomber, the B-17 Flying Fortress.

This wonderful aircraft could carry its bomb load up to well above 20,000 feet, where it might expect relative immunity from flak, and it could be made to bristle with heavy-calibre machine guns. Its remarkable stability not only made it an ideal bombing platform but also enabled it to be flown in tight formation so that with careful choreography and thorough training and discipline a massive protective firepower could be generated. Moreover, the B-17 had immense built-in strength and could still fly when heavily damaged. The Americans believed not only that the Anglo–German tactics of night bombing were strategically ineffective if not immoral; they also believed that they could build up formations of B-17s which would be able to fight their way to and from vital German targets in daylight. In daylight, they thought, they would be able to carry out precision bombing against key targets. It was, they believed, a matter of building up formations of sufficient size and of acquiring the necessary operational experience.

This idea alarmed the British, who knew it would not work. Churchill tried to persuade Roosevelt to abandon it and Portal, the Chief of the British Air Staff, tried to convince Arnold, Commanding General of the United States Army Air Forces, that no time should be lost in converting the B-17s and their crews to night operations. Roosevelt left the matter to Arnold and Arnold would not budge. Like Pershing before him, the American commander was not going to be taught by the British; American forces under American command would fight the American way. This meant that the United States Eighth Air Force, building up on British bases, had the mission of attacking German key targets by precision bombing in daylight and, in August 1942, under the command of General Ira Eaker, the first operational experiments, albeit against short-range targets in France, began.

The results, not surprisingly, were quite encouraging. Though the Eighth Air Force still lacked its own fighter component, the targets were at such short range that Royal Air Force Spitfires could afford a considerable measure of fighter cover. Moreover, the Germans had not yet adapted their tactics to meet these operations. Nor, on the whole, were they unduly concerned about targets in France at this stage of the war. In addition, the Americans tended to exaggerate massively the number of German fighters shot down by their B-17 gunners. In January 1943, General Eaker lifted his sights and the Eighth Air Force bombers opened their strategic attack upon German targets. Now began the acid test of the theory that disciplined formations of B-17 bombers, flying high in daylight, could fight their way through the German air defences, reach and destroy vital targets and then return in sufficient surviving strength to provide the nucleus for reinforcements and the launching of the next attack.

After nine months of this, the writing began to appear on the wall. First, the Americans found it much more difficult to carry out their precision bombing than they had envisaged, perhaps as a result of doing so much training and evaluation in the clear visibility of such climatically delectable areas as Texas. Over Germany they often found themselves looking down on nothing better than the top side of cloud. When they introduced radar to overcome this problem, they achieved approximately the same accuracy of aim as Bomber Command in its night area offensive. Even more important, however, were the losses which the American bomber formations began to suffer, especially when they appeared over Germany. Particularly severe losses were incurred on 17 August 1943 when a double-pronged attack was launched against Schweinfurt and Regensburg. For this, the largest American bomber operation to date, 376 B-17s were despatched. Three hundred and fifteen of them were considered to have carried out their attacks and sixty were destroyed. This loss rate, amounting to sixteen per cent of the despatched force, was about three times as great as any bomber force could afford to sustain over a period of more than a month or so. It was beginning to look as if the B-17 self-defending formations would not avail against the interceptor fighters and larger 'destroyers' of the Luftwaffe – the single-engined Me 109s and F.W.190s and the twin-engined Me 110s and Ju 88s. The approaching crisis of American bombing policy was now almost at hand. For the Grand Alliance it was one of the greatest severity and consequence.

The Allies were planning to invade Europe in the late spring of 1944 and thereafter to develop a major second front in Western Europe. The autumn, winter and early spring were therefore all the time that now remained in which the heavy bomber forces could, in general, adequately undermine the German war economy and, in particular, produce an air situation, or in other words, a sufficient degree of command of the air which would make this second front militarily feasible. The British were now firmly embarked upon a massively destructive area offensive against the great industrial centres of Germany, and though their casualties, mostly due to night fighters, had risen severely and were about to do so yet much more severely, the hope was that German industry would begin to stagger under the holocaust. The Americans continued to be more concerned with particular industries and they were now particularly concerned with the aircraft industry and that which produced its components. Their hope was that by concentrated efforts they could so reduce German aircraft production that the Luftwaffe would become incapable of sustaining its effort against the bomber formations. Of course, this aim also fully accorded with the grand strategy of the second front, since it would contribute to Allied air superiority over the beachheads and the future battle fronts. After nine months of action over Germany, during which the Eighth Air Force was increasingly reminded of the priority which was to be given to the destruction of the German aircraft industry and especially that part of it devoted to fighter production, Allied intelligence came to a singularly gloomy estimate of the position. In this period, it seemed, German single-engined front-line fighter strength had increased from 300 to 700. Twin-engined fighter strength had gone up from 370 to 590. Not only was the outlook bad; it was getting worse.

British Bomber Command was urged to give priority in its area attacks to towns particularly associated with the German aircraft industry, but the commander-in-chief, Sir Arthur Harris, would much have preferred it if somehow the American bombers could have been added as reinforcements to the climax of the general area offensive now about to be approached in the Battle of Berlin. This, however, was not to be, and the Americans resolved upon a second, more massive and, they hoped, decisive thrust against Schweinfurt.

From here came nearly half of Germany's entire production of ball bearings, the essential component of so much that moves and a key factor in the production of aircraft and their engines. The complex of ball bearing factories in Schweinfurt seemed to offer the bombers a prize without parallel in all Europe.

The weather over England on 14 October 1943 was not good. Large masses of deep cloud reaching down to low levels presented the B-17s with great problems in linking up into formations. Two hundred and ninety-one of them nevertheless succeeded in doing so, 149 from the 1st, and 142 from the 3rd, Bombardment Division. The B-24 Liberators of the 2nd Bombardment Division found the going too difficult and abandoned the mission. P-47 Thunderbolt fighters of the 8th Fighter Command, the fighter component of the Eighth Air Force, took off to cover the bombers as far as their range allowed. The rather longer-range P-38 Lightning fighters, recently arrived from America, by a strange irony were not declared operational until the next day. Thus covered, the 1st and 3rd Bombardment Divisions flew on approximately parallel tracks from East Anglia across the Low Countries and so to the area of Aachen. Thereafter, they diverged slightly, the 1st Division north about and the 3rd Division south about, towards Schweinfurt.

The point of this divergence marked the beginning of the severest air battle yet seen over Europe, for this was the operational limit of the range of the 8th Fighter Command Thunderbolts. These escort fighters, which had a tremendous diving speed, had earlier, when escorting shorter-range bombing operations, had considerable success against the defending German fighters, which were first surprised by their appearance and then by their performance. Now, however, they availed the B-17 crews little more than a temporary postponement of their ordeal. The Germans showed little reaction until the bomber formations came to the area of Aachen, about 240 miles from East Anglia and the limit of the Thunderbolt's operational range. At this point the Thunderbolts turned for home, and wave after wave of German fighters swept in, converging upon the bomber formations from the directions of Holland, Hamburg, Berlin, Munich and Paris. The German tactics, which had by now benefited from operational experience, were systematic and polished. The attacks were concentrated against the leading groups of bombers in turn. Twin-engined 'destroyers' broke up the formations by lobbing rockets into them from 1,000 yards or so and thus opened up the opportunities for numerous kills by their own cannon fire and that of the higher-performance single-engined Me 109s and F.W.190s. A fearful execution now set in as tangled American machines and bodies fell out of the sky at an alarming rate, and the formations which pushed on to Schweinfurt were already decimated when they got there: of the 291 which had set out, some twenty-eight were already destroyed while many others floundered in precarious condition. The worst losses had been suffered by the 40th Combat Wing, which was in the van of the 1st Bombardment Division. Of its forty-nine aircraft, one seventh already lay in ruins on the route to the target.

The surviving element of this shattered vanguard nevertheless apparently succeeded in placing more than half its bomb load within 1,000 feet of the aiming points in Schweinfurt, where, as the attack opened, the sky was clear and the visibility excellent. As the bombardment proceeded, however, some cloud drifted across the target area and the view was also obstructed by smoke and dust arising from the explosions and fires. In all, it seems that 228 Flying Fortresses arrived over their aiming points and that they dropped 395 short (United States) tons of high-explosive bombs and eighty-eight short tons of incendiaries on and immediately around the three main ball bearing plants. The probability is that 143 H.E. bombs fell within the curtilages of the plants and that eighty-eight of these made direct hits on the buildings themselves. The positions of the incendiaries, which fell with less accuracy than H.E. bombs, could not be plotted or subsequently discovered with so much precision. It was immediately apparent that the Americans had carried out their mission with the utmost gallantry and devotion to duty and that they had, in the face of fearful odds, achieved a remarkable degree of physical destruction in the target area. The two bombardment divisions now turned for home and followed closely parallel tracks south about. On the way a further thirty-two of their number, either succumbing to earlier wounds or becoming the victims of fresh German attacks, crashed to destruction in Germany or France. Others fell upon English soil and yet others came back onto their own runways immediately ready for the scrap heap. From the original force of 291, only ninety-three came through unscathed, and at least seventy-seven had made their last flights.

The cost to the Germans, though summed up for public consumption by General Arnold in the words 'Now we have got Schweinfurt' and expressed through combat reports as 186 German fighters destroyed, was in truth far less. Schweinfurt probably cost the Luftwaffe no more than thirty-eight fighters destroyed and twenty damaged and certainly not more than forty-three destroyed and thirty-one damaged. As for ball bearings production in Schweinfurt, the true loss amounted to about six weeks' production. As for the German war economy, it continued to expand by leaps and bounds. If the bombers could have maintained a sustained and prolonged assault upon the Schweinfurt factories and others producing ball bearings, if they could have dropped not 300 or 400 tons of bombs upon them but, over a period, 6,000 or 7,000 tons, then there might have been a different story. But, of course, they could not. It they had tried, on the terms of battle of October 1943, the Eighth Air Force would have ceased to exist long before the German ball bearings industry.

Despite the wonderful determination of the American crews and despite the optimistic public pronouncements of General Arnold, the operational lesson of Schweinfurt was simple and stark. It was that unescorted self-defending daylight bomber formation attacks upon major German targets were not a practicable proposition of war.

What courses were now open to the Americans? They could not retrain their bomber crews and convert their aircraft for the purpose of night attack. They had already left the decision until too late, for the process would have taken some two years to achieve. Nor, with the invasion of Normandy now fixed and imminent, could they redeploy their Eighth Air Force in another theatre of war. They could not stand by and leave the continued assault to Bomber Command unaided, for the British night assault could not in itself produce the direct and urgently necessary effect upon the air situation which was needed alike for the purposes of the invasion, the survival of the day bombers and, as events were about to demonstrate, the night bombers too. Finally, for reasons which Schweinfurt had decisively demonstrated, they could not continue the policy of unescorted day attack upon which, up to now, they had hung their hats. The only offensive policy open was, in fact, a direct assault upon the Luftwaffe, an attack upon its forces, not in production, but in the air. In such an attack bombing would be needed to draw up the German air defences but fighters would be needed too to engage and destroy them. Schweinfurt had also decisively demonstrated this.

Strangely, the idea of such a coordinated bomber and fighter offensive had been authoritatively, if only vaguely, mooted, and even more strangely the means of carrying it out were to hand. It was not until after Schweinfurt, however, that this mooting was taken seriously or these means properly harnessed.

The mooting was the work not of an air force general but of a civilian, Mr Robert Lovett, the Assistant-Secretary of War for Air. After visiting the Eighth Air Force in England in June 1943, he submitted a memorandum to General Arnold in which he insisted upon the need for effective long-range fighters to get to grips with the German air defences. He thought the need could to some extent be met by the provision of what he rather vaguely described as 'proper' petrol tanks for the P-47 Thunderbolts, but he was sure that P-38 Lightnings and P-51 Mustangs were going to be needed. Mr Lovett sent these suggestions to General Arnold on 19 June, but the general was in no great hurry. His reply was dated 10 July and in it he indicated that the Lightning had been regarded as the most likely solution of the problem. As we have seen, some squadrons of these aircraft were being sent to the 8th Fighter Command in England, but the urgency with which they were despatched and worked up was insufficient, as we have also seen, to enable any of them to fly operationally on 14 October. As to the third aircraft mentioned by Mr Lovett, the P-51 Mustang, there was even less sense of urgency. This was in spite of General Arnold's belief, as he told Mr Lovett in his memorandum of 10 July, that the P-51B Mustang, which was already in production, 'now looks the best' as the solution to the long-range fighter problem. By 12 August 145 of these aircraft had been delivered; none were sent to join the 8th Fighter Command in England. By 4 September, it was demonstrated that with drop tanks the P-51B had an endurance of 1,474 miles, but still there was little urgency about getting them to England. Of the first 673 P-51Bs which were to be produced, 333 were ordered not as long-range fighters, but as reconnaissance aircraft. In 1943 it was planned that no more than 180 were to be sent to England as long-range fighters.

Schweinfurt wrought a sudden and dramatic change in both production and allocation plans. On 30 October General Arnold ordered that all long-range P-38s and P-51s were to be withheld from reconaissance and reserved exclusively for the long-range fighter role with the Eighth Air Force in England. A crash programme of Mustang construction was begun, and before the war was over the North American Aviation Inc. had produced 14,000 of them. Such was the effect of Schweinfurt. Its importance can only be appreciated when the performance, role and achievement of these P-51 Mustangs is understood.

The origins of the Mustang are among the strangest in the history of aircraft production. Ordered by the British in substitution for the Curtiss fighters which they thought they wanted, it was built by the North American Aviation Inc. to a design which was supervised by the British. Coming into service with the Royal Air Force towards the end of 1941, it was relegated, owing to poor performance, to Army Cooperation Command and it was rejected by the Americans. A modified version with a Rolls-Royce Merlin 61 engine in place of the original Allison V-1710 was first flown in October 1942 but the result was still not good. Further modifications were made and the Packard–Merlin engine was tried. The result was the P-51B.

The original Mustang was capable of 388 m.p.h. at 5,000 feet but its performance decreased with altitude and was 366 m.p.h. at 15,000 feet. The new Mustang could do 375 m.p.h. at 5,000 feet, 425 m.p.h. at 15,000 and 455 m.p.h. at 30,000 feet. It could outpace the F.W.190, Germany's best fighter, by 50 m.p.h. up to 28,000 feet and by about 70 m.p.h. above that. It was faster at all heights than the latest Messerschmitt 109, the G, and it could out-turn and out-dive both the F.W.190 and the Me 109G. Its rate of roll was similar to that of the Me 109G but in this respect, and in this alone, it was slightly inferior to the F.W.190.

In addition to all this, the P-51B proved particularly suitable for modification for long-range fighting by the addition of droppable wing and belly petrol tanks. From these the pilot could draw the fuel to carry him to the most distant combat areas and, on arrival there, he could drop them and so become fully operational as an interceptor fighter of the highest performance. Here at last was the machine, long regarded by the British as a technical impossibility and yet as much their own invention as anyone's, which had the performance of a fighter and the range of a bomber. From its mongrel and hesitant origins, it was now propelled into vast mass production and hastened into operations with the 8th Fighter Command by the lesson of Schweinfurt on 14 October. Though still without its long-range tanks, the P-51B Mustang made its operational debut with the Eighth Air Force on 5 December 1943.

The Commanding General of the 8th Fighter Command, General W. E. Kepner, believed that the Mustang's range could be developed to Berlin and beyond, and so, despite the sceptics, it came to pass. By March 1944

Mustangs ranged all over Germany as far as Berlin. After that they extended their operations yet farther afield. The Eighth Air Force in England, now associated with the Fifteenth in Italy as the United States Strategic Air Forces in Europe under the supreme command of General Carl Spaatz, seized the opportunity, and within a few weeks, in a series of massive air battles provoked by their bombers and fought by their fighters, primarily their long-range fighters, they smashed the German command of the air in daylight over Europe. The bombers brought the Germans up and the Mustangs ensured that there were no areas, as before there had been beyond Aachen, in which they could operate at an advantage. Thus, all the other fighters on the Allied side, even including the by now vast numbers of Royal Air Force Fighter Command Spitfires, which since the Battle of Britain had multiplied in conditions of relative inaction, got their chance to open fire on the enemy.

The resulting command of the air in daylight, proved by the abrupt decline in the rate of American day bomber casualties despite the increasingly ambitious tasks which they took on, opened the way for the launching of the Allied armies into France, which was to be achieved on 6 June 1944, and it opened the way also for a gradual collapse thereafter of the German night air defences. Thus, Germany was exposed both to the threat of catastrophic destruction by bombing and to that of invasion from the west. Such was the phoenix which rose from the ashes of Schweinfurt.

Note on Sources

The main groups of unpublished sources upon which this chapter is based are:

1. *The correspondence, memoranda, reports, directives and other papers of the United States Army Air Forces*, which were collected after the war at the Research Studies Institute in Montgomery, Alabama, and in the Federal Records Center in Alexandria, Virginia. I owe it to the Rockefeller Foundation and the United States Air Force authorities that I was able to see these.

2. *The British Air Ministry files*, which until recently were held by the Air Historical Branch of the Ministry of Defence and which have now passed to the Public Record Office.

3. *The Speer Documents*, which were captured by the Allies in 1945 and which have now been returned from the Imperial War Museum, in whose Department of Documents microfilm copies of the most important are held, to the German Federal Government.

4. *Miscellaneous secondary reports and narratives* including the reports of the United States Strategic Bombing Survey, the British Bombing Survey Unit, *The Development and Production of Fighter Aircraft for the United States Air Force* by Doris A. Canham for the Historical Office Air Materiel Command (1949) and *Achtung Indianer* (1944), a history of the U.S. 8th Fighter Command.

The relevant specific references to these sources can be found in the British official history, *The Strategic Air Offensive against Germany* (see below).

Among the most important of the published sources are:

Arnold, General H. H., *Global Mission* (1951).

Bekker, Cajus, *The Luftwaffe War Diaries* (translated into English and edited by Frank Zeigler) (1966).

Caidin, M., *Black Thursday* (1960).

Craven, W. F., and J. L. Cate, eds, *The Army Air Forces in World War II*, 7 vols (1948–1958). This is the American official history. See esp. Vol. II, Ch. 20, by Arthur B. Fergusson.

Frankland, Noble, *The Bombing Offensive against Germany: Outlines and Perspectives* (1965).

Frankland, Noble, *Bomber Offensive: The Devastation of Europe* (1965).

Peaslee, B. J., *Heritage of Valour. The Eighth Air Force in World War II* (1964). The author flew on the Schweinfurt mission.

Speer, Albert, *Inside the Third Reich* (1970) (Eng. trans. by Richard and Clara Winston).

Webster, Sir Charles, and Noble Frankland, *The Strategic Air Offensive against Germany 1939–1945*, 4 vols (1961). This is the British official history. See especially Vol. II, Chs IX and XI, and Vol. III, Ch. XIII.

Ghurkas and men of the West Yorkshire Regiment advancing through difficult terrain towards Nungshigum

Chapter Eighteen

IMPHAL-KOHIMA

Sir Geoffrey Evans

KASE TOSHIKAZU, a Japanese Foreign Office official, when referring to the Imphal–Kohima battle in his book *The Eclipse of the Rising Sun* (published 1951), had this to say: '*Most of the force perished in battle and later of starvation. The disaster at Imphal was perhaps the worst of its kind yet chronicled in the annals of war.*'

Even if this last sentence is an exaggeration, and although the final knock-out blow was to come the following year at Meiktilla in central Burma, the fact remains that the defeat at Imphal was the greatest on land the Japanese had suffered in their history.

But, first, where are Imphal and Kohima? This is a question that not many inside India and certainly extremely few outside could have answered in prewar days. And what were the events that brought about this great battle, which made these two out-of-the-way places household names, at least in India and the Far East?

Four hundred miles, as the crow flies, north-east of Calcutta lies Manipur State on the eastern borders of Assam, with Imphal, its capital, standing in an open, healthy, fertile plain of 700 square miles, 2,500 feet above sea level and seventy miles from the India–Burma frontier by way of a track through the mountains to Tamu in the Kabaw Valley, along which the British and Indian soldiers retreated in 1942.

Surrounded on all sides by jungle-covered mountains, rising in places to 8,000 feet, that 'Lost World' of Conan Doyle's imagination was the only flat space on the north-east frontier of India adequate for the concentration of troops, airfields, dumps of supplies of all natures, hospitals and workshops necessary for operations on a large scale.

Satisfactory as it may have been as an area for the actual concentration, it suffered grave disadvantages from the fact that the rail communications from India were inadequate to meet the demands of a large force, while the 140-mile-long and twelve-foot-wide road forward from railhead (Dimapur) to Imphal had been built largely for bullock carts and for only a modicum of motor transport. Running as it did through gorges, up and down hairpin bends, and along the sides of mountains, liable to be cut off for days by landslides, and in places one-way, it was a dangerous and precarious main line of communication.

However, by late 1943, by dint of superhuman efforts on the part of India Command, the staff of Lieutenant-General W. J. Slim's Fourteenth Army, the engineers, imported and local labour and the medical officers (for malaria was rife), such progress had been made with the lines of communication as to enable the IV Corps (Lieutenant-General G. A. P. Scoones) to be made up to a total of three Indian Divisions – the 17th, 20th and 23rd – and the 254th Tank Brigade. At least two of the six airfields were approaching all-weather standard (during the monsoon, May to October, earth strips were unusable), reserves of supplies were increasing daily and the administrative installations were in place and working. In fact, preparations had reached a stage when offensive operations could be given serious consideration.

Ninety miles north of Imphal, and almost fifty from Dimapur, stands the capital of Nagaland, Kohima, at the summit of a pass between mountains 8,000 to 10,000 feet high and at a point where the road turns south to Imphal. At the time the battle took place, it was the headquarters of the district commissioner administering the loyal and courageous Nagas.

Meanwhile, what of the Japanese? In January 1942, when their Fifteenth Army invaded Burma, that country was entirely unprepared. By May the Allies had been driven out, the British to Imphal and India and the Chinese to China, thus permitting the Japanese to occupy the whole country up to the banks of the River Chindwin, to the Chinese frontier in the north and to Arakan on the Bay of Bengal.

The problem then facing them was: what should be their future strategy, consolidation or an advance into India? Opinion was divided, one school of thought favouring a further advance, the other, consolidation, for success had come more quickly than expected and the army, having overrun itself, needed time to reorganize.

Finally, the day was carried by the latter group, mainly because the two leading divisional commanders, one of whom was Lieutenant-General Mutaguchi, later to command the Fifteenth Army, were strongly of the opinion that the roadless, mountainous jungle between Burma and India, together with the highly dangerous diseases indigenous to that area, put a further advance out of the question.

So a policy of consolidation was adopted, while the British prepared to make Imphal the base for their future return to Burma. Thus for eighteen months the 600-yard-wide River Chindwin became the disputed boundary between the opposing forces on this front and the forests and mountains of the Kabaw Valley and Chin Hills a no man's land in which minor engagements and patrol clashes were frequent occurrences.

Then, following Major-General O. Wingate's first expedition into Burma on foot, there came a dramatic change in Japanese thinking, primarily due to the pressure exerted by the forceful Mutaguchi, whose opinion carried considerable weight in high places. So impressed was he by the way in which Wingate had overcome the problems of operating in this wilderness of mountains, jungle and rivers that he became convinced that, given good weather and adequate preparation, offensive operations on a large scale were both desirable and possible.

But there were other factors that also had a bearing: the British preparations – the airfields, the building of roads forward, etc. – had not gone unnoticed, and the Japanese realized that an offensive could not be long delayed; they knew, too, that the Chinese had reorganized and were pressing for an Allied offensive; morale at home had deteriorated as a result of the land and sea defeats suffered at the hands of General MacArthur, and a victory was needed to boost it. The capture of Imphal, therefore, had much to recommend it in the eyes of the Japanese High Command in Tokyo: not only would it raise morale among the Japanese people and undoubtedly lead to panic in India with consequent embarrassment to the Indian Government, but also, by depriving the British of their base, it would rule out any possibility of a British offensive into Burma for a long time to come and thereby deal a serious blow to the Allied cause.

Following a series of conferences and much coming and going between Tokyo, Singapore and Rangoon, the decision to capture Imphal was taken in September 1943, and General Kawabe, in command of Burma Area Army, a new headquarters introduced to control all operations in Burma, issued orders to Mutaguchi, now promoted to the command of the Fifteenth Army, to *prepare* plans for Operation U-Go, in other words the invasion of Manipur. To enable him to carry out his task, Mutaguchi was allotted the 15th, 31st and 33rd Divisions and the 1st Indian National Army Division, which was of unknown quality, being made up of prisoners-of-war taken in Singapore and other theatres in the Far East.

Nevertheless, there were still some, including members of Mutaguchi's own staff, who doubted the wisdom of the undertaking on the grounds that the troops available were insufficient and the difficulties of supplying them once across the Chindwin too great.

Turning to the Allied situation at the beginning of 1944, the front for which General Slim was responsible stretched from Ledo in the north to Maungdaw in Arakan – in a straight line about 600 miles in length – and roughly followed the line of the India–Burma frontier.

At Ledo the American general Joseph Stilwell, with a Sino–American force, was preparing for an arduous advance through appalling country towards Myitkyina, with the object of reopening the Burma Road to China: the IV Corps, on the central front and 250 miles south of Stilwell, watched a front of 200 miles from Homalin on the Chindwin to Tiddim in the Chin Hills, while 300 miles south-west in Arakan, the XV Corps (Lieutenant-General Sir Philip Christison) with the 5th and 7th Indian Divisions and the 81st West African Division was planning to advance down the Mayu peninsula from Maungdaw. Owing to the complete lack of lateral communication in the tangle of mountains between the IV and XV Corps, any reinforcement of one by the other entailed a road and rail journey back into India and forward again, an operation requiring three weeks to complete.

Because the dispositions of the IV Corps had been selected not only to cover the main approaches to Imphal, but also with a view to a further advance into Burma, its divisions were widely dispersed, and two of them could be likened to hammerheads on the end of flimsy handles.

The 17th Division (Major-General D. T. Cowan) was based on Tiddim, 160 miles south of Imphal, and connected with it by a mountainous road, in the dry weather described as 'a series of boulders joined together by dust';

during the monsoon it was deep in mud. Often closed by landslides, it was dependent on a bridge over the Manipur River, at times a torrent, at Milestone 130.

Eighty miles due east of Imphal, the 20th Division (Major-General D. D. Gracey), its headquarters set up near Tamu and its brigades pushing forward to the Chindwin and south down the Kabaw Valley, was better served by a metalled road fit for the heaviest tanks, along which a stream of lorries carried all that was required to form a base close to Tamu to support a force of two divisions in operations across the Chindwin. To cover the intervening ground between the divisions and to protect their flanks, patrols and local levies under the command of British officers watched for any move by the Japanese.

Finally, corps H.Q., the airfields, and the 23rd Division (Major-General O. L. Roberts), less one brigade in position around Ukhrul, together with all the supplies, petrol and ammunition, were congregated in and about Imphal. At Kohima the newly arrived 50th Parachute Brigade was engaged in training for jungle warfare.

On receipt of executive instructions from Tokyo early in January 1944, Kawabe based his strategy on diverting Slim's attention elsewhere and thereby forcing him to commit his reserves before the assault on Imphal was launched. To do so he ordered his commander in Arakan to open an offensive, Operation Ha-Go, against the XV Corps about a month prior to Mutaguchi's attack, and the date fixed for its opening was 4 February. On 19 January Kawabe ordered Mutaguchi to begin operations in the first week in March.

The essence of Mutaguchi's plan was similar to Kawabe's in that he aimed at drawing Scoones's reserve away from Imphal by a series of storming attacks from different directions, particularly on Cowan's isolated 17th Division at Tiddim. On 8 March, a portion of the 33rd Division, commanded by Lieutenant-General Yanagida, a talented though cautious soldier, was to launch a surprise attack from Yazagyo in the Kabaw Valley and cut the road to Imphal at Tongzang, forty miles north of Tiddim, thus severing that vital link; in addition, the road was to be cut at Milestone 100 to fend off troops sent to assist the 17th Division; simultaneously, besides attacking Tiddim itself, a strong column with tanks, under Major-General Yamamoto, was to advance on Tamu through the Kabaw Valley.

A week later, on the night of 14–15 March, by which time Mutaguchi expected Scoones would be fully occupied in extricating his 17th Division, the 15th and 31st Divisions, commanded respectively by Lieutenant-General Yamauchi, an erstwhile military attaché in Washington, and the courageous unconventional Lieutenant-General Sato, were to burst across the Chindwin between Homalin and Thaungdut. Having crossed the river, the 15th Division* was ordered to cut the Imphal–Kohima road a few miles north of

* This division had been moved from Thailand, and when operations began part of one regiment and some artillery were still on the way, owing to the interruptions of the lines of communication caused by Allied bombing.

Imphal and attack the base from the north-west, while the 31st Division advanced directly to the capture of Kohima to prevent reinforcements going to the relief of Imphal.

To complete the encirclement and destruction of the IV Corps, the 33rd Division, having eliminated the 17th Division, was to enter the Imphal Plain from the south and Yamamoto's force, on reaching Tamu, was to turn west and occupy the high ground above Palel overlooking the plain.

It was a bold plan, packed with surprises, but considerable risks were obvious in the supply of the 15th and 31st Divisions: all depended on the swift capture of Imphal, for it would be impossible to resupply them properly through the appalling country between them and their objectives. But the Japanese soldier was accustomed to living hard with a bag of rice tied to his belt, so, besides supplementing their food from the small villages through which they passed, units carried a month's supply with them, on elephants, mules and bullocks and on a proportion of their own fighting soldiers employed as porters. Mutaguchi considered these arrangements to be adequate because he estimated that Imphal would be taken in a month, after which his army would turn to the defensive before the monsoon set in.

In assembling the three divisions for their respective 'D' days, the maximum deception measures were to be taken to give the impression that the Japanese were only strengthening their positions along the Chindwin.

Thus, for the Japanese, the stage was set for the battle to come, the outcome of which meant so much to both contestants.

Whereas the future strategy of the Fourteenth Army and the IV Corps had been directed towards a limited offensive in the Kabaw Valley and the Chin Hills, plus Wingate's fly-in to the Katha area, with the object of reducing the pressure on Stilwell, by 3 February 1944 the accumulation of evidence of Japanese intentions made a new appraisal of the situation an urgent necessity.

For some time past, it had been known that only two enemy divisions (the 18th and 33rd) were facing the IV Corps, but as a result of vigorous patrolling and from other sources it came to light in December and January not only that the 18th Division had been relieved by the 31st, but also that an entirely new division, the 15th, had moved into the line around Thaungdut, on the Chindwin, bringing the total to three. Air reconnaissance also revealed a quantity of rafts in a tributary of the Chindwin near Homalin, which could only be for a crossing of the river; a new road had been built connecting Homalin with the Rangoon–Myitkyina railway at Indaw; the first tanks were reported to have been seen at the southern end of the Kabaw Valley, together with a fresh regiment and some heavy artillery. In fact there were many indications of an enemy build-up for an attack on Imphal.

On 4 February Operation Ha-Go opened as planned in Arakan, and though by 24 February the Japanese had been completely routed, losing more than half the number with which they had begun the attack, the operation had had the effect Kawabe hoped for and Slim had been forced to use his reserve.

In the meantime, Slim and Scoones, who were in close touch throughout since the Fourteenth Army's headquarters were at Comilla, only a short distance by air from Imphal, were planning to meet Mutaguchi's offensive if and when it came.

In Scoones's opinion, with which Slim agreed, the Imphal Plain was the key since its loss would prevent any further resistance. But if he fought a defensive battle with the corps so widely dispersed, with the possibility of one or both outlying divisions being cut off, he would be at a grave disadvantage. There seemed to be no alternative other than to concentrate the corps in and around Imphal: by so doing, his position would be more favourable, as he would be fighting the battle on ground of his own choosing. Moreover, because the surrounding country was open, full use could be made of Allied air superiority and his powerful Lee-Grant tanks could manoeuvre more freely and, of great importance, his communications would be considerably shortened.

When to withdraw the 17th and 20th Divisions from their forward positions was by far the most difficult decision to make. The British and Indian soldiers had reached their present positions with much blood and sweat and to bring them back without telling them the reasons, which for security reasons could not be divulged, could only have a bad effect on morale; if they were withdrawn and the Japanese did not attack it would be infinitely worse, but in view of the intelligence reports this was an unlikely contingency. With the initiative lying with the Japanese, timing was an all-important factor, and Slim, having accepted Scoones's plan, made it clear that he, Scoones, the man on the spot, should put it into effect when and *only* when he was as sure as he could ever be that the Japanese offensive had begun.

His fundamental aim being '*to hold the Imphal Plain and destroy any enemy who entered it*', Scoones intended, when the Japanese plans were clearer, to use the minimum to defend the vital approaches while employing the maximum for counter-attack. To this end, he ordered the 17th Division to be prepared to make a clean break when the moment came, and, moving to Imphal with all speed, blowing the demolitions on the Tiddim road as it withdrew, to leave one brigade to cover the southern end of the plain and come into the corps reserve.

The 20th Division, on the other hand, was to continue with its operations in the Kabaw Valley without moving further south, but on orders from the IV Corps Gracey was to concentrate his division near Tamu to cover the withdrawal or destruction of the stores in the base and the evacuation of the thousands of labourers working on the road, together with all the mechanical equipment. That completed, the 20th Division was to move back slowly to the Shenam heights overlooking Palel and hold them to the last.

By relieving the brigade of the 23rd Division at Ukhrul with the 50th

Parachute Brigade from Kohima and leaving three unattached battalions to watch the approaches to it, Scoones expected to have a reserve comprising the whole of the 23rd Division (who would also have the responsibility of destroying infiltration into the plain or onto the road to Kohima), the 17th Division less one brigade, and the valuable 254th Tank Brigade.

Finally, corps headquarters, the airstrips and various installations were to form themselves into 'boxes' or areas of all-round defence with ten days' supply of water, food and ammunition.

These orders, issued only to those who had to know, were sent out on 29 February so that they could come into force at the press of a button, but the burning question remained: when to press it.

Because he foresaw that Scoones's task was likely to be a hard one and now that the Japanese had been defeated in Arakan, making it possible to thin out the formations on that front, Slim, on 6 March, ordered 5th Division from Arakan to complete its concentration on the central front by 14 April. He also planned to bring in the 7th Division as soon as possible afterwards and thus to reform the Fourteenth Army's reserve.*

But there was one serious miscalculation in their appreciation of Japanese intentions which was to cause a major upset, for both Slim and Scoones considered that the maximum force the enemy could send against Kohima was one regiment,† whereas Mutaguchi had allotted a whole division.

To complete the picture, Operation Thursday, or Wingate's fly-in to the Indaw area, was due to begin on the night of 5–6 March, and after some uneasy moments when it was thought the Japanese had got wind of the plan it did, in fact, take place successfully.

The period of waiting was an anxious one for those 'in the know'. Reports of the enemy having been sighted here and there flooded into corps headquarters, but not until 10 March was first physical contact made with some of the 33rd Japanese Division at Tongzang. This was followed by the news that the enemy had also established road blocks at Milestones 100 and 109 on the Tiddim road and that the 20th Division had been attacked in the Kabaw Valley.

On 13 March, Scoones was in no doubt that the offensive had begun, so giving Cowan permission that morning to withdraw to Imphal he sent a brigade of the 23rd Division down the Tiddim road to help cover his retreat; at the same time he ordered Gracey to evacuate quickly the unarmed labour and machinery working on the road to Tamu.

But it was not until 5 p.m. the next day that the 17th Division began its withdrawal, with the result that twenty-four valuable hours were lost. The division, now cut off, faced a fighting withdrawal, in which the whole of Scoones's reserve was to be committed and his plan disrupted as the curtain rose.

* These divisions were relieved by the original reserve committed in Arakan.

† The equivalent of a British brigade.

Then, during the night of 15–16 March, information was passed to corps headquarters that strong Japanese forces were crossing the Chindwin near Thaungdut and Tonhe, and next morning it was learned they were heading for Ukhrul, where only one battalion of the 50th Parachute Brigade had as yet arrived.

Since Scoones's reserve had been committed so early, it was clear to Slim, on 14 March, that reinforcements from Arakan were needed immediately. The supreme commander, Admiral Mountbatten, having readily agreed to provide the necessary aircraft,* the 5th Division (Major-General H. R. Briggs), with its guns, jeeps and regimental mules, was flown into Imphal between 19 and 29 March, except for one brigade despatched to protect the crucial and practically defenceless Dimapur, where, out of a ration strength of 45,000, only 500 had ever fired a rifle. Furthermore, Mountbatten ordered General Sir George Giffard, commanding the Eleventh Army Group, to send Lieutenant-General M. G. N. Stopford and XXXIII Corps Headquarters, with the 2nd British Division, from India to the central front without delay.

To Mutaguchi in his headquarters at Maymyo, 200 miles in the rear, the situation at the end of March must have appeared very satisfactory, except for the delay to the timetable of the 15th and 31st Divisions caused by the resistance of the 50 Parachute Brigade in the area of Ukhrul between 21 and 26 March. Detachments of the 31st Division had cut the Imphal–Kohima road at Milestone 72 on 29 March, the remainder of the division was well on its way to Kohima, and the 15th Division was advancing on Imphal itself. The IV Corps was now completely isolated from the outside world except by air. As a result Operation Stamina, the greatest air supply operation in the history of war, was put into effect.

In some battles of long duration, it may sometimes be possible to say, in retrospect, that it was on such and such a day, long before the end, that the battle was won or lost, and 4 April 1944 is a good example.

On that day, all the divisions of the IV Corps were concentrated in and around the plain and holding a horseshoe-shaped front of almost 100 miles from Kanglatongbe in the north, through Nungshigum, Kameng, Shenam, Shuganu to Torbung on the Tiddim road. Unless an unexpected disaster occurred, Imphal was secure.

On that same day, Sato's 31st Division launched its first assault on the small garrison at Kohima, which was saved by the timely arrival of the brigade of the 5th Division flown to Dimapur. Even so, the heroic defenders had to fight desperately to hold their positions until relieved by troops of the 2nd Division on 20 April, but nearly two months were to elapse before Sato gave up attempts to capture the town.

* These largely came from the United States Army Air Force. There was no time to ask the President's permission but Mountbatten's action was subsequently approved in person by the President.

With the IV Corps concentrated and the 2nd Division having arrived at Dimapur, Slim decided that the time had come for counter-attack. On 10 April he ordered Scoones, while holding the Japanese 33rd Division at the southern end of the plain, to destroy Yamauchi's 15th Division on the north and east of Imphal and to place a force at Ukhrul to disrupt the enemy's communications with the Chindwin, after which he, Scoones, could turn to the destruction of the 33rd Division.

To Stopford, shortly to be reinforced by the 7th Division (Major-General F. W. Messervy) from Arakan, he gave orders to hold Kohima, to attack and destroy Sato's 31st Division and to open the road to Imphal at the earliest possible moment.

Six weeks of fine weather could now be expected before the monsoon broke in earnest. During this period the Japanese made fanatical attempts to break through the 17th Division in position about Bishenpur and the 20th Division at Shenam, where it is claimed that, in proportion to the size of the battlefield and the number of troops involved, more casualties were suffered by both sides than in any other engagement of the Second World War.

On 10 April a serious situation developed when troops of the Japanese 15th Division captured Nungshigum, an important hill only six miles east of Imphal, thus posing a direct threat to the Imphal 'box'. The only defences directly between the enemy and corps H.Q. were the 'boxes', largely manned by administrative troops. However, the position was retrieved three days later when a strong counter-attack involving infantry and tanks, supported by artillery and aircraft, drove the Japanese from the heights with heavy casualties. This was the nearest point to Imphal that the Japanese reached throughout the four months' battle.

As the days went by the 5th and 23rd Divisions made slow progress against the 15th Japanese Division, while the Allied air forces not only flew in stores and flew out casualties and unwanted personnel, but also gave magnificent close support to the troops on the ground and played havoc with the enemy's communications far back in Burma.

But it was the logistic position that presented the greatest anxiety for the British. When the road was first cut on 29 March, because Air Transport Command needed time to organize the airlift into Imphal, the ration scale for the IV Corps' 153,000 men and 11,000 animals had been reduced by a third as a precaution. Then, early in May, owing to the vagaries of the weather and shortage of aircraft and airfields, reserves had fallen to such a level that Scoones gave the middle of June as the latest date for the opening of the road, if rations were not to be further reduced or a proportion of the troops flown out. In the event, consequent on the action of the Air Officer Commanding, Third Tactical Air Forces, Air Marshal J. E. A. Baldwin, in reorganizing the aircraft and airfields, plus a lucky break in the weather, all demands were being met by the middle of June and fifteen days' reserve had been built up.

At Kohima, Sato was under pressure, but because of the extremely difficult country, the weather, the shortage of certain types of artillery ammunition, the necessity for the troops of the 2nd Division to acclimatize themselves to jungle warfare and, not least, the fighting qualities of the Japanese soldier, the British could not expect a quick success.

Despite urgings from some quarters for a breakthrough to the relief of Imphal, Slim, supported by Giffard, was convinced that the IV Corps could certainly hold out until the third week in June. He was satisfied that the enemy should continue to batter themselves to pieces against the Imphal defences, for the more casualties they incurred the fewer Japanese there would be to oppose a later advance into Burma, while the XXXIII Corps continued with its efforts to open the road. Furthermore, besides the battle casualties in men and material which the enemy were suffering, with the arrival of the monsoon the communications to the 15th and 31st Divisions would become impassable and both would face starvation.

For all these reasons, Slim transferred the greater part of his available resources to Stopford. His timing was indeed fortunate.

By the second half of April, Mutaguchi, realizing that his timetable was well behind schedule and that the early capture of Imphal was imperative, ordered Sato to send a regimental group from Kohima to attack Imphal from the north in conjunction with part of the 15th Division. Unfortunately for the Japanese, these orders, together with Sato's future plans against Kohima, fell into Slim's hands. Reaction was swift, and with Stopford's immediate increasing of the tempo Sato, considering that his chances of even holding his position would be drastically reduced if he denuded himself of a regimental group, cancelled the order for its move.

On the southern and eastern defences of the plain, the 33rd Division put in attack after attack without success, and for these failures Mutaguchi relieved Yanagida of his command in May, replacing him with the tough, experienced and resilient Lieutenant-General Tanaka. Both Sato and Yamauchi suffered a similar fate a few weeks later, to the detriment of Japanese morale in general.

Early in June the monsoon was in full swing. Mist and clouds shrouded the mountains, sluggish streams became raging torrents, all roads other than tarmac were quagmires. The British and Indian soldiers lived and fought in diabolical conditions but, unlike with the Japanese, their rations, monotonous though they were, came regularly and medical arrangements were of the highest order. And British, Indian and United States Army Air Force pilots never hesitated to fly through the worst weather conditions to deliver supplies and attack enemy positions.

Indeed victory was in sight when, on 4 June, the XXXIII Corps was poised to begin to clear the road and Sato was starting to pull out for a disorganized retreat to the Chindwin.

Perhaps it was in celebration of things to come that the morning of 22

June broke bright and sunny for the first time in many days to reveal the leading infantry and tanks of the 2nd Division about eight miles north of Imphal. The journey from Kohima had been a hard one because bridges had been blown, the road had been littered with mines, and Sato's rearguard had put up fierce resistance.

At 11 a.m., junction was made between the 5th Indian and 2nd British Divisions after three months of bitter fighting. The road was once again open. That night the first convoy of lorries, with headlights blazing, drove into Imphal.

But though the siege might have been raised the battle was by no means over, for Slim was determined to turn the defeat of the Japanese Fifteenth Army into a rout. However, he needed to assess carefully what could be asked of his soldiers. After months of hard fighting without relief, they were very tired. Malnutrition had lowered their resistance to disease, now on the increase with the coming of the monsoon, particularly scrub typhus, for which the accepted cure was careful nursing; but since quick evacuation to hospital was often impossible, men were dying in isolated positions in the jungle. Rain-sodden blankets had long been discarded and officers and men, their skins often covered with irritating sores, lay down in their saturated clothes to be bitten by leeches.

The country too made a pursuit all the harder and called for great physical effort. Because the mountains and rivers mostly ran from north to south, the follow-up would be against the grain of the country, entailing ascents and descents of mountains up to 4,000 feet high, along very narrow tracks, which were frequently washed away in places. More often than not they were shrouded in mist and cloud and a false step by man or mule meant death in the trees below. In contrast to the intense cold of the mountain tops, the valleys were hot, steaming and deep in mud, while rivers swollen by the monsoon rains would test the ingenuity of the engineers who had to devise means to cross them. For many units there could be no question of land lines of communication, and though pilots would be prepared to fly in the most dangerous conditions to drop supplies, there would be days when flying was quite impossible and the troops on the ground would suffer accordingly.

Nevertheless, all information pointed to the fact that conditions for the enemy were infinitely worse and Slim, confident that he could call on his men for one more effort, ordered Scoones and Stopford to carry out a relentless pursuit. If the 15th and 31st Divisions were given no respite, the opportunity to destroy them before they reached the Chindwin was there.

Messervy's 7th Division followed up Sato from the direction of Kohima, the 23rd Long Range Penetration Group worked round the rear of his retreating 31st Division and the 20th Division mopped up the remnants of the 15th Division in the vicinity of Ukhrul. At the same time as these operations were in progress the 23rd Division moved to encircle Yamamoto at

Shenam and the 17th Division made final efforts to smash Tanaka's 33rd Division at Bishenpur. There was plenty of evidence of the extent of the Japanese defeat. Without any control, for communications had gone, without food except for what could be obtained in the small villages, already pillaged in the advance, with no resupply of ammunition nor proper medical attention, it would be hard to imagine a worse state of chaos than that which existed in Mutaguchi's demoralized army.

On the tracks leading to the Chindwin and on the Tiddim road, the signs of despair and misery were rife. Japanese corpses lay half concealed in the oozing mud, some reduced to mere skeletons having fallen, exhausted, without boots and most of their clothing. Now and again the pursuing troops would come upon a knocked-out tank, the dead crew sitting inside in grotesque attitudes, or a bombed transport column, some of the charred vehicles standing by the side of the road while others lay smashed down the mountain-side.

Everywhere were rifles, ammunition and equipment discarded by men too worn out to carry them further. At times the evil smell of corpses denoted a makeshift hospital hidden in the trees, where men lay dead on the stretchers on which they had arrived, some with a bullet hole in the head, having been put out of their misery by their attendants before they left. Such prisoners as were taken – and there were very few – were in a ghastly state: half-naked, often wounded or suffering from malaria, dysentery or beri-beri, they were broken both in body and mind.

Yet, in spite of starvation, disease and the generally hopeless outlook, there were still small parties of Japanese prepared to fight and delay the pursuit: brave men indeed.

In vain did Mutaguchi try to stop the headlong retreat by issuing orders with which his subordinates either could not or would not comply, but by 10 July both he and Kawabe (both generals were relieved of their commands) concluded that the thought of further offensive operations was unrealistic. Ten days later orders were issued for the withdrawal of the Fifteenth Army to the line of the Chindwin, but by then numbers had already beaten the pistol and were across.

There are many factors to be considered when determining the enormity of the Japanese defeat and its effects on the Burma campaign as a whole.

Measured in terms of casualties, out of a total strength of some 100,000 who began Operation U-Go the Japanese losses amounted to 53,000, of which 30,000 were killed, missing or died later, while a large proportion of those who escaped suffered from wounds, disease and severe malnutrition. Furthermore, most of their tanks, guns and equipment were captured or destroyed. Until time was given them to rest, refit and receive reinforcements, the 15th and 31st Divisions were no longer fighting entities.

Against these colossal figures, the casualties suffered by the IV and XXXIII Corps were 12,000 at Imphal and 4,000 at Kohima, but of these many returned to fight again thanks to the excellent medical attention they received.

As for the wider strategical picture, Slim had always maintained that his best chances of making a successful re-entry into Burma lay in inflicting a major defeat on the Japanese *before* he crossed the Chindwin, since he was of the opinion that if he did not they could quickly concentrate against him far greater forces than he could possibly hope to maintain across the river. Unwittingly Kawabe had played into his hands by attacking Imphal, though there were many anxious moments, particularly in the early stages of the battle.

By his virtual destruction of the Japanese Fifteenth Army Slim achieved his strategical object. Although innumerable problems relating to terrain, weather, logistics, disease and the number of troops available remained to be solved, the way into Burma now lay open.

The high stakes involved are undoubtedly the outstanding feature of this great battle, because defeat meant disaster to the loser. Had the contest gone the other way, the repercussions can only be the subject of conjecture. The effect on Allied morale would have been very serious and the security of India put in grave peril, while any thought of the reconquest of Burma would have had to be postponed until the war in Europe was won.

Though the defeat of the Japanese in Arakan marked the turn of the tide, the victory at Imphal–Kohima was as decisive as any of the Second World War. For the Japanese, it meant that the myth of their invincibility had been exploded once and for all. The back of their army in Burma had been broken, the initiative they had enjoyed for so long had passed from them, and their days in occupation of Burma were numbered. So fast and so far did they withdraw that the Fourteenth Army had little difficulty in crossing the Chindwin. It was not until the enemy reached the line of the River Irrawaddy that stiff opposition was again encountered.

Note on Sources

Brett-James, Antony, *Report My Signals* (1945).

Brett-James, Antony, *Ball of Fire, The Fifth Indian Division in the Second World War* (1951).

Doulton, A. J. F., *The Fighting Cock, being the History of the 23rd Indian Division 1942–47* (1951).

Evans, Geoffrey, *Slim as Military Commander* (1969).

Evans, Geoffrey, and Antony Brett-James, *Imphal* (1962).

Kirby, S. Woodburn, *The War against Japan*, Vol. IV, (1965).

Mountbatten of Burma, Vice-Admiral the Earl, *Report to the Combined Chiefs of Staff by the Supreme Allied Commander South-East Asia, 1943–1945* (1951).

Roberts, M. R., *Golden Arrow, The Story of the 7th Indian Division in the Second World War, 1939–45* (1952).

Slim, Field-Marshal Viscount, *Defeat into Victory* (1956).

Swinson, Arthur, *Kohima* (1966).

Takagi Toshiru, *Imparu* (1949).

D-day: American troops struggling ashore at Omaha beach, 6 June 1944

Chapter Nineteen

NORMANDY 1944

Martin Blumenson

THE ANGLO-AMERICAN invasion of Normandy in June 1944 was decisive for the outcome of the Second World War because of what hung in the balance. It gave Germany probably the last opportunity to defeat the Allied partners in the West. It gave the Allies the chance to prove their crushing superiority over Germany. At the conclusion, no question remained as to who had won the war and who had lost.

Strategically, the Normandy landings came as no surprise. Both sides had prepared for the event long in advance of its occurrence.

From June 1940, the time of the French capitulation, when the British withdrew their troops from the European continent, they were possessed of the idea of returning. Within two weeks of the evacuation from Dunkirk, they served notice of their intention by launching a small raid on the German-occupied coast. This was the beginning of a consistent policy of hit-and-run operations to harass the Germans, compel them to stretch their defences over the periphery of Europe, and keep them in a constant state of tension and uncertainty. The best known of these operations were the spectacular descent and destruction at St Nazaire and the controversial landings at Dieppe in 1942. In large part these endeavours culminated in Normandy two years later.

The Normandy landings were also the historical extension of traditional British military policy. For an island people who had dealt with invaders, who had developed a maritime competence in the extension of empire, and who had a long experience in marine operations, amphibious ventures were natural. As early at least as the Continental wars during the late medieval period, through the imperial rivalries, the Napoleonic struggle, and the First World War, Britain knew how to move land troops by water and to sustain them overseas. The immediate shipment of an army to France in 1939 and the later excursions to Norway, as well as Normandy, followed the established pattern.

When the United States entered the Second World War after Pearl Harbor, it was a naval power like Britain. It too had an amphibious legacy: operations twice in Mexico, and military actions in Cuba, Puerto Rico and the Philippines, followed by the massive shipment of human and material resources to Europe in the First World War. Confronted with the necessity of fighting a two-ocean war at the end of 1941, the United States adopted categorically an earlier commitment to a Europe-first policy and immediately – early in 1942 – formulated and enunciated a strategy of building up stores of men and material in the British Isles for an eventual cross-Channel attack.

Despite the similarity of the British and American outlook, it was impossible to implement the idea at once. British near-exhaustion, together with first-hand knowledge of and respect for German strength, as well as American military weakness – a large and trained ground force was lacking

– combined to delay what both nations recognized would be the climactic offensive strike of the war, the cross-Channel expedition. At issue was only the matter of timing.

Although the Americans were impatient to close with and defeat the Germans so they could turn quickly to the Pacific and engage Japan, they realized the impracticability of rushing across the Channel. For the British would have to furnish most of the forces, and they were unwilling to jeopardize them in what they thought would be a risky throw of the dice. Faced with the British refusal to undertake a significant re-entry into the Continent in 1942, the Americans enlarged and trained their ground forces, sending a substantial proportion to England to prepare for a cross-Channel operation. Meanwhile, the Americans accepted the British peripheral concept as an expedient, and in November 1942 joined the British in an invasion of French North-west Africa.

This opened a new line of endeavour, and it led to the amphibious operations against Pantelleria, Sicily, southern Italy and Anzio. The invasion of southern France emerged out of these actions, although it was really a supporting arm of the main effort, the Normandy landings, which capped the Allied strategy against Germany.

The Allied invasions in the Mediterranean were important for many reasons. They built up a shared experience in command usages for the Allies, contributed to the development of special equipment and techniques, and provided increasing confidence in this form of warfare. Although each venture was important in itself to maintain Allied initiative, to push closer to the German homeland, and to stretch the German defences, and although each was perhaps even vital because of the possibility of Allied failure – each offered the Germans the chance to inflict a serious setback on the Allies – none was decisive. For the Allied steps across the Mediterranean constituted an approach march. In southern Italy the Allies faced the prospect of a long march up the peninsula ending at the barrier of the Alps; and in southern France the presence of Allied troops posed no immediate danger to valuable German holdings.

In contrast, Normandy gave the Allies access to a direct route – across a territory inhabited by a friendly population partially mobilized in the Resistance – to the German border. The space and time factor involved was considerably more disadvantageous to the Germans. The heart of their bastion was immediately threatened, not only militarily but also psychologically.

Rarely, if ever, had an operation been in preparation for so long. From the beginning of 1942, American troops and supplies were transferred to Britain in what was known as Bolero, the preliminary aspect of the cross-Channel attack, the build-up. Although the North African landings siphoned off much of this strength, the flow of American units and equipment to Britain continued so that whenever the movement across the Channel seemed to be feasible (for example, in the event of a sudden German collapse) forces would be ready to embark for the Continent.

American strategists hoped to launch a cross-Channel operation in 1943, but success in North Africa generated its own momentum. Sicily was simply too close to avoid. So the Allies continued to advance in the Mediterranean area at the expense of Bolero. Yet American insistence on starting to plan realistically for a cross-Channel operation led the Allies, in the spring of 1943, to agree to mount a cross-Channel attack a year later, in May 1944. They appointed Sir Frederick Morgan Chief of Staff to the Supreme Allied Commander (COSSAC) – although a commander had yet to be selected – and instructed him to draw up a plan of invasion.

Morgan and his staff produced an outline plan codenamed Overlord. It called for landings in the bay of the Seine and for expansion of the initial beachheads into a lodgement area defined roughly by the Seine and Loire Rivers. This would serve as the base for future operations to be launched towards Germany.

Meanwhile. the Combined Operations Headquarters under Lord Louis Mountbatten, deriving lessons from previous amphibious experience, was devising special equipment and procedures for the invasion. At the same time the Allied navies and air forces were gaining mastery of the seas and the skies, a condition essential for success and sufficiently nearly attained by early 1944.

It was then, after President Roosevelt and Prime Minister Churchill had met with Generalissimo Joseph Stalin at Tehran, that the Western Allies chose the men to carry out Overlord. They drew largely upon the experienced leaders in the Mediterranean theatre: Dwight D. Eisenhower to be the Supreme Allied Commander; Walter Bedell Smith to be his chief of staff (Morgan to be the deputy chief of staff); Sir Arthur Tedder to be the Deputy Supreme Commander; Sir Bernard L. Montgomery to head the British and Canadian ground forces; Omar N. Bradley to lead the American forces; Sir Miles C. Dempsey and George S. Patton, Jr, to command the field armies. In command of the Allied navies was Sir Bertram Ramsey. Directing the Allied Expeditionary Air Forces was Sir Trafford Leigh-Mallory. In general support were the British and U.S. strategic air forces under Sir Arthur Harris and Carl Spaatz.

As these men and others began in January 1944 to recast the general Overlord blueprint into the specific and detailed plans for the invasion, now called Neptune, the strategic bomber forces imperceptibly shifted their attacks from targets deep in occupied Europe to objectives related more closely to the landings. Their intent was to isolate the Overlord lodgement area and make it difficult, if not impossible, for the Germans to send reinforcements to the landing area; to this end, they destroyed bridges across the Seine, railroad yards, and other transportation facilities. They also struck coastal defences and other important installations useful to German opposition.

At the same time the Allies set into motion a gigantic deception plan named Fortitude. The object was to make the Germans believe that the Overlord landings would be made, not in Normandy, but rather in the Pas de Calais or Kanalküste. This region was the most logical place for invasion because it was on the other side of the Dover straits, the shortest distance from the English shore, which would facilitate not only the sea crossing but also close air support of the ground forces on the landing beaches. The Pas de Calais was where the Germans were installing mysterious giant launching pads, picked up by Allied intelligence, for the V-weapons yet to be fired against England. The region also gave access to good ports, which the Allies needed to sustain their troops on the far side of the Channel. It offered the most direct path to the German homeland.

During the first months of 1944, Allied troops trained and the authorities gathered stocks of equipment and supplies. Through Charles de Gaulle or, more specifically, Joseph Koenig, the Allied command imposed control over the French Forces of the Interior and alerted them to the impending invasion. Because the landing sites, roughly in the area between Carentan and Caen, offered no major ports, the Allies constructed two huge artificial harbours, one each for the British and American zones – a complex enterprise including obsolete ships to be sunk offshore to create a protected anchorage and floating piers to be towed across the Channel and connected by ramps to the shore. The Allies also accumulated vast numbers of a whole family of landing ships and craft, as well as various amphibious vehicles, to carry the assault troops and their appurtenances to the Continent. Because production difficulties delayed the delivery of an adequate number of these vessels, the invasion was postponed from May to June.

Optimum conditions of tide and light obtained for an invasion on 5 June, and during the early days of that month the vast and complicated Overlord machinery began to move. As troops were funnelled to ports of embarkation and loaded aboard ships, the air forces stepped up their attacks on the German defences near the coast, an enormous fleet of ships prepared to protect and to carry the ground troops across the Channel, and planes and gliders were held in readiness to fly airborne troops to Normandy.

All was set for the descent upon the Continent when a tempest buffeted north-west Europe. The storm, bringing rain, high winds and rough waters, made landings impossible. Eisenhower had to postpone the operation. Because the Allies had weather stations in Greenland and elsewhere in the Atlantic area, forecasters could predict clearing conditions on 6 June. With this information in hand, Eisenhower made his dramatic decision and ordered the venture to proceed.

With hopes that the Fortitude deception had persuaded the Germans to look for the invasion to come in the Pas de Calais, that the 24-hour delay had in no way been fatal to the multitude of delicately synchronized actions necessary for the landings, and finally that the weather conditions had lulled the German defenders into a false sense of security, the Allies launched the most significant operation of the war in the West.

The Germans knew that the invasion was coming but not exactly when or where. They had been more or less awaiting landings for almost four years, and the British raids had reinforced their expectations.

In the summer of 1940, Adolf Hitler believed he had won the war, and he confidently anticipated the conquest of England. The Battle of Britain blunted that ambition, and he turned his eyes to the East. In June 1941 he launched his massive onslaught against the U.S.S.R. – Germany was, after all, a land power. To protect his back in the West, a first-rate division was placed as garrison on the Channel Islands, which Hitler thought the British were sure to try to take; seven large coastal batteries guarded the shore between Boulogne and Calais; the Orginisation Todt started to construct bombproof U-boat shelters along the Atlantic coast, especially at Brest, Lorient, and St Nazaire; and army elements began to erect field fortifications at the most likely invasion sites along the Channel.

In May 1942, after the first Russian winter offensive and the American entry into the war had indicated that there would be no quick end to the conflict, Hitler began to think more seriously about defending in the West. He appointed Gerd von Rundstedt Commander-in-Chief, West, and laid down a basic order that coastal defences were to be so organized as to smash an invasion before the troops managed to come ashore, or, at the latest, immediately after they landed.

Shocked by the St Nazaire raid, although somewhat heartened by the Dieppe operation, Hitler evolved the idea of an Atlantic Wall. In August he ordered a line of fortresses to be constructed, including many strongpoints with machine guns and artillery pieces, to form a belt of interlocking fire. Troops manning this line were to be protected against air bombardment and naval shelling by concrete works.

At the end of September 1942, Hitler expanded his notion. The Atlantic Wall was to consist of the strongest possible defences, massive concrete fortifications offering the utmost physical and psychological strength, a total of 15,000 concrete and steel strongpoints guarded by 300,000 troops. Construction priorities were the U-boat pens, harbours, and beaches suitable for landings. He wanted the invasion stopped at the water's edge.

Unfortunately for his wishes, the war in the East against the U.S.S.R. and to a lesser extent the North African, Sicilian and southern Italian campaigns, drained manpower from the West; shortages of concrete and other materials, as well as of labour, hampered the programme. Nevertheless, an imposing series of defences arose along the coast from Denmark to Spain.

In October 1943, Rundstedt was less interested in concrete than in the quality of his combat troops. Admitting that the Atlantic Wall was valuable for fighting and for propaganda, he saw victory against an invasion in more orthodox military terms. He believed that the length of the coastline precluded strong defences everywhere. Consequently, the Allies were bound to get ashore somewhere. They could be beaten only by a powerful counter-attack rapidly mounted against invaders still lacking a firm beachhead. The problem was that the troop units assigned to the West were deficient in men, armaments and transport.

Hitler understood. In November he instructed that the coastline be further strengthened by fixed defences: artillery batteries, anti-tank defences, dug-in tanks, mines, and other like measures that stressed material rather than men. At the same time he agreed that if the Allied invaders somehow broke through this hard crust, they were to be overwhelmed by mobile reserves which were to be rushed up to counter-attack them.

To ensure the invincibility of the Atlantic Wall, Hitler that month transferred Erwin Rommel and his Army Group B headquarters to the West. Subordinated eventually to Rundstedt, Rommel inspected and improved the defences. During the first five months of 1944, he was responsible for building along the entire coast, but most of all in the Pas de Calais, a defensive belt three or four miles thick, consisting of many simple field experiments rather than a few huge fortifications, including underwater obstacles like hedgehogs, tetrahedra, and stakes slanting forward, all usually mined, to wreck landing craft, and poles planted in fields to prevent glider landings. Rommel's defences were designed to destroy the invasion in the first forty-eight hours. To this end he wanted all the troops concentrated in the coastal crust.

While Rommel was trying to get every soldier in the West dug in along the shoreline, Rundstedt was trying to retain a certain number of troops as a mobile reserve. Thus arose conflicting approaches to the problem of defeating the Allied invaders: by linear defence or defence in depth, by static warfare or mobile operations, by holding ground or launching a battle of annihilation, by depending on concrete or on armoured power, by destroying the enemy in their landing craft and on the beaches or inland.

If sufficient high-grade units had been available, both conceptions could have been implemented. Because of shortages of troops and materials, neither took precedence. Rundstedt contended that invaders would get through coastal defences no matter how thick the concrete and how formidable the works. Rommel argued that they had to be stopped at the beaches because Allied air attacks would destroy the mobile reserves moving up to counter-attack; and even if the mobile forces could launch their attack, they would never be able to regain the invasion beaches because of the efficacy of the long-range Allied naval guns.

Hitler never said which method he preferred, which is another reason why neither Rundstedt's nor Rommel's effort gained priority. As it turned out, both commanders worked harmoniously together when the invasion arrived.

Most of the senior German officers expected the Allies to appear at the

Pas de Calais, and there they concentrated their fortifications and their largest field army, the Fifteenth. Since German intelligence was unreliable – air and sea reconnaissance was restricted, news from neutral countries was confusing, reports from agents were sketchy – the Germans depended more on inference and logic than on information. In March 1944, and later in April and May, Hitler, apparently by intuition, warned that the invasion was likely to come in Normandy, where the Seventh Army guarded the tremendously long coast from the Somme River to the Loire.

In spite of any such warnings, the time and place of the invasion took the Germans entirely by surprise. Rommel was at home, on his way to visit Hitler. The Seventh Army was planning to hold a map exercise at Rennes for high-ranking commanders on 6 June. The bad weather led the Germans to think that landings were impossible.

Three airborne divisions, the 6th British and the 82nd and 101st U.S., initiated the invasion in the early hours of 6 June. The British, coming to earth east of Caen between the mouths of the Orne and Dives Rivers, were to protect the eastern flank of the beachhead. The two American divisions near Carentan were to protect the western flank and also to seize beach exits to facilitate egress for the amphibiously landed troops across marshes immediately behind the dune. Despite the inevitable dispersal of the airborne elements on the ground, groups quickly coalesced in the pre-dawn darkness and in a series of small-unit actions took their objectives.

Within the first hour after daylight – the time of touchdown varied according to place – the leading assault waves came ashore on five beaches. The Second British Army directed the I Corps, which landed the 3rd Division on Sword beach, near Ouistreham, and the 3rd Canadian Division on Juno, near Courseulles-sur-Mer; and the XXX Corps, which supervised the 50th Division on Gold, near Arromanches-les-Bains. The First U.S. Army had the V Corps directing parts of the 29th and 1st Divisions coming ashore on Omaha beach, near Vierville-sur-Mer and Colleville-sur-Mer; and the VII Corps landing the 4th Division at Utah, near Ste Mère Eglise.

To say that the invaders landed without difficulty on four of the beaches would be to understate, even to overlook, the fierce fighting – and the bravery of countless men on both sides of the contest – that took place everywhere, near the water's edge as well as immediately inland. The Germans reacted well even though bombers pounded their bunkers, naval guns shelled their installations, and French Resistance fighters sabotaged and otherwise interfered with their communications.

Only at Omaha beach was the issue in doubt throughout most of D-day. For Allied intelligence had failed to pick up the presence of a German division precisely in that area until just before the operation, when it was too late to change the landing plan. As a consequence, the Americans there found themselves frontally assaulting excellent German strongpoints skilfully defended. Subjected to a withering fire, many American troops were pinned down on the beach and unable to head for their immediate objectives. Yet even here, by the end of D-day, the defenders were overcome, and the invaders finally moved inland to occupy their designated positions.

The Allies broke through the German defensive crust by an overwhelming demonstration of power. Allied aircraft on 5 and 6 June flew 14,000 sorties of all types against inconsequential German opposition; 127 planes were lost. Close to 200,000 men, including about 25,000 merchant mariners, operated the British, American, Canadian, French, Dutch and other Allied ships directly involved in the invasion. About 26,000 troops were airlifted to France, and more than 130,000 were brought by sea. Sustaining casualties of about 10,000, the Allies put 156,000 troops and a substantial amount of supplies into Normandy on the first day of the invasion – despite the existence of the Atlantic Wall, which though formidable in appearance was but a thin crust after all.

In retrospect, the result could hardly have been otherwise. Yet on the eve of the invasion, when there was much that looked doubtful, Eisenhower acknowledged the hazardous nature of the operation. He scribbled a note and tucked it into his wallet. In case the invasion failed and he had to announce that failure, he was prepared to release the few words he had written on a piece of scrap paper, which accepted complete responsibility for the defeat.

The complexity of Overlord constituted one of its gravest dangers. A thousand things could have gone wrong: a rendezvous missed, a signal misinterpreted, a turn in the weather for the worse. Meshing together so many intricate pieces into a relatively smooth operation of such magnitude – even to the extent of maintaining the security that contributed to attaining tactical surprise – played a large part in the Allied success.

The Germans could have seriously disrupted the invasion by launching air attacks on the concentration of troops awaiting embarkation. Had the V-weapons been ready for employment only a few weeks earlier, they could have substantially interfered with the operation. If the Germans had learned definitely where the landings were to take place, they could have moved considerable numbers of the Fifteenth Army from the Pas de Calais to the Seventh Army area in Normandy. Had the calibre of the German troops been near the earlier high levels of youth, morale, training, equipment and supplies, the resistance on the beaches, even without the Atlantic Wall, would have been stronger.

But a single day of success by the Allies was no guarantee of ultimate victory. The beachheads were largely unconnected, still precarious, and still vulnerable. While the Allies turned their attention to reinforcing their initial assault waves, to consolidating the landings, and to pushing inland in order to gain depth and stability, Rundstedt and Rommel tried to mount the counter-attack that would drive the invaders back into the sea. The German efforts were in vain. By the end of the first week, as in all previous invasions, once ashore the Allies could not be dislodged.

The Germans continued to resist but with increasing hopelessness. Three weeks after the invasion, on 1 July, Rundstedt asked to be relieved and thereby conceded defeat. Two weeks later, on 17 July, Rommel was seriously injured by a strafing aircraft and removed from command. A few days afterwards, on 20 July, six weeks after the invasion, a small group of military men motivated by the hope of arranging an armistice executed a putsch that came close to assassinating Hitler.

Not until 7 August, two months after the Normandy landings, was Hitler able to launch a counter-attack at Mortain, and even this was less than whole-hearted, for some of the troop units refused to participate as ordered. Even the so-called miracle in the West, the reformation of a linear defence before the West Wall in September, was due more to a lack of Allied supplies than to German resurgence. The bitter defence along the approaches to the Rhine and the Ardennes counter-offensive were unable to conceal German bankruptcy and the fact that the Germans were senselessly and fatalistically operating on nerve alone.

All this the Allied invasion foreshadowed, not in detail but in general. Allied success on the landing beaches of Normandy, in addition to electrifying the world and giving heart to the people still occupied in Europe, showed clearly that Germany had irretrievably lost the war.

As early as 1943, Germany had been deprived of the initiative and was on the defensive everywhere. By 1944, the tide had definitely turned. Even the mission of the invading forces in Normandy was hardly to bring Germany to defeat, which had already been accomplished on the political and strategic levels; rather, it was to liberate Europe from the German occupation, which, like the Atlantic Wall, was a desperate and hollow show of force lacking viability and strength.

After the Normandy invasion, despite the bitter fighting that continued, the basic issue was no longer in doubt. The unconditional surrender of Germany was only a matter of time.

Note on Sources

Bradley, Omar N., *A Soldier's Story* (1951).
Butcher, Harry C., *My Three Years with Eisenhower* (1948).
Craven, W. F., and J. L. Cate, *The Army Air Forces in World War II*, Vol. III (1951).
Eisenhower, Dwight D., *Crusade in Europe* (1948).
Ellis, Major L. F., *Victory in the West* (1962).
Harrison, Gordon A., *Cross-Channel Attack* (1951).
Liddell Hart, B. H., ed., *The Rommel Papers* (1953).
MacDonald, Charles B., *The Mighty Endeavour* (1969).
Montgomery, B. L., *Normandy to the Baltic* (1947).
Morgan, Frederick, *Overture to Overlord* (1950).
Morison, Samuel E., *The Battle of the Atlantic* (1948).
Pogue, Forrest C., *The Supreme Command* (1954).

Ruppenthal, R. G., *Logistical Support of the Armies*, Vol. I (1953).
Ryan, Cornelius, *The Longest Day* (1959).
Speidel, Hans, *Invasion 1944* (1949).
Stacey, C. P., *The Canadian Army, 1939–1945* (1948).
Stacey, C. P., *The Victory Campaign* (1960).
Wilmot, Chester, *The Struggle for Europe* (1952).

Chapter Twenty

LEYTE GULF

Stanley L. Falk

BY THE SUMMER of 1944, a succession of staggering reverses had brought Japan to the brink of defeat. The great Japanese military force that had carved a mighty empire across east Asia and vast stretches of the western Pacific had suffered heavy losses in men, ships and planes. Allied offensives pressed relentlessly against a crumbling Japanese strategic perimeter and gathered increasing strength for the final crushing blows. From the central Pacific, the swift, powerful carrier and battleship flotillas of Admiral Chester W. Nimitz struck far and wide, devastating Japanese defences and seizing island after vital island in an unremitting drive toward the heart of Japan's empire. A second major enemy force, the armies of General Douglas MacArthur, with powerful air and naval support, had fought its difficult way up the island axis of the south-west Pacific in a punishing assault that threatened Japanese lines of communication to the vital Indies. And complementing these twin offensives were the strangling blows of American submarines and long-range bombers, striking repeatedly at Japanese shipping and rear area bases. By mid-June 1944, indeed, American victories in the Marianas had brought the Japanese home islands themselves within range of enemy heavy bombers.

In July, therefore, Japanese strategic planners took another look at the deteriorating situation. On the 24th, Imperial General Headquarters issued a comprehensive plan of defence to hold the Philippines, Formosa, the Ryukyus, the four main Japanese islands, and the Kuriles. Codenamed *Sho* (Victory), it involved a complicated scheme of manoeuvre to counter any enemy offensive with massive naval, air and land attacks in a climactic 'decisive battle' to determine the outcome of the war. Given the weakened state of Japanese combat units, however, none could be committed until the precise target of the enemy offensive was determined. Then, combined naval and air forces would attack at the last possible moment to destroy enemy transports and covering warships. In this manoeuvre, the once proud Japanese carrier forces, now all but stripped of first-line aircraft, would be reduced to a decoy role, to draw off the American battle fleet and bare the rest of the invasion force to Japanese naval gunfire and land-based air strikes. Any enemy troops who subsequently managed to get ashore could then be easily handled by the Japanese army.

The *Sho* plans required close timing and coordination. Skill in execution, no less than good fortune, would determine their outcome. And on their success or failure rested the fate of Japan.

Even as the Japanese prepared to implement *Sho*, a major American offensive was about to begin. In early September, after months of debate over targets and objectives, the United States Joint Chiefs of Staff approved plans for the invasion of the Philippines. MacArthur's forces, with the full support of Nimitz's fleet, would land on Mindanao in the southern Philippines in November and follow this with an assault on Leyte, in the central Philippines, a week before Christmas. But when preliminary air

The American carrier Princetown *burning fiercely after being hit by a Japanese dive bomber, 24 October 1944*

strikes by fast carrier task forces of Admiral William F. Halsey's Third Fleet – a part of Nimitz's command – encountered surprisingly light resistance, the invasion schedule was advanced. On Halsey's recommendation, plans for the seizure of Mindanao and other intermediate objectives were dropped in favour of a direct assault on Leyte on 20 October.

This change in plan meant that MacArthur would be operating initially without land-based air cover. Until he could establish airfields on Leyte itself, he would be dependent on the distant support of Halsey's Third Fleet and on the closer protection of Vice-Admiral Thomas C. Kinkaid's Seventh Fleet, which had the immediate mission of transporting and supplying the invasion force. Halsey's armada, with nearly 100 modern warships and more than 1,000 planes, was one of the strongest battle fleets ever assembled. But it was not under MacArthur's command, and Halsey retained the option of withdrawing his support of the beachhead should a more lucrative mission present itself. The Seventh Fleet, to be sure, was 'MacArthur's Navy' – as it was popularly called – but it was organized primarily for transport, bombardment and assault missions, and its air element, mounted on small, slow, unarmoured escort carriers, had only a fraction of the strength of Halsey's. In Halsey's absence, moreover, Kinkaid would have great difficulty defending himself and the beachhead against strong enemy naval forces while simultaneously providing air support to the invasion force ashore. In this divided command arrangement – of which the Japanese were unaware – lay the best hopes for the success of the *Sho* operation.

But the Japanese were also victims of a confused and divided command structure, which denied them the central control so necessary for execution of the complex *Sho* plan. This was especially true in the Philippines, where no single commander existed to coordinate the multi-faceted defence. Japanese army ground and air forces there – General Tomoyuki Yamashita's Fourteenth Area Army and Lieutenant-General Kyoji Tominaga's Fourth Air Army – were separate, independent units, each responsible to Field-Marshal Count Hisaichi Terauchi. He, in turn, had the entire army area command from the Philippines to Burma, and thus could devote only part of his time to coordinating operations in the Philippines. Naval forces were entirely separate. Practically all were a part of Admiral Soemu Toyoda's Combined Fleet. The major combat units, each an independent element responsible only to Toyoda, were these: Vice-Admiral Takeo Kurita's 1st Striking Force of battleships, cruisers and destroyers, located near Singapore so as to be assured a ready source of fuel; the carriers of Vice-Admiral Jisaburo Ozawa's Main Body, in the Inland Sea of Japan; and Vice-Admiral Kiyohide Shima's 2nd Striking Force, consisting of some cruisers and destroyers, also based in northern waters. Under separate commands, but also reporting to Toyoda, were naval air units in the Philippines and elsewhere. The Combined Fleet commander would thus have to control and coordinate all naval forces in the *Sho* operation, while Field-Marshal Terauchi had a similar responsibility for army units, and neither had a link with the other except through the separate Army and Navy Sections of Imperial General Headquarters.

Almost immediately, this disjointed command arrangement contributed to a major Japanese blunder. In mid-October, Halsey's carriers undertook heavy pre-invasion strikes against Japanese bases from the Philippines to the Ryukyus. After some hesitation, Toyoda independently directed implementation of the *Sho* plan by naval air units, in the mistaken belief that the invasion had actually begun. Terauchi, however, did nothing – although it probably would have mattered little if he had. Toyoda's premature commitment of his air units resulted in extremely heavy Japanese losses: in less than a week Halsey's flyers destroyed more than 600 Japanese naval aircraft, at small cost to themselves, crippling Toyoda's air arm. It was now impossible to carry out the vital initial air phase of the *Sho* plan, to defend Combined Fleet surface units against American air strikes, or to reinforce the relatively weak Japanese army air groups in the Philippines' flying cover for Yamashita's troops.

This error only served to compound the confusion among Japanese commanders, so that when the invasion of Leyte actually did begin a few days later there was a crippling delay in implementing *Sho*. American forces began preliminary landings on islands in Leyte Gulf – to the east of Leyte itself – on 17 October, following up with minesweeeping and clearing operations the next day. But not until the evening of the 18th, after considerable confusion among the various Japanese commanders involved, did the Army and Navy Sections of Imperial General Headquarters order the start of the *Sho* operation. And not for an additional thirty-seven hours did Toyoda actually issue execution orders to the Combined Fleet. Thus, when MacArthur's forces landed on Leyte itself on the morning of 20 October Japanese fleet units were still far away from Philippine waters. On top of the earlier Japanese air losses, this delay bid fair to frustrate the *Sho* objective of catching the American invaders in the midst of their landing operations.

Japanese hopes of crushing the enemy invasion force now rested almost exclusively on the guns of the Combined Fleet. But it was noon of 20 October before Admiral Kurita's powerful 1st Striking Force finally reached Brunei Bay, Borneo, his staging point for the attack. The greater part of this fleet would advance through the central Philippines, pass through the San Bernardino Strait, and then drive south to descend on Admiral Kinkaid's amphibious force in Leyte Gulf. Five battleships, including the 64,000-ton monsters *Musashi* and *Yamato*, twelve cruisers, and fifteen destroyers would sail with Kurita on this mission. A smaller and slower element commanded by Vice-Admiral Shoji Nishimura – two old battleships, a cruiser, and four destroyers – would follow a southern course and penetrate Leyte Gulf through Surigao Strait. Both of these units, it was hoped, would reach their destination at the same time early on the 25th, three days later than originally prescribed by the *Sho* plan, but by now the earliest they could hope to arrive. With luck, they could still catch Kinkaid between them. Admiral Shima's 2nd Striking Force, which by now had reached Formosan waters, would drive through Surigao Strait on Nishimura's heels – although their approach would not be coordinated.

Simultaneously with these manoeuvres, Admiral Ozawa's Main Body would be proceeding south from the Inland Sea. Ozawa had four carriers, two battleships partially converted to carry planes, three cruisers, and eight destroyers. Yet his offensive capability was practically nil. He mounted barely 100 aircraft, and his flyers were so unskilled that many were incapable even of landing on a flight deck. His mission, essential to the success of Kurita's attack, was to decoy Halsey's covering fleet away from Leyte. If he could, Ozawa was then to engage and defeat Halsey, but this was a forlorn hope and in any event hardly essential to the primary objective of luring Third Fleet protection away from Kinkaid.

Ozawa's sacrificial force was the first to sail, leaving the Inland Sea under cover of darkness late on 20 October. Fully expecting 'complete destruction', as he later put it, the veteran commander carefully made his way south. For a few days he would try to avoid enemy submarines and search planes. Only at the proper moment would he reveal his presence to Halsey.

Far to the south, Admiral Kurita's mighty flotilla completed refuelling early on the 22nd and sortied from Brunei Bay. Nishimura, proceeding along a shorter course, departed in the afternoon. Admiral Shima also left port on 22 October, moving south from the Pescadores towards the Philippines. The entire assault force of the Combined Fleet was now at sea, bearing with it the last real chance of success for the *Sho* plan.

The operation began poorly. Just after midnight of 22–3 October, a pair of American submarines sighted Kurita's battle force west of Palawan Island and alerted Halsey to the threat. Then, shortly after dawn, they moved to the attack. Their torpedoes sent two heavy cruisers to the bottom and so badly crippled a third that Kurita had to return it to Brunei with an escort of two destroyers. Although one of the submarines grounded on a reef and had to be abandoned, Kurita had lost five of his thirty-two warships, and his approach route was no longer a secret. He pressed on, nevertheless, and early on 24 October entered the Sibuyan Sea – in range, for the first time, of Halsey's aircraft.

The Third Fleet commander had spent the previous day preparing his carrier forces to attack both Kurita and Nishimura, who by now had also been discovered. But it was the Japanese who struck first. Early on the 24th nearly 200 bombers, torpedo planes and fighters took off from naval airfields on Luzon to hit the closest group of American carriers. Radar revealed their approach, however, and they soon ran into a determined force of Halsey's fighters. At the end of about an hour's combat, a third of the Japanese planes had splashed into the sea and the rest were fleeing homewards. They had downed only a handful of American aircraft and had failed to make a direct attack on a single warship.

At last, however, the Japanese did have some success. At approximately 9.40 a.m., from a low cloud off the port bow of the light carrier *Princeton*, a single dive-bomber made a shallow run on the American warship. Despite intense anti-aircraft fire, the Japanese pilot managed to drop his 550-pound bomb squarely on the carrier's flight deck. The bomb penetrated deep within the *Princeton*, where it exploded, set off secondary blasts, and hurled flaming aviation fuel throughout the ship's interior. Although the blaze seemed manageable at first, the *Princeton* was already doomed. At around 3.30 p.m. a great explosion shook the carrier, tearing apart her stern and throwing huge lethal fragments of steel into the midst of the firefighters and across the crowded deck of the cruiser *Birmingham*, which had drawn alongside to assist. With her upper decks covered with killed and wounded, the *Birmingham* had to pull clear of the stricken carrier in order to take care of her own casualties and repairs. The *Princeton*, once again fully ablaze, was abandoned. American torpedoes gave the *coup de grâce* to the flaming vessel, the first fast carrier to go down in two years. This loss, however, hardly satisfied Japanese objectives. Admiral Toyoda's air units, whose assigned role in the *Sho* plan had been to destroy enemy warships blocking the approach of the Japanese fleet, had not even partially achieved their mission.

Nor had army aircraft of General Tominaga's forces been any more successful in their attacks that day on Seventh Fleet units in Leyte Gulf. In a mass attempt to sink the great concentration of invasion shipping there, nearly all of these planes had struck again and again at the landing area throughout the 24th. The repeated assaults had forced American aircraft from the escort carriers to break off their ground support missions in order to protect the anchorage. But Tominaga's flyers had caused little damage to shipping. And nearly seventy Japanese planes – perhaps half the total number of attackers – had fallen victim to Admiral Kinkaid's fighters and anti-aircraft gunners.

Meanwhile, Admiral Halsey had been inflicting sharp punishment on the two Japanese surface forces driving towards Leyte Gulf. An initial attack by about a score of Third Fleet pilots on Nishimura's ships caused only light damage. But Kurita, who received the brunt of the air strike, was less fortunate. From just before 10.30 until the middle of the afternoon, five separate blows – a total of well over 250 sorties – staggered his force as it made its way doggedly through the narrow, reef-infested waters of the Sibuyan Sea. At a surprisingly low cost of only eighteen aircraft, American bombers and torpedo planes destroyed the mighty *Musashi* – although it took seventeen bombs and nineteen torpedoes to sink it – and sent a badly injured heavy cruiser limping back to Brunei Bay. Halsey's planes also smashed heavily at other Japanese warships, damaging especially their exposed communications and fire control equipment. Particularly harmful to the Japanese cause was the effect of the furious assaults on Kurita himself. 'We had expected air assaults,' recalled his chief of staff later, 'but this day's were almost enough to discourage us.'

At 3.30 p.m., finally, shaken by a number of false submarine alarms, and fearing continued air assaults in the confined waters of the San Bernardino Strait that now lay just before him, Kurita decided to reverse his course for a while. It was not until 5.14, when he felt that the approaching darkness ruled out further American air strikes, that he once again resumed his original course towards the strait. An hour later he received a brief directive from Toyoda that had been despatched to all naval units engaged in *Sho*: 'All forces will dash to the attack, trusting in divine assistance!' In response, Kurita informed Toyoda that he would 'break into Leyte Gulf and fight to the last man'.

While these events were taking place, the Japanese decoy force had at last gained Halsey's notice. During the morning, Admiral Ozawa had launched an unsuccessful air strike against the northernmost carrier group of the Third Fleet. The defenders had shot down about half the Japanese planes; the rest of Ozawa's flyers, incapable of making carrier landings, had flown on to Luzon. Then, late in the day, American search planes had finally located Ozawa. Halsey, who had been greatly concerned about the apparent absence of the Japanese carriers, felt that he 'now had all the pieces of the puzzle'.

There was no doubt in Halsey's mind that Ozawa constituted the main threat and was thus his primary target. Assessing the enemy forces confronting him, the Third Fleet commander quickly dismissed Admirals Nishimura and Shima. Kinkaid's larger and stronger units could easily defeat them. The powerful force under Kurita was clearly a greater threat, but returning carrier pilots claimed to have badly damaged the enemy armada – exaggerated claims that Halsey nonetheless accepted – and Kurita's uncertain manoeuvring before the San Bernardino Strait cast doubt on his will to continue forward. At the worst, reasoned Halsey, Kurita could 'merely hit-and-run', and Kinkaid should be able to handle this kind of problem as easily as the Nishimura–Shima threat.

The critical point about the Ozawa force was that it included most of Japan's remaining carriers – and the Third Fleet commander had no reason to suspect that they held less than their full complement of planes. Ozawa thus appeared to command the strongest and most dangerous of the Japanese striking forces converging on Leyte Gulf. For Halsey to allow him to approach any further seemed to make no sense. It would give the enemy commander the initiative, allowing him to shuttle planes back and forth between his carriers and Luzon, with the Third Fleet in the middle. It thus seemed clear to Halsey that he would have to attack Ozawa with enough force to destroy him altogether. By so doing, he would not only eliminate the primary threat to the Leyte invasion, but he would also achieve the more important strategic objective of wiping out a major and more decisive portion of the Japanese fleet.

Just before 8 p.m. on 24 October, Halsey directed the entire Third Fleet to move north after Ozawa. He radioed this decision to Admiral Kinkaid in Leyte Gulf, but, for a number of reasons, Kinkaid believed that strong Third Fleet elements were still covering the San Bernardino Strait to block Kurita's advance. In this, however, he was mistaken. Halsey assumed that Kinkaid had the San Bernardino Strait under aerial reconnaissance and that the Seventh Fleet commander could observe and defeat any effort by Kurita to break through. So he left not even so much as a destroyer patrol to cover the strait. Admiral Ozawa had thus managed to open the way for Kurita's assault. Incredibly, the Japanese scheme appeared to be working.

Further south, meanwhile, the small Nishimura force had been pushing on towards Surigao Strait. Kurita's earlier vacillation now meant that it was no longer possible for the two Japanese units to break into Leyte Gulf simultaneously. Mutual support was out of the question and Admiral Nishimura would have to attack on his own. Nor could he count on surprise. Admiral Kinkaid knew all about both Nishimura and Shima, and had prepared an elaborate reception.

Waiting to intercept and destroy the Japanese warships was the entire Seventh Fleet Bombardment and Fire Support Group. Rear-Admiral Jesse B. Oldendorf, in command, had placed his six battleships – five of which were survivors of the Japanese attack on Pearl Harbor – in a battle line across the northern end of Surigao Strait. Extending the flanks of this deployment were eight cruisers, while twenty-one destroyers took station ahead of the line, ready to attack down the strait. And in the southernmost position, at the entrance to Surigao Strait, thirty-nine motor torpedo boats lay in wait for the first sign of the enemy approach. Thus the two Japanese forces would have to brave an initial onslaught of torpedoes from the P.T. (patrol torpedo) boats and destroyers and then come under the devastating weight of heavy shellfire from the battleships and cruisers that capped the 'T' of their advance. It was a classic tactical formation, superbly planned and organized.

Straight into this ambush came Nishimura. An hour or so before midnight, 24–5 October, he reached the outer entrance to Surigao Strait and continued on unhesitatingly. Brushing aside the troublesome P.T. boats with little difficulty, he turned into the strait itself at about 2 a.m. Now his fate was sealed. Just after three, the first of three separate but well co-ordinated destroyer torpedo attacks struck the Japanese column. In an impressive demonstration of their traditional role, Oldendorf's destroyers blew one Japanese battleship in two, crippled the other, and sent two destroyers to the bottom. Less than half of Nishimura's force remained, and it was now in range of Oldendorf's heavier units. The American battleships and cruisers quickly finished the job, blasting Nishimura and his remaining battleships out of the water and sending the surviving Japanese warships, a damaged cruiser and a destroyer, fleeing south. The only major injury to the American side was a single destroyer heavily damaged in the confusion of the battle by friendly shellfire.

With Nishimura out of the way, it was time to take care of Shima, who arrived on the scene just as the former was disappearing. Uncertain about what had occurred, Shima suffered a torpedo hit on one of his cruisers, exchanged signals but little information with the fleeing destroyer from the Nishimura force, and then carelessly allowed his flagship to collide with Nishimura's surviving cruiser. By 5 a.m. he concluded that a further advance would only result in total annihilation. He took the prudent course, retiring swiftly south. American planes continued to pursue, however, exacting a further toll from the retreating Japanese warships for many days thereafter. Of the total of two battleships, four cruisers, and eight destroyers that had entered Surigao Strait on the night of 24–5 October, only a single cruiser and five destroyers survived for more than two weeks.

By dawn of 25 October, meanwhile, Admiral Kurita's heavy force had successfully passed through the San Bernardino Strait to the Philippine Sea and was advancing rapidly south along the coast of Samar towards Leyte Gulf. Although informed of the disaster in Surigao Strait, Kurita himself was not under attack. Indeed, he had yet to be detected, since neither Halsey nor Kinkaid realized that no one was guarding the northern approach to Leyte Gulf.

Just before seven, the astonished Kurita found himself face to face with the opportunity to attack an unexpected target: what appeared to be a huge American task force, consisting of half a dozen large carriers, many cruisers and destroyers, and possibly even one or two battleships. Never once during the entire action that followed did he realize that the apparent 'gigantic' battle fleet between him and Leyte Gulf actually included only six slow, tiny escort carriers, three destroyers, and four puny destroyer escorts. These vessels, under Rear-Admiral Clifton F. Sprague, were the northernmost of three similar Seventh Fleet task units supporting the Leyte beachhead.

Both Japanese and American commanders were caught off-guard by this sudden meeting, but Sprague was the first to recover. Quickly he launched his remaining aircraft, recalled those already out on ground support missions over Leyte, and sped as fast as he could for the inviting cover of a nearby rain squall. At the same time, he broadcast an urgent plain language radio cry for help. Within minutes the Japanese attacked, Kurita's powerful force charging the American formation and firing salvo after salvo of deadly shells. The worried Sprague began to doubt seriously, as he wrote later, whether any of his ships 'could survive another five minutes'.

Given the odds, this estimate was not unreasonable. Yet the tiny American force was to fight off the powerful Japanese fleet for more than two hours in a disorganized running battle that almost defies belief. Taking full advantage of rain squalls and smoke screens and displaying outstanding seamanship,

Sprague's vessels somehow managed to avoid destruction. Repeatedly the destroyers and frail destroyer escorts hurled themselves boldly at the heavier Japanese warships to cover the retreat of the vulnerable escort carriers. Overhead, Sprague's aircraft, unchallenged by any Japanese planes, struck again and again at the increasingly confused and frustrated Kurita. These gallant counter-actions forced the Japanese into evasive manoeuvres, broke up Kurita's tactical formations, badly damaged three cruisers, and sharply reduced effective command and control of the enemy force.

But the odds against the courageous Americans were too great. The sustained, heavy Japanese fire was overwhelming, and, despite some incredibly poor shooting, Kurita's gunners left almost none of Sprague's thin-skinned vessels unscathed. By 9 a.m. an escort carrier, two destroyers and a destroyer escort had succumbed to the weight of Japanese fire and slipped beneath the waves. Few of the other ships had escaped damage, and their continued existence against the overwhelming pressure seemed impossible. It appeared that Kurita must catch his fleeing quarry any moment and destroy him completely.

Then, as Sprague explained it, 'the definite partiality of Almighty God' saved the day. Kurita was by now thoroughly upset and bewildered. He had no clear conception of the actual battle situation. He felt that he had heavily damaged a powerful enemy fleet, but that the swift Americans were outrunning him. He feared increasingly heavy air attacks. And, above all, he was still anxious to get to Leyte Gulf. At 9.11, therefore, he halted the fight, directing his scattered vessels to reassemble to the north. The incredulous Sprague could hardly believe his eyes, and was only convinced of his good fortune by the insistent reports of his jubilant flyers.

Yet, having escaped disaster by the narrowest of margins, the tiny American force soon found itself under attack again, this time by a different enemy. Just that morning, the Japanese navy had unveiled a new weapon, the *kamikaze*, or suicide, bomber, whose pilot sought victory by deliberately crashing his explosive-laden plane into the deck of an enemy ship. Six Philippine-based *kamikaze* planes had attacked other Seventh Fleet escort carriers earlier in the day. Now, about an hour before noon, another suicide force hit Sprague.

Just as the Americans were beginning to relax after their escape from Kurita, nine Japanese planes came in just over the wave-tops, too low to be detected by radar, then shot up into the air close to their targets, and dived swiftly down onto their surprised victims. Despite punishing anti-aircraft fire, several of them crashed into or glanced off the sides of the vulnerable escort carriers. One carrier burst into flames and sank in half an hour. Others sustained heavy damage. Twenty minutes later, another *kamikaze* attack took a further heavy toll in damage and casualties, although it failed to sink any ships. This blow, as it turned out, was the last of the day for Sprague's battered force.

Admiral Kurita, meanwhile, had been making his final major decision of the battle. Having regrouped his scattered units, at about eleven o'clock he had once again turned south-west towards Leyte Gulf. But as he steamed towards his objective, he had begun to reconsider. He was convinced that he had already destroyed most of a large American carrier force, but felt that his action had thoroughly aroused the enemy, who, he was certain, now awaited him with overwhelming air and surface strength. Furthermore, he believed that by now the bulk of the American transports in Leyte Gulf had deposited their cargoes ashore and withdrawn. Did it make any sense, he asked himself, to risk destruction of Japan's last remaining battle fleet for the chance to eliminate a handful of empty transports? The answer seemed clear. At approximately 12.30, with the entrance to Leyte Gulf only forty-five miles away, Kurita abandoned his effort. His mighty force swung north and headed once more for the San Bernardino Strait and escape.

While Kurita and Sprague had been duelling, another one-sided battle had been raging several hundred miles to the north, where Halsey had finally made lethal contact with Ozawa. From 8.15 on 25 October until late that afternoon Third Fleet carrier planes smashed at the all but helpless Japanese decoy fleet. Of the seventeen ships that made up Ozawa's command, all four carriers, a cruiser and two destroyers were gone by evening. The remaining ships, defenceless against Halsey's superior force, would also have been doomed had not the Third Fleet commander been strongly distracted.

Just after eight, Halsey had received from Admiral Kinkaid the first of a number of increasingly frantic reports on Sprague's situation, accompanied by urgent requests for assistance. Halsey, however, was still convinced that Ozawa's carriers were the primary threat and thus his main objective. So he continued to close on the decoy force. At ten o'clock a strongly worded message arrived from Admiral Nimitz, who had been listening to Kinkaid's communications from his Pearl Harbor headquarters. This message, carelessly altered in handling, seemed to suggest that Halsey was after the wrong foe. At about eleven o'clock the Third Fleet commander finally changed his mind, reversed course with most of his units, and set off to rescue Sprague. He left a sizeable carrier force to try to finish off Ozawa, but took his battleships, and his frustration, south after Kurita. 'At that moment,' Halsey wrote later, 'Ozawa was exactly 42 miles from the muzzles of my 16-inch guns. . . . I turned my back on the opportunity I had dreamed of since my days as a cadet.'

But by now Kurita had made good his escape, slipping all but untouched through the San Bernardino Strait on his way back to Brunei Bay. Halsey had to content himself with catching a lone Japanese destroyer. His great fleet had travelled altogether about 600 miles in a fruitless chase north and then south without actually making surface contact with either of the two Japanese forces it was after.

The Battle of Leyte Gulf – fought entirely outside that body of water –

thus ended on a note of frustration for both sides. For the Japanese it signalled the defeat of the *Sho* plan, despite the amazing success of Ozawa's decoy mission. For the Americans, whose one-sided victory destroyed a major portion of the Combined Fleet and removed the main threat to the Leyte invasion, it was disappointing because of what might have been accomplished.

Few of the participants emerged with their reputations untarnished. The Japanese had begun with the highly complicated and hopelessly ambitious *Sho* plan, almost impossible of execution given their operational limitations and divided command. Admiral Toyoda made the first mistake with his premature initiation of *Sho*. Kurita compounded it with tactical errors and needless vacillation. Nishimura and Shima were helpless victims of the situation, but did little to improve matters with their poor ship handling. Only Ozawa made no mistakes, and his abilities were rewarded by good fortune.

The Americans also suffered from divided command, an error intensified by poor communications, misunderstandings, and Halsey's aggressiveness. Both Halsey and Kinkaid might have done better in watching San Bernardino Strait, and the former's inability to force a surface engagement with either Kurita or Ozawa overshadows what he did to both opponents from the air. Admirals Oldendorf and Sprague, like Ozawa, combined skill with luck, an unbeatable combination.

Weighing all the evidence in the light of the situation at the time, Halsey made the right choice in seeking out Ozawa. He could not ignore a major enemy carrier striking force that contained not only the bulk of Japan's remaining carriers but also apparently – and as far as Halsey could possibly know – a full load of combat aircraft. His failure to leave even a single destroyer covering the San Bernardino Strait is inexcusable, but would have been less so if Kinkaid's own aerial searches had been more aggressive. Even then, having made the proper decision to go north after Ozawa, Halsey probably erred in turning south again just as he was about to make the kill.

It also seems doubtful whether Kurita could have penetrated Leyte Gulf in any event, given the strength of Oldendorf's force and the unopposed air power of the Seventh Fleet escort carriers. Even if Kurita had somehow fought his way into the gulf, his surviving warships would have been too late to do significant damage or to delay MacArthur's operations on Leyte more than a week or so. It is this fact that justifies Kurita's own decision to turn back, perhaps the only correct choice he made in the entire battle.

Both sides thus committed errors. The important difference was that the Japanese mistakes were more frequent and more costly. In victory, the Americans sank one large and three light Japanese aircraft carriers, three battleships, six heavy and three light cruisers, and ten destroyers – a total of some 300,000 tons of Japanese combat shipping – and practically wiped out enemy naval air power. American losses – less than 40,000 tons – included a light carrier, two escort carriers, two destroyers, one destroyer escort, one P.T. boat, and relatively few aircraft.

The Battle of Leyte Gulf destroyed the Japanese fleet as an effective combat force and eliminated any further threat to American naval domination of the Pacific. It removed the primary danger to MacArthur's beachhead and secured his line of communications and supply. It thus ensured the reconquest of Leyte, and, therefore, the reconquest of all the Philippines, and the disruption of Japan's shipping lanes and access to the resources of the Indies. Leyte Gulf was exactly the type of 'decisive battle' that the Japanese *Sho* plan had contemplated. Unhappily for the authors of that plan, it turned out to be an American victory, which sealed the fate of Japan.

Note on Sources

Falk, Stanley L., *Decision at Leyte* (1966).
Field, James A., Jr, *The Japanese at Leyte Gulf: The* Sho *Operation* (1947).
Halsey, William F., and J. Bryan, *Admiral Halsey's Story* (1947).
Macintyre, Donald, *Leyte Gulf: Armada in the Pacific* (1970).
Morison, Samuel Eliot, *Leyte, June 1944–January 1945* (1963).
Woodward, C. Vann, *The Battle for Leyte Gulf* (1947).

United States Marine Corps artillery in action

Chapter Twenty-One

THE CHONGCHON RIVER

Robert O'Neill

THE SMASHING DEFEAT of the U.S. Eighth Army at the hands of the Chinese on the Chongchon River transformed the Korean War. In late November 1950, the Eighth Army was poised to deliver a final obliterating blow to the North Korean armed forces, but within six days of launching this offensive the whole U.N. army was fleeing southwards in considerable disorder. Seoul, the South Korean capital, was soon in communist hands. Under the command of General Matthew Ridgway the Eighth Army was able to win back a small portion of its December losses but, from the Chongchon onwards, there could be no question of ending the Korean War through a U.N. military victory. However, in ranking the Battle of the Chongchon River as one of the decisive battles of the twentieth century, one ought to place more emphasis on its consequences than on the actual course of the battle. In essence the action was merely an ambush on a grand scale in which one force was hurled back by another whose existence had remained a well kept secret. Yet, in common with all great decisive battles, the outcome of the tactics of the encounter broke the existing strategic relationship of the contenders and brought a new one into being.

The foundations of the Battle of the Chongchon River were laid during October 1950 when both the United Nations command and the Chinese deployed large forces into North Korea. The reasons for the U.N. advance to the Yalu River are many and varied, according to the several points of view of General MacArthur, President Truman, his senior advisers and America's allies.

Ever since the early days of the conflict, MacArthur had wanted to march into North Korea, to smash the North Korean People's Army and to occupy the territory up to the Yalu River. He reasoned that unless the armed forces of the North Koreans were completely broken and the whole of Korea brought under Syngman Rhee's rule the objects of the war would not be achieved and South Korea would continue to exist in peril of a second invasion from a revived North.

Truman was more cautious in his approach but was in fundamental agreement with MacArthur that re-unification of Korea under a democratically elected government was a major goal of the war. However, Truman had to balance the achievement of this goal against American objectives in terms of the global power balance. In particular, he knew he could not afford to become dragged into an extensive land war in east Asia which might seriously weaken the Western position vis-à-vis the Soviet Union in Europe. His dilemma in deciding how to balance his risks was heightened by vociferous demands from Syngman Rhee for rapid re-unification and by strong pressures from both the Republican Party and the American public at large. He could not, after the débâcle of American policy in China in 1949, appear to be soft on communist aggressors.

By mid-September Truman had taken his decision. On 15 September the

Joint Chiefs of Staff (J.C.S.) authorized MacArthur to conduct operations north of the 38th Parallel, provided that there was no indication or threat of Soviet or Chinese communist elements entering in force. In the event of such entry, no ground operations were to take place north of the 38th Parallel. This directive was followed by another on 27 September, informing MacArthur that his object was to destroy the North Korean forces and that he could cross the Parallel in the absence of entry or threat of entry of either Chinese or Soviet forces into the conflict. No non-South Korean troops were to be used in the provinces adjoining China and the Soviet Union.

MacArthur made his plans and communicated them to the J.C.S. for approval. In essence, he intended to divide his force, moving the X Corps, which had made the Inchon landing, by sea from the Seoul–Inchon area to Wonsan on the east coast. There the corps was to make an assault landing and press due westwards to Pyongyang. In the meantime the Eighth Army would thrust northwards from Seoul to meet the X Corps in a two-pronged drive on the North Korean capital. The U.N. forces would then have formed a strong line across the waist of North Korea to meet any ensuing major assault. This plan was approved by the J.C.S., and the Defense Secretary, George Marshall, sent MacArthur a personal message saying that he was to feel unhampered tactically and strategically in moving into North Korea. On 1 October South Korean forces advanced across the Parallel and MacArthur demanded from the North Koreans an immediate and unconditional surrender.

While these decisions and plans were being made in Washington and Tokyo, the Secretary of State, Dean Acheson, was ensuring the support of America's allies in the U.N. Eight of them introduced a vague motion into the General Assembly, bypassing the Soviet veto in the Security Council, and recommending that 'all appropriate steps be taken to ensure conditions of stability in Korea'. While the motion did not explicitly authorize the use of force to achieve the unification of Korea, its generality provided broad support for U.N. forces to cross the Parallel. The motion was passed on 7 October by forty-five votes for, five against, and seven abstentions. The Eighth Army rolled forward on 9 October and Truman removed the major restriction placed on MacArthur in the J.C.S. directive of 27 September. From then onwards he had authority to advance in the face of Chinese intervention, provided that 'in your judgment, action by forces now under your control offers a reasonable chance of success'. Provided that MacArthur did not call for reinforcement or escalation of the conflict, the only rein on his advance was his judgement as to what constituted 'a reasonable chance of success'.

The Chinese deployment of forces into North Korea appears to have been a response to the U.N. crossing of the Parallel. This is not to say that the Chinese had not been important sources of support, advice and encouragement to the North Koreans from the outset. Indeed, the movement of the

Fourth Field Army from south China to Manchuria which began in April 1950 suggests that the Chinese even then had an eye to the possible need to provide a backstop for the North Koreans. By mid-July there were about 180,000 Chinese soldiers in Manchuria and others were being concentrated in the Shantung peninsula. Attempts to mobilize Chinese public opinion against the Americans began soon after Truman had declared his support for South Korea. However, while the war was moving favourably for the North Koreans the Chinese took no direct part in it.

After the failure of North Korean attempts to eject the U.N. forces from Pusan in mid-August and in the face of a rapid U.S. build-up in Korea and Japan, Chou En-lai warned the U.N. of China's concern for North Korea and publicly stressed the friendship between them. After Soviet proposals for ceasefire talks, to include the Chinese, had been rejected in the Security Council in early September and MacArthur had brought off his gamble at Inchon, the tone of Chinese pronouncements on Korea became much sharper, and reports emanating from Peking suggested that a U.N. advance into North Korea could not be tolerated. The Indian ambassador to Peking, K. M. Panikkar, was told by Chou En-lai after the South Korean crossing of the Parallel on 1 October that if U.S. troops followed them China would offer resistance. After the fall of Pyongyang on 10 October a final warning was broadcast from Peking stressing that the Chinese people could not stand idly by in the face of the invasion of North Korea, because U.S. operations represented a direct menace to China's security.

The entry of hundreds of thousands of Chinese troops into North Korea began within a few days of this statement. The Chinese government evidently considered the dangers threatening the industrial heartland of Manchuria so great that it felt compelled to abandon its earlier policy of caution. China's best security against such a threat seemed to be the forward deployment of her own forces, despite the possibilities of escalation of the conflict to the nuclear level.

The U.S. administration's attitude to the Chinese warnings of their possible participation in the war was a combination of doubt and concern. Truman felt that Panikkar might have been a tool of the Chinese and that the Chinese could have been bluffing. It was argued in Washington that because the Chinese had not intervened in August, when a small contribution could have tipped the balance decisively on the Pusan perimeter, they would be unlikely to enter when the U.N. forces were in a position to inflict severe losses on their field formations. That the two contingencies were in no way of comparable strategic importance for the Chinese seems to have been overlooked in this reasoning. There was also hope in Washington that the Chinese would believe assurances that the U.S. had no designs whatsoever against them. In short, the U.S. and Chinese governments had no sort of effective relationship whereby attitudes of trust or suspicion could be convincingly conveyed from the one to the other. While both wished to avoid a direct conflict over Korea, misapprehensions built onto each other. The situation was reached in mid-October in which the Chinese felt that they finally had to go to war to protect Manchuria because of the way in which the U.S. was obviously ignoring their warnings. The Americans felt that to uphold the principles of collective security they and the South Koreans had to occupy North Korea. They were confident that the Chinese would interpret such action as posing no threat to themselves.

While the American misconceptions were based partly on inaccurate diplomatic interpretations, they were also founded on mistaken military assessments. The Far East Command (F.E.C.) provided the Department of Defense with the overwhelming part of its information on China and, during the critical weeks of decision-making in September and early October, F.E.C. assessments had continued to discount the possibility of Chinese or Soviet entry into the conflict in any way which could bring disaster to the advance into North Korea.

The execution of U.S. administration policy was complicated by serious tensions between the President and his commander in the Far East. On several occasions since the outbreak of the war MacArthur had given Washington cause for grave concern that he was prepared to overturn policy when it suited him. In July MacArthur had virtually ended the Truman policy of neutralization of Taiwan by his visit to Chiang Kai-shek and his subsequent public statements. When Truman had tried soon afterwards to deny publicly that there were substantial differences between himself and his military commander in the Far East, MacArthur had responded with his own public statement which indirectly castigated the Truman–Acheson line on China. In mid-August, MacArthur had gone even further in sending a message to the convention of the U.S. Veterans of Foreign Wars advocating U.S. defence of Taiwan and condemning those who opposed his view as appeasers and defeatists. Consequently, when the delicate problem of a possible direct conflict with China developed in early October Truman decided to fly to meet MacArthur to discuss the situation and to iron out problems between themselves on a personal basis. It is possible that Truman was also extremely concerned at the future course of MacArthur's actions with respect to the Soviet Union, for on 9 October two U.S. aircraft had accidentally attacked a Soviet airfield sixty miles from the Korean border. There was clearly a danger of a third world war unless such incidents were prevented in future.

MacArthur chose Wake Island and the two leaders met there on 15 October. The general apologized for the Veterans' convention message and assured Truman that victory was at hand as his forces swept northwards through the broken remnants of the North Korean People's Army. In reply to Truman's specific questions about the possibility of Chinese or Soviet intervention, MacArthur reassured him that there was very little likelihood of such a clash; and if the Chinese did manage to deploy 60,000 troops across the Yalu, the maximum number which MacArthur could foresee, they would be slaughtered by air power before they could reach Pyongyang. MacArthur went so far as to prophesy major reductions in his forces in December and January. The word went out to Allied nations. The Canadians decided not to send the brigade they had promised, much of the Royal Navy component of the U.N. forces departed in mid-November, U.S. ships crossing the Pacific with ammunition were turned back and General Bradley, chairman of the Joint Chiefs of Staff, asked for a division to be sent from Korea to Europe in January. Truman departed, alleging his complete satisfaction with the talks, and MacArthur returned to Tokyo to continue directing the advance to victory.

Beginning on 7 October, the X Corps was unscrambled from the Eighth Army near Seoul, put onto ships, and sent several hundred miles round to Wonsan. When the troop ships reached there on 19 October they had to wait for over a week until North Korean minefields had been cleared. In the meantime, as the commander of the Eighth Army, General Walker, had predicted, South Korean troops pressing up the coast had taken Wonsan. The Eighth Army made a surprisingly rapid advance to take Pyongyang on 19 October. Hence the laborious shipment of the X Corps to the east coast had been futile in terms of its original purpose, and several divisions had been taken out of operations at a time when they could have been exploiting the weakness of the North Koreans.

The possibility of linking the Eighth Army and the X Corps on a strong defensive line across the waist still remained, but MacArthur did not consider that the situation called for such caution. Rather he decided to use the X Corps to occupy north-eastern Korea, thereby maintaining his own direct control of operations by refusing to place the whole of the ground force under Walker's command. The X Corps commander, Major-General Almond, had retained his previous Tokyo posts of deputy commander and chief of staff to MacArthur. Almond and Walker were rivals, and the former had the advantage of a close personal relationship with the commander-in-chief. Consequently, for several reasons MacArthur was not disposed to disband Almond's independent command. The continued division of command meant that each force could advance at a different rate and that there would remain a wide gap of twenty to fifty miles between them. MacArthur held that the country between the two forces was too rugged for threatening enemy operations. However, throughout the advance northwards, North Korean guerillas were able to operate in this corridor and both the Eighth Army and the X Corps had to face attacks around their flanks. At least MacArthur was right in so far as the Chinese did not pour southwards through the gap.

Once plans had been made for a two-pronged advance, the question arose as to how far north the U.N. force should go. The J.C.S. directive of 27 September had prohibited the use of non-Korean troops in the provinces adjoining China and the Soviet Union. In effect this directive limited the advance of non-Korean units to a line just north of the waist of Korea, approximately fifty miles north of the Pyongyang–Wonsan line. Despite Truman's sweeping permission of 9 October for MacArthur to advance if prospects for success were 'reasonable', irrespective of Chinese entry, this particular limitation had not been removed. Yet, two days after the Wake Island meeting, MacArthur, on his own authority, advanced the line between some ten miles in the west and fifty in the east. On 24 October he abolished the line altogether. The J.C.S. reminded MacArthur that the earlier line had not been revoked by them. He protested, quoting Marshall's signal of 29 September that he was to have freedom in his *modus operandi* and claiming that the issue had been settled at Wake Island. Once again he had his own way. The MacArthur mystique evidently still carried weight in the Pentagon.

During the second half of October the Chinese moved eighteen divisions across the Yalu and into concentration areas over fifty miles inside North Korea. This movement of 180,000 men was made without discovery by U.S. or South Korean intelligence and must be regarded as a classic example of the achievement of complete surprise. The Chinese were aided by the disintegration of the U.S. intelligence organization which had taken place after the departure of U.S. occupation troops in 1948. Despite General Walker's efforts, a replacement organization had not become effective by November 1950. Furthermore, the Eighth Army lacked trained specialists who could take and interpret air photographs. Despite these deficiencies, in late October members of General Walker's intelligence staff were keenly looking for signs of Chinese involvement. They were by no means unaware that there was close cooperation between the Chinese and the North Koreans but daylight aerial reconnaissance, when weather permitted, discovered no signs of movement across the Yalu. A few Chinese prisoners captured in mid-October formed the basis for a hopelessly low estimate of 9,000 Chinese being in North Korea.

The Chinese did not achieve their surprise entirely through the deficiencies of the Eighth Army's intelligence service. They advanced with great skill, moving rapidly at night and halting two or three hours before dawn to camouflage men, animals and equipment. By the end of October the Thirteenth Army Group of General Lin Piao's Fourth Field Army had assembled in forward concentration areas north of the Chongchon River, from near Chongju in the west to the Chosin reservoir in the east, where it waited to engage the Eighth Army. Over a distance of 150 miles were concealed the Thirty-eighth, Thirty-ninth, Fortieth, Forty-second, Fiftieth and Sixty-sixth Armies, each of three divisions. During the first half of November they were reinforced by the Ninth Army Group of General Chen Yi's Third Field Army, consisting of the Twentieth, Twenty-sixth and Twenty-seventh Armies, each of four divisions. This force concentrated to fall on the flank of the X Corps near the Chosin and Fusen reservoirs.

Altogether nearly 300,000 Chinese, supported by North Korean remnants and guerillas numbering perhaps 80,000, were waiting for approximately 150,000 U.N. troops to walk unwittingly into them.

The Eighth Army crossed the Chongchon River on 24 October. General Walker had three corps, the I and IX U.S. and the II Republic of Korea (R.O.K.), a combined strength of some 100,000 men under his command. The I U.S. Corps, under Major-General Milburn, consisted of the 1st U.S. Cavalry Division at Pyongyang, and the 24th U.S. Infantry Division, the 1st R.O.K. Infantry Division and the 27th British Commonwealth Brigade, of U.K. and Australian battalions, at the front. The IX U.S. Corps, under Major-General Coulter, was made up of the 2nd and 25th Infantry Divisions. The II R.O.K. Corps, under Major-General Yu Jae-hung, included the 6th, 7th and 8th Infantry Divisions. Walker had disposed his forces with the I Corps on the left, advancing on axes which lay between the west coast road to Sinuiju and the northerly road from Kunu-ri to Chosan on the Yalu, and the II R.O.K. Corps on the right, advancing northwards on a 35-mile front from Kunu-ri to Yongwon. The IX Corps was engaged in protecting the army's rear areas from determined guerilla actions.

The battlefield which both U.N. and communist forces overlooked in late October was, in tactical terms, somewhat like a funnel bounded on the west by the sea and on the east by mountains, with its mouth at the Yalu and its neck at the Chongchon. Many small roads and tracks led southwards from the Yalu, through hilly but not particularly rugged country, converging on the narrow coastal plain which runs southwards from the Chongchon. The hilly terrain north and east of the Chongchon offered good cover for a concealed approach by a force which was not heavily dependent on roads. The funnelling effect imposed by the convergence of mountains and coastline is accentuated by the Chongchon and Kuryong Rivers flowing westwards at the choke of the funnel across the line of the roads converging on the coastal plain. Once a force advancing northwards had crossed the Chongchon via the three main points available, it faced both defeat in detail as it fanned out on an ever-widening front and complete interruption of its lines of communication by a flank attack down the valleys of the Chongchon and the Kuryong. In the event of such an advance being turned into a rout, the retreating troops would have to converge slowly back through the funnel, constantly exposed to attacks from the flank and the rear.

These dangers had been recognized by General Walker, and he was ready to react with caution if his forces encountered trouble. Elements of the 6th R.O.K. Division reached the Yalu on 26 October. Between 27 and 29 October the main body of the division was attacked and defeated by Chinese forces between Ongjon and Huichon. The northernmost regiment had to fall back in scattered groups although it did manage to bring back a bottle of Yalu water for Syngman Rhee as a token in support of his claim that his sovereignty embraced the whole of Korea. The 8th R.O.K. Division also had to fall back after a clash with the Chinese, and the 1st R.O.K. Division in its turn encountered a strong Chinese force near Unsan, fifteen miles north of the Chongchon on the central sector, and became locked for several days in an action in which the situation grew steadily worse for the South Koreans. General Walker ordered the 1st Cavalry Division up from Pyongyang to support the vital centre. In the first week of November the 8th Cavalry Regiment of this division and another of the 1st R.O.K. Division were overwhelmed. On the west coast things had gone better, and by 1 November the 24th U.S. Division was within twenty miles of the Yalu. Nonetheless, in view of the virtual destruction of the 6th R.O.K. Division on the right and the danger threatening the centre, Walker decided to pull back his forces to form a line along the Chongchon with a substantial bridgehead on the north bank towards the coast.

MacArthur's divided forces each went their separate ways in the following weeks. While the Eighth Army was moving back to consolidate around the Chongchon, the X Corps dispersed itself deep into the hills of the north-east, encountering some Chinese resistance on the left flank. MacArthur himself became very anxious about the possibility of meeting overwhelming numbers of Chinese troops and on 5 November he ordered a heavy air offensive over North Korea, including the Yalu River bridges at Sinuiju. This offensive infringed an earlier J.C.S. directive that no bombing was to occur within five miles of the Yalu, so there was considerable reluctance in Washington to permit MacArthur to carry out these raids. However, MacArthur claimed that his forces were being threatened with destruction if the flow of men and material across the Yalu were not stopped. Truman gave way on grounds of military necessity, breaking an obligation to consult with the British government before taking such measures, because he believed MacArthur's claim that the situation was urgent. In fact it was already too late for bombing the Yalu bridges as the Chinese troops were in their concentration areas in North Korea.

After 7 November Chinese pressure ceased, possibly to see whether there would be a diplomatic response from Washington. To make the point more explicit, on 11 November the Chinese Foreign Ministry announced that Chinese volunteers were fighting in Korea. However, MacArthur's intelligence staff in Tokyo continued to discount the mildly apprehensive views of the Eighth Army and X Corps and dismissed the fate of the 8th Cavalry Regiment as being due to failure to take adequate security precautions in the face of 'a small, violent, surprise attack'. Gradually MacArthur recovered confidence. He reverted to the belief that the Chinese would not intervene in great numbers and reassured the J.C.S. that if they did his air power would destroy them.

U.S. and U.N. assurances were given to the Chinese that the conflict would be confined to Korea and on 8 November they were invited to send a delegate to Lake Success to discuss reports by General MacArthur of having encountered Chinese troops. Chou En-lai insisted on linking such talks to the question of Taiwan and the matter proceeded no further. Truman and his senior advisers felt, despite considerable apprehension, that MacArthur's directive to proceed with the offensive should not be altered, believing that MacArthur had to be allowed at least to test the strength of the Chinese forces already in Korea. In fairness to Truman it should also be pointed out that Republican gains in recent Congressional elections had resulted in greater pressures for handling the situation with firmness. Had Truman decided to halt MacArthur at that point for longer diplomatic soundings, he would doubtless have been condemned out of hand by many, including MacArthur himself, as an appeaser, and very serious political consequences could have followed.

Walker's plan for his resumed advance was to bring the IX Corps into the centre, leaving the I Corps on the left and the II R.O.K. Corps on the right. MacArthur wanted Walker to move on 15 November, but the problems of adequately supplying a force of this size over the long and difficult lines of communication available were too severe for this date to be feasible. It was not until 20 November that the supply system was able to deliver the 4,000 tons required daily to meet the minimum needs of offensive operations, and even then one quarter of this amount was being delivered by air, impeding the forward deployment of the tactical air squadrons on which MacArthur had put such reliance in the worst case.

On 17 November Walker fixed the date of the offensive as the 24th. On the eve of what was designed to be the final thrust to finish off a successful war, the U.S. troops celebrated Thanksgiving Day with special rations. General MacArthur flew to visit the I and IX Corps as the advance moved forward on 24 November, reiterating his promise that his troops would be sent home for Christmas once they had reached the Yalu. After flying over the battlefield MacArthur returned to Tokyo to learn of a new J.C.S. suggestion that he should halt his troops on the hill-tops overlooking the Yalu valley. As before, MacArthur rebuffed this limitation on his grand design and, also as before, he was given his way.

The advance moved forward on the first day without opposition. On the second, in the central sector, the 9th Regiment of the 2nd Division, advancing north-east along the valley of the Chongchon, encountered the Chinese in prepared positions and was repulsed. During the night of 25–6 November the Chinese attacked the American companies on the hill-tops where they had halted. Casualties were heavy on both sides. The divisional commander, Major-General Keiser, was aware that he was being effectively blocked but did not judge defeat to be in the offing. He did not know until late on 26 November that the II R.O.K. Corps had disintegrated under the weight of a powerful Chinese assault, leaving the right flank of the Eighth Army wide open. The Chinese then swept in from the east, to the south of the Chongchon and behind the 2nd Division.

They were encountered at Wawon, just seven miles east of Kunu-ri, on 27 November by the recently arrived Turkish Brigade. The Turks had been sent towards Tokchon to reinforce the II R.O.K. Corps position before it was known that this formation had been destroyed. Despite a gallant fight the brigade was shattered. Small groups of Turks managed to escape and continued to fight. The 25th Division, on the 2nd Division's left, had a similar experience: they encountered the first Chinese on 25 November and were hard pressed during that night. Some readjustment followed next day but the division looked to continue the advance, albeit with caution.

After a second night of heavy Chinese attacks, 26–7 November, the 2nd Division had to readjust its regimental dispositions to provide some protection for its rear against the Chinese columns coming from the east. Another night of heavy fighting followed and, with his artillery bases under threat from across the Chongchon, General Keiser received permission to withdraw to the next line of hills to the south. The 25th Division also had a bad night on 26–7 November and had to begin to withdraw on the following day. The weight of Chinese attacks was sustained and the division was saved only by the depth of its centre. The Chinese were forced to make several setpiece attacks and vital time was won to withdraw to stronger positions.

From the point of view of the Eighth Army as a whole, the Chinese attack had grave implications. The right flank had been shattered. The 2nd Division was being forced back under heavy pressure on the right of centre, the 25th Division was withdrawing in the centre, and the two left flank divisions, the 24th and the 1st R.O.K., were in danger of being cut off across the Chongchon. Walker attempted to save the situation by using the 2nd Division as a shield around Kunu-ri, supported by the reserves, the 1st Cavalry Division and the 27th Commonwealth Brigade, further to the south, to hold off the Chinese long enough for the 24th, 25th and 1st R.O.K. Divisions to withdraw south of the Chongchon through the bottlenecks of the crossing points and the few congested roads of the coastal plain.

On 28 November, while General Keiser was beginning his withdrawal, General MacArthur announced to the Security Council that his forces were being engaged by over 200,000 Chinese and as a consequence the U.N. faced 'an entirely new war'.

The Eighth Army avoided tactical disaster in the following two days largely through the efforts and sacrifices of the 2nd Division in standing firm around Kunu-ri. On 29 November General Coulter authorized Keiser to withdraw to Sunchon, some twenty miles to the south of Kunu-ri, on the following day. In the meantime the 27th Commonwealth Brigade had marched to Sunchon to attempt to keep open the road down which the 2nd Division could make its withdrawal most directly. It was also possible for the 2nd Division to withdraw westwards via Anju and then south and east to Sunchon, but Keiser did not favour this route because it was longer and congested by the 25th Division. However, the problems of trying to use the direct route were revealed clearly by the fate of a small Turkish convoy which ventured up the Sunchon–Kunu-ri road ahead of the 27th Brigade on 29 November. After several ambushes, remnants of the convoy reached Keiser's headquarters. The Chinese were already across the road, although not yet in sufficient numbers to stop a whole division. However, by the 30th a whole Chinese division was dug in along six miles of the steep valley up which the road wound to its highest point, a pass approximately half-way to Sunchon.

The 27th Brigade attempted to clear the road but was unable to advance beyond the pass. Consequently on 30 November the 2nd Division had to run the gauntlet, so well described by S. L. A. Marshall in *The River and the Gauntlet*. Not knowing the strength of the Chinese ambush until they were caught in it, and unable to turn back, the 2nd Division's convoys suffered fearful slaughter, including over 3,000 casualties and most of the division's equipment. The only redeeming features of the catastrophe were the courage of those who kept their discipline and fought their way through the tangle of wreckage which blocked the road, and the humanity of those not seriously injured who assisted the thousands of wounded and dying as they choked the ditches along that fearful ribbon of death. The remnants of the division's artillery came through the pass before dawn on 1 December. The rearguard escaped more lightly via Anju. The Eighth Army, though still intact, was in full retreat with its rear elements under constant pressure. The Battle of the Chongchon had inflicted on the U.S. army its most serious reverse to that date. It set in motion a withdrawal which MacArthur, in moments of panic, claimed could lead to the evacuation of U.N. forces from Korea unless 'positive and immediate action' was taken directly against China.

In order to save the Eighth Army from a far worse mauling, MacArthur ordered a rapid withdrawal of 120 miles virtually to the 38th Parallel. In the event such a dramatic disengagement was not necessary as the furious six days of combat had exhausted the Chinese supply system and they were unable to maintain pressure on the Eighth Army for more than a few days. At least the break of nearly a month which followed provided time for the consolidation of a strong line further south – though it was unfortunate from the U.N. viewpoint that, in the state of low morale which had gripped the Eighth Army during 'the big bug-out', time was not better used. However, the rapidity of the withdrawal, made for the most part within a fortnight, meant that huge quantities of supplies and equipment had to be destroyed. Although only 13,000 casualties were suffered in the withdrawal, the economic and tactical losses were enormous.

It is not easy to apportion blame for the U.N. defeat. While many people from forward commanders to President Truman had felt considerable uneasiness in the preceding weeks, there was general agreement at least that MacArthur's policy of a drive to the Yalu should be tried. Certainly

MacArthur's confidence in the ability of his ground and air forces to handle the Chinese was misplaced, but he had no idea that they were facing 300,000 Chinese already in position. Undoubtedly MacArthur's optimism was founded on a failure of intelligence to discover the true state of affairs, but good intelligence is not to be taken for granted in a combat situation. MacArthur can be criticized for under-valuing Chinese resolve as well as capacity, but again many others from the Chongchon to Washington, New York and London shared the view that the Chinese were unlikely to enter the conflict at that apparently late hour after North Korea had been denied direct reinforcement when the battle for the Pusan perimeter was at its height in August. Nonetheless, in his words at the Wake Island meeting and in his messages to the J.C.S. and the Security Council, MacArthur made himself the standard-bearer of optimism when, as an experienced soldier who ought to have been fully aware of the hazards of intelligence, he should have shown a little more caution, particularly in the way in which he separated the X Corps from the Eighth Army. At least it is to his credit that he disengaged when he did instead of feeding the Eighth Army stubbornly into a mincing machine in an attempt to justify his predictions. However, more credit would have been his due had he kept cooler in reverse and not flown to the opposite extreme of threatening evacuation of his forces from Korea. Perhaps, rather than trying to find severe fault with all those who went along with MacArthur, it would be more to the point to credit the Chinese with the achievement of perfect tactical surprise in the face of a powerful enemy, coupled with the courage and skill to turn this advantage into a major victory.

The consequences of the battle scarcely need to be dwelt on. The X Corps, already in difficulties on 28 November, had to be withdrawn on the orders of the J.C.S., thereby rendering pointless all the losses to the main thrust caused by transferring the corps to Wonsan in October. MacArthur's reputation as a commander was severely damaged and his whole command felt a lack of leadership until the arrival of General Ridgway to replace General Walker, following his death in a jeep accident on 22 December. The MacArthur–Truman relationship deteriorated sharply as MacArthur compounded his loss of the President's confidence by calling repeatedly for expansion of the war into China. The final crisis was not far ahead for the man who had been a heroic figure to many Americans for a decade.

For Truman himself, the defeat created an atmosphere fraught with peril. His policy of attempting to limit the war in the Far East in order to preserve the strength of the Western alliance in the more vital area of Europe came under much greater pressure from the Republicans. Ably supported by Acheson, Truman weathered the crisis but it provided one more argument for his political opponents to use against him for the remainder of his term in office.

When uncertainty regarding the future course of the conflict was at its height in late November Truman considered and rejected use of the atomic bomb. However, he did not have sufficient duplicity to hide the matter completely from the penetrating questions of journalists. Great consternation was caused thereby in the capitals of America's allies, particularly London. The Prime Minister, Attlee, flew to Washington to urge moderation, and out of these talks came clear recognition that U.N. aims no longer embraced unification of Korea but extended only to the preservation of South Korea. From henceforth the only feasible solution to the conflict could be a negotiated bargain. Military force still had a long and bloody role ahead of it in Korea, but its new objectives were so subtle that the doctrine of limited warfare became increasingly unpalatable in the West, particularly to those who had to risk paying its heaviest price.

The Chinese emerged from their victory as a major world power which could no longer be treated with contempt. However, through this elevation Chinese relations with the U.S. degenerated very sharply and subsequent Sino-American hostility has been a major influence in world politics until very recent times. The Chinese army established a reputation at the Chongchon which was to be well maintained in the three following years of bitter fighting. Chinese military prowess has cast a long shadow in many capitals, great and small, ever since. Had the Chinese not proved masters of the Chongchon field in November 1950 the course of world history since then must have been profoundly different.

Note on Sources

Dean Acheson's *Present at the Creation* (1970) is an indispensable source for understanding the development of major aspects of U.S. foreign policy during the Korean War, particularly the relationship between Truman and MacArthur, the limits Truman felt bound to observe in east Asia for the sake of the U.S. strategic position in the world at large, and the shortcomings of the President's chief advisers in October and November 1950.

Roy E. Appleman's *South to the Naktong, North to the Yalu* (1961) is the U.S. official history of military operations in 1950 up to the eve of the Battle of the Chongchon. Appleman gives a detailed account of U.S. strategy and tactics leading to the abortive plan for the final drive to the Yalu, based on full access to the records of participating formations, units and individuals. He provides a good critical analysis of command relationships and staff failings.

The River and the Gauntlet, by S. L. A. Marshall (1953), is the most detailed history of this battle available, written on the basis of field research in Korea soon afterwards. Some readers may find the volume excessively concerned with tactics and insufficiently with strategy but Marshall would make no apology for his structure. It is an excellent account of operations at the level of forward companies with much to teach even the participants about the conduct of the battle.

Richard Neustadt's *Presidential Power* (1960) is an analysis of the ways in which a U.S. president can exert his authority based on three case studies of important decisions taken by President Truman, including the dismissal of General MacArthur. The author was a White House aide during the Truman years and has, in this book and elsewhere, made a notable contribution to political science.

David Rees's *Korea: The Limited War* (1964) is the best general history of the Korean War, written with great insight and conciseness. Despite the breadth of Rees's topic, his treatment of the wider international antecedents and consequences of the Chinese entry into the war is probably unsurpassed.

John W. Spanier's *The Truman–MacArthur Controversy and the Korean War* (1959) is a very thorough and detailed account of the clash between the President and his commander-in-chief in the Far East between 1950 and 1951, providing a scholarly perspective on one of the most important chains of cause and effect which led to the surprise on the Chongchon.

Vol. II of Harry S. Truman's *Memoirs, Years of Trial and Hope* (1956) is the President's account of his years in office, including his own perspective on the factors which led him to underrate Chinese intentions in October and November 1950.

Finally, Allen S. Whiting's *China Crosses the Yalu* (1960) is a masterly analysis of Chinese policy in the months which preceded their entry into the war.

Chapter Twenty-Two

DIEN BIEN PHU

Stewart Menaul

IN THE YEAR 1883, in the wake of colonial expansion in Asia, Vietnam became a French protectorate and remained under French control until 1954, except for a short period of occupation by the Japanese in the Second World War. Although France was overwhelmed by the advancing German armies in 1940 and large areas of the country including Paris were occupied for the remainder of the war, France continued her colonial rule of what had become known as French Indo-China. Even under Japanese occupation France continued to administer the territory until the Japanese took over in 1945 and granted Vietnam independence under Japanese protection with Boa Dai as emperor. With the eventual defeat of Japan by the Allies, France restored colonial rule on the prewar pattern, which the Vietnamese people, particularly those in the north, could hardly have been expected to greet with rapture.

As early as 1941 the Central Committee of the Indo-Chinese Communist Party had announced its determination to liberate the whole of Vietnam from foreign domination. The instrument of its policy was to be a politico-military organization known as the Viet Minh under a dedicated international communist named Nguyen Ai Quoc, soon to change his name to the more notorious and familiar Ho Chi Minh. When the Japanese surrendered to the Allies in August 1945, Ho Chi Minh had already assumed control of large areas of north Vietnam. Claiming the support of the majority of the Vietnamese people, he called on the Emperor Boa Dai, now established in the ancient capital city of Hue, to abdicate and on 2 September 1945 Ho proclaimed the Democratic Republic of Vietnam. After formal elections which confirmed him as president and elected a National Assembly in which the Viet Minh won most of the 400 seats, Ho demanded the total withdrawal of the French from Indo-China and the complete independence of Vietnam.

In 1946, France agreed to recognize the Democratic Republic of Vietnam as a free state, but within the French union, and proposed that a referendum should be held to determine whether north, central and south Vietnam were prepared to unite under the regime established by Ho Chi Minh. Lengthy discussions in Hanoi and Paris failed to produce accord on the major issue of total independence for Vietnam, and as a result incidents of armed violence increased throughout the northern part of the country, culminating in the decision by Ho Chi Minh, in December 1946, to mount offensive operations against all French forces in north and central Vietnam. Another phase in Vietnam's seemingly endless struggle for independence and freedom was about to begin, but the vast majority of the Vietnamese people were totally unaware of the real political complexion of the new so-called Nationalist Front under Ho Chi Minh which was claiming to represent them in Hanoi.

The man destined to command the Viet Minh forces in the campaigns which followed was Vo Nguyen Giap who, despite the emotional eulogies written and spoken about him, was not a military genius. Indeed, on assuming command of the Viet Minh forces he was totally uninformed on the

French parachute troops fly in to reinforce the Dien Bien Phu garrison, 21 November 1953

principles of warfare and inexperienced in any kind of combat. His philosophy of guerilla warfare in the early days of his military campaigns in Vietnam was based on Chinese teaching and was quite simple. He often proclaimed it to his troops in the field: the support of the local population is an important factor in waging guerilla warfare; if it can be won peacefully well and good, but if it cannot then other methods must be used. This philosophy he was to translate into action for more than two decades, often with total lack of concern for the suffering inflicted on local populations or the heavy losses which his troops endured in attacks against the French and, subsequently, in the second Indo-China war, against the Americans and their allies.

Giap was born in 1910 the son of a farm labourer. At school, and later at Hanoi University, he was a brilliant student but a hot-head, seldom out of trouble with the authorities. He was the outstanding pupil of his year at Hanoi University and was selected for further studies in Paris, but in 1938 he left the academic environment to devote his time to the cause of communism and to the ultimate unification of Vietnam as an independent state under a communist regime. When the Second World War began, Giap joined Ho Chi Minh in China to study guerilla warfare. He stayed until 1941, when he returned to his native land to begin the process of building up communist guerilla units supported by a communications and logistics infrastructure. By 1945 the Viet Minh cadres were several thousand strong, based mainly in the north close to the Chinese border. Though armed and equipped mainly by the Chinese, they also managed to cull rifles and ammunition from the French, the Japanese, and even the Americans, who had openly supported the Viet Minh in 1944. Thus, when the offensive against the French began in 1946, Giap had an army of about 60,000 men, inexperienced in guerilla warfare but tolerably well trained and well versed in the philosophy of guerilla tactics as expounded by Giap.

After suffering many setbacks at the hands of the better equipped and better trained French forces, the Viet Minh were compelled to leave the cities and towns for the greater security of the countryside. They moved north towards the Chinese border where in 1949 direct contact was established between Ho Chi Minh and Mao Tse-tung. More and better equipment was supplied by the new Communist Chinese regime and more recruits for Giap's forces were trained in China, so that the Viet Minh gradually extended their control over large areas of the north Vietnamese countryside. They were also active in south Vietnam, in the Mekong delta and around Saigon, and in 1953 a number of divisions crossed into Laos to link up with the pro-communist Pathet Lao. The expansion of communist activity and the successes which they could legitimately claim, especially in the Red River delta area, persuaded the French that little real headway was being made against Giap's guerillas. In 1953 the French government appointed a new commander-in-chief, General Navarre, to take over from General de Lattre de Tassigny, who had returned to France for reasons of health. During his tour of duty in Indo-China, de Lattre had been no more successful in countering Giap's guerilla tactics than his predecessors, Generals Leclerc, Salan and Raoul. The new commander-in-chief was convinced that the tactics adopted by the French throughout the previous six years had not been and could not be successful. Furthermore, with the end of the Korean War China was diverting large quantities of modern arms and equipment, including heavy vehicles, artillery, anti-aircraft guns, machine guns and rifles, to the Viet Minh. Giap by this time had upwards of 120,000 men, well trained and well armed, with as many more available in the countryside if and when required.

General Navarre, after a thorough appraisal of the situation, decided upon a new strategy in which he contended that the only hope of inflicting a crippling defeat on Giap's guerillas was to draw them into setpiece battles, in which he was convinced the French forces would be successful. He chose the valley of Dien Bien Phu as the place for the first major confrontation and, he hoped, the beginning of the re-establishment of French dominion over Indo-China.

The village of Dien Bien Phu lies in a valley less than twenty miles from the Laotian border and 100 miles west of Hanoi. It is just seventy-five miles south of the Chinese border. The climate has two distinct seasons: winter, which prevails from November to April, is cool and damp with fine drizzle, while the summer months from May to October are characterized by heavy rains with occasional typhoons, and the temperature often climbs into the nineties. The valley of Dien Bien Phu is surrounded by densely wooded hills, and in the summer months collects more rain than almost any other area in the country. Weather considerations, therefore, largely dictated the timing of initial preparations for and the subsequent conduct of the Battle of Dien Bien Phu. The first operation, to establish a French base complete with airfield and fortified against enemy assault, began in November 1953. It was planned to use the base as a springboard for offensive actions against the enemy in the surrounding jungles, to cut his lines of supply, and ultimately to lure him to setpiece battles against superior French forces. Not unnaturally the dry season was selected for mounting the campaign, and on 20 November 1953 the first airlift of French airborne troops was despatched from Hanoi to the valley. This was an air drop operation under the command of General Dechaux, commanding the French air force in Indo-China, accompanied by General Cogny, commanding French forces in north Vietnam, who took command of French troops once the air drop was complete. The total available strength of sixty-five French transport aircraft (C-47s) was deployed.

The Viet Minh were known to be in the area and to have a headquarters in the village, so some opposition was expected. But the air drop was not exactly a model of military precision. The 1,500 paratroops were to have been dropped on three main zones, to the north, west and south of the village. Some landed well away from their allotted dropping zones, and while making their way back to prearranged rallying points were subjected to ambush by the Viet Minh. In the middle of the afternoon of 20 November a further 700 paratroops, with additional equipment, were air-dropped into the valley without opposition. Casualties were relatively light, and by nightfall the village of Dien Bien Phu was in French hands under the command of General Cogny. In the immediately surrounding hills was the 148th Regiment of the Viet Minh army and in the jungle further to the rear the 316th Division consisting of three regiments of infantry and an artillery battery of heavy 120-mm mortars and 75-mm recoilless rifles.

The French garrison of three battalions, commanded by Colonel de Castries, who took over when General Cogny returned to Hanoi, was equipped with automatic rifles and supported by artillery and mortars. Their immediate task was to erect defences and repair and improve the small airstrip to the north of the village so that additional equipment and supplies could be flown in from Hanoi. Transport aircraft of all types were in desperately short supply (less than 100), and French forces deployed in small units all over north, central and south Vietnam relied heavily on air transport for resupply and reinforcement. The Viet Minh forces in the Dien Bien Phu area under the command of General Hoang Van Thai, on the other hand, had neither air transport nor air support. Their supplies were transported mainly on bicycles or on the heads of thousands of porters (coolies), often over terrain that would have daunted the best trained troops the French could muster. Throughout the campaign the Viet Minh logistic supply lines were almost entirely activated by endless columns of human transport, though they had up to 600 heavy trucks supplied by the Soviet Union, which were used when suitable roads or tracks were available.

At the end of the first week there were 4,500 French troops in the valley of Dien Bien Phu. The garrison was the largest in the area, and in addition to the central command post, based on the village, there were strongpoints forming an outer ring of defences. These posts were known as Béatrice, Gabrielle, Anne-Marie, Dominique, Huguettes, Françoise, Elaine and Claudine, with Isabelle further to the south, guarding the only effective escape route from the valley if things went wrong. Even at this early stage it had become clear to the commanders on the spot that the basic materials and equipment required for the construction of solid defensive systems for the headquarters and airfield at Dien Bien Phu and the strongpoints on the periphery of the valley, about thirty miles in perimeter, could not be provided by airlift from Hanoi unless the French air force was considerably reinforced, since there was no suitable alternative means of transport.

Dien Bien Phu was well known to the French authorities, who had to relinquish it to the Japanese when they invaded Indo-China in the Second World War. The French reoccupied it when the Japanese surrendered in

1945, but lost it again to the Viet Minh in 1952. The importance of the valley, giving easy access to northern Laos, was well appreciated by both the French and Viet Minh High Commands, and Giap was quick to appreciate that reoccupation of the valley of Dien Bien Phu by the French would present a potential threat to his guerilla strongpoints in the area and, more importantly, to his logistic supply lines already being extended into Laos. It now fell to General Navarre to pit his not inconsiderable military experience and skill against the wily Giap. Navarre, of course, had his headquarters in Saigon, in south Vietnam, from which he paid flying visits to the controlling headquarters of French forces in the north at Hanoi commanded by General Cogny and to subordinate field headquarters, including Dien Bien Phu, scattered throughout north Vietnam. Giap, on the other hand, remained with his forces in the field most of the time, and his intelligence of French forces and deployments was far greater than the French suspected.

Early in December 1953 it became known that the Viet Minh were preparing to move two infantry divisions supported by artillery from the Red River delta to the highlands in the north-west of Vietnam. This was a clear indication that Giap was probably preparing to concentrate a vastly superior force in the hills surrounding the valley of Dien Bien Phu with the aim of thwarting French plans. The French, in analysing this intelligence information, faced a serious dilemma in that they did not have the necessary forces to mount an offensive against these divisions on the move or against their logistic supply lines. Dien Bien Phu was still a relatively lightly held air-head and garrison and it would clearly have been inappropriate to take forces from the garrison itself and redeploy them against Giap's divisions headed for the valley. Here was a cogent early warning of France's inferiority in numbers which went unheeded and was to prove costly in the months ahead.

After a visit to Dien Bien Phu and discussions on site with General Cogny and his staff from Hanoi, General Navarre returned to Saigon and prepared his now famous directive which finally committed the French in Indo-China to a decisive battle with the communist forces at Dien Bien Phu. On 3 December 1953, the directive was despatched to General Cogny in Hanoi and to Colonel de Castries at Dien Bien Phu. The directive envisaged holding Dien Bien Phu at all costs and in particular the airfield into which supplies and reinforcements would be flown and from which casualties would be evacuated. Other strongpoints in the surrounding area were to be given up if necessary in order to reinforce the garrison and its strongpoints at Dien Bien Phu. Air support and air resupply were to receive top priority and the French air force in north Vietnam was directed accordingly. A further four battalions of infantry, supported by five batteries of 105-mm artillery and two batteries of 75-mm recoilless rifles together with heavy mortars were despatched to the garrison. But even these reinforcements could not by any stretch of the imagination have been considered sufficient to pit against the Viet Minh divisions converging on the valley, nor could the very limited air support available have been expected to provide continuous resupply and reinforcements to meet the kind of attack which the communists were preparing to mount with overwhelming numbers. But the French High Command did not appear to appreciate this somewhat obvious fact and persistently underrated the Viet Minh's ability throughout the campaign.

By 1 January 1954 the French garrison, with its bizarre mixture of French, Algerian, Foreign Legionnaires (consisting of Germans, Italians, Spaniards and East Europeans), Vietnamese, Laotian, Moroccan and African troops, totalling nine battalions, was established within lightly constructed defensive wire compounds, supported by strongpoints and 'hedgehogs'. They had constructed some reinforced gun emplacements and dug-outs from the limited local material available and the meagre supplies flown in from Hanoi, and were apparently prepared to take on three Vietnamese divisions well armed and generously supported by artillery and mortars. The Viet Minh also had reliable and highly functional lines of communication not readily susceptible to air interdiction even if the French had had the air power to do it, which they had not.

Giap had learned from bitter experience that it was prudent to attack only when the chances of success were high, but once a decision to attack had been reached, even if losses might also be high, he demanded that units committed to action must be resolute in pressing home their attacks irrespective of losses. The way to counteract modern armaments, he argued, was to 'display boundless heroism'. The price of victory in the Battle of Dien Bien Phu would be high, but success for the Vietnamese forces over the French forces besieged in the valley would herald the defeat and humiliation of French forces throughout Vietnam and probably the end of French colonial rule in South-east Asia.

In December 1953 the French had begun their sorties against the enemy in the jungles and on the hills surrounding the valley, making contact with locally recruited tribesmen in an attempt to establish reliable intelligence of enemy positions and movements. As the airstrip north of the village was now in full operation, supplies of both reinforcements and logistics continued to be flown in and units operating in the jungle had the advantage of light spotter aircraft (Crickets) and, if necessary, cover by fighter bombers from the French air force and navy (Bearcats, Helldivers and Corsairs) which were able to operate from the strip. But, as a portent of what was to come, one of the first infantry patrols to venture into the hills only a few miles from Dien Bien Phu was almost totally annihilated by communist forces who lured them into a cleverly arranged ambush. These were not roving bands of undisciplined guerillas, but part of the 176th Regiment of the 316th Division of the Viet Minh army, which had recently moved into the hills and jungle surrounding Dien Bien Phu. In less than a month it became clear that deep penetration patrols by French forces were an expensive and not wholly reliable means of obtaining intelligence of enemy positions and movement, and it came as no surprise to outside observers when, towards the end of January, French activity was confined to probing sorties within the perimeter of the valley itself, by now almost completely surrounded by Viet Minh forces. The only useful road (41) was controlled by the communists less than seven miles from Dien Bien Phu and not even air strikes could dislodge the enemy from their strongpoints.

The communist forces relentlessly tightened the ring around the valley until most of the French strongpoints came under artillery and mortar fire from 75-mm and 105-mm guns. By the beginning of February the first direct artillery fire from fixed positions in the hills landed on the airstrip damaging aircraft and buildings. At the same time, the enemy began using anti-aircraft guns against French transport aircraft ferrying in supplies and reinforcements to the airstrip. Colonel de Castries now had to recast his tactics so as to concentrate attacks on enemy artillery and anti-aircraft positions with counter-artillery and mortar fire supplemented by air strikes by B-26 bombers and Bearcat fighters using bombs, rockets and napalm. When French commando units attempted to attack enemy artillery and mortar emplacements which had been positively identified, they were invariably driven back with heavy losses. The Viet Minh 308th, 316th and 304th Divisions supported by an artillery division were now identified dominating the hills to the north and north-east of the airstrip, and it is difficult to understand how any French commander could have believed that a force of ten battalions, which was all that was available in the whole Dien Bien Phu complex, could dislodge an enemy more than four times his strength, occupying strategic positions overlooking the garrison area and growing stronger every day. The French had suffered a string of defeats with heavy casualties at the hands of the communist forces in the previous month, and even the introduction of a few tanks (a total of ten were operational in Dien Bien Phu) made no real difference to the effectiveness of French counter-attacks against an enemy by now well established in a ring around the valley. By mid-February, de Castries reported to Hanoi that casualties since the reoccupation of Dien Bien Phu in November amounted to thirty-six officers, ninety-six N.C.O.s and 836 men – or virtually a whole battalion. To make matters worse, headquarters in Hanoi felt compelled to order a limit on the use of ammunition of all kinds.

The real siege of Dien Bien Phu can be said to have started on 13 March. Hurried attempts had been made to fortify the central sector and the outlying strongpoints against enemy artillery and mortar fire and the inevitable infantry attacks which the French knew must come, but Dien Bien Phu was not sufficiently strong to withstand the bombardment which was eventually hurled against it. General Navarre, in his original conception of the military strategy for Dien Bien Phu, had envisaged the possibility of a siege and had even formulated plans for evacuation if it became impossible to sustain operations against the Viet Minh or hold the base, but neither he nor his staff at the headquarters in Saigon nor General Cogny and his staff in Hanoi could provide the garrison with the men, guns, ammunition and materials needed for either a siege or an evacuation. Every movement in Dien Bien Phu and on the strongpoints could be observed and plotted by the enemy; consequently the firepower he was able to bring to bear was both heavy and accurate.

Throughout the build-up and during the battle, one of the most impressive performances by the communists was their ability to maintain logistic support of a large force over a prolonged period. The French had nothing like the air strike capability that would have been necessary effectively to interdict the enemy's lines of supply and communications, which stretched back to the Chinese border. Even today, many historians and chroniclers of the Dien Bien Phu siege do not appear to appreciate that the total number of aircraft available to the French in Indo-China in 1954 (French air force and navy) was less than would have been used by the United States army in a battalion strength operation in South Vietnam fifteen years later. The strike aircraft that were available to the French did not have the means to find and destroy logistic supply depots or the routes over which supplies were conveyed, which for the most part were virtually jungle tracks. On the few occasions when important road junctions or river crossings were identified, the small weight of bombs which could be dropped on them made little difference to the continuity of the communist supplies. At best, the French could muster only seventy strike aircraft, made up of fighters, fighter bombers and light bombers, with occasional sorties by four-engined heavy transports used as bombers. Nor did the French aircraft escape unscathed from enemy anti-aircraft fire, particularly the transport aircraft on the approaches to Dien Bien Phu.

On the evening of 12 March, it was clear that the Viet Minh had completed their build-up and in accordance with Giap's well known tactics were about to deliver their first major assault on the garrison. The French not only totally underestimated the Viet Minh's strength and capability, but they also grossly overestimated their own. It is known that the communist strength on the eve of the first assault numbered about 48,000, while the French garrison totalled 11,000, of which probably no more than 8,500 could be considered as trained, reliable troops. As the battle progressed, the communists added at least another 11,000 to their total while the maximum the French were able to fly in or air-drop was 4,000. The communists were supported by more than eighty 105-mm howitzers, twenty-five 75-mm howitzers, and twenty heavy 120-mm mortars. They had thirty-six heavy 37-mm anti-aircraft guns (Russian) and at least fifteen 75-mm pack howitzers. They also had thirty recoilless rifles and Russian rocket-launchers. The French had six batteries of 105-mm howitzers, four 155-mm howitzers, and three companies of 120-mm heavy mortars attached to strongpoints Claudine, Anne-Marie and Gabrielle: a total of twenty-four medium and four heavy artillery pieces, twenty-four heavy mortars and four 0.5 calibre anti-aircraft guns for use against enemy infantry attacks.

The communist assault began as expected with an artillery and mortar bombardment of the airstrip, during which aircraft and storage and maintenance facilities were destroyed. Strongpoint Béatrice to the north-west of the airstrip was subjected to accurate and continuous artillery and mortar fire, causing heavy casualties among the French forces, until it was eventually overrun by communist infantry after fierce hand-to-hand fighting in which the remaining French forces were almost entirely wiped out.

Strongpoint Gabrielle to the north of the airstrip, which was thought to be the best constructed in the entire Dien Bien Phu complex, proved to be the most vulnerable. It had more troops (mostly Algerian), guns and ammunition than any of the others. The morale of its defenders was high, but, like most French predictions, its estimate of the strength of the enemy, his location, and his fighting ability, had been highly inaccurate. While the French correctly guessed that the assault would begin with an artillery and mortar bombardment in the early hours of the morning and had asked for air support in the form of flares to be dropped over estimated enemy positions, they quickly discovered that they were powerless to interrupt the withering and deadly fire from enemy batteries concealed in the surrounding hills. In the opening phases all the officers from the strongpoint were either killed or wounded. A counter-attack, mounted from the central sector at Dien Bien Phu by French infantry with tank support, failed. It was intercepted by Viet Minh infantry and compelled to retreat. In the meantime, waves of Viet Minh infantry were throwing themselves against the barbed wire perimeter of the main defences on Gabrielle until the remaining French defenders were compelled to retreat in daylight in full view of the enemy occupying the surrounding hills and jungle. They managed to reach the other strongpoints at Anne-Marie and Huguette, but their losses were heavy: at least 800 casualties to add to the 700 already suffered during the assault on Béatrice.

Enemy losses were even heavier, as was to be expected of troops indoctrinated in the belief that 'heroism was the best answer to superior firepower'. Thousands perished against the barbed wire entanglements as machine gun bullets tore into their ranks, but still they came on until the piles of dead provided stepping stones on which others following could clamber over the wire entanglements. Reserves appeared to be no problem to the communists, and the morale of the victorious Viet Minh troops was in stark contrast to the French in the central sector at Dien Bien Phu as the siege ring tightened with each succeeding day. In Hanoi, General Cogny, sensing that the loss of Dien Bien Phu was highly likely if not inevitable and that the military situation throughout the Red River delta was deteriorating, was reluctant to respond to appeals from Colonel de Castries for reinforcements from other units deployed in north Vietnam. General Navarre in

Saigon had just as stubbornly resisted Cogny's requests for troops from south Vietnam to be redeployed to the north, but eventually a further battalion of paratroops was dropped on the beleaguered garrison to replace the heavy casualties suffered in the first forty-eight hours of the battle.

Anne-Marie was the next to fall. Not only was it totally inadequately defended and an easy target for enemy artillery and mortar fire, but its defenders, who were mostly locally recruited T'ai troops, deserted *en masse* as the communists began their attack. The enemy effort in the opening phases of the battle had been prodigious and obviously could not be sustained indefinitely, so the Viet Minh forces now rested and regrouped for six days while maintaining artillery and mortar fire on all remaining French positions. By now the ring around the strongpoints in the north had been closed, isolating Isabelle to the south, which was still holding out against determined enemy attacks with mounting losses. The rainy season was close at hand and began to interfere with air attack and air support operations. Air resupply, already hazardous from enemy anti-aircraft fire, became more erratic and unreliable as weather conditions deteriorated. The area around the garrison was bare of vegetation and pockmarked with shell and mortar holes. Heavy rain converted it into a veritable bog which made movement, even within the wire defences, extremely difficult. French attacks on anti-aircraft positions, now well established in the hills surrounding the village, afforded some relief to the vulnerable C-47s, but could not prevent the expansion of the enemy's anti-aircraft defences, which became more numerous and more accurate as the perimeter shrank with each succeeding enemy assault.

On 29 March the next phase of the Viet Minh offensive began on what were known as 'The Hills', to the east and south of the airstrip and east of the Nam Yum River. The French regarded these hills as vital to the continued defence of the central control post of the garrison and the airstrip. Most of the Hill positions were held by Moroccan and Algerian forces, with a sprinkling of French paratroops in Dominique and Elaine. Rain was now falling regularly, which interfered with the air drop of much needed supplies, especially medical equipment for the mounting casualty list in the hospital. As usual, communist artillery and mortar barrages preceded the attack upon the Hills. Waves of infantry, oblivious of the slaughter of their comrades in front of them, stormed through minefields and wire defences to capture four of the five major defensive positions. French casualties were heavy, and many Algerian and locally recruited forces broke and ran for the jungle. The ability and will of the garrison to resist were further weakened by more than 2,000 casualties. Losses of artillery and mortar pieces were also heavy and ammunition was running short. Attempts to dislodge the enemy from two of the hills were partially successful, but at the cost of further heavy losses. Meanwhile, a relieving column from Isabelle which attempted to reach the village was routed, and from that moment on Isabelle was totally isolated and no further attempts to help the main garrison were made.

On 1 April General Giap personally assumed command of Viet Minh forces at Dien Bien Phu. He knew that peace negotiations were soon to begin in Geneva and victory at Dien Bien Phu was vital to any discussions on the independence of Vietnam. On 2 April the communists resumed the offensive with an attack on Huguettes to the north and west of the airstrip. With the help of four tanks, the French mounted a determined counter-attack against superior Viet Minh forces, now close to the northern end of the airstrip. Combined artillery and air strikes took an awesome toll of enemy infantry to bring the total of communist casualties since the siege began to well over 9,000 and compel Giap to call for reinforcements from his reserves located in the jungle to the rear of the Viet Minh lines. His replacement problem, of course, was relatively simple when compared with that of the French, whose losses were again heavy, and while they gained temporary respite from relentless pressure by the Viet Minh, and some reinforcements were air-dropped, these only postponed the ultimate and inevitable outcome of the unequal struggle.

On 10 April the French counter-attacked against Elaine, with support from air strikes and artillery, in the hope of retaking some of the hill positions. The communist reaction was the same as in previous encounters. Waves of fanatical infantry hurled themselves against the withering fire from French automatic rifles, but this time they faltered and the French recaptured and held part of Elaine. For the first time Giap began to question the credibility of his tactics as he counted the mounting losses sustained in his attempts to tighten the ring round Dien Bien Phu. He decided on a more cautious approach and intensified a system of trench-digging operations as a means of closing on the French positions while hoping for a lower casualty rate. This provided some respite for the hard-pressed garrison and relative quiet descended on Dien Bien Phu for more than a week, interrupted by occasional shelling and air strikes against communist positions. Air drops were beginning to fall more and more into enemy hands as anti-aircraft fire became more concentrated and the drop areas more restricted. For General de Castries (promoted brigadier-general in the field) resupply became a choice – or rather a permutation – of ammunition, reinforcements, medical supplies and food, all of which were now scarce commodities in Dien Bien Phu. Not surprisingly relations between the various unit commanders in the garrison had become strained and the defence was conducted more and more by a committee rather than by a commander and his staff. Even the field promotion of Colonel de Castries did not make a great deal of difference.

On 24 April, while Dien Bien Phu was slowly dying in the inexorable grip of the communist stranglehold, a new drama was being enacted in Paris, Washington and London. As the situation worsened, the French appealed to the United States for air strikes against the communist positions at Dien Bien Phu and against their logistic supply lines stretching back to the Chinese border. The proposal was to use B-29 bombers, which the French claimed could so devastate the communist positions that there would be at least a chance to reinforce the garrison and perhaps save Dien Bien Phu. The British were asked to join in, but apart from the political implications of United States and British involvement in the conflict it was clear to experts in Britain, who knew the capability of bombers against jungle targets, that decisive results could not be achieved in a short time by bombing attacks alone. Britain had experienced similar problems in Malaya. Dien Bien Phu was now so congested, with enemy units close to French positions, that bombing attacks could not be made by high-level heavy bombers without inflicting casualties on the French garrison. After four days of intense discussions the proposed operation, known as Operation Vulture, was abandoned. Those who took part in the discussions with the French in London felt deeply sorry that it was not possible to help them, but they knew it was already too late to save Dien Bien Phu.

Two other operations were proposed and partially planned: one was designed to relieve the garrison with a force from Laos which was to link up with air-dropped forces from Hanoi; the other was a desperate break-out operation to save what could be salvaged of the garrison at Dien Bien Phu. They were known respectively as Operations Condor and Albatross. Both would have required air support on a scale far beyond the capacity of the French air force in Indo-China. The tragedy was that the French did not appear to appreciate the volume of air lift and air strikes that would be required to support relieving columns moving in the jungle while, at the same time, maintaining support for the garrison at Dien Bien Phu. The French also totally overestimated the effects of air strikes by light bomber or fighter-bomber aircraft in weather conditions which often prevented aircraft from accomplishing their missions. It was hardly surprising that in the event both these operations failed.

Supplies of ammunition, food and reinforcements continued to be dropped on Dien Bien Phu in a haphazard fashion, but despite the efforts by the French air force and civilian pilots the strength of the garrison was still only just over 5,000 fighting troops, and artillery and mortar support had been reduced by nearly half. There were nearly 1,000 wounded in the hospital and makeshift casualty stations, and desertions were becoming more frequent. Giap's forces, on the other hand, numbered about 35,000, with at least 20,000 reserves, and they had overwhelming artillery, mortar and anti-aircraft support. The garrison at Dien Bien Phu had been reduced to less than a mile square to the south of the airstrip and the enemy had pushed his trenches to the very edge of the remaining garrison defences. This meant that supplies air-dropped to the desperate defenders more often than not fell in enemy-held territory. Communist anti-aircraft fire had been further intensified, and to add to the difficulties of air drop and air strike operations the monsoon had broken in all its fury.

On 29 April the Viet Minh directed a devastating barrage of artillery and mortar fire on the remaining garrison area. They were literally firing down from the hills, previously captured in bitter hand-to-hand fighting, onto the remaining French positions. There were few reliable dug-outs or communication trenches left in the garrison by 5 May, and the French were running out of ammunition. They had come almost to the limit of human endurance and, with declining morale at what they considered to be the indifference of the outside world to their plight, they knew that the end could not be far off and that no amount of resupply or reinforcement could now prevent the communists from capturing the garrison.

On 6 May the final assault began with a merciless attack by artillery, mortars and rockets, accompanied by a new and unexpected form of firepower, which proved to be high explosives tunnelled under French strongpoints and fired by remote control. The devastation created had the effect of slowing down the advancing waves of Viet Minh infantry, which further increased their casualties, but French air strikes proved to be self-defeating as they now killed as many French troops as they did those of the enemy. Despite great gallantry on the part of the remaining French forces, particularly the legionnaires and paratroopers, they could not stave off the mass of infantry attacks which eventually overwhelmed them. Many of the dug-outs in Dien Bien Phu were defended to the last bullet and the last man, and only when the Viet Minh had captured the entire area did General de Castries submit to the Viet Minh officers who entered his control point in the centre of Dien Bien Phu. The time was 5.30 p.m. on 7 May. The battle for Dien Bien Phu was over. Isabelle fell at about the same time. The relief forces (Condor) from Laos never reached Dien Bien Phu or Isabelle, though they got within sight of the latter in time to see it fall.

The siege lasted just fifty-six days. In that time a total of 4,000 reinforcements were flown in or air-dropped to replace casualties to the French garrison's original strength of 11,000. Between 13 March and 7 May, 6,500 tons of supplies were parachuted into the garrison at Dien Bien Phu, or roughly 120 tons a day, of which less than 100 tons a day reached the defenders. At the end of the battle there were just over 9,000 troops left in the garrison, including more than 2,000 deserters who could not get through the Viet Minh lines. (These were mostly North African, Vietnamese and locally recruited T'ai troops who threw down their arms and ran, only to find they could not escape through the tight cordon of Viet Minh troops. They were deserters within their own lines – a unique situation – and were captured with the remnants of the garrison when Dien Bien Phu fell.) The French casualties were 2,200 killed, 6,000 wounded, and 6,000 prisoners-of-war, of whom more than half died in prison camps. Although the Viet Minh had no air support of any kind they destroyed forty-eight French aircraft over the valley and sixteen on the ground, and damaged many more. Viet Minh casualties can only be estimated, but it would seem that at least 8,000 were killed and 15,000 wounded; it could well have been more.

To emphasize the deficiency in planning, the overestimation of French capability and the underestimation of the enemy in the Dien Bien Phu siege, the most striking comparison is the siege of Khe Sanh in South Vietnam in 1968 when two North Vietnamese divisions (over 20,000 men) besieged a garrison of 6,000 United States and South Vietnamese forces. The siege lasted seventy-eight days, and in that time United States airmen flew more than 24,000 attack sorties in which they dropped over 95,000 tons of bombs. They also flew 1,200 airlift sorties during which over 12,000 tons of supplies were delivered to the garrison. Enemy casualties at Khe Sanh were even higher than at Dien Bien Phu, but the garrison held out entirely due to the right application of air power in the right strength at the right time. There was no repetition of Dien Bien Phu throughout the whole of the second Indo-China war between 1964 and 1973.

After nearly every battle the winner indulges in self-gratification and rarely embarks immediately on detailed post mortem analysis, much less recrimination, though he is often quick to exact retribution from the vanquished. The loser initially attempts to convert a defeat into a glorious defensive victory, before dissecting every facet of the battle to find out what went wrong, who was responsible and what punishment should be visited upon the guilty. Instant historians, in recording the battle or campaign, sometimes invent factors to substantiate their own pet theories of why the battle was lost or won, so that all too often those who took part in the event begin to wonder if they are all talking about the same contest, until the official historians correct the balance. Dien Bien Phu was no exception. The causes of French failure were many and varied and are still argued about today, but the most obvious and generally agreed major contribution to the defeat of French forces at Dien Bien Phu was persistent French underestimation of the enemy's capabilities, together with invariable overestimation of their own, particularly in logistic supply.

On the other hand, the major factor that ensured success for the Viet Minh was their ability to operate in and use the jungle terrain or the delta with equal ease. The solution to their logistic supply problem was simple but effective. They were able to bring superior firepower to bear on the French and to maintain it despite heavy losses. The French logistic supply organization in support of their forces at Dien Bien Phu virtually collapsed. They did not possess the aircraft needed to maintain even a relatively small garrison, and, with the experience of the U.S. forces in South Vietnam nearly two decades later to draw upon, it is surprising that Dien Bien Phu held out as long as it did. But gallantry in battle is not enough: the French made too many mistakes in the planning and execution of the Battle of Dien Bien Phu. Yet it must be regarded as one of the most famous and decisive sieges of modern times. It signalled the end of French colonial rule in Indo-China and heralded the collapse of French colonial rule everywhere, but not, alas, the longed for peace in Vietnam. More than twenty years later that unhappy, war-torn country saw the final chapter of a politico-military struggle which may be said to have begun where Dien Bien Phu ended. Has peace really come to Vietnam?

Note on Sources

I am grateful to my many friends in Vietnam for their help and guidance in understanding the Vietnamese situation and for the information given to me during my visits to Vietnam, to witness and discuss Vietnam's struggle for independence; I am particularly indebted to Colonel Cao Xuan Ve, soldier, scholar, and friend.

I am indebted to the late Bernard B. Fall whose account of the Battle of Dien Bien Phu in his book *Hell in a very Small Place* (1966) is an indispensable source of information; to Colonel Jules Roy whose *La Bataille de Dien Bien Phu* (1963) is invaluable as a historic record of the siege by a Frenchman; to the late Otto Heilbrunn, to Paddy Honey and to many others. Above all, I am indebted to the late Général d'Armée André Beaufre who until his death in March this year was Director, Institut Francais d'Etudes Strategiques. General Beaufre saw service in Indo-China during his distinguished military career and I gladly acknowledge his help and advice during our many discussions on Vietnam, in public, on radio and television, and in private.

Chapter Twenty-three

TET OFFENSIVE

Bernard Brodie

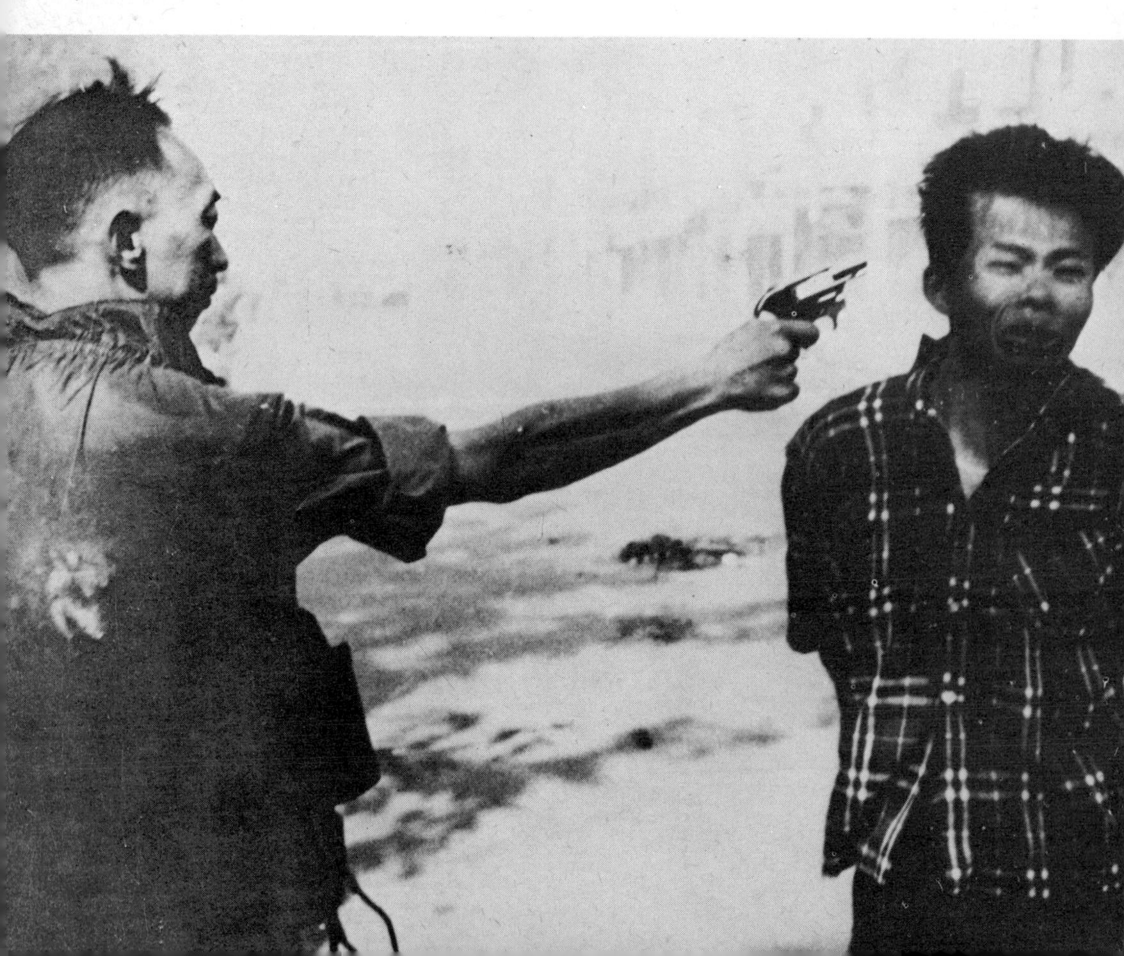

THE TET OFFENSIVE of 1968 differs in its main characteristics from virtually all other struggles usually collected under the words 'decisive battles'. First, as the name applied to it suggests, it was not even in the normally accepted sense of the term a 'battle'. More significantly, it was probably unique in that the side that lost completely in the tactical sense came away with an overwhelming psychological and hence political victory. And there can be no question of its decisiveness.

Battles are often called 'decisive' which actually changed little the flow of events but which because of their spectacular attributes serve as convenient historical markers in describing those events. The Battle of Leyte Gulf in 1944, described by Stanley L. Falk elsewhere in this book, had more floating tonnage involved in it than any other naval battle in history, and it marked the last despairing sortie as a major fighting force of a proud navy with a half-century's tradition of victory. Because blunders were committed on both sides, it is easy to imagine different outcomes for the battle, but none is imaginable that could have changed the outcome of the Pacific War. Admiral Halsey's fleet was too overwhelmingly superior to be defeated. The Tet Offensive, on the other hand, which could have only one tactical outcome, does not simply mark but actually caused the beginning of the end of American participation in the Vietnam War, with all the strategic and political consequences that flowed from that withdrawal.

One could argue that the American turnabout was bound to come sooner or later in any case, but the chain of events which that offensive certainly precipitated included the political demise of the President in power in the United States. His successor was therefore bound to be committed to withdraw, but that successor, Richard Nixon, demonstrated in his first four years of power how protracted could be the withdrawal of a President reluctant to face its consequences.

With a little stretching of the imagination one could hold also that the Tet Offensive marvellously exemplifies Clausewitz's famous doctrine, which he held to be central to his entire teaching, that the political aim of any war must guide and dominate not merely the national commitment to that war but also its very strategy. The main difficulty with that statement is that we in the West cannot now be sure, and may indeed never be sure, just what was in the minds of those governing North Vietnam, and especially in the mind of their defence minister, General Vo Nguyen Giap, in planning and launching the Tet Offensive. As we shall see, opinions in the West concerning what he intended to achieve vary widely. But if he really intended what he in fact achieved, then he must stand out as one of the most brilliant strategists in all history. That may be allowing him too much; on the other hand, those who hold that he was expecting a tactical victory and had no idea that his inevitable tactical defeat would nevertheless bring in its train fabulous strategic and political gains are setting him down as stupid – a conclusion that ill accords with the other accomplishments of this man, including the

Brigadier-General N. N. Loan shooting a Viet Cong prisoner. The Viet Cong was captured in Saigon during the Tet fighting

1954 victory at Dien Bien Phu. The latter battle, unlike Tet, was a tactical victory rather than defeat, but it also returned disproportionate strategic and political rewards. Statesmen or generals who are merely lucky are rarely so consistently and extravagantly lucky.

The military events of Tet in 1968 are individually on a small scale and, to the usual student of military history, hardly even interesting. They were essentially isolated but simultaneous guerrilla actions taking place in urban settings, and the two things most remarkable about them are, first, the degree of surprise achieved by the attackers, and second, the fierce determination that the latter showed in resisting to the death the counterattacks of their militarily superior opponents. Clausewitz confessed to knowing very little about guerrilla war, which made virtually its first appearance during his lifetime in the Iberian peninsula from 1808 to 1814 (inspiring the 'Horrors of War' depicted by Goya), but he hesitantly offered as a basic principle of guerrilla warfare that the guerrillas must not risk too much lest their losses dampen their ardour. In Tet the guerrillas ventured all, and a large proportion of them gave their lives in doing so.

Tet is the lunar new year, the celebration of which, always a major event in Vietnam, was scheduled to begin in 1968 on the evening of 29 January. In preparation for this holiday President Nguyen Van Thieu, after consultation with his American Allies, announced a thirty-six-hour cease-fire to be effective from the evening of 29 January to the early hours of 31 January. Because of enemy troop activity, however, an exception was made for the zone of I Corps, the northernmost of the four Corps zones into which South Vietnam was administratively divided. The Viet Cong for their part announced a seven-day Tet truce to begin on the evening of 27 January. The latter move was a subterfuge which in itself fooled nobody, inasmuch as it had to be viewed in the light of reports during January from agents and prisoners that a Viet Cong and North Vietnamese offensive was impending, and United States troops were in fact placed on full alert several days before Tet. However, the nature of the attack was not at all predicted. General William C. Westmoreland in his official report admits: 'It did not occur to us that the enemy would undertake suicidal attacks in the face of our power. But he did just that.'

Possibly because of a mixup in coordination, the enemy attack was launched in I and II Corps Zones twenty-four hours ahead of the attack in the remainder of South Vietnam. This gave the Allies some additional warning, but still did not reveal the nature of the attack in the Saigon area, which was in III Corps, where it began late on the 30th. In addition to Saigon, assaults were mounted against thirty-six of the forty provincial capitals, five of the six autonomous cities, sixty-four of the 242 district capitals, and about fifty hamlets. The most important city attacked besides Saigon was the old Imperial capital Hué, far to the north in I Corps Zone.

In preparation for the attack the Viet Cong went to extraordinary lengths to assemble and hide supplies and to infiltrate troops in civilian disguise into the cities to be attacked. Their forces operating in the Delta (IV Corps Zone) were drawn upon to reinforce those operating in the vicinity of Saigon. Otherwise they used mainly local forces, and the North Vietnamese Army was used mostly for backup except in the operations round Dak To in the northwest corner of II Corps Zone.

Despite the American alert, large numbers of South Vietnamese soldiers were on leave for Tet, and their units were in most cases about half strength. Nevertheless, in most of the cities attacked the South Vietnamese Army threw back the attackers within a few hours or at most two or three days. Very heavy fighting continued, however, in Kontum City, Ban Me Thuot, Can Tho, and Ben Tre, and in Saigon and Hué the battle was protracted into the middle and latter parts of February. At Dak To, where a more conventional attack was being pressed by the 1st Division of the North Vietnamese Army, the battle continued until the end of February.

At Saigon the attack began at night with a sapper assault on the American Embassy, but this was contained by midmorning of the following day. The Viet Cong coordinated this attack with assaults on the Presidential Palace, the Vietnamese Joint General Staff compound, the Tan Son Nhut Airbase complex, and even the Phu Tho Race Track, which became their base of operations and held out the longest. According to the Westmoreland Report, enemy forces consisted of 'elements of eleven local force battalions', which can hardly be considered a large number of men. Still, in order to deal with these attacks, General Westmoreland was obliged for the first time to put American combat forces into Saigon, and by the end of the second day some seven American battalions were operating within the city in support of South Vietnamese Army and National Police forces, and many more U.S. battalions occupied positions along roads leading to the city in order to block enemy reinforcements. To quote again from the official report: 'Except for breaching the wall and entering the grounds of the U.S. Embassy, the only successes against a government target were brief incursions into the rear of the Vietnamese Joint General Staff compound and into two remote areas of Tan Son Nhut Airbase.'

The fighting at Hué was on a much larger scale and more protracted. Regular units consisting of eight battalions made up of both the Viet Cong and the North Vietnamese Army were able to infiltrate under the concealment of low fog, and these were later reinforced by another Viet Cong battalion and units from two North Vietnamese Army divisions. Before the battle was over some sixteen North Vietnamese battalions, as well as those of the Viet Cong, had been identified in and around Hué. The troops quickly captured most of that portion of the city on the south bank of the Perfume River, and they later seized the bulk of the northern half including the Imperial Citadel. U.S. marines drove them from most of the south bank within the first few days, but the battle for the Imperial Citadel was fierce and prolonged, lasting until 25 February. The fighting inevitably resulted in heavy damage to the city and especially to the historic Citadel, with some 116,000 residents of the city being made homeless, almost entirely from the firepower of American and South Vietnamese aircraft and artillery, which included large naval guns operating from off the coast.

In all the areas of major combat the Communist forces were surrounded and usually fought to the death. Their losses were therefore heavy, but they could hardly have been as heavy as were claimed officially by the Americans and South Vietnamese. At Hué, for example, the Americans claimed 5,000 enemy killed within the city and an additional 3,000 to the immediate north, but they admitted the loss of only 500 U.S. and South Vietnamese soldiers killed. Inasmuch as the latter were doing most of the attacking against troops sheltered behind heavy fortifications, it is hard to understand such a disparity of losses in favour of the attackers, despite their monopoly of artillery and air power. Similarly, the claim for enemy dead in the entire Tet Offensive rose to 45,000 by the end of February, while Allied losses in dead were put at 1,001 U.S. and 2,082 South Vietnamese and other Allied personnel.

These losses do not include civilian casualties. There is no doubt that in Hué the enemy rounded up and executed a large number of government officials and school teachers, but whether those deaths reached the 1,000 figure originally mentioned in the Westmoreland Report (later raised to 3,000 in some retrospective reporting) must also be under the same shadow of doubt. The entire discredited system of 'body counts' for determining enemy dead has such a scandalous history in the Vietnam War that there would have had to be an extraordinary and inexplicable shift to virtue during the Tet Offensive for one to accept as even nearly correct the figures for enemy dead claimed by the Allies. Still, there is no doubt that the Communist enemy, and especially the hard core Viet Cong, paid a heavy price for what in the end turned out to be a demonstration only, with Allied positions everywhere regained.

Such, in briefest outline, were the military events of Tet. Why, then, did they result in such a tremendous and finally decisive blow to the Allies, who not without some justification called themselves the victors? The answer lies partly in the shatteringly painful truth of a long buildup of illusion. It lies also in a story of how generals in Washington outsmarted themselves in trying to use the results of Tet as leverage to secure a larger mobilization of American forces. And behind all this was the growing weariness of the American people with a war of rather dubious relevance to themselves, which suddenly after three years appeared to be no closer to its end than it had been at the beginning. Besides, their own generals, including and especially Westmoreland, had been assuring them (and probably themselves) as late as the preceding December that the war was almost won.

President Lyndon B. Johnson and General Westmoreland quickly pronounced the Viet Cong offensive a costly failure. The Viet Cong, said Westmoreland, had simply sought 'to cause maximum consternation in South Vietnam'. But, as one American news reporter put it in the same week: 'If that was their sole purpose, the Communists had clearly scored a resounding victory.' The same reporter told of one U.S. official in Saigon saying: 'If you ask me, I'll tell you for the record that this was simply a desperate suicide action on the part of the Viet Cong. But privately, I'm stunned.' Stunned, too, were Americans at home, who sat before their TV sets watching the spectacle of U.S. troops storming their own embassy in Saigon to oust the guerrilla invaders. There were several other related incidents to help stun the American populace, including a photograph on the front pages of leading American newspapers showing a General Loan of the South Vietnamese National Police coldly executing by pistol shot a bound and boyish-looking Viet Cong captive. And the beginning of the offensive had followed by only a few days the capture for the first time in a hundred years of an American naval vessel, the U.S.S. *Pueblo*, taken by some North Korean naval forces as she approached too near their shores. It appeared that American power was spread very thin indeed in the western Pacific. It began to appear also that the news reporters, whom the Administration in Washington had been so roundly condemning for their 'negative attitudes' in their accounts of the ineptness and corruption of the South Vietnamese government and the excessive optimism of their own leaders, civilian and military, were right after all.

Naturally, the shock was much greater in South Vietnam itself, where the Tet Offensive demonstrated in the most costly and effective manner that after all these years of war and 'pacification', and despite three years of combat involvement by the ultrapowerful United States, no part of the country was safe, neither any rural area nor the heart of Saigon. No doubt the executions in Hué had been intended to accentuate exactly this conclusion. However, it had always been widely understood that without large and direct military support by the United States the South Vietnamese government would not only fail to protect its people but would inevitably succumb. The decisiveness of Tet must therefore be sought not in its effects on the South Vietnamese people, whose government in any case had never attracted their support, but in its effects on the American commitment to the war.

Direct American commitment to the war, as compared with extending aid to France, had begun with the French departure in 1954, following their defeat at Dien Bien Phu in May of that year. The Geneva Conference of 1954 and its attendant Declaration had provided for the two Vietnams, North and South, with the proviso that elections be held within two years to determine the government of a unified Vietnam. But in the previous year President Dwight Eisenhower had already in a speech announced that the fall of Vietnam to Communism would be 'of the most terrible significance to the United States', and in April of 1954 in a press conference he had presented the famous analogy to falling dominoes. During the Dien Bien Phu crisis he had been willing to intervene with air power on the side of the French as urged by his Secretary of State, John Foster Dulles (and also by his Vice-President, Richard Nixon), but only in collaboration with the British Government, which Prime Minister Winston Churchill quickly refused. Immediately following the Geneva Declaration, Secretary Dulles, who was determined that South Vietnam should not fall to the Communists, patched together the South-east Asia Treaty with its attendant organization (SEATO) which named South Vietnam as one of the so-called 'protocol powers' to be covered by whatever protection the Treaty afforded.

The United States had sponsored in October 1955 the election of Prime Minister Ngo Dinh Diem to the presidency of South Vietnam, to replace the irrelevant playboy Emperor Bao Dai established by the French, and more significantly had supported Diem in his refusal to hold the elections called for in Paragraph 7 of the 'Final Declaration' of the Geneva Conference. President Eisenhower later communicated in his published memoirs the views he had held in 1954, which no doubt had not been changed by 1956 despite the accession of Diem: 'I have never talked or corresponded with a person knowledgeable in Indochinese affairs who did not agree that had elections been held as of the time of the fighting, possibly 80 per cent of the population would have voted for the Communist Ho Chi Minh as their leader rather than Chief of State Bao Dai.' Ho Chi Minh and his followers were no doubt of the same opinion, which is why they had signed the Declaration in the first place, thus giving the French a gracious way out.

The Diem refusal to hold elections was inevitably followed by the revival of military activity by what was now called the Viet Cong, mostly South Vietnamese Communists trained in and supported by the North, though the Ho Chi Minh regime preferred for a time to hold to a pretence of non-involvement. The Eisenhower Administration naturally gave military support to Diem, not only in the form of vast amounts of matériel but also of so-called 'military advisers', who were professional U.S. military personnel attached directly to what was now called the Army of the Vietnam Republic (A.R.V.N.). During Eisenhower's time the number of these advisers did not exceed 800, but with the increase in fighting which coincided with the Administration of President John F. Kennedy the number grew to almost 17,000, many of the advisers taking part directly in combat actions.

We now know that President Kennedy was determined not to let the involvement grow, and that shortly before he was cut down by the assassin's bullet in November 1963 he had ordered the initiation of a drastic reduction in American military advisers in Vietnam, to proceed by approximately 1,000 per month. In the first month after his death the first thousand was in fact withdrawn. However, the man who succeeded him in the presidency, and who achieved election to the office on his own merits by overwhelming majorities in the following year, was of markedly different convictions.

President Lyndon B. Johnson certainly did not desire to send American combat troops to Vietnam and to become involved there to the extent he did: but much more than Kennedy he shared the simplistic Eisenhower view that a Communist victory in Vietnam would be an unmitigated disaster for the United States. The kind of advice that President Kennedy forthrightly rejected when General Maxwell Taylor and Mr Walt W. Rostow, supported by Secretary of State Dean Rusk and Secretary of Defense Robert McNamara, had advocated in their memorandum of November 1961, in which they advocated a 'hard commitment to the ground', that is, the despatch of American combat troops, was some three and a half years later to fall on more receptive ears.

President Kennedy knew that there was an enormous difference between sending advisers to operate individually with Vietnamese troops and sending American combat forces as organized units to take part in the fighting. President Johnson no doubt understood that there was a difference, but when the South Vietnamese government seemed once again on the verge of collapse at the beginning of 1965 he was willing to cross the chasm. In March and April of that year decisions were executed which made the United States an open and full-fledged participant in the fighting against the Viet Cong and soon also the North Vietnamese. By the time of the Tet Offensive three years later this commitment had risen to 525,000 American troops in Vietnam, at which time the total of American fatalities there was something in the neighbourhood of 30,000.

The United States being a democracy, enjoying freedom of the press and other news media, no war of the dimensions of that in Vietnam is going to be adequately supported by the people unless (a) their government has convinced them and keeps them convinced that the war is being fought for important national interests, and (b) they see signs of a steady progression towards victory. A high increment of (a) naturally reduces the need for (b), and to some extent vice versa, inasmuch as victory in itself, or at least avoidance of defeat, is generally accepted as an important national interest, regardless of the initial motivation for going to war.

The United States had had some fairly recent experience with these matters in the Korean War, which had broken out in June 1950 during the spring floodtide of containment doctrine and cold war psychology. Though the U.S. intervention was immensely popular at the outset, abroad as well as at home, this popularity suffered a sharp decline five months later with the countering intervention of Communist China and a resulting heavy defeat of American arms. Following his firing of General Douglas MacArthur for insubordination in April 1951, President Harry Truman's popularity rating as measured in the leading opinion polls plunged to the lowest level (23 per cent) suffered before or since by any president, except for President Nixon's rating just before his resignation. General MacArthur had advanced the cry: 'Fight to win, or get out' – a notion that simplistically but with great popular effectiveness cut through the involved reasoning of limited war doctrine. Even though the December defeat had been brilliantly redeemed by the success of the spring 1951 offensive under General Matthew Ridgway, the Korean War remained unpopular, because of the seeming interminability of the armistice negotiations, which dragged on into the presidential elections of November 1952, and largely accounted for Eisenhower's overwhelming victory. He had electrified the nation with the simple phrase: 'I shall go to Korea.'

The Johnson Administration had forgotten all the significant lessons of Korea save one. Truman, having no large number of ground troops at his disposal, had at the very outset of American commitment to Korea called up the reserves, officers and men who had already fought the long, hard war that had ended five years earlier. These were men who had kept their reserve status without any idea that they would be called back so soon, and for a war that impressed them as being far less necessary than that in which the enemies included Hitler and in which the precipitating event for the United States was the Pearl Harbor attack. Anyway, why not leave the fighting to those who had not yet fought? Throughout the war the reservists called back to active duty formed with their families a reservoir of bitterness that greatly contributed to the unpopularity of the war. President Johnson, however, had the advantages of the large expansion of conventional forces, especially ground troops, that President Kennedy had pushed for reasons that had more to do with Europe than with Vietnam. The expanded army made it unnecessary for President Johnson to call up the reserves, and he was determined not to do so. This decision happened to be counter to the thinking of the Joint Chiefs of Staff, especially of their chairman, General Earle Wheeler, and this had much to do with the aftermath of Tet.

The military in the United States, as in other democratic countries, cherish an idealized image of themselves as politically neutral servants of the state and of its constitutionally determined government. Their duty as they see it (or at any rate, say it) is simply to carry out their orders, for the wisdom or unwisdom of which they hold themselves not responsible. To a remarkable degree they do in fact so conduct themselves, but the conception is nevertheless much too idealized to be true. Military officers are deeply inculcated with the requirement for obeying orders, but like people in other professions they present wide personal variations. Some who achieve high rank will show a considerable propensity for influencing the orders they receive. General MacArthur was a perhaps outstanding example of this propensity but certainly not a unique one.

An old axiom in the United States Army forbids the fighting of a land war on the Asian continent, and this axiom did indeed at times give pause to various senior officers. But there is also overriding commitment to 'mission achievement'. Thus, once the military involvement in Vietnam reached serious proportions, the bias of the military, and especially of those on the spot, was for more rather than less involvement, and for a more rapid buildup of the necessary power, in order to achieve success.

The most pervasive form of giving effect to this bias was to send home optimistic interpretations of how the war was progressing. For a variety of reasons, including the mere passage of time and hence some diminution of innocence, the Vietnam War elicited from many Americans quite different responses from those of the Korean War. People of intellectual bent were from an early period quite divided about American military participation in Vietnam, and this was bound to result in publication of a good deal of informed and sophisticated criticism of what the United States was doing and where it was going. The effectiveness of this criticism was bound to mount with the American casualty figures and with the passage of time that seemed not to bring the United States nearer to a victorious end. The military leaders in Vietnam and at home, and not the military alone, naturally viewed these expressions of negative public opinion as an obstacle to mission achievement, and therefore as something to be combated. They felt they could help their government as well as themselves by (a) accentuating their already strong institutional bias to report progress, and (b) withholding information potentially damaging to their position.

Mr David Halberstam in *The Making of a Quagmire* (1964) gives us a vivid account of the pressures put upon him and his colleagues by senior American military officers and Embassy officials during his eighteen-month stint in Vietnam as a reporter for the *New York Times*. His stay there ended shortly after the assassination of Diem, which preceded by three weeks the assassination of President Kennedy. It was thus a period well before the commitment of American combat forces but when American involvement was nevertheless considerable. A report published at home which cast doubt on the roseate predictions or assessments of the official news handouts in Vietnam was likely to result in the author's being greeted at his next encounter with a top military officer by the tart question: 'Whose side are you on?' Even Secretary of State Dean Rusk was not above putting such a question under comparable circumstances.

We may also assume that however imperfectly these officers could control independent channels of reporting, they could control their own very well. There is much evidence to indicate that the President and his advisers, including the Joint Chiefs of Staff, were fed a steady diet of news through official and therefore secret channels which stressed and exaggerated the favourable and diminished or suppressed the unfavourable. And they clearly placed more credence in what came to them through official channels, the volume of which may well have swamped their reading time, than in the contrary reports of people whom they did not know and did not trust. President Johnson would plaintively exclaim to doubting Washington reporters at a press conference: 'If only you could read the cables on my desk!'

Enemy body counts were held to be an important measure of progress, possibly because of Secretary of Defense Robert McNamara's well-known predilection for graphs and figures. Credit for bodies would be negotiated among junior line officers before some operation that was expected to produce such bodies, for commendations and decorations; hence promotions depended on fulfilling the desires of one's seniors in this respect. The same bodies might be counted two or three times by different air and ground combat units, and whether the bodies were truly those of enemy troops or merely of civilians who happened to get in the way was a matter not to be too closely investigated.

Worst of all was the corruption, for political reasons, of all the concerned intelligence agencies, military and civilian. Mr Samuel A. Adams, a former C.I.A. analyst, has vividly and depressingly exposed this corruption, on the basis of his own firsthand experience, both in a *Harper's* article (May, 1975) and as a witness at the trial of Dr Daniel Ellsberg. Army intelligence had instructions in late 1967 to keep its estimate of the total of Viet Cong troops in South Vietnam to some figure under 300,000, which meant that just before the Tet Offensive they were estimating 270,000, or just about half the number indicated by data available to the C.I.A. The C.I.A. went along with this doctoring of figures on the orders of its then director. Mr Richard Helms. Apparently a larger figure would have embarrassed the President, because it would require him to face up to a decision either to increase drastically the number of American troops in Vietnam or to pack up and go home.

For comparable reasons the later indications of a vast network of Viet Cong and North Vietnamese agents within the army and government of South Vietnam were totally suppressed, because such data, along with the irrepressible evidence of the most intense, pervasive, and blatant pecuniary corruption of South Vietnamese officials, would show how hollow was any hope for the 'Vietnamization' of the war.

No large organization like the Army can fool people outside without also fooling itself. Knowledge that figures have been doctored under orders must be kept close, and those responsible for encouraging such orders may neglect to remember that they have done so. When in November 1967 General Westmoreland returned to Washington and in a press conference announced that 'the enemy is running out of men', he was basing that estimate on fabricated figures, but he was almost certainly unaware of doing so. He no doubt believed what he was publicly saying – that the war was virtually won and that American troops would soon begin coming home. If he believed it, so probably did the Joint Chiefs, and so almost certainly did the President and his advisers. The public was glad to have these gratifying assurances, but it was becoming wary of what it was being told. The leading opinion polls were showing a steady rise in the proportion of people ready to agree that American entry into the war had been a mistake and a steady fall in President Johnson's popularity.

General Taylor was given to reiterating the remark he made before a

Senate committee in 1966, that the French had lost their Vietnam war not at Dien Bien Phu but in Paris. This was intended as a warning to Americans. One could of course have replied that Paris was indeed the natural and appropriate place for the French Government to make policy, and that especially at the time Taylor was making these remarks, it was difficult to fault the French decision. Still, Taylor anticipated better than he knew what would be the place of decision with respect to Tet.

As we have seen, General Westmoreland's immediate, and quite natural, response to the liquidation of the Tet Offensive was to claim an overwhelming victory. Tet, he said, was the enemy's 'last gasp' effort, a sign that Hanoi had decided that 'protracted war was not in its long-range interest'. The hard core of the Viet Cong, he asserted, had been committed and was now destroyed. Had the Joint Chiefs let it go at that, the chances are that the shock of the recent events would have been absorbed, and the war would have continued on its weary way, more or less unchanged.

However, their Chairman, General Wheeler, thought he now saw his chance finally to get the mobilization of the reserves that he and his colleagues had so long desired. Cautioning Westmoreland by cable not to sound so sanguine, he added that 'the United States is not prepared to accept defeat in Vietnam' ('defeat' had been entirely missing from Westmoreland's conception of what had happened to him). He then sped to Saigon, where he persuaded Westmoreland that if he requested sufficient reinforcement he could shift to a really offensive strategy. Upon his return to Washington, he conveyed to the President Westmoreland's endorsement of the Army's request for 206,000 additional troops for Vietnam, in addition to the 525,000 American troops already there.

As it happened, Secretary of Defense McNamara (who in the President's eyes had turned 'soft' on Vietnam) was in the process of being replaced by Mr Clark Clifford, an old Truman and later Johnson aide long known as a certified hawk. President Johnson's instructions to the outgoing McNamara and the incoming Clifford were to consider how the Army's request could be met. To McNamara this was another problem to be 'managed', that is, to be provided with a practicable solution that would meet the President's desires. To the fresher Clifford, however, who was sworn in on 2 March, it was a prompting to take a wholly new look at the situation. Actually, Clifford's personal conversion concerning the war had been proceeding for some time, and the events of Tet had given it a strong impulsion. He probed the Joint Chiefs for their assessment of the battlefield effect of adding the additional troops requested, but received only 'vague and unsatisfactory' answers.

Mr Townsend Hoopes, then Under-Secretary of the Air Force and hence in a position to observe and to participate in what was going on, describes in his excellent *The Limits of Intervention* (1969) the battle that then ensued to change the President's mind about the war. Secretary Clifford was a skilled lawyer, and he now applied his extraordinary forensic skill to the problem. In this he was assisted not only by some high-level members of the Administration but also by a group of elder statesmen, with former Secretary of State Dean Acheson as their chairman, known as the Senior Advisory Group on Vietnam. This group met on 25 and 26 March to hear briefings about the course of events in Vietnam. It soon became clear that most of them, including and especially former hawks like Dean Acheson, Cyrus Vance, and McGeorge Bundy, had defected from their previous support of the war. The choice being between escalation and the reverse, they were strongly in favour of the latter.

This was shocking to the President, who was then undergoing some political shocks as well, for the successes that month on the hustings of Senators Eugene McCarthy and Robert Kennedy, both running for the presidential nomination on antiwar platforms, showed that the Democratic Party was in revolt. For this combative and stubborn President, an entire reversal of his policy, and hence acknowledgement of error and defeat, was not possible without some violent thrashing about, but on 31 March, just one month after the final liquidation of the Tet Offensive, he gave the famous speech in which he announced the halting of the bombing of North Vietnam except for a small area in the extreme south, called upon 'President Ho Chi Minh to respond positively, and favourably, to this new step toward peace', and, perhaps most significantly because it was irreversible, announced his own withdrawal from the presidential race.

It was still to take five years for the final American withdrawal from Vietnam and another two years for the ending of the war through the collapse of the South Vietnamese government of President Nguyen Van Thieu, but the President's speech of 31 March 1968 pretty nearly assured the latter result. After all, Trafalgar preceded Waterloo by ten years.

In his memoirs, *Swords and Plowshares*, published four years after Tet, General Maxwell Taylor avowed himself still unable to understand why Giap and his colleagues took the decision to launch the offensive. 'One must admit,' he says, 'that the enemy put on a good show.' But, says Taylor, 'out of the 84, 000 men who, we estimated, were committed to the immediate Tet Offensive, over 30,000 were killed in the first two weeks of the fighting. In the first six months of the year, the number of enemy killed in action approached 120,000.' He compares this offensive to Hitler's sacrifice of his last combatworthy divisions in the Battle of the Bulge.

The least that could have been expected of Taylor would have been a drastic downward revision of the figures for enemy dead from those originally claimed, or perhaps no reference to figures at all. That Tet should have had such a bad influence within the United States Taylor ascribes entirely to the malevolent influence of television – a commonly held conclusion based on absolutely no study and leaving many critical points unexplained.

Other American military officers too have written articles describing Giap as a bungling amateur, not at all deserving the respect accorded him because of what appear, falsely, to be his achievements. An amateur Giap certainly is, in the sense that there is no West Point or Sandhurst in his training. However, he is not unique in this respect among the great military captains in history. One would anyway expect that a man with the small resources of a North Vietnam who succeeded in getting the better of the greatest military power in the world, which happens for the detractors mentioned above to be their own country, should on a strictly pragmatic basis be rated more generously.

The official American explanation of Tet is that Giap expected his planned military actions to provoke a great uprising in his favour among the South Vietnamese troops and people, with total victory to follow in one fell swoop. The fact that no such uprising occurred and that losses were so heavy among the Viet Cong and North Vietnamese troops committed argues, according to this version, an enormous blunder and total failure on the part of Giap. The assumption seems to be that he was saved from the penalties of his errors only by something tantamount to treason within the United States.

General Westmoreland's official *Report on Operations in South Vietnam* during the period of his command there says, for example:

> It is difficult to believe that the enemy would have sacrificed those experienced and hard-core cadres if he had not expected to succeed. . . . Another strong indication that he entertained high hopes for a decisive victory, is the fact that throughout the country, and particularly in the Delta, he impressed into his military units large numbers of untrained, local Vietnamese, many of whom were very young and others very old. This move had all the signs of a one-shot, go-for-broke attempt.

Surely one cannot have it both ways. To say that the troops sacrificed were too good to be spared is inconsistent with the latter argument quoted, which can be interpreted to suggest exactly the opposite. And one has a different idea about the first part of the argument if one scales down drastically the initial American claims of enemy fatalities, as everything indicates they should be scaled down. There is no doubt that the price paid by Giap was heavy, but there is no strong indication that it was disproportionate to what he expected to pay or to the results he expected to achieve.

There are other indications that an uprising was not within the expectations entertained by Giap. First, he had an extraordinarily extensive and efficient intelligence network in South Vietnam. The Viet Cong even had an agent who was an adviser to President Thieu on American policy. It is possible that he could have made so egregious an error despite good intelligence, but most unlikely. Second, there is no evidence that he prepared the South Vietnamese for any uprising or that he resorted to any kind of special propaganda effort during the offensive itself. On the contrary, as a careful RAND study shows, the propaganda complement to the military action was conspicuously absent. To be sure, the executions in Hué, rather too promptly carried out to suggest expectations of a long stay, undoubtedly had a propaganda intention, but it was the opposite of that which one would characterize as an appeal for an uprising.

The expected 'uprising' interpretation simply does not hold water. It is a desperate attempt to show madness in the enemy's method, a weak effort to project upon him a Bay of Pigs mentality. Giap knew the forces he was confronting, and he would have had to be of very weak mind indeed (which we know from his writings as well as his actions that he is not) to assume that the forces he was committing to great cities like Saigon and Hué could actually capture and hold those cities – and those are the two cities where they actually held out the longest. In towns where the strength of the attackers was so slight that they held out for only a few hours, we may be sure that he did not expect them to hold out indefinitely.

Naturally, we cannot attribute to him the expectation of the totality of what really happened. He could hardly know that a General Wheeler would play into his hands, or that a Clark Clifford would be in the right place with the right frame of mind and the right skills to play the role he did. Giap expected his offensive to have a great shock effect on the South Vietnamese and especially the Americans, and it most certainly did. He might even have expected the shock to start an avalanche of sorts. The avalanche just happened to be a lot bigger than anyone could possibly have expected.

Note on Sources

In preparing this chapter I have used mainly the following sources:

Adams, Sam, 'Vietnam cover-up: playing with numbers', *Harper's* (May 1975), pp. 41–73.

Giap, General Vo Nguyen, *The Military Art of People's War*, selected writings of the author, ed. by Russell Stetler (New York: Monthly Review Press, 1970).

Halberstam, David, *The Making of a Quagmire* (New York: Random House, 1964).

Henry II, John B., 'February, 1968', *Foreign Policy*, No. 4, Fall 1971, pp. 3–33.

Hoopes, Townsend, *The Limits of Intervention* (New York: McKay, 1969).

Pohle, Victoria, 'The Viet Cong in Saigon: tactics and objectives during the Tet Offensive', RAND Corporation Memorandum RM-5799-ISA/ARPA, January 1969.

Taylor, Maxwell, *Swords and Plowshares* (New York: Norton, 1972).

Taylor, Maxwell, *The Pentagon Papers*, Senator Gravel Edition, 5 vols. (Boston: Beacon Press, 1971–72).

Westmoreland, General William C., *Report on Operations in South Vietnam, January 1964–June 1968;* contained in *Report on the War in Vietnam*, by Admiral U. S. G. Sharp, Commander in Chief Pacific (Washington: U.S. Government Printing Office, 1968).

Also files of *Newsweek*, *Time*, and the *New York Times*.

I should like also to acknowledge with thanks the assistance, in an interview, of Mr Brian Jenkins of the RAND Corporation, who, however, is not responsible for and does not fully share the interpretation I have placed on events.

Authors' Biographies

LOUIS ALLEN was educated at the Universities of London, Paris and Manchester. He now teaches French literature at the University of Durham. He served as a Japanese-speaking intelligence officer in South-East Asia during and after the Second World War, and has since written many books and articles on it, including forthcoming works on Singapore and on the Japanese surrender, as well as *Sittang* – chosen by the Military Book Society – which deals with the last battle of the Burma campaign, and a history of modern Japan, *Japan: the Years of Triumph*. He is also a theatre and literary critic, and a frequent broadcaster, and he was for several years chairman of the B.B.C. North-Eastern Regional Advisory Council.

CORRELLI BARNETT was born in London in 1927, and educated at Trinity School and Exeter College, Oxford. From 1945 to 1948 he served in the army. Starting in 1952 he spent eleven years in public relations, first in industry and then in a consultancy.

His previous books, *Marlborough*, *The Desert Generals*, *The Swordbearers*, *Britain and Her Army* and *The Collapse of British Power*, have all won high praise. In 1970 he won the Royal Society of Literature Award for *Britain and Her Army*.

He was historical consultant to, and part author of, the B.B.C. Television series *The Great War* (1964), and historical consultant to, and author of, the B.B.C. Television series *The Lost Peace 1918–33* (1965) and *The Commanders* (1973). He won the 1964 Screen Writers' Guild Award for the best British television documentary script.

He is a Fellow of the Royal Society of Literature, a member of the Council of the Royal United Services Institute for Defence Studies, and chairman of the Literature Panel of the Eastern Arts Association.

MARTIN BLUMENSON was educated at Bucknell and Harvard Universities. He served in Europe during the Second World War, and later in Korea. He has been Professor of Military and Strategic Studies at Acadia University in Nova Scotia, holder of the Ernest J. King Chair at the Naval War College, and Mark W. Clark Professor at The Citadel, and is now Visiting Professor of Military History at the Army War College. Lieutenant-colonel retired, he has had ten books published, among them two volumes in the official series *U.S. Army in World War II*, as well as *Rommel's Last Victory*, *Prelude to Monte Cassino* and *The Patton Papers*.

BRIAN BOND was born at Medmenham in Buckinghamshire in 1936 and educated at Sir William Borlase's School, Marlow, and Worcester College, Oxford. After teaching history at Exeter and Liverpool Universities he became Lecturer in War Studies at King's College, London, in 1966. His principal publications in military history include *Victorian Military Campaigns*, *The Victorian Army and the Staff College*, *Chief of Staff* (2 vols) and *France and Belgium 1939–1940*. He is currently engaged on a study of Liddell Hart's military theories, and is also editor of the new yearbook *War and Society*.

BERNARD BRODIE was born in 1910 and received his doctorate at the University of Chicago. He is now Professor Political Science at the University of California, Los Angeles.

He has been a writer on strategic affairs for thirty-five years, having first made a name for himself through his works on seapower and naval strategy in the early days of the Second World War. He was a proponent of the idea of mutual nuclear deterrence and one of the originators of the idea of limited war at the time of the Kennedy and Johnson administrations when such thinking was unfashionable; he was also a critic of the war in Vietnam.

He has written the following books: *Sea Power in the Machine Age*, 1941; *A Guide to Naval Strategy*, 1942; *The Absolute Weapon*, 1946 (editor and co-author); *Strategy in the Missile Age*, 1959; *From Cross-Bow to H-Bomb*, 1962 (co-author with Fawn M. Brodie); *La Guerre Nucleaire*, 1965; *Escalation and the Nuclear Option*, 1966; *War and Politics*, 1973.

ALVIN D. COOX, who holds a Ph.D. from Harvard University, is Professor of History and Director of the Centre for Asian Studies at San Diego State University, California. Previous associations include the Japanese Education Ministry, the Johns Hopkins University, the University of California and the University of Maryland. A resident of Japan for twelve years after the Second World War, he has written the books *Year of the Tiger*, *Japan: The Final Agony* and *Tojo*. He also collaborated with S. Hayashi on *Kogun: The Japanese Army in the Pacific War* and with M. Schneps on *The Japanese Image* anthology. The recipient of Rockefeller Foundation post-doctoral grants, Dr Coox won the Trustees' Outstanding Professor Award of the California State University system in 1973.

CHRISTOPHER DOWLING was born in Wellington, New Zealand, in 1940 and educated at Highgate School and Oriel College, Oxford, where he specialized in military history. After a year in industry he returned to Oxford to complete a D.Phil thesis on naval history during the Napoleonic Wars. He is a former Councillor of the Navy Records Society and since 1966 has been Keeper of the Department of Education and Publications at the Imperial War Museum. With Noble Frankland he is editing a series of works on the politics and strategy of the Second World War

JOHN ERICKSON was born in 1929 and educated at South Shields High School and St John's College, Cambridge, doing his military service with The King's Own army intelligence. As a student he did research into East European history at Cambridge and the University of Vienna, and he was appointed Research Fellow of St Antony's College, Oxford, in 1956. He has lectured at several British and American universities, his most recent appointment being as Lees Knowles Lecturer at Cambridge n 1972. Professor of Defence Studies at Edinburgh University since 1967. His publications include: *The Soviet High Command 1918–1941*, *Panslavism* (ed.), *The Military-Technical Revolution* (ed.), *The Armed Services and Society*, *Soviet Military Power* and *The Road to Stalingrad* (Soviet–German War), Vol. 1, 1975.

LIEUTENANT-GENERAL SIR GEOFFREY EVANS, K.B.E., C.B., D.S.O., D.L., was born in 1901, and educated at Aldenham School and The Royal Military College, Sandhurst. He served in the Middle East and Burma during the Second World War.

Between 1940 and 1942 he saw service, both on the staff and in command of a battalion, with the 4th Indian Division at Sidi Barrani and Keren, and in the Western Desert offensive of 1941–42, before being appointed commandant of the Staff College at Quetta in 1942. From late 1943 until the conclusion of the Burma Campaign, he served in the Fourteenth Army as a brigadier on the General Staff and as a brigade commander in Arakan, where he commanded the Sinzweya Box during the Japanese 'Ha–Go' offensive. During the Imphal battle he commanded a brigade and, in its closing stages, the 5th Indian Division. As commander of the 7th Indian Division he took part in the reconquest of Burma. His last appointment was G.O.C.-in-C Northern Command before retiring in 1957. The four books he has written about the war are *The Desert and the Jungle*, *Imphal* (with Antony Brett James), *The Johnnies*, and *Slim as Military Commander*.

STANLEY L. FALK was born in New York City in 1927. He holds a Ph.D. in History from Georgetown University, Washington, D.C., and served three years in the U.S. army. He is now Chief Historian to the United States Air Force, and has also participated in the official historical programmes of the United States Army and Joint Chiefs of Staff. Before assuming his present position, he was for several years Professor of International Relations at the Industrial College of the Armed Forces, Washington, D.C. He is the author of five books on the Second World War, the most recent of which is *Seventy Days to Singapore*, as well as articles, reviews and other works on military history and national security affairs.

NOBLE FRANKLAND was born in 1922 and educated at Sedbergh and Trinity College, Oxford. During the war he served as a navigator in Bomber Command and was awarded the D.F.C. From 1956 to 1960 he was Deputy Director of Studies at the Royal Institute of International Affairs. Since then he has been Director of the Imperial War Museum. With Sir Charles Webster he was the author of the official history *The Strategic Air Offensive against Germany*, which was published in four volumes in 1961. His other works include *Crown of Tragedy: Nicholas II* and *The Bombing Offensive against Germany*. Dr Frankland is vice-chairman of the British Section of the International Committee for the Second World War and was historical adviser for the recent Thames Television series, *The World at War*.

ALISTAIR HORNE was born in 1925 and educated in Switzerland, the U.S.A. and Great Britain, taking a degree in English literature at Jesus College, Cambridge. He served in both the R.A.F. and the Coldstream Guards during the Second World War, ending up as a captain attached to security intelligence, and he spent three years as foreign correspondent in Germany for the *Daily Telegraph* (1952–5). His first book, *Back into Power* (1955), was a study of postwar Germany. Between 1962 and 1967 he completed a trilogy on Franco–German conflicts, based on the Siege of Paris (1870), Verdun (1916), and Sedan (1940). The second of these, *The Price of Glory*, was awarded the Hawthornden Prize in 1963. He also cooperated with the B.B.C. on the *Great War* series. Other recent books by him include *Death of a Generation*, *The Terrible Year: The Paris Commune*, and *Small Earthquake in Chile*. He is currently at work on a study of the Battle of Austerlitz in 1805, and on a full-scale history of the Algerian War of 1954–62.

BIBLIOGRAPHY

General Sir William Jackson, G.B.E., K.C.B., M.C., A.D.C. General M.A., was born in 1917 and educated at Shrewsbury, the Royal Military Academy, Woolwich, and King's College, Cambridge. Now one of the most senior serving generals in the British army, he has had a long and balanced military career as regimental officer, staff officer and senior commander. During the Second World War he saw active service in Norway, North Africa, Sicily, Italy and the Far East. After the war he turned to writing military history as a hobby; his books include *Attack in the West*, *Seven Roads to Moscow*, *Battle for Italy*, *Battle for Rome*, *Alexander of Tunis as a Commander* and *North African Campaigns*. His last appointment was Commander-in-Chief, Northern Command, and he is now the Quartermaster-General.

Peter Kemp was born in 1904 and educated at the Royal Naval Colleges at Osborne and Dartmouth. He specialized in submarines and was invalided following a submarine accident in 1928. After being on the editorial staff of *The Times* he was recalled for naval service in 1938 in the Naval Intelligence Division. He rejoined *The Times* in 1946 but left in 1949 to become Naval Librarian and head of the Naval Historical Branch in the Admiralty, retiring in 1969. He was simultaneously assistant editor of the *R.U.S.I. Journal* from 1949 to 1959 and editor from 1959 to 1969. He has written many books and articles on naval subjects and edited two volumes of the First Sea Lord papers of Lord Fisher for the Navy Records Society.

Christopher Lloyd was born in 1906 and educated at Marlborough and Lincoln College, Oxford. He has lectured at Bishop's University, Quebec, the Royal Naval College, Dartmouth and the Royal Naval College, Greenwich, where he was also Professor of History from 1962–6. His publications include *The Navy and the Slave Trade*, *The Nation and the Navy*, *Medicine and the Navy*, *William Dampier*, *The British Seaman*, *Mr Barrow of the Admiralty: A Life of Sir John Barrow 1764–1848.*

Malcolm Mackintosh was born in 1921 and educated at the Edinburgh Academy and Glasgow University. He served in the British army from 1942 to 1944 in the Middle East, Italy and the Balkans, latterly as a liaison officer with the Soviet army in Rumania and Bulgaria. After graduating in 1948, he worked in the B.B.C.'s Overseas Service for twelve years, then became consultant on Soviet affairs to the International Institute for Strategic Studies in London. His publications include *Strategy and Tactics of Soviet Foreign Policy* and *Juggernaut: A History of the Soviet Armed Forces.*

Air Vice-Marshal S. W. B. Menaul, C.B., C.B.E., D.F.C., A.F.C., was born in 1915 and educated at Portadown and the R.A.F. College, Cranwell. He is currently Director-General of the Royal United Services Institute for Defence Studies, London, an appointment he has held since 1968 when he retired from the Royal Air Force after a distinguished career in peace and war. He is a specialist in nuclear weapons and nuclear strategy. He lectures widely on military affairs and is a contributor to many journals, including *International Defence Review*, *Defence*, *World Forum*, *R.U.S.I. Journal* and *NATO's Fifteen Nations*. He broadcasts frequently on defence matters in this country and in the United States, travels extensively, and has visited Vietnam on a number of occasions.

Richard Natkiel, who researched and produced the map section at the back of the book, is head of the cartographic department of the *Economist*. He has made a study of the campaigns and battles of the Second World War and was responsible for the cartography in Purnell's *History of the Second World War* as well as many other books on this subject. More recently he was commissioned by Weidenfeld and Nicolson to produce the maps for the *Atlas of the Second World War*.

Robert O'Neill was born in 1936 and educated at the Royal Military College of Australia, Melbourne University and Oxford University, from which he holds a D.Phil. He served with the Australian army in Vietnam from 1966 to 1967 as an infantry captain and was mentioned in despatches. After lecturing in history at the Royal Military College of Australia from 1967 to 1969, he became a Senior Fellow in International Relations in the Research School of Pacific Studies of the Australian National University, Canberra. In 1970 he was appointed by the Australian government to write a history of Australia's role in the Korean War, and in 1971 he became head of the Strategic and Defence Studies Centre of the Australian National University. He is a member of the Editorial Board for the Publication of Australian Documents on Foreign Policy and a period editor of the *Australian Dictionary of Biography*. During 1973 he worked at the Imperial War Museum, London, on the history of Australia's role in the Korean War. His publications include *The German Army and the Nazi Party, 1933–39*, *Vietnam Task* and *General Giap, Politician and Strategist*.

Alan Palmer was born in 1926 and educated at Bancroft's School, Essex, and at Oriel College, Oxford. He served in the Royal Navy from 1944 to 1947 and was head of the history department at Highgate School, London, from 1953 to 1969. He is now engaged primarily on historical writing and research. His books on historical topics include *The Penguin Dictionary of Modern History*, *Napoleon in Russia*, *The Lands Between*, a history of Eastern Europe in the nineteenth and twentieth centuries, and *Russia in War and Peace*. He is also the author of an account of the Macedonian Campaign (1915–18), *The Gardeners of Salonika*, and he has written biographies of Metternich, Tsar Alexander I, George IV, and Frederick the Great. His latest biography, *Bismarck*, will be published in the spring of 1976, and he is at present preparing a study of Kaiser William II.

Captain Stephen W. Roskill, C.B.E., D.S.C., Litt.D., F.B.A., R.N., was born in 1903 and joined the Royal Navy in 1917. He was educated at the Royal Naval Colleges at Osborne, Dartmouth and Greenwich. During the Second World War he served both on the Naval Staff and in command of H.M.N.Z.S. *Leander*. In 1948 he was invalided from the navy and appointed Official Naval Historian to the Cabinet Office. From 1949 to 1960 he wrote *The War at Sea 1939–1945*, the official naval history, and in 1961 he was appointed Lees Knowles Lecturer at Cambridge University. He has lectured in many British, American and Commonwealth universities at various times, and contributes regularly to various learned journals in England and America. His other books include *The Navy at War*, *The Strategy of Sea Power*, *A Merchant Fleet in War* and *The Art of Leadership*.

Harrison E. Salisbury was born in 1908 and educated at the University of Minnesota. From 1930 to 1949 he worked for United Press in Chicago, New York, London and Moscow and as foreign news editor. He joined the *New York Times* in 1949 as Moscow correspondent, remaining in that post until 1955 when he joined the staff in New York. He eventually reached the post of associate editor in 1972, from which he has now retired. He won several awards for his reporting from Russia, and later from Vietnam, including the Pulitzer Prize in 1955. He is the author of several books on the Soviet Union, including *The 900 Days, The Siege of Leningrad* and *War Between Russia and China*. Among his other books are *The Eloquence of Protest, Voices of the Seventies, The Many Americas Shall Be One*, and *To Peking – and Beyond*. In 1972 he made a six-week tour of China and the first visit by an American correspondent to North Korea.

PETER SIMKINS was born at Greenford, Middlesex in 1939 and educated at Ealing Grammar School and King's College, London, where he specialized in war studies. In 1961 he was appointed archivist and research assistant to the late Captain Sir Basil Liddell Hart, with the task of cataloguing the latter's papers (prior to their eventual transfer to the Centre for Military Archives at King's College). In 1963 he joined the staff of the Imperial War Museum, becoming Keeper of the Department of Exhibits in 1965. He has contributed articles to Purnell's part-work histories of the First and Second World Wars and edited *The Illustrated Book of World War II.*

SIR JOHN WHEELER-BENNETT, G.V.C.O., C.M.G., O.B.E., F.B.A., was born in 1902 and educated at Malvern College, but owing to ill-health he was unable to go up to Oxford. In 1924 he founded the Information Service on International Affairs, which subsequently became the Information Department of the Royal Institute of International Affairs, of which he was a member of the Council for sixteen years, specializing in American, German and Irish affairs. During the Second World War he served in Britain, the U.S.A. and Europe with the Ministry of Information, the Foreign Office and SHAEF, and he was later attached to the British prosecution team at the Nuremberg Trials. In 1946 he became first British editor-in-chief of the captured German Foreign Ministry archives.

He was a founding Fellow of St Antony's College, Oxford, in 1950 and has been a visiting professor and scholar-in-residence at various American universities. In 1958 he published the official *Life of King George VI*, and he was knighted the following year and also appointed Historical Adviser, Royal Archives. He is a trustee of the Imperial War Museum.

His numerous works of history and biography include *Hindenburg, the Wooden Titan*; *Brest-Litovsk, the Forgotten Peace*; *Munich, Prologue to Tragedy*; *The Nemesis of Power: the German Army in Politics*; *John Anderson, Viscount Waverley*; and, with Anthony Nicholls, *The Semblance of Peace: the Political Settlement after the Second World War.*

Index

1. To differentiate where necessary, the symbols WWI and WWII are used for the two World Wars.
2. Air forces are filed under their titles: e.g. Royal Air Force, USAF, and Luftwaffe.
3. Aircraft are usually under makers' names and numbers: e.g. Me 109, FW190, and Zero.
4. Military forces of all countries are filed under the title ARMIES; this head is then broken down alphabetically by formation, nationality and number: e.g. Army (British) 8th, Brigade (Indian) 44th, Corps (German) 21st Panzer.
5. Naval units are generally shown by the ship's name, nationality and type: e.g. *Akagi* (Japanese) carrier.
6. The various operations occur under the code name: e.g. Citadel (German) operation.

INDEX

INDEX

INDEX

INDEX

INDEX

INDEX